PENN STATE STUDIES IN ROMANCE LITERATURES

PENN STATE STUDIES IN ROMANCE LITERATURES

Editors
Frederick A. de Armas
Alan E. Knight

Refiguring the Hero:
From Peasant to Noble in Lope de Vega and Calderón
by Dian Fox

Don Juan and the Point of Honor:
Seduction, Patriarchal Society, and Literary Tradition
by James Mandrell

*Don Juan
and the
Point of Honor*

Don Juan and the Point of Honor

Seduction, Patriarchal Society,
and Literary Tradition

James Mandrell

The Pennsylvania State University Press
University Park, Pennsylvania

Publication of this book has been aided by a grant from The Program for
Cultural Cooperation Between Spain's Ministry of Culture and United
States' Universities.

Library of Congress Cataloging-in-Publication Data

Mandrell, James.
    Don Juan and the point of honor : seduction, patriarchal society,
and literary tradition / James Mandrell.

        p.   cm.
    Includes bibliographical references and index.
    ISBN 0-271-00781-8 (alk. paper)
    1. Don Juan (Legendary character)   2. Honor in literature.
3. Spanish literature—History and criticism.   I. Title.
PN57.D7M33   1992
860.9'351—dc20   91-10220
                                                            CIP

ftw

ADS 6262

It is the policy of The Pennsylvania State University Press to use
acid-free paper for the first printing of all clothbound books.
Publications on uncoated stock satisfy the minimum requirements of
American National Standard for Information Sciences—Permanence of
Paper for Printed Library Materials, ANSI Z39.48–1984.

for Martha and Melissa
and for Rob

Porque no es así como quiera el oficio de alcahuete;
que es oficio de discretos y necesarísimo en la
república bien ordenada.

—*Cervantes*, Don Quijote

Contents

Acknowledgments

Early versions of parts of this study were published in *Hispania; Bulletin of the Comediantes;* "*Malevolent Insemination*" *and Other Essays on Clarín,* edited by Noël Valis; and *Letras Peninsulares.* I am grateful for the permission of the editors and publishers to include that material here in revised form.

The debts incurred during the research, the writing, and the rewriting of this book are countless; to thank all of those who helped me in one way or another would be impossible. Yet it would be the meanest form of ingratitude not to mention the following. First, earlier studies of Don Juan and of seduction have profoundly influenced my own work in ways with which the authors might or might not agree; I therefore acknowledge the unwitting contributions of Leo Weinstein, Jean Rousset, Shoshana Felman, and Carlos Feal, even as I exempt them from potential criticisms for the manner in which I have used their insights. Second, I thank several of my friends and colleagues, all of whom have been stimulating, provocative, and generous with their comments and criticisms. I extend my gratitude to Richard Macksey, Harry Sieber, John Irwin, Eduardo González, Deanna Shemek, Kathleen Myers, Robert Molla, Dian Fox, Benigno Sánchez-Eppler, Jane Hale, Richard Lansing, Lawrence R. Schehr, Robert C. Spires, and Noël Valis. Very special thanks are due Lou Charnon-Deutsch, and, above all, Gregory L. Lucente and Paul R. Olson.

A Note on Translation

Unless otherwise noted in the Works Cited, translations are my own. Although decisions regarding what to include only in translation and what to give in the original and translation are inherently difficult, in those instances in which citation from the original language is not germane to the argument, I generally include only the translation; otherwise, and in the case of most literary texts, both the original and its translation appear. Published translations have occasionally been modified to reflect more accurately the sense of the original. Titles of works mentioned in passing are usually given in the original; dates given in the text for works refer to the original date of publication and not to subsequent editions or translations, even if citations are from later versions.

Introduction

*One pays dearly for immortality: one has to die several times while still
alive.*

—*Nietzsche,* Ecce Homo

It is virtually a tradition of studies of Don Juan to begin by noting
that this character is one of the great creations of Western literature, comparable to Oedipus, Narcissus, Hamlet, Don Quijote, and
Faust. It goes without saying that this sort of opening is a tradition
precisely because the comparison points up a significant difference
between Don Juan and his comrades in literary and cultural renown.
Whereas it is customary to speak of Sophocles' Oedipus, Ovid's Narcissus, Shakespeare's Hamlet, Cervantes's Don Quijote, and Goethe's
Faust, with respect to Don Juan, there are simply too many equally
important works to single out one version as more significant than any
other. To Molière's *Dom Juan* (1665) one could add Mozart's *Don Giovanni* (1787); to Dumas's *Don Juan de Marana ou la chute d'un ange*
(1836), one could respond with Shaw's *Man and Superman* (1901–3); to
Torrente Ballester's *Don Juan* (1963), one could add John Berger's *G*
(1972). If one were to suggest that the author of the first version of Don
Juan's story be given pride of place, an enormous practical problem
comes into play: What is the first Don Juan play and who is its author?
Because the story of Don Juan is usually viewed as comprising two
complementary parts—the one the history of a dissolute libertine, the
other the motif of the double invitation—Tirso de Molina's *El burlador
de Sevilla y convidado de piedra* [The Trickster of Seville and the Stone
Guest] (c. 1630) is generally considered the first identifiable or first-
known, if not to say simply the first, work in which Don Juan appears.
There are, however, two difficulties with this designation. First,

Tirso de Molina is the pseudonym of a Mercedarian friar, or so we think. Despite extensive documentation, this piece of information, though generally accepted as fact, is far from indisputable; and the same is true for the attribution of *El burlador de Sevilla,* since the publication history of this drama is confusing in the extreme. Moreover, there are two seventeenth-century versions of "Tirso's" *comedia, El burlador de Sevilla* and *¿Tan largo me lo fiáis . . . ?,* both of which have partisans and detractors.[1] It is, then, difficult if not impossible to speak of Tirso's Don Juan in the same way that we discuss any of the seemingly comparable characters mentioned as Don Juan's literary cohorts.

A host of similarly contradictory issues compounds the uncertainty with regard to the "first" version of Don Juan's story. In his *Love in the Western World,* Denis de Rougemont comments, "The way in which the mystical character of Don Juan stirs the emotions of women and fascinates the minds of some men is to be accounted for, I fancy, by his *infinitely contradictory* nature" (209). Kierkegaard's *Either/Or: A Fragment of Life, Edited by Victor Eremita* is symptomatic of these types of contradictions, which can be characterized as indecision and/or undecidability. As the title indicates, there is an ongoing play on indecision cast as opposition that begins with the title, continues with the opening play on philosophical discussions of the distinction between inner and outer, then concludes with aphoristic comments on marriage and women ("Marry, and you will regret it. Do not marry, and you will also regret it. Marry or do not marry, you will regret it either way" [1:38]).

---

1. These three problems—the question of authorship, of the publication date (and the problem of dating in general), of textual priority—constitute the most pressing issues facing textual critics and literary historians who work with *El burlador de Sevilla.* For important discussions of the question of authorship, see Gerald E. Wade, and the earlier article written by Wade in collaboration with Robert J. Mayberry; and Alfredo Rodríguez López-Vázquez. See also Ruth Lee Kennedy's biographical work. On the dating of *El burlador de Sevilla,* see Wade; and D. W. Cruickshank. Of course, most discussions of these problems include at least some treatment of this question. The issue of textual priority—of the greater aesthetic and technical merits of *El burlador de Sevilla* or *¿Tan largo me lo fiáis?*—is the most problematic of the three. Major contributions on this topic have been made by María Rosa Lida de Malkiel, who extensively refutes Joaquín Casalduero's claim that *El burlador de Sevilla* is to be preferred to the other version of the *comedia* ("Sobre la prioridad"). In connection with this, see Casalduero, *Contribución* 12–13, 19–73. Michael D. McGaha is in essential agreement with Lida de Malkiel, while dissenters include Daniel Rogers, "Fearful Symmetry"; Albert E. Sloman; and Xavier A. Fernández, "¿Cómo se llamaba el padre de Don Juan?" "En torno al texto," "Precisiones diferenciales," "Estudio preliminar" (3–65). The latest salvos in this debate are those of Luis Vázquez, "Documentos toledanos," Rodríguez López-Vázquez (2–14), and Luis Vázquez in the introduction to his recent edition of the *princeps* of *El burlador de Sevilla.*

In sum, these distinctions are the very contrasts between the documents associated with the nameless "A" and with "B," who is also known as Judge William. In a sense, Kierkegaard's philosophical inquiry into the question of either/or embodies the contradictions involved in treatments and interpretations of Don Juan, contradictions having to do with the ways in which Don Juan's story ends, with the putative virility of the *burlador* or trickster, and with questions relating to the possible social effects of such a figure.

Given the contradictions that reside in Don Juan as a character and the many divergent literary and critical treatments that he has stimulated, it should come as no surprise that I shall focus primarily on the elements in Don Juan's story that anticipate or call for rewriting and revision; it is one of my basic contentions that an impulse toward retelling is central to the story in virtually every version. I shall consider, then, the reasons for which Don Juan's story has exercised—and continues to exercise—such imaginative power in Western cultural traditions. In other words, what is it about Don Juan that sparks such interest and controversy?

Because my primary interests here are those of writing, revision, and the relationship between a text and various notions of interpretation, my point of departure will be precisely those issues in relation to works in which Don Juan or an avatar of Don Juan figures prominently. Beginning with the letter in Tirso's *El burlador de Sevilla* and continuing with the letter and the lists in José Zorrilla's *Don Juan Tenorio* (1844), the literary works to which most attention will be given are Adelardo López de Ayala's *El nuevo don Juan* [The New Don Juan] (1863), Clarín's *La Regenta* [The Judge's Wife] (1884–85), Jacinto Octavio Picón's *Dulce y sabrosa* [Sweet and Savory] (1891), and Azorín's *Don Juan* (1922) and *Doña Inés* (1925). The critical works will include studies of individual literary texts, discussions of Don Juan in historical terms, as well as other treatments of history (literary, social, cultural), philosophy, anthropology, and literary theory.

The reasons for dealing with these specific literary texts, and not others of equal or possibly even greater canonical or aesthetic interest, have to do with canonicity *and* interest, the relations between and among the works and the literary canon *and* the potential interest of these texts for the type of analysis proposed here, which is not to suggest that I have selected only those works most susceptible to this analysis, although certainly that must be taken into account. Rather, I include in the discussion a range of texts, including classic, canonical works as well as works considered to be of lesser historical or aesthetic merit, texts in which Don Juan figures prominently and in which literature and its social values are implicated. In so doing, I argue for the validity of my general interpretation of Don Juan while offering detailed readings of specific literary works. Moreover, I situate my general interpretation within the Spanish canon so as to be able to demonstrate the imaginative power of Don Juan within one specific literary tradition, the ongoing process of reinterpretation within Spanish literature. Because I propose a *theory* based on Don Juan as a literary character and a social principle, my mode of analysis can be extended to other texts. Yet to do so here—to include detailed discussions of Molière's *Dom Juan,* Mozart's *Don Giovanni,* Shaw's *Man and Superman,* Pérez de Ayala's *Tigre Juan* and *El curandero de su honra* (1926), Unamuno's *El hermano Juan* (1939), Torrente Ballester's *Don Juan,* Berger's *G,* and so forth—would result in an encyclopedic volume. My intention is not to write a *history* of Don Juan, but to elucidate a theory that responds to the historical vicissitudes of the character *and* his interpretation. I therefore leave to others the development of similar interpretations with respect to literary texts not treated in this study.

The relationship between a literary text and its interpretation as it pertains to meaning has been a seminal topic from the time of the patristic scholars to the present. Aquinas, for instance, asserts in the *Summa Theologiae* apropos of allegory in Scripture that there are four levels of meaning or significance that progressively lead us towards the revelation of the state of eternal life: the historical or literal, the allegorical as such, the tropological or moral, and the anagogical. Through scriptural exegesis, readers are brought to a realization of the fullness of God's meaning, a meaning that resides in the text and that is gradually revealed to the individual (*Christian Theology* Ia, 1, 10). A more extreme rendering of the way that literature acts upon an individual is found in Robert Penn Warren's discussion of "pure" and "impure" poetry, in which he equates the poem with the monster Orillo in Boiardo's *Orlando Innamorato* and the critics with Orillo's adversaries who would master him. Unlike the adversary, however, who was, in fact, able to subdue Orillo by dismembering him, the critic has "only one way to conquer the monster" that is poetry: "you must eat it, bones, blood, skin, pelt, and gristle. And even then the monster is not dead, for it lives in you, is assimilated into you, and you are different, and somewhat monstrous yourself, in having eaten it." Having consumed the poem, the critic becomes the poem, gives "the monster—the poem—a chance to exhibit again its miraculous power" (3).

These views of literature and its power contrast markedly with contemporary theories of interpretation in which meaning inheres in the individual reader and is validated by an interpretive community. Yet even the most willful of readers, those accused of reducing a text to fit their own theories, are eventually drawn back into the dynamics of the text they would explicate and thereby master through interpretation. This inescapable return to the text can be demonstrated by a series of commentaries on and interpretations of one of the more talked about yet unreadable texts of the last twenty years, the missing letter in Edgar Allan Poe's "The Purloined Letter."

Jacques Lacan was one of the first to try to read the letter. In the opening essay of the French edition of his *Ecrits* (1966), the transcription of a "seminar" given in 1955, Lacan discusses the letter in terms of larger questions concerning his theories of the Symbolic order and its relationship to the Oedipal triangle. His position was subsequently subjected to a scathing reading by Jacques Derrida ("Le facteur de la vérité"), in which Derrida twits Lacan—and psychoanalysis in general—for a reductive insistence on "triangulation," on viewing all relationships in terms of the multiple triangles of the family romance. These two readings in turn spawned Barbara Johnson's suggestive rereading ("The Frame of Reference," in *The Critical Difference* 110–46), where, while admitting to a distinct sympathy for the discourse of each of her predecessors regarding the purloined letter, Johnson reveals Derrida's inherent recuperation of precisely those strategies *and* weaknesses of Lacan. Yet, in this game of critical one-upmanship, Johnson herself takes a position with respect to the others, one that corresponds to Poe's original formulation of the King, the Queen, and the Minister in his story of Dupin's masterful genius of detection. As John T. Irwin insightfully demonstrates, all of what Johnson refers to as a critical "round-robin," in and of itself almost a version of Poe's game of even-and-odd, is, in fact, to be found in "The Purloined Letter." In other words, Poe's story not only serves as the text and catalyst for the readings of Lacan, Derrida, and Johnson, it anticipates and structures their outcome: it influences the nature of the subsequent critical discourse. However strong or willful a reading might be, however reductive in its attempt to force a text to conform to a particular theoretical posture, interpretation takes place within parameters established by the text itself.[2]

---

2. Shoshana Felman adds her own interpretation in "The Case of Poe: Applications/ Implications of Psychoanalysis," in *Jacques Lacan and the Adventure of Insight* (26–51). Poe's "The Purloined Letter" also figures, via Lacan, in Felman's suggestive "Turning the Screw of Interpretation," which takes into consideration several issues pertinent to this study of Don Juan, namely, letters and the nature of reading and interpretation.

My interest in this particular series of texts and commentaries on the letter has less to do with the discourse of Lacan as opposed to that of Derrida—or Johnson as opposed to that of the theorists she interprets—than with the dialectic of interpretation and recuperation at work here, particularly as these explications relate to their "host" text. As Charles Altieri has said in regard to Derrida's work, these "texts exemplify a form of pure constitution, of writing on other writing aimed to manifest the way we can make the seams in one discourse the creative ground of another" (26). This series of texts—Poe, Lacan, Derrida, Johnson, Irwin, texts as commentaries and commentaries as texts open to interpretation—strikes me as instructively similar at key points to the vicissitudes of Don Juan, of the letter, and later the list in Don Juan's story. In other words, this refraction of text and commentary in relation to Poe, of constant reading and rereading as related to rewriting, can also be found at work in Don Juan.

If Poe's short story and the critical exchange that it has stimulated form the central theoretical touchstone for my study, it is only one of a number of contemporary theoretical concerns that have influenced my literary interpretations in particular and my views of Don Juan in general. Also germane is the question of desire as it has been interpreted in psychoanalytic, anthropological, and literary contexts. I refer to the Lacanian "name of the father," René Girard's "mimetic desire," and Harold Bloom's "anxiety of influence."

For Lacan, the desire of the individual—as expressed in the Freudian Oedipus complex, especially as it is implicated in culture—is responded to by an authoritative no from society in the guise of the (symbolic) father. Guy Rosolato, following Lacan, defines the "name of the father," or paternal metaphor, in this way: "A distinct person, that is to say, perceived as capable of alternating his word and his desire, he becomes the forbidding authority. Original and autonomous author of laws, he becomes their principle, to be both feared and admired, since the child delegates to him, through the omnipotence of his thoughts, a limitless power, though unclear in its reasons, a power that both protects and punishes" (39). Particularly in his guise as an agent of God, the symbolic father embodies and adumbrates the complex set of laws by which society—and the individual as constituted in society—is controlled. This set of laws, rather, this authority, is not only materially *real* but also *symbolic,* manifest in those conventional systems of signs within which action and social interaction take place, including and appearing most obviously in the powers that determine the uses and ends of language, especially as the speaking subject constitutes himself discursively in relation to those around

him. Lacan says of this complicity between the father, language, and
the Law:

> The primordial Law is therefore that which in regulating mar-
> riage ties superimposes the kingdom of culture on that of a na-
> ture abandoned to the law of mating. The prohibition of incest is
> merely its subjective pivot. . . . This law, then, is revealed clearly
> enough as identical with an order of language. . . . It is in the
> *name of the father* that we must recognize the support of the
> symbolic function which, from the dawn of history, has identified
> his person with the figure of the law. (*Ecrits* 66–67)

By linking the Law with language by means of the incest taboo, Lacan
shows the extent to which relations between individuals are emblem-
atic of larger social concerns. What seems to be a local question—
relations between individuals in the family structure—can be generalized to the workings of society and, for Lacan, the importance of
language in social interactions.

The importance of the "name of the father" as a type of social structure in the story of Don Juan is obvious yet crucial. As a figure both
symbolic and real, the father incarnates a variety of social functions
that would seem to tend toward the containment and punishment of
the *burlador*'s social anarchy. Yet once the importance of this version of
the Law is acknowledged, the question must be posed: Why is Don
Juan's perfidy not brought to an end by precisely those figures that
ought to be held responsible for his actions?

One possible response is to be found in two distinct but complementary theories proposed by René Girard, the one having to do with what
is called mimetic (or triangular) desire, the other concerning the nature and function of ritual (or sacrificial) violence in society. Girard's
interest in desire and in its conflictual nature is similar to that of
critics working within the framework of the Oedipus complex; but he
shifts the emphasis from the schema proposed by Freud and developed
by Lacan and others to a triangular framework attentive to rivalry,
imitation, and questions of representation, all of which verge on some
form of social and/or cultural violence. Girard's mimetic desire occurs
when an individual subject desires an object *because* it is desired by
another subject, here designated as the rival: desire is modeled on the
wishes or actions of another. Philippe Lacoue-Labarthe says that

> the basic hypothesis upon which rests Girard's famous analysis
> [is that] every desire is the desire of the other (and not immedi-

ately desire of an object), every structure of desire is triangular (including the other—mediator or model—whose desire desire imitates), every desire is thus from its inception tapped by hatred and rivalry; in short, the origin of desire is mimesis—mimeticism—and no desire is ever forged which does not desire forthwith the death or disappearance of the model or exemplary character which gave rise to it. (12)

Desire does not take place only between a subject and an object, one and an other, but involves a third person, this third being the one who mediates, conditions, and controls to an extent the original desire.

In Girard's terminology, mediation can be either internal or external, can take place either inside or outside the particular world of an individual. For example, in his explanation of internal mediation, as in Stendhal's *The Red and the Black,* a character "will desire any object so long as he is convinced that it is desired by another person who he admires. The mediator here is a *rival,* brought into existence as a rival by vanity, and that same vanity demands his defeat. . . . This means that one is always confronted by two *competing* desires. The mediator can no longer act his role of model without also acting or appearing to act the role of obstacle" (*Deceit, Desire, and the Novel* 7). In external mediation the situation is otherwise. Girard cites the case of *Don Quijote,* because the knight-errant models his desire on Amadís, without affecting the mediator in the least. Thus, the essential difference between the two types of mediation, internal and external, is that in the latter the mediator is inaccessible, and in the former it is all too real.

Although it would be tempting to see in the notion of internal mediation yet another version of the Oedipus complex, Girard cautions against such a reductive move. In a critique of Freud's notion of triangular desire as expressed in Oedipal terms, Girard remarks:

> Freud does not understand that the mediator's desire is the essential factor in the desirability of the woman. The subject needs the desire of his rival to sustain and to legitimize his own desire. In Oedipal terms, this would mean that the son wants the father's desire to sustain and legitimate his desire for the mother. If there is one thing that the Oedipus complex will not allow, it is certainly that. It would mean that the mother is not desired "for herself," that she has no independent value of her own, that she is desired primarily as an object for the father. In addition, it would mean that the father is not the incarnation of the law

against incest. The two pillars of the Oedipus edifice crash to the ground. (*"To double business bound"* 67)

For Girard, each term in the triangle that is mimetic desire is necessary and dependent on the others, which means that the "more the father is a father in the sense of the law, the more unlikely it is that he will be a mimetic rival. He may be an ideal model, he may be a hated tyrant, but the mimetic rival is something else again. Far from being compatible and combining easily, the role of the father as an incarnation of the law and the role of the mimetic rival are normally separate and divergent" (*"To double business bound"* 68). Mimetic desire is therefore distinct from the Freudian notion of the Oedipus complex, although there are similarities in structure if not in function.

We will have occasion to consider Girard's notion of ritual sacrifice and its importance for understanding Don Juan's story in the literary discussions that follow. Suffice it to say for now that Girard's theories are suggestive in that they take into account the role of literature in the determining of individual actions (i.e., the external mediation found in *Don Quijote*) and the function of imitation in relation to rivalry. In this sense, Girard's work parallels that of Harold Bloom, particularly Bloom's theories of poetic "misprision" or misreading. According to Bloom, a young poet, or "ephebe," does battle with his precursors, specifically a "strong" poet, in order to stake out his claim to independence and originality: "Poetic history . . . is held to be indistinguishable from poetic influence, since strong poets make that history by misreading one another, so as to clear imaginative space for themselves" (*The Anxiety of Influence* 5). Working within a system of six revisionary ratios—expressed as psychic defenses, rhetorical tropes, and symbols of extremes—Bloom elaborates an ingenious means of reinvigorating a historical approach to sources and influence, all the while rehabilitating the concept of the author as an agent of literary creation. Although the six revisionary ratios as Bloom presents them in *The Anxiety of Influence* and elsewhere are, in and of themselves, suggestive tools in literary analysis, it is in Bloom's conception of literary history in toto that the pertinence of his work for the study of Don Juan is to be found. Because there are so many versions of Don Juan's story, because Don Juan's literary—and putative social and cultural— immortality has been purchased at the price of his resurrection, how are we to understand the impulse toward repetition at work here?

These various theories relating to interpretation, desire, social structures of rivalry, and imitation provide a means for approaching the topic of Don Juan from a number of different, yet related, perspectives,

and of understanding the contradictory nature of the *burlador*. Therefore, ways in which a text determines its exegesis, the dynamics found
in Poe's "The Purloined Letter" and in the various commentaries on
the story, and other contemporary theories of literature all structure
and provide the theoretical framework for my treatment of Don Juan,
but other theoretical concerns underlie and are indeed central to individual considerations. In chapter 1, I shall suggest how a literary text,
or a body of texts, can determine the outcome of the discussion of that
text. By examining the critical "myth" of Don Juan, we shall see how
the interpretations mirror the literary texts they study, in terms both
of the strategies of presentation and argumentation and of ideology.
Chapter 2 demonstrates how the common literary device of a text
within a text, the letters and lists in Tirso's *El burlador de Sevilla,*
Zorrilla's *Don Juan Tenorio,* and López de Ayala's *El nuevo Don Juan,*
can raise significant questions in the interpretation of those same
texts. Tying this critical tool to the topics of honor and seduction—the
one a key issue in the study of Spanish literature and society, the other
a central concern with respect to Don Juan's story—I shall show how
these texts evidence various concerns with respect to authorial originality and immortality as well as to social harmony and well-being. Chapter 3 focuses on the ways in which a literary text not only can shape
subsequent discourse but can also serve as an implicit or explicit
subtext for other works of literature and for the roles of individuals in
society. In a close reading of four novels, Clarín's *La Regenta,* Picón's
Dulce y sabrosa, and Azorín's *Don Juan* and *Doña Inés,* Don Juan's
beneficial social role is once again presented, this time in terms of the
role that the reader plays in relation to Don Juan. Finally, in chapter 4,
the discussion centers on anthropological, psychological, and cultural
theories of society and of Don Juan in order to propose a variety of ways
that a literary text and the notions of interpretation and recuperation
might explain and partake of more general aspects of patriarchal social
relations.

Alongside the broadly historical presentation of critical and literary
approximations of Don Juan is another type of study that examines the
burlador from the perspective of the author and the reader, and from
the optic of literary tradition and then the social implications of seduction. The first two chapters are, generally speaking, concerned with
authorial interpretations of the *burlador,* be those interpretations critical or literary. Therefore, the first half of the book is oriented more
toward questions of literary tradition than social history, although
social issues are indeed involved in the literary analyses. The third and
fourth chapters are more openly interested in social mechanisms as

they are understood and interpreted first, by readers of novels in which Don Juan appears and seduction is involved; and second, by social theorists, even if, once again, literary questions are brought into the discussion. There are, then, a number of related issues that figure in this study, and any or all of them might play a role in the discussion of a particular literary text, interpretation, or theory.

Although it is true that the readings of the individual texts can and do stand alone, I intend to establish a collective force to the argument, one that becomes more apparent in the later chapters as various historical, cultural, and theoretical issues touched on previously are more extensively developed. By means of detailed literary analyses and extensive citation from and considerations of other texts, I show the extent to which seduction is a social and a literary phenomenon of which Don Juan is a primary representative and agent. I contend that the many different texts cited here form, for better or worse, a significant part of our cultural patrimony and have determined the nature and tenor of our discourse on culture and society. The issue of right or wrong with regard to some of the more speculative considerations of cultural and social theory ought, therefore, not to enter into play. More important is the currency of the various notions considered here, and the extent to which they shape our ideas with respect to literature and culture.

What should emerge from this series of readings is a view of Don Juan that stresses the peculiar moral force of the figure in patriarchal culture as well as the ethical appeal of the figure and his story to individuals involved in the ongoing interests of social stability. In other words, Don Juan should emerge as (1) a social force in patriarchal society and culture, a force that, given the nature of patriarchy, is necessarily seen as socially positive; (2) a force operative at the level of language and rhetoric; and (3) a character whose story and vicissitudes are still meaningful today. This is not to say that I view Don Juan as a positive social force or patriarchy as a desirable social system; I do, however, claim that Don Juan is a positive force *in* patriarchy. If anything, this reading of Don Juan is critical of the character as a social and cultural phenomenon. If the readings of the individual literary texts, read through the optic of Don Juan, seem severe, so be it. I fully intend to reveal the substance of a character who, because familiar, seems innocuous, when, in fact, he is far from benign. In this sense, then, the literary texts, though implicated in the cultural processes by which Don Juan's message is transmitted and perpetuated, cannot, in and of themselves, be faulted for *what* they portray. Neither can they be faulted, because of their involvement in literary tradition, for the *way* they portray Don Juan. Yet, to refuse to recognize the nature of this literary character and the texts of which he is a part is to acquiesce in the perpetuation of the type of imaginative power, the seduction, exercised by the *burlador*. We must not surrender to that seduction, however attractive it, and the literary texts that embody it, may be.

1

The One and the Same: Meaning and the Critical Myth of Don Juan

> *Don Juan continually hovers between being idea—that is, power, life— and being an individual. . . . Don Juan is a picture that is continually coming into view but does not attain form and consistency, an individual who is continually being formed but is never finished.*
> —*Kierkegaard, "The Immediate Stages or the Musical-Erotic,"* Either/Or

The imaginative power of Don Juan and his story is undeniable given the countless versions that exist, among them some of the canonical works of world literature. Yet I would go so far as to suggest that the imaginative power as it resides in Don Juan's role as a seducer is limited not only to *literary* treatments but to *critical* considerations as well. In this sense, so powerful is Don Juan—and his story—that the apparent distinctions to be made between literary and critical versions are difficult to sustain, which is to say, the critical approximations end up recapitulating the story of Don Juan in substance and in style. It is important, therefore, even before discussing the literary texts treating the *burlador* or trickster, to see what is at work in critical studies so as to understand how, and eventually why, Don Juan exercises such seductive power in literary and sociocultural domains. By focusing on a category of discourse that supposedly unites the literary and critical domains, myth, and its invocation in studies of Don Juan, we will eventually be able to see how what passes for exegesis becomes, in the process of explication, a profoundly ideological force in the restatement of dominant social and cultural values. This critical restatement will in turn lead us to confrontation with the inevitable uncertainty about Don Juan's meaning.

The first drama in which Don Juan appears as an identifiable protagonist is Tirso de Molina's *El burlador de Sevilla y convidado de piedra* [The Trickster of Seville and the Stone Guest] (c. 1630), but the origins of this literary figure are nevertheless uncertain. All that can be said safely is that the story is understood to comprise two distinct aspects, both of which were first brought together by Tirso: the first is the history of a dissolute libertine, the second, the motif of the double invitation. This is not to set aside the question of origins, either in a practical or in a theoretical sense. Various critics have attempted to trace the oral legend of the *burlador* and have often suggested as a precursor a Castilian romance first transcribed by Juan Menéndez Pidal. This romance was explicitly and extensively discussed by both Ramón Menéndez Pidal and Víctor Saíd Armesto and had actually been proposed earlier as an oral precursor by Emilio Cotarelo y Mori. As for the double invitation, Dorothy Epplen MacKay has documented the widespread diffusion of this motif and has noted that it is not exclusively Spanish. Recent studies, such as that of Trinidad Bonachera and María Gracia Piñero, have done little to improve or modify the work of these predecessors; and the origins of the story of Don Juan continue to be obscure, as do the sources for *El burlador de Sevilla*.

Alongside these practical studies on the origin of Don Juan there exists a series of more or less theoretical investigations into the origins of the figure. The theoretical focus of these studies may appear to derive from the literary texts themselves, but in most cases, historical or not, the primary interest at a theoretical level has had to do with the origin of Don Juan and his role in society and culture. In other words, this Don Juan is not the protagonist of any single work, nor can he be limited to any single or specific textual rendering. Indeed, as many critics would have it, Don Juan is not even primarily a literary character. Instead, Don Juan appears in a variety of guises as the "popular" or "mythical" Don Juan.

In truth, the popular or mythical version of Don Juan is at least as old as the mid-nineteenth century, at least as old as the major critical—as distinct from literary—treatments of the character. Still, the introduction of this "type" of Don Juan only serves to refocus and to restate a serious question pertaining to contemporary studies of the figure and of his story: Is Don Juan a *popular* figure or a *literary* character? On the one hand, Don Juan is undeniably popular; his story in its many forms continues to attract considerable attention. On the other hand, given the imprecise connotations of the term *popular*, particularly as it is associated with the term *myth*, critical exegesis must contend with opposing forces as it tries to reconcile popular "response" with concrete textual bases.[1]

1. See, for instance, José Alberich's discussion of Don Juan's popularity. For a different perspective, see Timothy Mitchell; and my "Nostalgia and the Popularity of *Don Juan Tenorio*."

The problem would appear to stem from the impossibility of separating the popular Don Juan from the literary Don Juan. But this is not the problem; it is a result of the problems inherent in *not* separating the popular Don Juan from the literary Don Juan, since Don Juan, according to most critics, is unmistakably literary *and* popular. To be more exact, he is a literary figure that, by means of his popularity, has transcended any representation that can be limited to one or even to many specific texts, which in turn means that the whole of the story of Don Juan appears to be greater than the sum of its parts.

The distinctions made here between literary versions of Don Juan and critical references to the popular or mythical Don Juan are more descriptive than analytic. They do not draw on the concepts of the Russian Formalists (*fabula* and *sjuzhet*), the Structuralists (*histoire* and *discours*), or more recent theorists, such as Seymour Chatman (story and discourse).[2] Rather, the distinctions made and terms used are intended to be much less charged, to carry much less critical and theoretical baggage. With respect to the "story" of Don Juan, then, I refer to the general outline of events, more particularly, to the story as found in Tirso's *El burlador de Sevilla*. As for the distinctions between literary and critical versions, between literary texts and what is called the myth, I show that such distinctions are ultimately confusing, that they are based not only on misused terminology but also on an implicit attempt to recuperate the ideological subtexts at work in the various versions of Don Juan's story.

Of course, different texts or bodies of texts excite different critical responses and provoke varying vocabularies. In the case of Don Juan, as a literary character and as a kind of synecdoche—as a character who now represents the whole of a story that has been told and retold in wildly disparate manners—the crucial problem confronting any scholar is one of unity. How can so many Don Juans be dealt with systematically, synthetically, and exhaustively? How can every difference in the various representations of the character be brought into relationship with the preponderance of similarities, and thereby into consonance with the large corpus of Don Juan texts? More plainly, how can there be so many Don Juans and what can we do with them? Obviously, one way to introduce unity is by means of a synthetic taxonomy, by creating a hypothetical unity. In many respects, this has been the function of the "popular" or "mythical" Don Juan. With the creation of a nonliterary figure, a figure that depends not on textual representation but instead on popular imagi-

---

2. Chatman discusses all of these distinctions. But see Barbara Herrnstein Smith's pointed critique of Chatman's position.

nation and cultural tradition, any discrepancies can be systematically attributed to the individual and to the individualization—what Luis Muñoz González refers to as the "personalization"—of the character. In this way, every manifestation of the character of Don Juan gains access to the larger domain of his cult and transcends the specificity and therefore the limitations of any single text.

For these reasons, the figure of Don Juan has been associated in critical discussion with the term *myth;* and the basic assumption of contemporary treatments of Don Juan is that he is a mythical figure and, by extension, that his story in toto is a myth. The popular and literary dimensions of the character support this movement toward a hypothetical unity. Yet the preference for this terminology has only emerged over the last half-century or so and has established itself at the expense of such previous terms as "legend" and "theme," both of which had been used regularly in other periods to describe Don Juan and his story. In fact, in the late nineteenth and early twentieth centuries, these terms, along with myth, were practically synonymous, adopted without qualification or definition.[3] However, with the advent of more extended critical discussion of the figure of Don Juan, myth became the term most often used to describe the character. Most recently, several critics have demonstrated a strong interest in justifying, not merely asserting, the status of Don Juan's story as a myth.

Although currently widespread in studies of Don Juan, the term *myth,* when applied to Don Juan, is not as unproblematic as it might seem. But the troubling nature of the word has as much to do with myth as a critical term as it does with the question of Don Juan's status as a myth. First, it is difficult, if not impossible, to arrive at a general critical consensus as to what constitutes a myth. As G. S. Kirk notes in his authoritative study *Myth: Its Meaning and Functions,* "There is no one definition of myth, no Platonic form of a myth against which all

---

3. Myth is the primary designation of Don Juan and his story in many critical treatments. It is nonetheless important to distinguish between those cases in which use of the term is significant per se and those in which it is merely a convenience. For our purposes, the most interesting instances are the following: Gregorio Marañón, "Notas"; Francisco Agustín; Ramiro de Maeztu; Joaquín Casalduero, *Contribución;* Guillermo Díaz-Plaja; Francisco Maldonado de Guevara; Antonio de Salgot; Pedro Salinas; Oscar Mandel; Francisco Fernández-Turienzo; Víctor Valembois V.; Luis Muñoz González; Jean Rousset; Maurice Molho, "Oedipe-Burlador," "Sur le discours idéologique," "Trois mythologiques"; Shoshana Felman, *The Literary Speech Act;* and Carlos Feal. Theme and/or legend, but not myth, are used almost exclusively in Víctor Saíd Armesto; Georges Gendarme de Bévotte; Angel Valbuena Prat; Leo Weinstein. See also Ricardo Fernández de la Reguera, and Gladys Crescioni Neggers, who use myth and legend interchangeably.

actual instances can be measured" (7).[4] Second, there are almost as many working definitions of myth as there are treatments of the topic of mythology, a situation that should induce critics and scholars alike to handle the term with a measure of caution. Unfortunately, such has not been the case. In the criticism of Don Juan, the term has frequently been used as a convenience—as a sort of methodological shorthand the result of which is a hypothetical coherence—or as a descriptive tool in the service of taxonomy, despite extensive rhetoric to the contrary. In those few instances in which there appears to be an important reason for its use, myth turns out to be an ideologically motivated term employed to perpetuate the "myth" of a myth of Don Juan and not to clarify the literary figure and the problems inherent in his textual representation.

Thus, the designation of Don Juan as a mythical figure is neither a simple nor an isolated move. It depends on (and develops out of) the gradual emancipation of the fictional character of Don Juan from any specific text or from the domain of the written word. In other words, it depends on precisely what Ramón Pérez de Ayala referred to as the impossibility of seeing Don Juan for the first time, even as it is contingent upon the contradictory fact of Don Juan's textual specificity, on his nature as a figure who exists only by means of texts ("Don Juan," *Obras completas* 3:170–75). This paradoxically divided existence forms the basis for most critical treatments of Don Juan. Unlike Kirk, who believes that there is "no Platonic form of a myth," many critics of Don Juan base their comments on the conviction that there is, if not a Platonic form, at least some form of the essential Don Juan and his story against which every manifestation of the character must be measured.

Yet myth, when applied to Don Juan, does not always assume these explicit configurations and does not necessarily embody a complex set of ideas. Early uses of the term are characterized by a blatant disregard for clarity and continuity in the choice of terminology. Gregorio Marañón, for instance, in "Notas para la biología de Don Juan" [Notes for a Biology of Don Juan], a historically significant essay first published in 1924, begins by discussing the "theme of Don Juan," then follows with "sexual myths," and finally ends with "the myth of Don

4. See also Kirk's penetrating "On Defining Myths." Other interesting contemporary discussions include Roland Barthes, *Mythologies;* Walter Burkert (especially 1–34); Marcel Detienne, "Rethinking Mythology"; and René Girard, *The Scapegoat* (particularly 25–44, 95–99). See too the discussion between Burkert and Girard, inter alia, in Robert G. Hamerton-Kelly, *Violent Origins.*

Juan" ("Notas," *Obras completas* 4:75–93).[5] Since Marañon never explains his choice of terms, there is no way of knowing if his reading of
Don Juan derives from some systematic understanding of this terminology, or if his choices are arbitrary. Only as time passed and the term
became more embedded in critical tradition was more attention paid to
questions of terminological validity. As a different kind or category of
Don Juan figure, the mythical Don Juan possesses his *own* history; he
is the protagonist of another, not entirely autonomous body of texts, the
theoretical and critical response to the literature itself. Because of this
other textual tradition, there is some validity to discussions of the
literary Don Juan on the one hand and of the popular Don Juan on the
other. It remains to be seen, however, how hard and fast the distinctions between literary and critical treatments really are, and also what
exactly distinguishes Zorrilla's Don Juan, to give only one example,
from the popular Don Juan of one of his exegetes.

As a means of exploring the nature of these distinctions, I shall
outline the history of this so-called popular or mythical Don Juan as he
manifests himself in the various scholarly and critical texts. The uses
of the terms *myth* and *mythical* will form the focal point of the discussion, but only because this "mythical" Don Juan permits the easiest
and most immediate access to an entire series of critical and theoretical
problems. The discussion begins as a historical overview of invocations
of myth as a useful or valid term and continues with a detailed analysis
of two of the most significant treatments of the problem, Jean Rousset's
Le mythe de Don Juan [The Myth of Don Juan] (1978) and Maurice
Molho's "Trois mythologiques sur Don Juan" [Three Mythologies on
Don Juan] (1978). Eventually, literary treatments will come into play,
including Prosper Mérimée's *Les âmes du purgatoire* [Souls in Purga-
tory] and Byron's *Don Juan,* in order to contrast the critical and popular Don Juan with his literary forebears. Finally, after discussing Don
Juan as myth, I will consider the questions of meaning and indecision
in terms of two more recent books, Shoshana Felman's *The Literary
Speech Act: Don Juan with J. L. Austin, or Seduction in Two Languages* (1980) and Carlos Feal's *En nombre de don Juan (Estructura de*

    5. This essay was first published in 1924 in José Ortega y Gasset's journal *Revista de
Occidente*. It was republished in 1937 in *Cinco ensayos sobre Don Juan* [Five Essays on
Don Juan], which includes contributions by José Ingenieros, Ramiro de Maeztu, Américo
[de] Castro, and Ramón Pérez de Ayala. This is a crucial volume, as it brings together the
work of critics who, while not necessarily in agreement on the appropriate interpretation
of Don Juan and his story, nevertheless agree upon the importance of the figure for
Spanish culture.

un mito literario) [In the Name of Don Juan (The Structure of a Literary Myth)] (1984).

One of the first critics to attempt an explanation of the use of the term "myth" was Ramiro de Maeztu in his essay "Don Juan o el poder" [Don Juan or Power], first published in *Cinco ensayos sobre don Juan* (1937). At least from a theoretical perspective, Maeztu's attention to the details of terminology constituted an advance on the work of his contemporaries. In contrast to Marañón, Ingenieros, Pérez de Ayala, and Castro, Maeztu says clearly and consistently that "Don Juan is a myth; he has never existed, does not now exist, and will never exist except as a myth. . . . the imaginative substance of the figure of Don Juan depends precisely on his condition as a myth" (*Don Quijote, Don Juan y la Celestina* 87–88). Yet Maeztu's position is obviously not based on exclusively literary grounds. He concludes the above passage by saying, "The figure of Don Juan is more popular than literary" (88). For Maeztu, the mythical nature of Don Juan results from and depends on the figure's capacity to engender popular, not literary, response. Don Juan is not limited to one text, is not "literary," but is instead entirely "imaginative": Don Juan exists in the minds of the public and is, therefore, a myth.

Antonio de Salgot's argument in *Don Juan Tenorio y donjuanismo* [Don Juan and Don Juanism] (1953) coincides with the general outlines of Maeztu's discussion of this point by claiming, "In reality, the very fact that the theme of Don Juan has endured and continues to endure is obvious proof that it is a theme linked to human nature. Don Juan is a myth, in the sense of an allegorical fiction of something that we all look for and experience, but that we can never quite define" (151). Salgot bases his assertion of Don Juan's status as a myth first on the durability of the Don Juan theme and then on the way in which that theme is bound to human nature. Myth arises precisely from this collective yearning for an indefinable aspect of the real world. Expanding on the notion of Don Juan's popularity, Salgot arrives at an interesting if naive consideration of the durability of the myth. In so doing, he espouses a view of myth that is patently psychological and, more importantly for studies of Don Juan, Jungian.

This psychological aspect of the myth is treated somewhat more explicitly in Guillermo Díaz-Plaja's *Nuevo asedio a Don Juan* [A New Siege on Don Juan] (1947), although in this case, too, the analysis lacks rigorous development. In his conclusion, Díaz-Plaja situates the "myth of Don Juan" in "the marginal zone—between life and books. . . . (in) the diffuse zone in which myth lives and breathes." In the context of this formulation, other distinct pairs of opposing or complementary concepts are mentioned: "life and history"; "reality and legend"; "testimonies of a living or of a psychological reality" (123). But within this discussion, the basic opposition is between two types of reality: first, an observable physical reality, and second, a historical reality ("living and historical forms"), which is composed among other things of literary discourse ("life and books"), legend ("reality and legend"), and the psychologically real ("a living reality . . . a psychological reality"). For Díaz-Plaja, the historicization of Don Juan is only possible given the textual representation of history and the events upon which that history is based. At the same time, this notion of history is incomplete without the psychological elements proper to history, "a psychological reality," that is implicitly collective.

Because *legend,* one of the key terms in Díaz-Plaja's study, refers to the fictional elaboration of something historically verifiable, and because it embodies both a textual and historical reality, it serves the author well. But there is also a historical dimension to Díaz-Plaja's predilection for the term. Legend was a common term in Don Juan criticism following the publication of Georges Gendarme de Bévotte's seminal *La légende de Don Juan* [The Legend of Don Juan] (1911) and the earlier, and equally significant, book by Víctor Saíd Armesto of the same title, *La leyenda de Don Juan* (1908). Gendarme de Bévotte's study, the first truly comprehensive historical treatment of Don Juan to be written in the twentieth century (Felipe Picatoste's study was probably the first comprehensive historical treatment), cuts across national boundaries in its diachronic survey of various representations of the character.

Saíd Armesto's book, on the other hand, is a much more partisan document; the extensive argument is intended as a refutation of those who would detract from Don Juan's Spanish heritage, and principally of Arturo Farinelli who, in a pique of anti-Hispanic nationalistic fervor, asserted that Don Juan was certainly not of Spanish heritage, but of Italian origin ("Don Giovanni"; *Don Giovanni*). Taking up the cudgels for Spanish tradition, Saíd Armesto provides examples from both oral and written literature to support the thesis that Don Juan derives from a historical Spanish legend with a lengthy tradition of literary convention behind it. For this reason, the word *legend,* when used in discussions of Don Juan, assumes a particular sort of historical imperative in terms of a peculiarly Spanish history. Díaz-Plaja's use of the term recalls these earlier studies of Don Juan with the result that, in this context, legend is at once historical, literary, and, more significantly, popular. By virtue of its association with early oral narrative, legend functions as the rubric under which historical reality assumes an organic coherence.[6] The myth of Don Juan is inscribed, then, in the margins of sociocultural reality and literature and is neither purely real nor textual. Instead it transcends both categories in such a way that it combines aspects of each of them. Don Juan can legitimately be the object of empirical study—because there is a concrete textual basis for such study—and he can also extend beyond fiction into everyday life: he can be both "imaginative" and popular.

If the psychological aspect of these early treatments of Don Juan and myth seems either reductive or facile, consider the ground staked out by Jean Rousset in *Le mythe de Don Juan*. Despite being both more polemical and more theoretical, Rousset's work relies on the same concepts and terminology discussed earlier, and it does so while offering little in the way of elaboration. Rousset prefaces his discussion of the "invariable" and "variable" elements of Don Juan's story by asking if it is possible to speak of Don Juan as a myth. His initial answer hesitates between the opposing possibilities, "between yes and no" (5). Yet the ambivalence of this response is dispelled by his subsequent treatment of the problem. For Rousset, the story of Don Juan is based not only on the presence and possibility of death ("*la* mort"), but on the "Dead Man" or "Dead One" as represented by the Statue, "on the active presence of the Dead Man, of the animated Statue," which is to say, the true protagonist is not Don Juan, but the sepulchral Statue of the deceased Commander (6). In this way, the story of Don Juan taps into the "profound" substratum of Christianity and the death cults of ancient (pagan) myth and ritual. This deeper level of signification permits Rousset to replace the usually accepted origin of Don Juan, Tirso de Molina's *El burlador de Sevilla,* with an "enduring power over the collective consciousness," locating the origins of the myth not at an identifiable moment in history but, once again, in a stratum of collective human experience that transcends both history and the specificity of any given text (7). Here popularity is rendered in terms of that which is familiar to all by means of an inherited collective experience of past cultural history. In Rousset's reading, Don Juan has been displaced by and reduced to the univocal avatar of the

6. Not everyone agrees with this assessment of the popular, legendary nature of Don Juan. Frederick A. de Armas, for instance, rejects an approach that advocates an exclusively folkloric or legendary (i.e., oral) tradition and suggests a reading that takes into account the literary tradition of the Cid ("The Guest of Stone").

figure of expiatory Death and divine intervention, and he now resides in the collective (un)conscious.[7]

The repeated references by these critics to the collective nature of Don Juan (to the importance of Don Juan for collective human experience and to the impossibility of understanding Don Juan if only the "literary" aspects of his story are taken into account) echo Jung's notion of the collective unconscious. As such, these formulations reproduce the problems inherent in Jungian treatments of the origin of the mythic sign. For Jung, myth is only indirectly referential and does not operate at purely an individual level; myth as an object of investigation cannot be explained except as an aspect of the totality of all of human experience. The meaning of myth, then, cannot be discovered by tracing the history of an individual's everyday and emotional experiences (as for Freud), but only by examining the past history of an entire culture, by examining the "collective unconscious." In discussing poetry, Jung says, "I am assuming that the work of art we propose to analyse, as well as being symbolic, had its source not in the *personal unconscious* of the poet, but in a sphere of unconscious mythology whose primordial images are the common heritage of all mankind. I have called this sphere the *collective unconscious*" ("On the Relation" par. 125; emphasis in the original). But in analytical terms, the problem with the collective unconscious is that it is virtually inaccessible. Theoretically, the origin of the "primordial image," or "archetype," is empirical and historically verifiable. More important, it is grounded in the emotional experiences of the race and is therefore barred from human perception, since "only by *inferences* drawn from the finished work (of art) can we reconstruct the age-old original of the primordial image" ("On the Relation" par. 126; my emphasis). In these terms, the discursive space opened by a discussion of Don Juan and myth becomes limitless, entirely speculative, at the same time that it is a priori limiting because it necessitates the return to a text that can be characterized as somehow insufficient. The individual manifestations of the myth are thus reduced to being viewed as symptoms of a larger cultural truth that cannot be fully or directly apprehended. This means that any appeal to a normative or popular version of the Don Juan figure or of Don Juan's story grants privilege to critical speculation at

7. Most recently, Beryl Schlossman has claimed with respect to Rousset's "myth" of Don Juan, "The mythical reading moves toward an ultimate identity; Rousset sees it in the form of Death, his structural common denominator. . . . Rousset's emphasis on Death uses the function of myth to sacrifice the erotics of Don Giovanni in the interests of ethics and brotherly love" (353–54).

the expense of specific textual representation. The historical dimensions of the various versions of the story are likewise absorbed by an ahistorically collective process of classification.

This sort of ahistorical collective classification recurs, however, even in later, non-Jungian interpretations. Indeed, the basic oppositions essential to these earlier studies—popular as opposed to literary, oral presentation as opposed to written representation—continue to be paramount to an ambitious treatment of the topic of Don Juan and myth. In "Trois mythologiques sur Don Juan," a title that all but names the article's inspiration and methodological bias in the work of Claude Lévi-Strauss, Maurice Molho vigorously explores those aspects of Don Juan's story that pertain to the question of his status as a myth. Unlike earlier critics, however, Molho does not use his discussion merely as a preface or conclusion to a more general treatment of Don Juan. Rather, the issue of Don Juan's status as a myth is the question at hand, and Molho pursues his investigation not only in abstract argumentation but also by means of close readings of specific texts.

Given the detailed and extensive nature of Molho's remarks, his lengthy essay bears careful analysis. In "La subversion du mythe" [The Subversion of the Myth], the first part of the essay, Molho examines "the myth in an oral version collected in Seville in 1830 by Prosper Mérimée in the form of two little stories [*historiettes*], each of which constitutes an amusing subversion that is significant to the extent that it purports to free itself from traditional mythic discourse" (75). The second study concerns *El burlador de Sevilla* and the "mythical structure" of that drama, from which Molho "attempts to disengage the meaning in view of its relation to a specific moment in the moral history of Europe" (75). The last (and in this context, the least relevant) part deals with the *Festin de Pierre* and the often-discussed double invitation.

Despite the inclusion of *Les âmes du purgatoire* and of the *Festin de Pierre*, the principal focus of the essay is Tirso de Molina's *El burlador de Sevilla*. In a paradoxical move, *El burlador de Sevilla* (in Molho's notation, "*DJ₁*"), is designated as the starting-point of the Don Juan myth. Earlier in this same essay, Molho tries to obscure the origins of Don Juan's story in order to initiate his proof of the figure's mythical nature (an argument that I shall address shortly). But Molho avoids confronting the problematic issue directly by claiming that *El burlador de Sevilla* is the first work in which "the mythical structure" of Don Juan "is found realized at the outset," and that it therefore is representative of "an original state" of the myth (10–11). As such, Tirso's drama merits being acknowledged as the first *textual* representation of Don Juan. More to the point, DJ_1 is also what Molho (openly adopting Lévi-Strauss's terminology) calls the "reference myth," or "key myth" ("Trois mythologiques" 35; *The Raw and the Cooked* 1–2). In other words, *El burlador de Sevilla* is the manifestation of the myth against which all others will be measured; it is of necessity Molho's Platonic form of the Don Juan story for the simple reason that "there is no DJ_0" (35).

The advantages of a "reference" or "key myth," both for Molho and for Lévi-Strauss, are primarily heuristic. But the notion is not without problems. The critic must distinguish between those elements that are, strictly speaking, textually specific and those that inhere in the mythical structure. As Molho puts it, "One thus runs the risk, if one is not careful, of analyzing not the mythic discourse at all, but that in which the artist has dressed the myth, which is not pertinent in strict mythology" (36). Fortunately, however, "the two structures—that of the myth and that of the object that reveals it—are indissociable" (37). The two structures are mutually constitutive because they are indivisible, because they are one and the same. The critic is spared the effort of delimiting the distinct properties of each because every individual manifestation of the myth necessarily expands the parameters of the known variants. The task of the critic, therefore, is to find "a strong coefficient of generalization, which can be uncovered by analysis" (37).

Molho's search for this strong coefficient of generalization in the mythical structure of *El burlador de Sevilla* and in the myth per se is based on Lévi-Strauss's well-known methodology as set forth in "The Structural Study of Myth." The core of this approach, and the centerpiece of Molho's analysis, is the systematic displacement of the syntagmatic elements of the myth into a paradigmatic grid in which the myth is represented as a "two-dimensional chart" (*Structural Anthropology* 2:217). The arrangement is such that reading from left to right and from top to bottom corresponds to the diachrony of the narrative, while reading the columns from left to right, each as a unit, reveals the synchronic structure. Lévi-Strauss describes the aim of the procedure in this way: "Were we to *tell* the myth, we would disregard the columns and read the rows from left to right and from top to bottom. But if we want to *understand* the myth, then we will have to disregard one half of the diachronic dimension (top to bottom) and read from left to right, column after column, each one being considered as a unit" (*Structural Anthropology* 2:214; emphasis in the original). For Lévi-Strauss, the important distinction is between telling and understanding; and in Molho's analysis, the syntagmatic disposition of *El burlador de Sevilla*, the text qua text, is thereby rejected for a paradigmatic "structure" of relationships organized as patently structuralist binary oppositions in order to reveal the "mythological discourse."

The result of Molho's dextrous critical two-step—in which the distinction between telling and understanding is only one more variation on the notion of opposition so crucial to his study—is a reading of *El burlador de Sevilla* that emphasizes the contradiction between Don Juan's perversion of monogamy and the subsequently ineffective affirmation of the monogamous relationships by various male characters in positions of some authority, as well as the contradiction between the Statue's supernatural killing of Don Juan and the King's inability to ensure social stability vis-à-vis marriage (i.e., institutionalized monogamy). These contradictions clearly point to the substitution of monogamy and Christian fear (what Molho refers to as "mortification") for Eros and passion. This means that "the myth of Don Juan is nothing other than that of the origins of monogamy" (50). *El burlador de Sevilla*, then, and consequently the myth of Don Juan, is the text by which society explains the opposition between desire on the one hand and the need for the institution of a (Christian) social stability on the other. In Lévi-Strauss's terms, Don Juan's story constitutes the process by which conflict in society is dialectically resolved, since "mythical thought always progresses from the awareness of oppositions towards their resolution" (*Structural Anthropology* 2:224).

There are two serious weaknesses in Molho's analysis. First, it is questionable whether or not Molho's conclusion constitutes an "anthropologically" sound judgment of the texts in question. In *El burlador de Sevilla*, the possibility and importance of monogamy are very much in evidence prior to Don Juan's intrusion, and Christian marriage is not instituted as a result of his affronts. Rather, and as we shall see, Don Juan is a catalyst toward this reaffirmation of monogamy, if not the outright cause, in a scenario in which matrimony is tantalizingly invoked and less surely upheld. It is not, then, an either/or choice between desire and monogamy. Don Juan stimulates the impulse toward social stability as represented by marriage and plays a role in the proper channeling of desire in *El burlador de Sevilla*. Strictly speaking, then, Molho is straining his argument when he asserts that the myth of Don Juan both recounts and represents the origins of monogamy; wherever monogamy originated and however it was rationalized in the seventeenth century, Tirso does not confront either topic, even though monogamy is a forceful and significant issue in the drama.

Second, Molho's insistence on the adequacy of the term *myth* remains

troubling. As the epigraph to his second study indicates (which is taken
from Lévi-Strauss and reads, "Tout mythe, du seul fait qu'il existe,
énonce un discours cohérent" ["Every myth, by the very fact that it
exists, expresses a coherent discourse"]), the essence of myth for Molho
is its unity, the unity of its discourse as well as the possibility of creating endless reproductions of the same truth: in this case, that truth
pertains to the origins of monogamy. But Lévi-Strauss also says that
"the unity of the myth is never more than tendential and projective and
cannot reflect a state or a particular moment of the myth. It is a
phenomenon of the imagination, resulting from the attempt at interpretation; and its function is to endow the myth with synthetic form and to
prevent its disintegration into a confusion of opposites" (*The Raw and
the Cooked* 4). The unity of myth in these terms is a "projection," the
act of interpretation itself, which is to say, the unity brought to the
myth by the "mythologist" or critic. We can take this one step further.
Although the "synthetic form," the result of the critic's interpretive
labor, prevents the myth from "dissolving into a confusion of opposites," that confusion of opposites is *also* the result of interpretation
because it is the heuristic base on which the critic constitutes his
reading. The rejection of the syntagmatic disposition of the plot as
embodied in the text engenders, then, not a paradigm, as Molho and
Lévi-Strauss would have it, but another syntagma, *another story*. So
the story of Don Juan that Molho, via Lévi-Strauss, would transform
into an easily comprehensible form of social discourse is nothing more
than a retelling of an elusive and ephemeral original "text."

In a somewhat different context, Lévi-Strauss affirms that this possibility of conversion is precisely the point: "We define the myth as consisting of all of its versions; or to put it otherwise, a myth remains the
same as long as it is felt as such. . . . Therefore, not only Sophocles, but
Freud himself, should be included among the recorded versions of the
Oedipus myth on a par with earlier and seemingly more 'authentic'
versions" (*Structural Anthropology* 2:217). Yet by this logic Lévi-
Strauss's own version of Oedipus is not itself exempt from being considered as a "source" of the myth; because there is no privileged textual
basis, no single authoritative or authentic version, no text is closed to
the act of interpretation. Even those texts that are assumed to be
somehow different from the works that they undertake to study are, in
fact, open to interpretation and analysis. In this way, the methodology
adopted uncritically by Molho converts "Trois mythologiques sur Don
Juan" into another version of the story it pretends to study. Molho's
interpretation becomes part of his discourse of monogamy, not only an

explication of Don Juan but also a perpetuation of his meaning, whatever that meaning might be.[8]

As the first study in his essay demonstrates, however, Molho is clearly unaware of the many ways in which this shift from telling to understanding works on a theoretical level, a failing that has serious consequences for his entire enterprise. Molho begins the essay by pointing out what is *not* known of Tirso's play. The lack of information regarding the first performance and the publication of the drama, the uncertain authorial attribution, and the fact that there is no definitive text, all contribute to the impossibility of situating the drama in a specific historical moment, or, for Molho, of positing the origin of the myth. This move on the part of both Rousset and Molho corresponds to the historical claims made by other critics, most notably those who emphasize the "legendary" nature of Don Juan and who detect a lengthy literary precedent for *El burlador de Sevilla* (a past that would include Ovid's *Ars Amatoria* as well as other works).[9] As Molho recognizes, however, the distinction between oral and written literary representation is crucial because a textual tradition is different from an oral tradition. He both bridges and exploits this gap with his presentation

8. Of course, both Lévi-Strauss and Molho would argue that this new version of the story, this new syntagma, was constructed by means of their critical elaboration at a level higher than that of the story in its analyzed form. This corresponds to dialectical philosophy and to the dialectics of Lévi-Strauss's own approach. The new version, the *critical* version, sublates (or sublimates) the syntagmatic and paradigmatic versions so as both to represent and to subvert, to include and to discount, the material under scrutiny. Nevertheless, Molho, like Lévi-Strauss, ignores the possibility of the sublation of his own version, which focuses attention on his methodology and finally on the problematic nature of his manipulation of the literary texts. In this regard see Herrnstein Smith, who remarks of narrative and plot summaries of a novel, "Not only will different summaries of the same narrative be produced by people with different conventions, habits, and models of summarizing, but even given the *same* conventions, their summaries will be different if the motives and purposes of their summarizing are different. . . . Each of these summaries would simplify the narrative at a different level of abstraction. . . . It is evident, moreover, that each of these summaries would, in effect, be another *version* of the novel: an abridged and simplified version, to be sure. . . . My point here is that what narratologists refer to as the basic stories or deep-plot structures of narratives are often not abstract, disembodied, or subsumed entities but quite manifest, material, and particular retellings—and thus versions—of those narratives, constructed, as *all* versions are, by someone in particular, on some occasion, for some purpose, and in accord with some relevant set of principles" (217–18). See also Barbara Johnson's discussion of citation and paraphrase in "The Frame of Reference," *The Critical Difference* 110–46.

9. See Agustín; Díaz-Plaja; Arturo Farinelli, "Don Giovanni," *Don Giovanni,* and "Cuatro palabras"; Fernández de la Reguera; Pérez de Ayala, "Don Juan" (1937), in *Obras completas* 3:343–90; and Salgot.

and analysis of *Les âmes du purgatoire,* in which Mérimée recounts two versions of Don Juan's story as an introduction to his own version of Don Juan (a fact that Molho chooses to ignore, going so far as to excise from his citation of Mérimée the paragraph that makes the introductory nature of this material obvious). By beginning his discussion of the myth of Don Juan with these paragraphs from Mérimée, Molho in effect creates an oral tradition for Don Juan's story: "We shall approach the myth not from the perspective of DJ_1, but with the help of two late versions that Prosper Mérimée quotes . . . which were collected, it seems, in the streets of Seville" (11). These oral versions of Don Juan's story are then opposed to the written version of Don Juan, and are used to subvert the "traditional mythic discourse."

The "historiettes" do not, however, simply "subvert" the myth. Molho reads the two oral versions against *El burlador de Sevilla* "in order to see that they are a rigorously inversive replication" (31).[10] The proof of this most rigorous of inversions lies in the historical and social climate of Spain, and more particularly in the differences between the Spanish seventeenth and early nineteenth centuries. The "traditional" myth as found in Tirso's drama "is therefore nothing more than an edifying ritual of repression" (32). This "ritual of repression" repeats itself, moreover, in the later plays by Zamora and Zorrilla as a celebration of the "Spaniards' gregarious and self-repressive reaction" (32). Mérimée's "historiettes," on the other hand, represent an oral version of "a secret and blasphemous cult" (33), indeed, a version in which Don Juan, as a diabolical force, is fully able to triumph over the Commander. This contradiction, according to Molho, "is the very one that overcomes, from variant to variant, the mythical structure DJ_1" (33).

10. For Lévi-Strauss, inversion figures as a key transformation in the process of a myth's transmission. Lévi-Strauss explains: "Thus we arrive at a fundamental property of mythical thought. . . . When a mythical schema is transmitted from one population to another, and there exist differences of language, social organization, or way of life that make the myth difficult to communicate, it begins to become impoverished and confused. But one can find a limiting situation in which, instead of being finally obliterated by losing all its outlines, the myth is inverted and regains part of its precision" (*Structural Anthropology* 2:184). For Molho, this "rigorously inversive replication" is just one of many logical steps in the course of a myth's transmission and, more important, transformation. Nevertheless, it must be noted first, that Lévi-Strauss is speaking primarily of myths that have been transmitted from one *culture* to another. This means that, while cultures can be distinct for reasons of time or period, the emphasis remains on problems of language, social organization, and way of life. Second, as Mary Douglas has succinctly pointed out apropos of Lévi-Strauss's analysis of "The Story of Asdiwal" and the problem of inversion, "opposition is a pliable concept in the interpreter's hands. The whole notion of dialectic rests on the assumption that opposition can be unequivocally recognized" (60).

Unhappily, Molho's emphasis on *Les âmes du purgatoire* is entirely misplaced. Mérimée's story opens with these words:

> Cicero said somewhere, I think in his treatise *On the Nature of the Gods,* that there were many Jupiters—a Jupiter in Crete, another on Olympus, another somewhere else—so that there was not a city in Greece of any importance that didn't have one of its own. All of these Jupiters have been made into one to whom all of the adventures of each of his namesakes have been attributed. This explains the prodigious number of great exploits ascribed to this god.
>
> The same confusion is found with regard to Don Juan, a character whose celebrity closely approaches that of Jupiter. Seville alone had several Don Juans; many other towns had their own. At one time, there was a separate legend for each. In time, they all merged into one.
>
> However, on closer consideration, it is easy to separate them out, or at least to distinguish between two of the heroes, namely, Don Juan Tenorio, who, as everybody knows, was carried off by a statue of stone, and Don Juan de Maraña, whose end was completely different.
>
> The stories of the lives of both men are nearly the same: only the denouement distinguishes them. There is an ending for every taste, as in the plays of Ducis, which conclude happily or sadly, according to the sensibility of his readers.
>
> As to the truth of this story or, rather, of these two stories, there is no doubt. The provincial patriotism of the people of Seville would be gravely offended if one were to question the existence of these libertines who have rendered suspect the genealogies of their noblest families. . . .
>
> I have attempted to give to each of these Don Juans the part that belongs to him in their common careers of wickedness and crime. For lack of a better method, I have tried to tell of Don Juan de Maraña, my hero, only those adventures that do not, by right of prescription, belong to Don Juan Tenorio, so familiar to us through the masterpieces of Molière and Mozart. (*Les âmes du purgatoire* 351–52)

In passing, note that Molho takes Mérimée's "legends" and turns them into "myths," distorting the character of the prefatory material. Yet Molho's real fascination with *Les âmes du purgatoire* stems not from the semantic possibilities of the text, but, rather from Mérimée's open-

ing moves. Indeed, Molho's analysis recuperates the vicissitudes of the
introductory paragraphs to Mérimée's story of Don Juan de Maraña:
both begin with a tale that is told, an oral version of the story of Don
Juan, and then turn to consider written versions of the same story.

Still, Mérimée's account of the two oral versions of Don Juan's story
is obviously nothing more than a frame for his own fictional account of
Don Juan de Maraña. The opening paragraph in which he accurately
refers to Cicero's *De natura deorum*—most likely to the discussion of
the three Jupiters (3.21)—is an attempt to grant privilege to his own
version of Don Juan: just as Crete's Jupiter is only one aspect of the
collective "myth" of that god, *Les âmes du purgatoire* is another part of
the larger legend surrounding the figure of Don Juan. Molho, however,
does not treat the quotation from Mérimée in these terms. He sees in
the frame story an oral version of a myth and not a modification of the
well-known topos of affected modesty so common in literary prefaces.
Moreover, at least in this case, Molho is a trusting soul. He accepts
Mérimée's word that the "historiettes" were, in fact, "collected . . . in
the streets of Seville" ["recueillies . . . dans les rues de Séville"] with
only the addition of a cautionary "it seems" ["semble-t-il"]. We are left
with his opposition between written Don Juans—*El burlador de
Sevilla, No hay plazo que no se cumpla ni deuda que no se pague, Don
Juan Tenorio*—and Mérimée's oral versions. Yet the oral versions are,
in fact, not strictly so; they were collected and written out and are,
therefore, part of a text presented as if it were part of an ongoing oral
tradition. What Molho regards as a subversion of the Don Juan myth
can be understood as a frame story that is in reality exemplary in its
imitation of traditional exordia.

The fact that Don Juan exists only as a function of a *literary* text is
thus effaced once more, although in a manner distinct from that associated with those critics who resort to such notions as the Jungian collective unconscious. Whereas (in Jungian terms) the situation of Don Juan
in the collective unconscious renders his myth inaccessible except
through various incomplete manifestations, Molho subverts the written
Don Juan (*El burlador de Sevilla* as the "key myth") by opening it up to a
putative oral version and by finding the story as written to be so restricted that the only possible interpretive accommodation is through
"subversion" and "inversion." Molho then replaces Don Juan's story as a
progression through time with a paradigmatic "synthetic form," a hypothetical and static coherence that is dependent upon arbitrarily designated critical categories. The term *myth,* then, when used in application
to the story of Don Juan, brings unity (of plot, of characters, and of
meaning) to a seemingly disparate collection of texts and literary forms

by permitting the critic to disallow the importance of any discrepancies, by enabling him to incorporate differences into the sum total of all possible versions. Behind this simultaneous recuperation and denial of difference—recuperation in its critical accomodation by means of the concept of myth; denial in that any significant alteration in meaning is attributed to a structural variance—rests the concept of history. Although Molho believes that the details of the myth may be altered in individual representations according to the needs of a specific historical moment, the myth per se retains its integrity.

This essential integrity, of course, is the point of Rousset's classification of the "invariable" and "variable" elements of the myth. An analogous moment occurs in Molho's essay during his discussion of *El burlador de Sevilla,* but with slightly divergent, though nonetheless important, consequences when he emphasizes the sameness of Don Juan's seduction of Isabela, Tisbea, Doña Ana, and Aminta. According to Molho, difference is important here only insofar as each woman represents a new conquest for Don Juan. Even if they are different women, the seduction remains the same act in which the meaningful element of the repetition is the essentially identical nature of each seduction. This allows Molho to claim that each seduction is *equally* important and categorically *identical* just as he will go on to assert that the responses of the various male characters are in essence the *same response.* As we have seen, the effect of this procedure is to shift attention from the diachronic aspects of the story to the representation of the events as synchronic and invariable repetitions of a single action. But this procedure is nothing more than the logical outcome of an appeal to a normative and all-encompassing version of Don Juan's story, a version that can never be fully portrayed or apprehended. It thereby amounts to nothing more than the denial of the meaningful nature of the progression through time of individual textual representations in order to invoke the atemporal nature of myth. In this way, the oppositions instituted as critical categories—the opposition between an oral and written "text"; popular and literary versions—point to granting privilege to one category over another. The *text* representing Don Juan's story, the word as written, becomes the handmaiden of the *myth* of Don Juan. To say, therefore, that myth, when used in application to Don Juan, enables the critic to disallow the importance of difference is to say that the critics who both invoke and justify invocation of the term *myth* do so in order to legitimate their increasing distance from the text, since they implicitly confer greater importance on that which is not written.

This point is not minor. Mérimée, for example, is obviously aware of

the dynamics of written representation and the role that the figure of
Don Juan plays in the mechanics of storytelling. To return to the introductory paragraphs of *Les âmes du purgatoire,* the trajectory of the
frame story is not merely one from oral to written versions—from the
two "historiettes" to Molière and Mozart—in which the end result is an
accomodation of his own version. Mérimée moves from a curious yet
entirely accurate reference to Cicero, through the multiple Don Juans
of Sevilla and the two Don Juan stories, in order finally to assert his
desire to distinguish himself from Molière and Mozart. But this is a
summary of only the most salient features of the prefatory material.
We must ask what holds this sequence of ideas together. And why a
story about Don Juan? Does Mérimée simply intend to legitimate the
multiple Don Juans by means of the reference to Cicero? Even given
Molho's procedures, it is somewhat misleading to comment, as Molho
does, on Mérimée's use of Cicero in terms of Jupiter alone. To do so is to
posit a movement in Mérimée's prefatory material from a discussion of
an individual god (with many and various manifestations) to an
oblique reference to two renowned authors of works treating Don Juan.
The point of the reference to Cicero is not just that there are many
Jupiters, but that each significant town has its own Jupiter in order to
suggest its importance and to enhance its reputation. Likewise, and
this is the point of Mérimée's invocation of Cicero's *De natura deorum,*
any author of merit claims his right of association with other significant authors, in Mérimée's case, with Molière and Mozart. Not only has
Mérimée distinguished himself and his hero from the canonical versions of Molière and Mozart, he has also employed a traditional literary
figure in such a way that the grounds for comparison are implicitly
established and his filiation from Molière and Mozart is explicitly
stated, a filiation again suggested when Mérimée mentions the noble
families of Sevilla. Every detail in the paragraphs introducing *Les
âmes du purgatoire* therefore contributes to the creation of a literary
history in which Mérimée, as an author, takes his place alongside the
canonized immortals of the recent past. Don Juan, as the protagonist of
these works, is thus the link between and among all of these authors,
the means by which they all come together.

   That an author should attempt to suggest his eminence both by
returning to a well-known literary character and an oft-told story and
by gesturing towards those eminent predecessors who have treated
that character and story is not peculiar to the early nineteenth century.
Horace advises the Pisos in the *Ars Poetica* to do the same thing. On
the subject of the material appropriate for an author's attentions and

talents, Horace counsels either the invention of a story that is internally consistent, a story in which each element contributes to the consonance of the whole, or the adherence to a sure tradition: "Aut famam sequere aut sibi convenientia finge" ["Either follow tradition or invent what is self-consistent"] (line 119). But Horace leaves little doubt as to which of the two options is to be preferred:

> Difficile est proprie communia dicere; tuque
> rectius Iliacum carmen deducis in actus,
> quam si proferres ignota indictaque primus.
> publica materies privati iuris erit, si
> non circa vilem patulumque moraberis orbem,
> nec verbo verbum curabis reddere fidus
> interpres, nec disilies imitator in artum,
> unde pedem proferre pudor vetet aut operis lex.
> (lines 128–35)

[It is hard to treat in your own way what is common: and you do better to spin into acts a song of Troy than if, for the first time, you were to give the world a theme unknown and unsung. Public matter shall be of a private right if you do not linger along the beaten path, if you do not seek to render word for word as a slavish translator, and if in your imitating you do not put yourself into a tight spot, out of which either shame or the laws of genre will keep you from retracing your steps.]

For Horace, language, and that which language engenders, exists as a *res communis,* as something not only familiar to all humans, but also as something shared by all. Thus, an author who wants to demonstrate his worth can best do so by undertaking a project previously essayed by another, by handling familiar material with originality so as to make that which is common, personal ("publica materies privati iuris erit" ["public matter shall be of a private right"]). In this way, an author's claim to greatness is necessarily measured against the achievements of others; it thus depends on his ability to master and to remake material already in the public domain (see Brink 103–9; Norton 190–91). Mérimée's story, if not a conscious response to Horace's injunction, makes use of Don Juan precisely in the manner advocated by the author of the *Ars Poetica.* Don Juan's story functions as the common ground, as the *res communis,* between the nineteenth-century author of *Les âmes du purgatoire* and several major literary figures of the recent past, who are significant for having treated the same topic. Don Juan allows Mérimée to extrapolate his own heritage and thereby to construct a genealogy for his own literary endeavors.[11]

A reference to Horace would be gratuitous at this point were it not for the fact that Byron uses a line from the *Ars Poetica*—"Difficile est proprie communia dicere"—as the motto of his own epic version of Don Juan's story. What serves only as an oblique confirmation of the reasons for Mérimée's invocation of Cicero's multiple Jupiters instead figures prominently as the epigraph to another treatment of Don Juan. But it is no coincidence that Horace is mentioned on the opening page of Byron's *Don Juan*. Byron was well acquainted with Horace's epistle to the Pisos—having translated it earlier under the title of *Hints from Horace*—and the didactic spirit of the *Ars Poetica* perfectly suits the moral intent of Byron's poem.[12] As Jerome J. McGann, one of Byron's more insightful readers, puts it, "*Don Juan* is intended, first, to correct the degenerate literary practices of the day; and second, to expose the social corruption which supports such practices" (65). Thus, according to McGann, "The point of *Don Juan,* insofar as it is a literary manifesto, is to clarify the nature of poetry in an age where obscurity upon the subject, both in theory and practice, was becoming rampant. . . . *Don Juan* was an attempt to restore poetry to its proper place and functions, both for its own good and for the benefit of the world it was meant to serve" (78, 165).

Byron himself leaves little doubt as to his intent in the poem. In the Preface and Dedication (both of which were suppressed by the author prior to publication of the first two cantos), he openly names the objects of his ire, taking first Wordsworth, the Lake Poets, Coleridge, and then

11. J. W. Smeed makes a similar point when he remarks that Don Juan is a character who is "bound to provoke strong feelings for or against him and who invites constant reinterpretation as moral views and social circumstances change. No doubt, second- and third-rate minds will have been drawn to him for the wrong reasons, seeing in this universally familiar character an easy option which seemed to reduce the need for original invention. . . . But more exacting and fastidious writers were drawn to this well-worn theme for precisely the opposite reason: because it challenged them to perceive and reveal fresh meaning in it. . . . The Don Juan legend is something like a popular tune on which countless composers have written variations" (150).

12. *Hints from Horace,* a free translation of the *Ars Poetica,* was completed in Athens in 1811 but not published until 1831, subsequent to Byron's death. Byron translated the passage in question, "Difficile est proprie communia dicere," as " 'Tis hard to venture where our betters fail, / Or lend fresh interest to a twice-told tale" (*Poetical Works* 1:296, lines 181–82). On Byron and Horace, see Jerome J. McGann 69–79. For a discussion of Byron's use of Don Juan's story, see M. K. Joseph 162–82.

Robert Southey, Britain's poet laureate, to task for their literary pretensions and for their ignorance of poetic tradition: in short, for their complete disregard for the power of poetry. Moreover, in a letter written to his publisher, John Murray, from Genoa on 25 October 1822, Byron explains that *"Don Juan* will soon be known by and bye for what it is intended a *satire* on *abuses* of the present states of Society" (*Letters and Journals* 10:68). A backward glance at Horace thus serves to confirm both Byron's didactic intent (for Horace's message is certainly didactic) and his strong belief in poetic tradition. Furthermore, the epigraph in its most literal meaning stresses the difficulty of speaking on common things in an appropriate manner and sets the tone for the early cantos of Byron's poem, which Byron characterizes in his first extended reference to *Don Juan* in a letter to Thomas Moore written from Venice on 19 September 1818 as being "a little quietly facetious upon every thing" (*Letters and Journals* 6:67).

But how does Don Juan as a character and protagonist fit into this recollection and recuperation of poetic tradition? Is he as important to Byron's undertaking as the Horatian motto would seem to indicate? Byron certainly thinks so. In the opening five stanzas of Canto I, four of which (stanzas 2–5) were added subsequent to the suppression of the Dedication and Prologue, he introduces his protagonist and then he reviews other possible candidates for the role:

1

I want a hero: an uncommon want,
    When every year and month sends forth a new one,
Till, after cloying the gazettes with cant,
    The age discovers he is not the true one;
Of such as these I should not care to vaunt,
    I'll therefore take our ancient friend Don Juan,
We all have seen him in the Pantomime
Sent to the devil, somewhat ere his time.

2

Vernon, the butcher Cumberland, Wolfe, Hawke,
    Prince Ferdinand, Granby, Burgoyne, Keppel, Howe,
Evil and good, have had their tithe of talk,
    And fill'd their sign-posts then, like Wellesley now;
Each in their turn like Banquo's monarchs stalk,
    Followers of fame, 'nine farrow' of that sow:
France too, had Buonaparté and Demourier
Recorded in the Moniteur and Courier.

3

Barnave, Brissot, Condorcet, Mirabeau,
    Petion, Clootz, Danton, Marat, La Fayette,
Were French, and famous people as we know;
    And there were others, scarce forgotten yet,
Joubert, Hoche, Marceau, Lannes, Dessaix, Moreau,
    With many of the military set,
Exceedingly remarkable at times,
But not at all adapted to my rhymes.

4

Nelson was once Britannia's god of war,
    And still should be so, but the tide is turn'd;
There's no more to be said of Trafalgar,
    'Tis with our hero quietly inurn'd;
Because the army's grown more popular,
    At which the naval people are concern'd:
Besides, the Prince is all for land-service,
Forgetting Duncan, Nelson, Howe, and Jervis.

5

Brave men were living before Agamemnon
    And since, exceeding valorous and sage,
A good deal like him too, though quite the same none;
    But then they shone not on the poet's page,
And so have been forgotten:—I condemn none,
    But can't find any in the present age
Fit for my poem (that is, for my new one);
So, as I said, I'll take my friend Don Juan.
                    (*Poetical Works* 5:9–10, lines 1–40)

Some critics of Byron's *Don Juan* have done the poet a grave disservice by discounting the importance of stanzas 2–5. For example, in his commentary on the composition of the poem, Truman Guy Steffan says, "It is a little strange that Byron, who tried so hard for animation, should have nodded so drowsily when he let his accretive habit overburden the beginning of the poem. . . . These four new pessimistic octaves interrupt the continuity of stanzas 1, 6, 7, 8, but the appeal of a favorite negative theme (futility) and the delight in allusive amplification override his narrative concern" (71).[13] This viewpoint is not only mistaken,

13. Steffan also includes in this same volume a chronology of Byron's composition of *Don Juan* that is interesting for its confirmation of the reading of the opening stanzas of

it constitutes a crucial misreading of the opening stanzas of the first canto of the poem. Far from interrupting the flow of the opening stanzas, the addition of the four stanzas sets the tone for and states the didactic intent of the verses that follow. As a conceptual whole, the first five stanzas of Byron's *Don Juan,* when read in conjunction with the epigraph from Horace, demonstrate the extent to which Don Juan is recognized and cherished by Byron as a literary character, as a character important for the dense literariness and the sense of tradition Don Juan lends a text.

For both Mérimée and Byron, Don Juan is a character who recalls and, indeed, who embodies a series of other texts. But this idea of Don Juan's essential *literariness* is opposed to the critical notion of the mythical Don Juan that we have been describing. Although as a literary character he is dependent on textual representation (in turn this dependence is crucial to the aims of Mérimée and Byron), the mythical Don Juan, as a kind of broadly nonliterary—or at best only partially literary—character, is used as a means of evading the specificity of any given representation. As such, myth and the mythical Don Juan are used to validate the strategic moves of the critics: not merely the move away from a given text, at best a banal issue, but the move away from *all* questions of representation, writing, and rewriting, raised by *any* version of Don Juan's story.

In fact, questions related to writing and rewriting ought to be at the heart of any treatment of Don Juan, particularly any broad or historically based treatment. To use Mérimée's examples of the Molière and Mozart–Da Ponte versions, it is a matter of record that neither author, neither Molière nor the librettist Da Ponte, was without "assistance" in the writing of his version of the story. Molière looked to two previous French works, both entitled *Le festin de Pierre ou le fils criminel,* by Dorimon and Villiers (see Gendarme de Bévotte 1:64–66, 84–96; Weinstein 32). Da Ponte's *Don Giovanni,* on the other hand, was loosely based on and at times freely taken from other Italian versions of the story, particularly Bertati's libretto for Gazzaniga's opera of nearly the same name (Weinstein 61–62). Although the Molière and Mozart–Da Ponte versions are recognized as masterpieces, far superior to other works of the same period, neither is without precursors serving to provide the later works with certain forms, ideas, and even specific

---

the poem given here. It is obvious that Byron added the stanzas in question *after* he had made the decision to publish the first two cantos without the Dedication and Prologue. In other words, Byron used the additional material to restate and to reformulate the intent of his poem (300–301).

lines. The complexity of this textual tradition is one of the salient reasons why myth, in this context, is so problematic. As an ahistorical and atemporal critical category, myth allows the critic to avoid all issues of writing and rewriting, as well as specific texts, in the search for either the so-called *original* Don Juan or *real meaning* of the story, Lévi-Strauss notwithstanding.

Given the prominence of these issues of writing and rewriting—and they are significant both in a broadly historical sense and in regard to the specific texts in question—saying that Don Juan is a myth becomes even more problematic when his status as a literary character, as an effect of the written word, is taken into account. An oral origin is not a demonstrable fact, but only the inference of those anxious to sustain the thesis that Don Juan is a mythical character. Don Juan's story is, therefore, not a myth, but a *mythology,* that is, a special kind of discourse that has as its primary attribute the fact that it is written. Moreover, in this instance, mythology is not merely a discourse on myth, but, in Marcel Detienne's terms, a *mythography,* the writing of or on myth.[14] Thus, the literary and critical versions of Don Juan's story, the written texts per se, constitute not myth and mythology respectively, but always a kind of mythography, a writing that always refers to some other like or related text.

In this sense, E. T. A. Hoffmann's short story "Don Juan" (1813) is instructive. The action of the story involves attendance at a performance of Mozart's *Don Giovanni.* After the first act of the opera, a woman, Donna Anna, enters the narrator's box and the two converse before the singer returns to the stage, to perform, it later seems to the narrator, under extreme emotional duress. After dinner, the narrator returns to the theater and his room where he jots down his impressions of the opera and its characters for his friend Theodore. Later, he detects

14. Detienne says, "Mythology is written. There is no mythology, in the Greek sense, except in mythographic form, in writing, through the writing that traces its boundaries, that outlines its figure. And it is through an illusion, that, since the nineteenth century, mythology has come to be the speech, the song, and the voice of origins" ("Rethinking Mythology" 52). See also Detienne's *The Creation of Mythology.* Charles Segal takes Detienne's observations as his point of departure in his "Greek Tragedy: Writing, Truth, and the Representations of the Self," remarking, "The oral culture of early Greece is mediated for us by writing, and the search for the preliterate substratum may be another form of Western man's perpetual longing for a primordial world of innocence and simplicity. When writing becomes the major force not only in recording, but also in creating and shaping myth, we may be dealing with 'l'illusion mythique' rather than with the genuine, first-degree myth of an oral culture; and access to a realm of pure myth, uncontaminated by the reflective and distancing processes of recording them, becomes ambiguous, uncertain, and paradoxical" (108–9).

the scent of Donna Anna's perfume only to learn the next day that the woman who sang Donna Anna died at the same hour that he noticed her perfume. Rather than yet another version of Don Juan's story, Hoffman's retelling is more properly an *interpretation*. As Leo Weinstein points out, "In attempting to evaluate Hoffman's contribution to the Don Juan legend, it must be borne in mind that his short story is not a new version but rather an interpretation of a previous version, that of Mozart and Da Ponte. Up to this point, every author who had advanced a new view on Don Juan had supported it by means of a play, but Hoffman merely presents a new interpretation—the execution of it is left to others" (76). In fact, the distinction between a version and an interpretation, or, in Lévi-Strauss's terminology as appropriated by Molho, between telling and understanding, reveals itself in the case of Hoffman's "Don Juan" to be difficult to sustain; and the short story poses a number of questions related to this discussion. What was intended in this short story? Is it, indeed, "merely" an interpretation or is it to be read as a literary text? Are the two that different, or are they one and the same?

To return to Molho's essay, we have seen how his structuralist study of myth both turned on him and turned his analysis into one more version of that which he was explicating. Molho distorted Mérimée's introductory paragraphs to *Les âmes du purgatoire,* turning legend into myth, and he transcribed "oral" tales into "true" traditional oral tales, all in order to retreat from considerations of the question of textual representation. As a result, he failed to take into consideration writing and rewriting as meaningful parts of Don Juan's story. Nonetheless, it is important to see that mythology, in the sense of Detienne's "mythography," was at work in both Mérimée's and Molho's discourse: in the former in the writing out of the "historiettes" and in their attribution; in the latter in his effort to conceal the traces of his own discourse by relying on the language of mythology. In the course of his essay, Molho recapitulates the narrative strategies of Mérimée's introduction and version, even down to his appeal to a transcendent or trans-textual force in order to legitimate his interpretation: whereas Mérimée uses the statue, Molho invokes myth and history. The difference between the literary and critical versions, at least as suggested by this comparison, is that the one openly asserts its reliance on and filiation from prior textual models while the other acknowledges a methodological debt that, far from concealing its strategies, underscores its unwillingness to consider the precise nature and form of its discourse.

To call Don Juan a myth is not, then, the gross error that it might

seem. Depending on how myth is defined and delimited, Don Juan is or
is not a mythical figure; it really is not a difficult question, in large
part because it tends to ignore or to sidestep the most significant aspects of the problem itself. But Don Juan is without doubt a mythology.
He is a character in a story that has been written and rewritten; and he
is the product of a set of discursive practices common to the modern
world (see Detienne; and Barthes, *Mythologies* 109–59). The critical
versions of the story we have considered here ignore the rhetorical and
literary aspects of the various textual representations of the character
Don Juan; instead of integrating these crucial details into their interpretation as a study of the mythography of Don Juan, they suppress
them and speak of the more ephemeral, the mythical, Don Juan. As a
result, their interpretations become ideological recapitulations.

The distinction between myth and mythology, between the atemporal
unity of mythic discourse and some sort of unity that is both diachronic
and centered in the act of writing, is both theoretically and conceptu-
ally difficult. At the heart of this distinction lies, as we have seen, the
apparent difference between literary and critical notions of the importance of Don Juan and his story. This distinction presupposes, however,
that there is, in fact, a difference between the two approaches to Don
Juan, and that this difference is, moreover, significant enough to create
two distinct discourses on the same subject, two discourses that differ
in manner but not in essence. Yet this appeal to difference constitutes,
in and of itself, a critical ploy designed to distance the criticism from
the act of writing on Don Juan so as to deny the intrusion of literary,
that is, nonobjective, aims. In fact, as Shoshana Felman's recent work
on Don Juan in general (and on Molière's *Dom Juan* in particular)
demonstrates, the criticism, the critical myth of Don Juan, can indeed
recapitulate in manner as well as meaning the literature treating the
mythology of Don Juan and his story.
    Felman's *The Literary Speech Act: Don Juan with J. L. Austin, or
Seduction in Two Languages* is a sophisticated and innovative handling of many of the questions pertinent to the present study in that
the author articulates the rudiments of a sensitive and useful approach
to the problem of relating the literary and critical treatments of Don
Juan and his story, although she explores the similarities between two
types of discourse not necessarily concerned with the same topic as
opposed to two distinct forms of discourse that ostensibly treat the
same subject. Intended as "a meditation on promising, in such a way
that the place of the literary will become the meeting and testing
ground of the linguistic and philosophical, the place where linguistics

and philosophy are interrogated but also where they are pushed beyond their disciplinary limits" (11), the book foregrounds the linguistic aspects of Don Juan's role as a seducer and then proceeds to use this grammar of seduction as a means of reading John Austin's formulation of speech-act theory as read through Emile Benveniste's important "corrective" in "Analytical Philosophy and Language." After asserting that "the myth of Don Juan's irresistible seduction . . . dramatizes nothing other than the success of language, the felicity of the speech act," and that to "seduce is to produce felicitous language," Felman concludes in a truly Lacanian fashion that the

> desire of a Don Juan is thus at once desire for desire and desire for language; a desire that desires *itself* and that desires its own language. Speech is the true realm of eroticism, and not simply a means of access to that realm. To seduce is to produce language that enjoys, language that takes pleasure in having "no more to say." To seduce is thus to prolong, within desiring speech, the pleasure-taking performance of the very production of speech. (28)

Verbal pyrotechnics aside—and it is abundantly obvious that Felman's performance is intended as a seductive example of her own viewpoint, as one more mythographic version of Don Juan's story—Felman's point is that desire in Don Juan manifests itself in two ways. The first of these is as a desiring for desire, which would explain the quintessential seriality of Don Juan's seductions, the lusting after a state of *perpetual* desire; the other is as a desire for language as constituted in language, a desire that in turn creates its own language. It is possible to recognize in these distinctions the fundamental features of the differences between literary and critical treatments of Don Juan, precisely the distinctions drawn thus far. In terms of Don Juan and of Austin (and, according to Felman, Freud, Lacan, Nietzsche, among others), the seductive promise reveals the nature of its duality both as the making of a promise and as the knowledge that the promise will not (and cannot) be kept. Moreover, from the fictional Don Juan to the historically verifiable Austin (and Freud, etc.), the discourse of the various figures is open to the misinterpretation that is another constitutive element of the promise, what Felman views as the Austinian distinction between the performative and constative aspects of language. Because Felman believes that the nature of Don Juan's promise is to be misunderstood, the promise cannot but be broken; likewise, Austinian (and Freudian, Lacanian, Nietzschean . . .) theories have been the subject of critical controversy precisely because their inherent theoretical and rhetorical complexities have caused the promise of intelligibility and comprehension to be broken as well.

All discourse can thus be viewed as a kind of performance that attempts to seduce (by one means or another) and to reconstitute itself (by means of the self-referentiality of its rhetoric). In so doing, such discourse fails to fulfill the letter of its word even as the performance is the completion of the promise. But if it is true that the promise appears in Austin in a meaningful way as well as in Don Juan's story, it is also true that, in Felman's theoretical rerendering of Don Juan's story, literary works manifest more explicitly the desire for desire while critical treatments, including Felman's own, demonstrate a more acute concern for matters of language, perhaps because of their interest in the linguistic artifact. The openness with which Felman treats these issues, however, does nothing to dispel the suspicion that Don Juan himself is concerned, indeed, most preoccupied with issues related to language. Furthermore, the critical texts in question make manifest their own desire as they search for a discourse suitable both to render Don Juan's desire comprehensible and to conceal their recapitulation of that desire.

In some ways, then, Felman's point is a banal restatement of a critical cliché; certainly the ancient authorities, Quintilian, Cicero, and Horace included, would not be surprised to hear of such a high value being placed on the rhetorical and suasive aspects of a text. In part, the shortcomings of Felman's study stem from her running roughshod over differences of presentation that are significant elements of Don Juan's story and history. For example, she never adequately distinguishes between the performative qualities of a text (the written argument) and of a drama (the text brought into the domain of the spoken word). Nonetheless, Felman asserts that the "sequence of scenes delineates the direction of a trajectory, indicates the direction Don Juan's movement" (46), buttressing my own insistence on the diachrony of Don Juan's story. Because, however, she is unwilling to forgo completely the atemporal interpretive domain gained by referring to the mythical aspects of the story, the sense of movement she elucidates takes place, paradoxically, in a temporal void. Don Juan "is no longer master of the direction or meaning of his movement: heading toward the future, he moves toward the past" (48). In this way Don Juan is caught in the warp of time, coming and going according to the rules of Felman's binary opposition.

Felman's theories of Don Juan and seduction founder, therefore, on the all too familiar shoals of myth criticism. But even though *The*

Literary Speech Act is not entirely convincing, it serves as a useful index of what can be achieved by isolating the one event from which all others derive, the seduction. It also helps by demonstrating the ways in which the linguistic aspects of specific texts can be analyzed, in this case the Molière and Mozart–Da Ponte versions, to say nothing of theoretical tracts. Felman thus formulates the means by which the distinctions between literary and critical versions of the story can be understood. Seduction, as embodied in the performative speech of the promise, is shown to be at work in two types of discourse, literary and critical; as such, it constitutes the common ground for interpreting these two languages. But must Don Juan return us to the past as Felman implies? Perhaps not. Don Juan might just mean the opposite of what the various texts themselves seem to suggest.

This possibly antithetical position is addressed by Carlos Feal in *En nombre de don Juan (Estructura de un mito literario)*. In broad terms, Feal believes that "In the name of Don Juan it is possible to articulate another law, another mode of existence," one that will lead the individual and society beyond the oppositional structures of patriarchy and matriarchy to some other type of social order. At the level of the individual, Feal shows how this articulation occurs primarily—if not exclusively—in terms of the male, who, it seems, incarnates reason (that which is inherently masculine and patriarchal) but fails to embody the essence of love (that which is inherently feminine and therefore matriarchal). Don Juan's literary role is to represent and to act out this feminine law of the heart, defying in the process the patriarchal order expressed as the Lacanian "name of the father." According to Feal, Don Juan responds to a feminine desire for, or "fantasy" of, liberation by furnishing the means by which woman can escape from the strictures of man: "What Don Juan gives—or what he supposedly gives—is a type of love different from that offered by other men, a love that, in its apparent rejection of social norms, the oppressors of women, permits woman to articulate her own defense and the law of the heart" (116–17). This is not to say that Don Juan is, in fact, a positive force with respect to women, love, and personal freedom; for Feal, Don Juan defies *all* of humanity by undermining the social order of patriarchy and by tricking women into believing that he offers them a truly passionate love. In this sense, Don Juan does not embody or characterize a new social order per se; he merely points in a perversely negative way to the conditions for or possibility of an egalitarian world.

The law of the father and the law of the heart constitute an opposition that plays itself out in various ways in *En nombre de don Juan*. On the one hand, each law corresponds, supposedly, to a specifically masculine and feminine form of desire. On the other, these laws are similar to the traditional distinction in Hispanic culture and criticism between honor, that which accrues to men but inheres in the comportment of women, and love as unbridled passion, an impulse that would subvert the "name of the father" in order to assert its own law of freedom. Feal's argument begins at the level of the individual, in the guise of the male who must learn to incarnate the "feminine fantasy" of Don Juan. It extends, however, to the domain of the social, where the hierarchical roles of power in the family, which find expression over and again in the basic opposition of male and female but more significantly in the relationships between father and daughter and mother and son, might eventually reach a point of equilibrium at which man is both father *and* son and woman is both mother *and* daughter.

As Feal puts it, "It is necessary for the masculine and the feminine to interpenetrate one another [*se interpenetren*], instead of mutually excluding each other, so that the law does not degenerate into privilege, the abuse of one sex by the other" (125). I shall comment in a moment on the precise terms that Feal uses to describe this commingling. Suffice it to say for now, this hypothetical equilibrium is modeled on a dialectical transcendence of the patriarchal and matriarchal distinctions, which constitutes the central paradox of the myth of Don Juan as posited by Feal. In a world in which this type of egalitarian reciprocity figures as the primary social order, Don Juan would not need to exist; to transcend the distinctions that he defies—patriarchy and matriarchy—is to eliminate the need for a force like Don Juan in society. Therefore, "Don Juan rises once again on his own ruins as a form of utopia. . . . This is the final moment of self-completion, one that points not to the past, but to a beyond, a future time, irremissibly future" (5). In the name of Don Juan, Feal discovers utopia, which means that Don Juan does *not* have to return us to the past.

This is far different from other contemporary interpretations of Don Juan's meaning. Michel Serres, for example, in "The Apparition of Hermes: *Dom Juan*" (1968) draws, implicitly at least, on Stendhal, who observes, "Don Juan disclaims all the obligations which link him to the rest of humanity. In the great market-place of life he is a dishonest merchant who takes all and pays nothing" (173). Thus, Serres asserts that Molière's "*Dom Juan* is a complete treatise on giving and counter-giving" (12) in which "whoever will not join the chain of commerce, nor pass along the peace pipe he has received, finds himself condemned to death" (5). The drama enacts various principles of exchange and profit, demonstrating that "Don Juan is not alone, the solitary hero outside the common law, the pretext vs. the text. The false exchange generates the protective cell" (11). If Serres sees a principle of exchange, indeed, of capitalism drawn out to its logical extreme and run amok, given the element of profit involved, then Michel Foucault, writing of the "unnatural" or "perversion" in *The History of Sexuality* (1976) sees Don Juan as a man obsessed with sex:

> Underneath the great violator of the rules of marriage—stealer of wives, seducer of virgins, the shame of families, and an insult to husbands and father—another personage can be glimpsed: the individual driven, in spite of himself, by the somber madness of sex. Underneath the libertine, the pervert. He deliberately breaks the law, but at the same time, something like a nature gone awry transports him far from all nature; his death is the moment when the supernatural return of the crime and its retribution thwarts the flight into counternature. There were two great systems conceived by the West for governing sex: the law of marriage and the order of desires—and the life of Don Juan overturned them both. (1:39–40)

We shall return to Serres's economic consideration of Don Juan as a model of exchange in the last chapter of this study. For now, note how distant these two interpretations are from Feal's vision of a utopia. Far from offering a means of escaping from the present chaos, Don Juan appears in these brief considerations as an *agent* of chaos, as an integral part of our modern-day world.

Still and all, Feal marshals an impressive amount of evidence in support of his thesis. However, the psychoanalytic theory conditions, rather than merely supports, the conclusions brought to light by the literary interpretations. As recent readers of Freud, Lacan, et al., have pointed out, there is an undeniably forceful patriarchal subtext at work in psychoanalytic theory, one that holds that the woman as such is a lack or void waiting to be filled by—interpreted by—man. For Feal to ignore, then, the feminist rereadings of Freud via the Lacanian rereadings, the powerful critiques of, say, Luce Irigaray or Sarah Kofman, is to exclude the woman once again, to silence the woman's voice that he would liberate, especially since Juliet Mitchell's sensible *Psychoanalysis and Feminism,* which he cites, is, in fact, an *apology* for Freudian misogyny. The irony at work here is patent: the dialectical articulation of life beyond patriarchy and matriarchy is constituted on the nondialectical discourse of the psychoanalytic *patri*mony. The "interpenetration" of which Feal speaks, however metaphorically, becomes the *penetration* of matriarchy by patriarchy. In practical terms this means that Feal's notion of Don

Juan as a "feminine fantasy" becomes one more version of the *masculine* fantasy of what *women* fantasize about, a kind of wishful thinking that probably begins in earnest in the nineteenth century with Byron's *Don Juan* and that culminates in the twentieth century, perhaps with Shaw's *Man and Superman* (1901–3), with Don Juan as the seduced, not the seducer, or as women as the tricksters who feign interest in Don Juan, as in Edmond Rostand's *The Last Night of Don Juan* (1921).

Byron's poem begins in the first canto with the seduction of the sixteen-year-old Don Juan by a twenty-three-year-old woman, Donna Julia, the consequences of which he is forced to flee. The second and third cantos treat the relationship between Juan and Haidée in scenes that are tinged by the narrator with an aura of illicit sensuality: they are "happy,—happy in the illicit / Indulgence of their innocent desires" (5:165, lines 97–98). Even love is invoked in negative terms in these two cantos in what might be read as a recapitulation of Dante's *Inferno*, Canto 5: "Oh Love! thou art the very god of evil, / For, after all, we cannot call thee devil" (5:153, lines 1639–40). Indeed, when the love between Juan and Haidée is reintroduced at the beginning of Canto 3, the narrator asserts, "We left Juan sleeping, / . . . / And lov'd by a young heart, too deeply blest / To feel the poison through her spirit creeping, / Or know who rested there; a foe to rest / Had soil'd the current of her sinless years, / And turn'd her pure heart's purest blood to tears" (5:161, lines 1, 4–8). Innocent lovers are unwittingly sinful, love is at fault. The poem continues in this vein with other scenes of seduction in which the women always prevail upon the passively innocent Juan, with, for example, the libidinous empresses. So prevalent is this presentation of the way of things, Harold Bloom has remarked that "Byron's Don Juan shares only a name with the hero of the legend or of Mozart. At the root of the poem's irony is the extraordinary passivity and innocence of its protagonist. This fits the age, Byron insists, because its overt heroes are all military butchers. The gentle Juan, acted upon and pursued, sets off the aggressiveness of society" (Introduction, *Lord Byron's* Don Juan 3). Not only does Juan's passivity suit, as Bloom suggests, Byron's age, it acts as a foil for the poet himself, as a representation of Byron. Byron's "innocent" hero masks the seductive reality of which he is, in fact, a part. Furthermore, Byron's poem demonstrates the critical uncertainty regarding Don Juan—is he or is he not a threat to society—in its own structural avoidance of closure: Byron defers that closure, that completion, to the process of reading and interpretation, or even indefinitely.[15]

15. In her provocative study of the fragmentary nature of Romantic verse, Marjorie Levinson says of *Don Juan*, "it is clear that the irresolution which characterizes *Don*

As I shall argue in the pages that follow, Don Juan's complicity in the reality of which he is a part, his role in patriarchal society and culture, is a constant in literary treatments of the character, a constant that is oftentimes revealed by the critical indecision regarding his meaning. Contrary to Feal's position, therefore, Don Juan does not defy both patriarchy and matriarchy. Rather, Don Juan shows how matrimony forms part of the social patrimony of men; in this context, it seems justifiable to ask how a "myth," which appears in the seventeenth century yet is, by definition, inexorably linked to the past, can lead to Feal's "beyond, a future time, irremissably future." Once again, the critic is bound up in the literary complexities he is attempting to explicate. Although Feal attempts to escape from the weight of the past as it affects Don Juan, he, too, is caught in the dual movement at work in Felman's analysis: he "is no longer master of the direction or meaning of his movement: heading toward the future, he moves toward the past."

Popular—or mythical—and literary, oral and written, past and present—these are the issues inexorably involved in the interpretation of Don Juan in his many versions. Don Juan's story is an exceptionally powerful one, not only seductive in its ability to engender commentary, but also surprisingly preemptive in its capacity to control what would pass as explanation and analysis.[16] In fact, once labeled a myth, Don Juan becomes an ineradicable force in the world, like Mother Earth, the sun, the moon. Whatever one *hopes* to find in the many texts treating the

---

Juan describes neither the relationship of one canto to its successor, nor the terminal condition of the work as a whole. The poem's (in)famous irresolution occurs within each canto and through the author's digressions and his disruptive posturings. The subject of *Don Juan* is, we see, its methods: acts of interpretation and uses of context" (67–68). Franco Tonelli advocates a similar position with respect to Molière's *Dom Juan*, of which he remarks, "The play is in fact composed as a free collage of scenes that undermines any causal linking. As the action unfolds, it appears to be struggling to find a suitable 'END,' at any rate, an end grounded on univocity of meaning. It actually ends on a flamboyant *coup de théâtre* with the protagonist sent to burning hell by a statue, while his servant Sganarelle remains on stage screaming that he has been cheated out of his salary" (441).

16. This is similar to Derrida's critique of Lacan's reading of Poe's "The Purloined Letter." Derrida asks of Lacan in particular and psychoanalysis in general: "what happens in the psychoanalytic deciphering of a text when the latter, the deciphered itself, already explicates itself? When it says more about itself than does the deciphering (a debt acknowledged by Freud more than once)? And especially when the deciphered text inscribes in itself *additionally* the scene of the deciphering? When the deciphered text deploys more force in placing onstage and setting adrift the analytic process itself, up to its very last word, for example, the truth?" ("Le facteur" 414).

figure, the fact remains that Don Juan continues to do one thing over and over again: to seduce, women and men, readers and critics alike. That critical treatments have not been able to "cure" Don Juan of this quirk of behavior demonstrates to what extent seduction is the essence of Don Juan. It is necessary, therefore, to turn to the evidence provided by the literary texts in order to find out what exactly is involved in seduction. This treatment will comprise two similar but distinct enterprises: the literary aspects of Don Juan and his story as well as the ways in which Don Juan operates in and has an effect on society. Moreover, we will discuss Don Juan's importance to the authors of his story and his effects on readers, all of which means that we will consider the meaning that he bears alongside the interpretations to which he has given rise.

Don Juan and the Author: Honor and Seduction

It may seem odd to link the topics of honor and seduction affirmatively rather than contrastively, to discuss honor *and* seduction rather than honor *or* seduction. But in the story of Don Juan, these topics are indeed inextricably linked positively, not negatively, and they are complementary rather than contradictory. Honor and seduction are involved in Don Juan's story in a variety of ways and at a number of levels; the two topics are, not surprisingly given their literary exposition, oftentimes explored in the context of writing and reading, activities that are frequently coded as inherently masculine (see Gilbert and Gubar 3–44). Moreover, with respect to treatments of Don Juan, honor and seduction have a part to play in issues of literary tradition, since the question of "why Don Juan?" is implicitly invoked with each author's rewriting and reconsideration of this story. It is necessary, therefore, to discuss these topics in a historical context, in this case in terms of three dramas, Tirso de Molina's *El burlador de Sevilla y convidado de piedra* [The Trickster of Seville and the Stone Guest] (c. 1630)[1], José Zorrilla's *Don Juan Tenorio* (1844), and Adelardo López de Ayala's *El nuevo Don Juan* [The New Don Juan] (1863).

---

1. Despite the fact that there is some question as to the authorship of *El burlador de Sevilla* as well as controversy over the textual relationship between *El burlador de Sevilla* and *¿Tan largo me lo fiáis . . . ?* (see Introduction, note 1), I have opted to follow the traditional attribution and to use the more common *El burlador de Sevilla* in Joaquín Casalduero's popular edition.

By dealing with honor and seduction from the optic of literary tradition and with the author's choice of protagonist, we shall see, this time in literary texts, the nature of Don Juan's imaginative *and* social power at work.

The tendency in the many historical treatments of Don Juan is to look only at the broad outline of the topic and not at the literary and historical contexts of the individual works. In the case of *El burlador de Sevilla,* this means that this *comedia* is generally analyzed in such synoptic studies in relation to later plays and literary texts to the exclusion of the dramatic tradition out of which it grows. Yet a consideration of Tirso's drama in the context of dramatic precepts of the Spanish Golden Age as well as in the context of other *comedias* reveals on the one hand the extent to which Tirso writes within a highly self-reflexive literary framework, and on the other how certain issues relating to language are also characteristic of other Golden Age texts. With respect to discussions of *Don Juan Tenorio* and *El nuevo Don Juan,* the comparisons with the immediate significant literary predecessor are both more apparent and more insidious; literary analysis inevitably becomes secondary to comparing and contrasting two distinct literary texts. Although such comparisons can indeed be instructive, here I shall show how and why a consideration of *El burlador de Sevilla* in terms of Golden Age literary concerns relates to a general study of Don Juan and, furthermore, the ways in which rewriting and revision can help us to understand the ongoing interest in the story of the *burlador* or trickster.

Language and Seduction in *El burlador de Sevilla*

> *Amor, degno maestro*
> *sol tu sei di te stesso,*
> *e sol tu sei da te medesmo espresso;*
> *tu di lègger insegni*
> *ai più rustici ingegni*
> *quelle mirabil cose*
> *che con lettre amorose*
> *scrivi di propia man ne gli occhi altrui . . .*
>   —*Torquato Tasso,* Aminta

The literary climate of Counter-Reformation Spain in the first half of the seventeenth century was charged with conflict over a number of issues, the most significant of which involved disputes between the *culturanistas* and *conceptistas* (concerning the nature and function of poetic discourse), and the so-called battle over the direction of Spanish theater, both of which had moral implications.[2] In the latter case, the disagreement centered on the differences between the neo-classicists (or neo-Aristotelians), who advocated "classical" dramatic form and an explicit ethical intent, and the exponents of the *comedia nueva* or new drama, led by Lope de Vega, who adhered to the notion of "aesthetic" unity and who championed popularity and commercial viability. The neo-classicists, probably following Horace but drawing inspiration and authority from Aristotle, insisted on a more narrowly conceived notion of the *comedia,* while Lope, among others, advanced the cause of the more loosely defined drama that was then popular in the theaters.

With the perspective gained from a distance of three centuries, the differences between the various factions do not appear great. After all, Tirso's most famous dramas—*El burlador de Sevilla y convidado de piedra* and *El condenado por desconfiado,* to say nothing of the saints' plays—are hardly amoral or unethical, particularly when viewed in terms of the Counter-Reformation and the emphasis on religious ortho-doxy. Nevertheless, the polemic over the theater was so vitrolic and the sponsors and patrons of the individuals involved so powerful that on 6 March 1625 Tirso was banished from Madrid and forbidden to write secular poetry by the Board of Reformation of the Council of Castilla on the grounds that he wrote works "that are secular [*profanas*] and that offer evil incentives and examples" (quoted in González Palencia 83).

These conflicts aside, the importance, even predominance, of Aristo-telian dramatic precepts in early Spanish drama and dramatic theory is well known. Although the *Poetics* was not available in Spanish trans-

---

2. In fact, the two conflicts parallel and spill over into one another. Generally speak-ing, *culteranismo* refers to foreign influences, principally Latin, on word choice and turns of phrase in Spanish, and *conceptismo* has to do more with conceptual subtlety, what some have called wit. With respect to the differences between *conceptismo* and *cultera-nismo,* see Andrée Collard. See also Alexander A. Parker, who comments, "The belief, once universally held, that these are two antithetical styles, *culteranismo* being a poetic style that indulged in florid play with words, while *conceptismo* was a prose style that ingeniously played with ideas, is no longer tenable" (Introduction, *Polyphemus and Galatea* 10); and Paul Julian Smith, who notes, "The distinction has been discredited: Quevedo both imitates Góngora and makes use of the *culto* vocabulary he ridicules elsewhere. Gracián, supposed theorist of *conceptismo,* draws more freely on Góngora than on Quevedo. The distinction between the two schools is one of degree rather than essence" (*Quevedo on Parnassus* 25). On the question of the *comedia,* see Joaquín de Entrambasaguas; Edward C. Riley; Sanford Shepard; Duncan Moir; Ruth Lee Kennedy; and Juan Manuel Rozas.

lation until 1626, it appeared in Latin versions in 1498 and 1536, and in Castelvetro's Italian translation in 1570. More important, Francesco Robortello's 1548 commentary on the *Poetics* rendered more accessible Aristotle's thoughts on tragedy, the seminal notions on which Golden Age drama and dramatic theory were to be based. To these imported editions and commentaries of Aristotle we can add Spanish treatises, among them Alonso López Pinciano's monumental *Philosophia antigua poética* (1596), Juan de la Cueva's *Ejemplar poético* (1606), Lope de Vega's *Arte nuevo de hacer comedias en este tiempo* (1609), Ricardo de Turia's *Apologético de las comedias españolas* (1616), Francisco Cascales's *Tablas poéticas* (1617), and Jusepe Antonio González de Salas's *Nueva idea de la tragedia antigua* (1632–33). Despite the number and range of treatises, the conflicts among competing dramatists and theories are in some ways moot. For all the bitter rhetoric and punitive measures, the *comedia,* in its many shapes and sizes, continued to be written along lines derived from an essentially Aristotelian concept of dramatic form. There are, however, obvious and significant differences of opinion among various theorists and dramatists that reveal divisions along lines not entirely to be expected.

The most important of these differences have to do with the nature of drama, plot, and the role of imitation. Again, Aristotle is the figure of most significance for a consideration of these topics; few of the dramatists, despite other conflicts, offer marked divergences from the precepts established by the *Poetics*. For instance, Aristotle presents the key notion of drama as the imitation of an action: "Tragedy, then, is a process of imitating an action which has serious implications, is complete, and possesses magnitude; by means of language. . . . the imitation of the action is the plot, for by 'plot' I mean here the structuring of the events" (1449b, 1450a; Else 25–26). López Pinciano misreads Aristotle in a strange way, scrambling plot (*fábula*), imitation, and "the work," so that the "work itself" stands apart from its imitation, the *mythos:* "la fábula es imitación de la obra . . . no ha de ser la obra misma" ["the plot is an imitation of the work . . . it is not the work itself"]. The apparent justification for this alteration is that "las ficiones que no tienen imitación y verisimilitud, no son fábulas, sino disparates . . . [tales como los] libros de cauallerías, los quales tienen acaescimientos fuera de toda buena imitación y semejança a verdad" ["fictions that are not imitations and verisimilar are not plots, but absurdities . . . as are chivalric novels, which contain situations well beyond any worthy imitation of or similarity to truth"]. Imitation does occur, then, at the level of worldly action, but López Pinciano makes an almost Platonic distinction between *fábula* and the work per se in order to distinguish (again following Aristotle) between poets and historians, between those who "imita[n] en sus escritos a la cosa" ["imitate the thing in their writings"] and those who "escriuen a la cosa como ella fué, o es, o será" ["write of the thing as it was, is, or will be"] (1:8). In this instance, the "work" is both the historical event and the literary work at hand. López Pinciano's argument conflates what are in Aristotle separate discussions of, on the one hand, mimesis and plot, and, on the other, poets and historians.

For his part, Lope de Vega, in the *Arte nuevo de hacer comedias en este tiempo* [New Art of Writing Drama in this Age] is more direct in his formulation and considerably clearer than either Aristotle or López Pinciano. Translating Robortello's commentary virtually word for word in this passage, as elsewhere throughout the *Arte nuevo,* Lope proposes as the *comedia*'s end the imitation of the actions of men: "Ya tiene la Comedia verdadera / su fin propuesto, como todo género / de poema o poesis, y éste ha sido / imitar las acciones de los hombres / y pintar de aquel siglo las costumbres" ["Now, the true *comedia* has its proposed aim, like any genre of poetry or *poesis;* and this has been to imitate the actions of men and to paint the customs of the times"] (*Arte nuevo* 51, 285, [310]). Here, instead of drama being the imitation of an action in which men play a part ("an imitation of an action [that] is enacted by certain people" [*Poetics* 1449b; Else 26]), the actions derive from the men themselves. Despite his polemic with the neo-classicists, Lope deviates only slightly from Aristotle's general outline and remains well within an Aristotelian concept of drama and dramatic form.[3]

Only Tirso diverges markedly from the views of his contemporaries, and he does so by locating mimesis in the self-referential moment of the drama itself. In *Los cigarrales de Toledo* [The Country Estates of Toledo] he remarks that "la Comedia . . . es una imagen y representación de su argumento" ["the *comedia* . . . is an image and a representation of its plot"] (125). The drama, by which we are to understand the play as it is seen onstage, is not only the imitation of an action, but also an instance of self-referentiality in that the representation of the events of the drama entails an enactment of the processes by which

3. The primary point on which Lope deviates from Aristotle, as do many sixteenth- and seventeenth-century dramatists, including Tirso, concerns the so-called doctrine of the unity of time. On the issue of the unity of time and the *comedia,* see Lope, *Arte nuevo* 128–31, 292–93, [317–38]; and Tirso, *Los cigarrales* 124–26. On Lope's dramatic precepts, see Rinaldo Froldi; Juana de José Prades's discussion in her edition of *El arte nuevo;* M. Romera-Navarro; Margarete Newels; and Federico Sánchez Escribano and Alberto Porqueras Mayo.

those events, the drama, came to be represented or acted out. This is nowhere more evident in Tirso's *comedias* than in Serafina's speech in *El vergonzoso en palacio* [The Timid Youth at Court], the drama preceding this discussion in *Los cigarrales de Toledo,* where she includes in a collection of epithets the statement that the *comedia* "es de la vida un traslado" ["is a transcription of life"] (line 773). This translation or transcript of life is, of course, the drama itself in which the stuff of the real world is first recast and then played out. Tirso thus complicates the equation in which the *comedia* is equivalent to the imitation of an action by introducing a new variable: the argument in its written form. In so doing he ostensibly releases his own works from the limitations of a theory based solely on verisimilitude and the imitation of reality. Moreover, that Tirso's statement occurs in a discussion of what has mistakenly been referred to as the Aristotelian unity of time makes this notion of dramatic representation all the more meaningful for us. Tirso demonstrates an awareness both of the issues at stake and, in the context of the analogy that he uses in this notion's development, of the importance of what he considers to be the dramatist's *materia prima,* language itself.[4]

One of the effects of this notion of drama and the dramatic text is, in Henry W. Sullivan's words, to keep

> the play always in an illusory realm. Tirso uses this design to promote his protagonist (usually a woman) to an unusually privileged position with respect to the remaining *dramatis personae,* who become collective dupes or victims in a metatheatrical situation. Since the dramatic universe never ceases to be a theater, a representation of its action, the protagonist can slip in and out of a multitude of roles, assumed identities and effortlessly spun fictions, in order to control the actions of the rest. (77)

As we shall see, Tirso's *burlador* is precisely one of these "privileged" characters, a consummate actor. More important, this new variable, the *argumento* or plot of the script, also creates the possibility of a radically different reading of Tirso's dramatic works. Drama is no longer merely a representation of events in the world; it is also an articulation of the dramatic text as it pertains to the event of the drama itself, to the drama's presentation.

---

4. In his excellent study of Tirso's dramatic theories, Francisco Florit Durán has considered some of these same issues. Paul Julian Smith makes a similar point with regard to Tirso (*Writing in the Margin* 145–46).

I am suggesting that *El burlador de Sevilla* in particular and Tirso's dramatic works in general have a dual focus. In one sense, the dramas are highly self-conscious, addressing issues pertinent to literature, and are, therefore, self-referential. In another sense, the dramas have a worldly focus; as Francisco Florit Durán puts it, the "essential aim" of dramatic representation, "in the hands of the dramaturge, is that of maintaining the theatrical illusion, that is, that the spectators will regard the *comedia* as the dramatization of a slice of life" (87–88).[5] In other words, Tirso wants to eat his cake and to have it, too: he acknowledges that his *comedia* is indeed a literary text, but he then attempts to conceal that fact from the spectator. What results is a curious tension between specifically literary concerns and worldly action, a tension that reveals itself, not surprisingly, in terms of language.

The importance of language in *El burlador de Sevilla* is best approached contextually. If the first appearance of Don Juan as an identifiable character is in Tirso's *comedia*, this is not to say that there are no precursors of Don Juan in literary infamy. Throughout the Western literary tradition there are characters, scenes, even whole texts that anticipate either the (mis)adventures or the attitudes of the *burlador*. Within the Spanish Golden Age alone there are several works in which figures similar to Don Juan appear, including three *comedias*, *La fianza satisfecha* [Payment in Full] (attributed to Lope de Vega), Juan de la Cueva's *El infamador* [The Slanderer], and Juan Ruiz de Alarcón's *La verdad sospechosa* [The Suspect Truth].

Of more apparent similarity to Tirso's Don Juan is the scurrilous protagonist of *La fianza satisfecha*, Leonido. In this *comedia* Leonido kills his mother, blinds his father, tries to rape his sister, and rejects religion; then, when Christ speaks to him in the last act of the *comedia*, Leonido repents and commends his soul to the infinite mercy of God's love. For Willis Barnstone, Leonido surpasses Don Juan to become a type of existential hero embarked on a process of "purification": "Before he can find himself, he must violently reject all values given him by others. He must purify himself by wiping out all traces of personal and social morality" (289). In another assessment that attends closely to the evidence offered by the text and by the historical and literary contexts, William M. Whitby and Robert Roland Anderson question Barnstone's analysis and assertions. They propose that "Lope's message to the Spaniards is that of St. Paul to the Romans. . . . If for even the greatest of sinners such as Leonido there is salvation, the implica-

---

5. In *The Limits of Illusion,* Anthony J. Cascardi discusses a similar process, the tension between illusion and worldly action, in terms of Calderón.

tion is that everyone can have hope. . . . In the exaggeration of sinful man and in the representation of God's infinite mercy through the Christ figure lies the universality of *La fianza satisfecha*" (69).[6] As a drama, *La fianza satisfecha* becomes a cautionary tale about the wages of sin even as it puts forth the hopeful message of possible redemption.

Despite, therefore, the similarities between the protagonist of *La fianza satisfecha* and Don Juan—which, I would suggest, are in fact similarities only in that each character takes a dim view of social convention and also takes a shortsighted approach to worldly action as a means of obtaining divine immortality—*El infamador* and *La verdad sospechosa* offer a much more powerful means of understanding what is at the heart of Don Juan as a character and of *El burlador de Sevilla* as a *comedia. El infamador* is, as its title indicates, about language, specifically, about the nefarious uses to which language can be put, in this case the impugning of a man's honor by defaming a woman to whom he is linked either by blood or by matrimony. Leucino's actions in the play are not the crucial aspects of his threat to society. Rather, what he says about various women, although *false,* assumes the guise of *truth,* and his language therefore undercuts the very fabric of social contracts. It attacks individuals where they have both the most to lose and to gain: in terms of what other people think and say about them. What is *said* is endowed with absolute value apart from its veracity or falsity.

This same issue is involved in *La verdad sospechosa,* in which the protagonist Don García is, to put it bluntly, a liar.[7] During the course of the *comedia,* he toys with issues of identity in pursuit of the woman he loves, concealing himself behind another name. His games with language—that he both is and is not who he says he is and that he confuses the identities of two women in the play—have the unsettling consequences of forcing him to marry a woman he does not love and to lose the woman he does: Don García must marry the wrong, but also the right, woman. At the same time, his habit costs him all respect. As his noble father Don Beltrán explains it, blood ties can do nothing to protect the honor of an individual given to wicked deeds and habitual vices. In sum, "Todos los vicios al fin / o dan gusto, o dan provecho; / mas de mentir ¿qué se saca / sino infamia y menosprecio?" ["In the end, all vices either

6. See also Bruce W. Wardropper's skillful reading of this *comedia* in "*La fianza satisfecha,* a Crudely Mangled Rehash?" in which he makes passing comparisons between Leonido and Don Juan Tenorio.

7. The connection between *El infamador* and *El burlador de Sevilla* is suggested by Leo Weinstein along with the example of Leonido in *La fianza satisfecha.* Joseph E. Gillet examines this same topic in some detail.

give pleasure or profit. But what can be derived from lying other than infamy and contempt?"] (lines 1460–63). If *El infamador* is about the destructive power of language in the social arena, *La verdad sospechosa* demonstrates that same power in terms of the individual. These plays are, then, about language and honor as they function in society; they demonstrate, moreover, how language and personal honor go hand in hand.[8]

The intimate connection between language and honor is, of course, a central topic in the study of Spanish literature, perhaps the single great topic from the Middle Ages to the present. The epic *Poema de Mío Cid* (thirteenth century) treats questions of honor, as does *El conde Lucanor* (1335), in which the author Don Juan Manuel has Patronio abjure, "Et deuedes saber que en·las cosas que tannen a·la fama, que tanto aprovecha o enpeçe lo que·las gentes tienen et dizen commo lo es verdat en si" ["And you should know that in questions of fame or reputation, what people believe or say is true is as important as the truth itself"] (382); and in Mateo Alemán's picaresque novel *Guzmán de Alfarache* (1599/1604) the protagonist laments: "¡Oh ... lo que carga el peso de la honra y cómo no hay metal que se le iguale! ... que diz que mi honra ha de estar sujeta de la boca del descomedido y de la mano del atrevido, el uno porque dijo y el otro porque hizo lo que fuerzas ni poder humano pudieran resistirlo" ["Oh ... how heavy is the weight of honor; there is no metal to equal it! ... they say that my honor is subject to the talk of the insolent and the hand of the bold, to the one because he said, to the other because he did what neither force nor human power can resist"] (1:266).[9] One of the most succinct expressions of what honor is—as well as its linguistic cast—can be found in Lope de Vega's *Los comendadores de Córdoba* [The Commanders of Córdoba].[10] Here Lope says that honor "es una cosa / que no la tiene el hombre" ["is something that man does not possess"]. Thus,

---

8. On this aspect of *La verdad sospechosa*, see Alan K. G. Paterson; and William R. Blue, who says, "The two elements in the play that create the tensions and expose the basic conflicts that occur when moral statements stand side by side with immoral or amoral acts are lying and honor" (59).

9. There is oftentimes a distinction made between "honor" and "honra," one that traditionally has to do with "a sense of honor" and "honor" per se. As Américo Castro says, "*Honor is*, while *honra* belongs to someone, is acted out and is in motion throughout one's life" (*De la edad conflictiva* 69). *Honor* represents the abstract concept of honor while *honra* is its worldly aspect. A slightly different view of honor is formulated in Julio Caro Baroja, "Honor y vergüenza." See also Gustavo Correa; and Bartolomé Bennassar.

10. Donald R. Larson has an extended discussion of this *comedia* and the topic of honor (38–54). Melveena McKendrick, however, views the presentation of honor in *Los comendadores de Córdoba* with some skepticism ("Celebration or Subversion?").

> honra es aquella que consiste en otro;
> ningún hombre es honrado por sí mismo,
> que del otro recibe la honra un hombre;
> ser virtuoso hombre y tener méritos,
> no es ser honrado; pero dar las causas
> para que los que tratan les den honra.
> El que quita la gorra cuando pasa
> el amigo ó mayor, le de la honra;
> el que le da su lado, el que le asienta
> el lugar mayor; de donde es cierto
> que la honra está en otro y no en el mismo.
>   (290b–291a)

[honor is that which inheres in others. No man is honorable in and of himself; rather, he receives it from others. To be virtuous and meritorious is not to be honorable, but to cause others to honor one. He who removes his hat when passing a friend or an elder honors him, as does he who seats him at his side or in the place of honor. From this it is plain that honor rests with others and not with oneself.]

Honor is otherness, something apart and distinct from the individual involved. In Julian Pitt-Rivers's words, it is "entitlement to a certain treatment in return" (22). Moreover, honor is both to be found in and upheld by language. As Harry Sieber has remarked of the sixteenth-century picaresque novel *Lazarillo de Tormes,* "Honor . . . is ultimately the property of the community at large and is subject to continuous affirmation or attack" (96).

If language serves as the primary arbiter of personal worth in Spanish society, if honor has a predominantly linguistic cast that cannot be completely controlled by an individual, then the crucial and topical nature of *comedias* like *El infamador* and *La verdad sospechosa* is immediately apparent. With respect to Don Juan, the quintessential seducer, and *El burlador de Sevilla,* it is important to recall, first, that the title of the second of the two versions of Don Juan's story, *¿Tan largo me lo fiáis . . . ?,* comes from Don Juan's response to the many warnings of his downfall at the hands of Divine Providence. In other words, it is Don Juan's *linguistic* reaction to the world that confers upon this *comedia* its title. Second, even the title of *El burlador de Sevilla* has its origins in the text of the drama: as Don Juan notes, "Sevilla a voces me llama / el burlador, y el mayor / gusto que en mí puede haber / es burlar una mujer y dejalla sin honor" ["All of Seville calls me *the trickster.* And my greatest pleasure is to trick a woman and to leave her without honor"] (lines 1313–17; see also lines 1485–89). Finally, the link between the *burlador*, his name, and his role as a seducer, which is explicit in this last quotation, emphasizes the connection between the quasi-contractual nature of the exchange of trick for honor.

Yet what, precisely, are the linguistic aspects of Don Juan's seductions? Common critical wisdom holds that the four seductions in Tirso de Molina's *El burlador de Sevilla* are important in an external, referential sense and in an internal structural one, that they serve to prove a point regarding Spanish society in general as well as to establish the structural frame and dramatic rhythm within the *comedia*.[11] The social point of the seductions is straightforward enough: Don Juan respects neither the conventions of his own class (the nobility) nor those of his inferiors (the peasantry). Women of all classes qualify as potential objects of his desire. This fact, along with the division of the quartet of women into two noblewomen (the Duquesa Isabela and Doña Ana) and two *villanas* or peasants (Tisbea and Aminta) allows for a special kind of symmetry of action in the drama. Don Juan moves from the seduction of an aristocrat to the seduction of a peasant, accomplishing his goal with apparently equal ease. So when Don Juan flees from Doña Ana, the third of his victims, it is only to be expected that he will end up with Aminta, since earlier he quite literally fell into Tisbea's arms while fleeing from the consequences of his seduction of Isabela. The drama is, therefore, organized around the social symmetry of the four seductions, around the way one seduction logically follows another.

Each seduction, moreover, proves a different social point as Don Juan infringes upon one aspect of the codes of honor after another. As A. A. Parker puts it, "none of the four seductions perpetrated by Don Juan is merely a sin of sexual indulgence; each one is aggravated by circumstances that make it heinous" ("The Spanish Drama of the Golden Age" 694). Beyond his sinful desire to seduce, Don Juan transgresses the social codes in many other ways: he betrays his friendship with the Duque Octavio; he violates the unwritten rules of hospitality; he abuses his friendship with the Marqués de la Mota; he murders a man; and he disrupts Aminta's wedding, this final affront constituting the profanation of a sacrament. Seduction, despite its primary importance in the action of the play, is therefore only a secondary aspect of the

11. For an elaboration of this point of view, along with a discussion of the concomitant social implications, see A[lexander]. A. Parker, "The Spanish Drama of the Golden Age." For a structural interpretation of seduction in the drama, see Casalduero, Introducción, *El burlador de Sevilla* 13–23.

drama in toto, part and parcel of a general chaos stemming from one individual's desires and actions. Indeed, the main problem in *El burlador de Sevilla* is the social containment of Don Juan's anarchy, so much so that it is to this problem that Don Juan's uncle, Don Pedro Tenorio, his father, Don Diego Tenorio, and even the king of Spain all devote their considerable energies.

The dramatic symmetry created by the four seductions is further buttressed at the levels of action and dialogue. In the cases of the noblewomen, Don Juan gains access to their chambers by assuming the guises of their suitors, first of Octavio and then of the Marqués. The key to his success is his essentially theatrical nature, his willingness to play at being someone else. With the peasants, however, the situation is completely otherwise. On each occasion the *burlador* is announced by his manservant Catalinón as Don Juan Tenorio; when necessary, Catalinón goes so far as to give the full particulars of his master's status and origins. Don Juan, then, does not seduce Tisbea and Aminta by means of the adoption of a disguise but instead by playing the role into which he was born, that of the noble and commanding *caballero* or gentleman. The distinctions between the social status of his various victims are revealed and emphasized by the divergent methods used to enjoy their favors, reinforcing the similarity of the seductions.

Despite the apparent symmetries of structure, action, and dialogue, there are subtle differences between and among the episodes involving the four women in *El burlador de Sevilla* that encourage a far different reading of the meaning of seduction in the drama. Repetition of the act of seduction is not meaningful only in a formal sense insofar as it underscores the congruity of action and dialogue and drives home the point about the wages of sin. Rather, seduction, because of its prominence and predominantly linguistic cast vis-à-vis the promise, suggests the linguistic issues that will be elaborated upon and eventually resolved during the course of the *comedia*.[12] Moreover, these scenes of seduction serve as a significant index of Don Juan's progression through and development in the drama. Each individual seduction is carefully presented in such a way as to complement the preceding action and to provide more

12. On the notion of the promise in Don Juan, see Casalduero, *Contribución* 19–39; Xavier A. Fernández, "Estudio preliminar" 18–25; and Shoshana Felman. These three critics are not the first to adduce the importance of the promise. Edouard Barry mentions it in his edition of *El burlador de Sevilla y convidado de piedra* (247); as does Américo Castro in his second edition of the *comedia* (306). M. L. Radoff and W. C. Salley comment negatively on the remarks of their predecessors, to which Castro responds in his third edition of *El burlador de Sevilla* (207). Leo Spitzer backs him up in Spitzer's review of the new edition.

information about how Don Juan achieves his goal in a society that would supposedly repress him, his desires, and his actions. Don Juan's transgressions are not just cumulative, serial aggravations that add up to his punishment. They constitute a progressively complex exploration of the nature of language as it functions in the world: initially as Don Juan's tool in seduction and, finally, as the means of his undoing.

The linguistic concerns of *El burlador de Sevilla* are apparent from the earliest moments of the drama. Opening in medias res with the final moment of a lover's rendezvous, the first scene demonstrates the crucial importance of the promise for the success of Don Juan's endeavors. Furthermore, this scene quickly establishes the two fundamental enigmas on which the subsequent action will be based: while the Duquesa Isabela shows a man out of her chambers, she discovers that the man she assumes to be her lover, the Duque Octavio, is instead somebody passing himself off as the duke:

ISABELA.	Duque Octavio, por aquí podrás salir más seguro.
DON JUAN.	Duquesa, de nuevo os juro de cumplir el dulce sí.
ISABELA.	¿Mis glorias serán verdades, promesas y ofrecimientos, regalos y cumplimientos, voluntades y amistades?
DON JUAN.	Sí, mi bien.
ISABELA.	Quiero sacar una luz.
DON JUAN.	Pues, ¿para qué?
ISABELA.	Para que el alma dé fe del bien que llego a gozar.
DON JUAN.	Mataréte la luz yo.
ISABELA.	¡Ah, cielo! ¿Quién eres, hombre?
DON JUAN.	¿Quién soy? Un hombre sin nombre.
ISABELA.	¿Que no eres el duque?
DON JUAN.	No.

(lines 1–16)

[ISABELA.	Duke Octavio, you will be able to leave more safely through here.
DON JUAN.	Duchess, I once again swear to you to fulfill my sweet promise.

ISABELA.	All of my dreams will come true? The promises and offers, presents and courtesies, desires and friendships?
DON JUAN.	Yes, my precious.
ISABELA.	I want to strike a light.
DON JUAN.	Why?
ISABELA.	So that my soul can testify to that which I have just enjoyed.
DON JUAN.	I will kill the light.
ISABELA.	Oh, heavens! Who are you, sir?
DON JUAN.	Who am I? A man with no name.
ISABELA.	You are not the duke?
DON JUAN.	No.]

The role played by the promise in this scene is patently obvious: one form of "enjoyment" is exchanged for another as Don Juan swears once again to fulfill his "sweet promise" in return for Isabela's favors.[13] The two questions posed by this scene are also obvious: Who is the "man with no name"? How did he succeed in getting into the Duquesa's bedchamber? The force of these issues aside, they are not the only points of interest here. Indeed, this scene is pivotal to the *comedia;* the exchange between Don Juan and Isabela points not only to the practical questions of identity and behaviour but also to the classical mythology that forms the underpinnings of Don Juan's scenario.[14]

To begin with the underlying myth, we need only look as far as the figure of desire par excellence, Eros, or, in his Roman guise, Cupid. Cupid's importance does not stem simply from his ability to incite desire in others (although this aspect of desire does come into play later on). Rather, the key is to be found in the history of Cupid's own consummated desire, in the story of Cupid and Psyche. As told by Apuleius in the *Golden Ass,* Books 4–6, Cupid's desire to possess Psyche is fulfilled, in spite of the express wishes of Venus, his mother, only under the condition that the mortal Psyche never see her semi-immortal lover's face. Cupid must come to Psyche in the dark of night and leave before dawn: he is a presence that is sensed in every way but that cannot be

13. Useful commentary on this opening scene is offered by Manuel Durán and Roberto González Echevarría; and Arturo Serrano Plaja.

14. Robert ter Horst proposes a different type of mythological understanding of this *comedia.* Rather than working in the context of classical mythology, he speaks of the creation of what Marcel Detienne would call a mythography, which functions as a subtext for the drama ("The *loa* of Lisbon").

seen. This prohibition creates desire in Psyche, who, growing increasingly dissatisfied and mistrustful, decides that she must see her lover. While he sleeps, she takes a light to Cupid's bed, whereupon she is so excited by his beauty that, in her emotion, she allows a bit of hot oil to drop on the sleeping god. The oil awakens him, and, because Psyche has failed to keep her word, Cupid flees from her. Psyche's curiosity— her desire to see as well as to possess Cupid—disappears (and is paralleled by the god's flight) at the moment that desire is consummated. Despite this consummation, one desire succeeds another, and Psyche is launched upon a series of trials as she attempts to regain her lost lover. As in other myths and tales involving sight and prohibition—for example, the myth of Orpheus and Eurydice and the biblical accounts of Noah and his children and of Lot's wife—the desire to know or to possess is heightened by denial and, once consummated, is punished either by the absence of desire or by the necessity of creating a new, even more futile, wish. Only by endlessly deferring gratification or by creating the conditions for the enactment of a new scene of desiring can longing be perpetually present.

Cupid's status as a semi- or near-immortal being deserves explanation here, because later this quality will enter into our discussion of Don Juan. According to Plato, Eros was a *daemon,* whose role was to serve as an intermediary for mortal men and the gods. In Plato's *Symposium,* Socrates explains how he learned of Eros from Diotima:

> Yes, but what can he [Love] be, then? I asked her. A mortal?
> Not by any means.
> Well, what then?
> What I told you before—halfway between mortal and immortal.
> And what do you mean by that, Diotima?
> A very powerful spirit, Socrates, and spirits, you know, are halfway between god and man.
> What powers have they, then? I asked.
> They are the envoys and interpreters that ply between heaven and earth, flying upward with our worship and our prayers, and descending with the heavenly answers and commandments, and since they are between the two estates they weld both sides together and merge them into one great whole. They form the medium of the prophetic arts, or the priestly rites of sacrifice, initiation, and incantation, of divination and of sorcery, for the divine will not mingle with the human, and it is only through the mediation of the spirit world that man can have any inter-

course, whether waking or sleeping, with the gods. And the man who is versed in such matters is said to have spiritual powers, as opposed to the mechanical powers of the man who is expert in the more mundane arts. There are many spirits, and many kinds of spirits, too, and Love is one of them. (202d,e, 203; Hamilton and Cairns 555)

Cupid, as a *daemon,* is neither purely mortal nor immortal, but, rather, mediates the divine and the earthly. As Apuleius's retelling of the myth of Cupid and Psyche makes explicit, Cupid (Eros, love) enables Psyche (the human soul) to become immortal; the conclusion of the myth is the happy reunion of the lovers and the conferral of immortality on Psyche. In other words, Cupid is the force by which the human soul can be bound to the gods in love and can thereby achieve immortality (see Tatum 48–68).

In *El burlador de Sevilla,* the connections between the drama and the myth of Cupid and Psyche are both multiple and important.[15] In terms of the drama in general and the opening scene in particular, Isabela's desire to see her lover recapitulates Psyche's desire to see Cupid. With the fulfillment of the putative "Octavio's" desire, Isabela seeks the fulfillment of her own wishes, and Don Juan solemnly swears to fulfill his promise. As confirmation of this promise, Isabela wants to strike a light, but this wish is frustrated, as is the desire to know the name of her lover. The opening scene toys with the notion of consummated desire in a such a way that Don Juan always achieves his goal and, in fact, does so precisely as he denies, by deferral, the fulfillment of the desires of another. Similarly, Psyche's constant trials, her attempts to regain possession of Cupid, are displaced in an odd way in Tirso's drama. The frustration of Isabela's wish to see "Octavio" and the public revelation of her transgressions force her to try to clear her name, to regain her now-impugned honor and to reunite herself with her real lover: she is thereby subjected to a series of trials of her own. In addition, the consummation of Don Juan's desires means that he must seek new objects, and so is likewise forced to desire anew. The daemonic Cupid who creates erotic desire in others and who succeeds in fulfilling his own has become the (mortal) Don Juan whose desires are apparently fulfilled *only* by disrupting the social fabric, by disjoining and disuniting those couples created by the erotic love he panders.

---

15. In fact, the myth of Cupid and Psyche appears to be particularly important for the *comedia,* as Frederick A. de Armas demonstrates in *The Invisible Mistress* (15—20, 72–75, 115) and again in *The Return of Astraea* (185–86).

Although the mythological underpinnings of the drama are clearly suggested in the opening scene, there still remain the problems of "who" and "how," since Don Juan's identity is not, in fact, fully revealed until much later in the first act. This does not mean, however, that the character who seduced the Duquesa remains anonymous. When his uncle, Don Pedro Tenorio, undertakes to punish the man who was caught in the Neapolitan palace, he learns that the culprit is none other than his nephew. When Don Pedro orders the *burlador* to reveal who he is, Don Juan complies by answering, "Ya lo digo: / tu sobrino" ["I already told you: your nephew"] (lines 53–54). Identity is established first and foremost by blood ties, and Don Juan remains a "man with no name" throughout these opening scenes, until Catalinón reveals various details about the *burlador*'s family and mentions his name to Tisbea at the beginning of the second scene of seduction (lines 570–78). With the unintended help of his name and noble lineage— unintended since he enjoins Catalinón in this same scene to keep his name a secret after the servant has already given Tisbea the full particulars (lines 679–84)—Don Juan proceeds with his plan to seduce the *pescadora* or fisherwoman.

The scenario is not, however, quite as straightforward as it might appear. The obstacles in this instance are, if anything, even greater than in the case of Isabela. As is indicated by Tisbea's name (Thisbe) and, somewhat less significantly, by her social status, Don Juan must surmount the many social and personal barriers separating him from the object of his desire. This episode derives much of its significance, then, from the ways in which Don Juan bridges the gap created by social differences and, more important, the expectations created by these differences, as well as that created by the more significant though symbolic inaccessibility of Tisbea. Consequently, the revival of Don Juan from his faint after the shipwreck occasions a remarkable and illuminating assessment of the *burlador*'s role in just this type of situation. After Catalinón has left his master in Tisbea's care and she has revived the *burlador,* Don Juan first asks where he is, to which Tisbea coyly responds, "Ya podéis ver; / en brazos de una mujer" ["As you can see, in the arms of a woman"] (lines 582–83). This provides enough temptation to put him in fine form, and he replies: "Vivo en vos, si en el mar muero. / Ya perdí todo el recelo / que me pudiera anegar, / pues del infierno del mar / salgo a vuestro claro cielo. / ... / Y en vuestro divino oriente / renazco, y no hay que espantar, / pues veis que hay de amar a mar / una letra solamente" ["I live in you, though I die at sea. I have lost any distrust that might have drowned me, since, from the hellish sea, I emerge into your clear heaven. ... And in your divine Orient I am reborn; do not worry, since you can see that from love (*amar*) to sea (*a mar*) there is but one letter"] (lines 584–88, 593–96).

The basic opposition immediately established in this passage is between life and death. The first line is a not too subtle sacrilege in which Don Juan situates his life in Tisbea and leaves his symbolic death behind him in the sea. Furthermore, this initial dichotomy extends to the contrast between the "hellish sea" and "your clear heaven," which is, however, also terrestrial since it is "*your* clear heaven." What was alluded to in the first line of the citation, a kind of collapsing of baptism and rebirth as suggested by Don Juan's emergence from the sea, is subsequently confirmed by Don Juan's rebirth into the world as represented by Tisbea. The religious overtones are struck most clearly here, particularly after the reference to the "hellish sea." The essential oppositions between life and death, Tisbea and the sea, heaven and hell, all resolve into "amar" and "mar," which, as Don Juan shrewdly observes, are strangely alike, separated from each other by only one letter.

This would all be so much verbal virtuosity except that the figure bridging these oppositions is Don Juan himself. Don Juan makes the transition from life to death, from the sea to Tisbea's arms, from hell to heaven in precisely the same way that "de amar a mar hay una letra solamente." Moreover, his linguistic facility re-creates and reorders experience in such a way that the one possibility of uniting the opposing figures resides in him. To get from "amar" to "mar" requires the introduction of language, beginning, appropriately enough, with the first letter of the alphabet, the letter that joins "mar" to "amar." Once Don Juan situates language, and the experience of the world through language, in his own gift of speech, the performative nature of the promises he will later make to Tisbea is both fulfilled, at least in his terms, and abrogated, in Tisbea's.[16] With his promise, Don Juan believes he has done what was expected of him since he is, in essence, the spoken word and since he gives himself as such. As Shoshana Felman puts it:

> Although he has no intention whatsoever of keeping his promises, the seducer, strictly speaking, does not lie, since he is doing

16. The term performative is taken from Austin's *How to do Things with Words,* in which he says that the word "indicates that the issuing of the utterance is the performing of an action" (6). It refers to that class of speech in which to say something is also to do it: for example, to promise, to bet, etc. See also Emile Benveniste, who offers what might be called a "corrective" to Austin's formulation, a topic that is taken up by Shoshana Felman (*The Literary Speech Act* 19–22).

no more than playing on the self-referential property of these performative utterances, and is in effect accomplishing the speech acts that he is naming. The trap of seduction thus consists in producing a *referential* illusion through an utterance that is by its very nature *self-referential:* the illusion of a real or extralinguistic act of commitment created by an utterance that refers only to itself. . . . While the seducer appears to be committing himself, his strategy is to create a *reflexive, self-referential debt* that, as such, does not engage *him.* (*The Literary Speech Act* 31–32)

Whether or not the seducer lies, whether or not debt can be self-referential, Don Juan, at this point in the trajectory of *El burlador de Sevilla*, believes in the possibility of self-referentiality, in the inherent completion of a linguistic performative. It is important, however, to realize that there are certain limitations involved in this schema: if Don Juan implicitly situates himself as the locus of language, as a kind of discursive logos, his choice of words nevertheless points to the controlling force of language as it functions in society. This emphasis on language derives not from Don Juan alone, but is a system of exchange mutually agreed upon by Don Juan and Tisbea. As the peasant astutely remarks, "Mucho habláis" ["You talk so much"]. But Don Juan, not to be outdone, replies even more smoothly, "Mucho entendéis" ["You understand so much"] (line 695). Whereas the one flatters the other's gift of speech, the second flatters the powers of comprehension of the first. Flattery, of course, demonstrates the crucial nature of language. For Marc Shell it emphasizes the creative powers of language: "Verbal flattery is the art of supplementing (or even creating) nature with words so that the listener, not acquainted with nature or willing to forget it, believes more in words than in things. . . . Language is the economic go-between, apparently mediating desires and their satisfaction" (120). If there is any doubt as to the linguistic emphasis in these scenes, Tisbea tells Don Juan, "Yo a ti me allano / bajo la palabra y mano / de esposo" ["I submit myself to you on your word and hand as a husband"]; later, after she has been tricked, Tisbea laments, "Engañóme el caballero / debajo de fe y palabra" ["The gentleman tricked me, in the name of good faith and his word"] (lines 938–40, 1017–18). Don Juan, then, gives his word in this exchange, as he did in the first instance, but he does so without intending to fulfill the desire of the other individual involved.

Although we are somewhat closer to understanding the first scene of the drama—the identity of the "man with no name" is now known—we

still do not know precisely *how* Don Juan gained access to the Duquesa's chambers, even though it seems clear that language is somehow implicated in the entire process. The question of "how" remains a
mystery only until the third seduction, Don Juan's encounter with
Doña Ana. The stage is set for this *burla* or trick when Don Juan and
the Marqués de la Mota scheme together to deceive Beatriz, a woman of
questionable honor. In order to fool Beatriz into thinking that Don
Juan is the Marqués, the nobleman gives his red cape to the *burlador*.
The plan is for Don Juan to present himself to Beatriz, to pretend that
he is the Marqués, and, presumably, to partake of the woman's favors.
The Marqués does not realize, however, that this role-playing fits into a
larger, much more scurrilous plan. Instead of being one of the tricksters, the Marqués has given Don Juan the means by which the nobleman himself will become one of the tricked: the red cape that Don Juan
now wears is also the sign by which the Marqués is known at the home
of his beloved cousin, Doña Ana.

Earlier in these scenes involving the Marqués and Doña Ana, Don
Juan was entrusted by one of Doña Ana's ladies to deliver a missive to
his aristocratic friend. His curiosity piqued by the *papel* or piece of
paper, Don Juan opened the note and read this message:

> "Mi padre infiel
> en secreto me ha casado
> sin poderme resistir;
> no sé si podré vivir,
> porque la muerte me ha dado.
>   Si estimas, como es razón,
> mi amor y mi voluntad,
> y si tu amor fue verdad,
> muéstralo en esta ocasión.
>   Porque veas que te estimo,
> ven esta noche a la puerta,
> que estará a las once abierta,
> donde tu esperanza, primo,
> goces, y el fin de tu amor.
> Traerás, mi gloria, por señas
> de Leonorilla y las dueñas,
> una capa de color.
>   Mi amor todo de ti fío,
> y adiós."
>   (lines 1325–43)

["My faithless father has secretly betrothed me to another without my being able to resist. I do not know if I will be able to live, since he has all but killed me. If you hold my love and my wishes in high regard, as you ought, and if your love is true, prove it on this occasion. And so that you might see in what regard I hold you, tonight, come to my door, which will be open, at eleven, and you will enjoy your hope and the object of your desire. You must wear, my dear, a red cape as a sign to Leonorilla and my *dueñas*. I trust you with all my love. Farewell."]

Unable to resist the opportunity offered to him, Don Juan relays the message, but not the missive itself, to the Marqués, adding one piece of misleading information not found in the original *papel:*

Para vos, marqués, me han dado
un recaudo harto cortés
   por esa reja, sin ver
el que me lo daba allí;
sólo en la voz conocí
que me lo daba mujer.
   Dícete al fin que a las doce
vayas secreto a la puerta,
(que estará a las once abierta),
donde tu esperanza goce
   la posesión de tu amor;
que llevases por señas
de Leonorilla y las dueñas
una capa de color.
                (lines 1384–97)

[Through that grille, Marquis, I was given a most courtly message to be passed on to you. I couldn't see who it was that gave it to me, but, by the voice I could tell it was a woman. In sum, it says that you are secretly to go to the door at midnight (which will be open at eleven) where you will be able to take possession of your beloved. As a sign for Leonorilla and the *dueñas,* you must wear a red cape.]

All of the pertinent information is included in this recitation, and there are even some near-exact syntactical and semantic repetitions of the letter. But Don Juan has added that the Marqués is to present himself at Doña Ana's door at twelve midnight instead of eleven o'clock as suggested in the letter. Because he emphasizes voice in his delivering of the contents of the message, we are given to understand that the message was delivered to him in oral and not written form. Yet earlier, in the exchange between Don Juan and Doña Ana's servant and in Don Juan's subsequent dilation on the subject of the message, the essence of the missive as a physical object, as a piece of paper, was particularly stressed (lines 1297–99, 1305–9, 1321–23).

Because Don Juan has not been entrusted with a mere message but a piece of paper, a letter, he has created the conditions for a far more cleverly vile *burla* than the one that he and the Marqués had planned together. Instead of going to the home of Beatriz, Don Juan goes to the home of the beloved Doña Ana, where he is assured of gaining access because he is wearing the requisite sign. This third seduction comes to an abrupt end when Doña Ana realizes that the man in the red cape is not the Marqués. Her cries for help bring her father, Don Gonzalo de Ulloa, who Don Juan is forced to kill in order to make his escape. As a final twist to this series of events, Don Juan returns the cape to the Marqués, who is then taken prisoner for his presumed part in the slaying of Don Gonzalo.

Doña Ana's seduction thereby resembles the opening scene of *El burlador de Sevilla* insofar as neither scene of seduction in which a noblewoman is involved shows Don Juan at work.[17] Rather, each scene is brought to a close within the play even as the events leading up to those final moments are external to the drama per se. The point of the first and third seductions would seem to be the discovery of the imposter and not the actual fact of the seduction. Tirso, however, makes one significant addition to the presentation of the third seduction: although the play does not portray the seduction of Doña Ana, it does represent the events leading up to Don Juan's entry into the home of the Ulloas. The inclusion of these scenes involving Don Juan, the Marqués, Catalinón, and Doña Ana's servant provides us with the answer to the second question posed by the opening scene of the drama. How does Don Juan gain access to a noblewoman's chamber? He does so both by being an especially adept opportunist, who skillfully takes advantage of and manipulates the personalities and intricate events surrounding him, *and* by being a consum-

17. Early commentators—including Gendarme de Bévotte, Castro, Radoff and Salley—are as confused as more recent critics as to whether or not Doña Ana is actually seduced. Wardropper, for instance, seems to think not ("*El burlador de Sevilla*" 70), but there has been continuing discussion. See Vicente Cabrera; Luis González-del-Valle; and José M. Ruano de la Haza.

mate actor (see Douglas Rogers, *Tirso de Molina* 33; Sullivan 77). More important, Don Juan, as an actor, takes his cues from a written text, in this instance, Doña Ana's letter, and he does so by concealing that it is a written text that gives him his words.

The essence of Doña Ana's letter, the *papel,* therefore, furnishes the *burlador* with his next role or *papel* in the drama. Enclosed in the *papel* sent to the Marqués is a dual message fully apprehended by Don Juan in his role as its bearer. When he says of the appearance of the letter, "A mí el papel ha llegado / por la estafeta del viento" ["A letter (dramatic role) for me has arrived, delivered by the wind"] (lines 1308–9), he not only comments on the surprisingly unexpected manner in which the letter for the Marqués materializes, but also on the way another role "arrives," a role that seems written for him alone. This initial commentary on and reading of the letter, along with his later recitation to the Marqués of the missive's contents—his re-presentation, as it were, of the contents of the *papel*—anticipate his eleven o'clock performance at Doña Ana's house. Indeed, he contrives with the Marqués only *after* he has relayed his version of the letter's contents to its proper destination, which is to say, he dons the red cape and assumes his role only after he has appropriately prepared himself for the part he is to play. To the question of "how," we must answer, then, that Don Juan is a masterly interpreter of the *written* word.

Doña Ana's letter itself is not, however, an object of momentary importance. Not only does the *papel* provide Don Juan with the role he plays in the third seduction, in the fourth seduction it also provides him with the means by which he convinces Batricio that Aminta, Batricio's new wife, had already promised herself to the *burlador.* Don Juan explains to Batricio: "Al fin, Aminta, celosa, / o quizá desesperada / de verse de mí olvidada / y de ajeno dueño esposa, / esta carta me escribió / envïándome a llamar, / y yo prometí gozar / lo que el alma prometió" ["In sum, Aminta, jealous, perhaps desperate at finding herself forgotten by me and the wife of another, wrote me this letter asking me to call. And I promised to enjoy that which her soul promised"] (lines 1864–71). Don Juan again assumes the role intended for another, this time portraying a wronged lover. Doña Ana's letter to the Marqués describes a situation that might not be unlike the triangle of Don Juan, Batricio, and Aminta. In the context of this new seduction, Don Juan becomes the *papel*'s destination while Batricio is cast as the wrongful and unwanted husband, and the letter is attributed to the presumably illiterate Aminta. Don Juan is indeed adept at intercepting and representing *papeles;* but he is equally skilled in *re*interpreting those texts and roles with another end in mind.

Don Juan's skill as an actor—as an interpreter and reinterpreter of
the written word—is developed in the fourth and final seduction in the
domain of the spoken word and social discourse, conflating the presentation of his modus operandi in the second and third seductions (in
which, in the seduction of Tisbea, the discussion centered on questions
of the spoken word and, in the case of Doña Ana, the question at hand
pertained to a written text). During the pastoral interlude of the scenes
involving Aminta and her wedding party, the fourth victim says upon
hearing Don Juan's seductive words, "No sé qué diga; / que se encubren
tus verdades / con retóricas mentiras" ["I don't know what I ought to
say. Your truths are concealed in rhetorical lies"] (lines 2051–53). Her
averral of doubt points to the inherently linguistic aspects of the
burlador's skills, and to the fact that Don Juan seduces when the moment is most propitious for exercising his facility with the spoken
word. Like Tisbea, Aminta exacts a promise from her would-be lover, in
response to which Don Juan solemnly swears, "Juro a esta mano, señora, / infierno de nieve fría, / de cumplirte la palabra" ["I swear by this
hand, señora, a hell of freezing snow, that I will honor my word"] (lines
2068–70). Seduction in *El burlador de Sevilla* appears first to be much
more than a structural device and, second, to have much more to do
with questions of language than is usually acknowledged. As seduction
is related to the promise, it suggests certain types of contractual obligations that are not specific to sexual relations between men and women,
but, rather, that have as much or more to do with society as a whole.
Thus, we must look at other aspects of the *comedia* if we are to understand the ways in which Don Juan's linguistic facility allows him to
deal with the world at large.

The reinscription of Don Juan's linguistic facility and of his reliance on
a text takes place primarily in the context of his interactions in the
exclusively male world of affairs of state and honor in a progression
similar to his development over the course of the four seductions. This
progression takes shape as a series of increasingly violent skirmishes
and encounters between the *burlador* and his male antagonists, beginning with the intrusion of the Rey de Nápoles (King of Naples) and his
men during the final moments of Don Juan's rendezvous with Isabela.
In the first instance of such an encounter, Don Juan's perfidy is opposed
to the moral rigor of the Rey de Nápoles and his agent, Don Pedro
Tenorio. In the scenes involving Tisbea, Don Juan has brief—and in
appearance not hostile—contact with the fishermen, including Tisbea's suitor, Anfriso. With his attempt on the honor of Doña Ana, the
conflictual nature of these assaults on traditional mores intensifies,

resulting in Don Juan's open combat with Don Gonzalo. Finally, with the seduction of Aminta, the second and third scenes of seduction collapse into one as Don Juan tricks Batricio, the husband, and proceeds to seduce Aminta with the help of her father, Gaseno.

The situation of the opening scene is recapitulated in inverse fashion in the scene with Gaseno. Where Don Juan committed an affront to the King and had to be duly punished, he now proceeds by receiving the father's blessing. What appears to be an act of submission—"a su padre voy a hablar / para autorizar mi engaño" ["I am going to speak with her father so as to authorize my deceit"] (lines 1906–7)—is, in fact, another *burla*. Don Juan will trick the father in much the same way that he tricked Batricio and will play on the avarice of both the father and the daughter. Like the scenes of seduction, then, these confrontations between and among the male characters follow a carefully plotted path in which specific moments and conflicts are seemingly reworked to Don Juan's advantage.

The principle by which these encounters are ordered is basic to the play's action in that it entails the same types of distinctions in social hierarchy that are at work among the four female victims. In this male preserve, however, the hierarchy is established with respect to the designation of the character who gives the orders and the *burlador*'s subsequent disobedience. Moreover, this dialectic of command and disobedience recurs in all of the scenes of confrontation engendered by Don Juan's seductions, always in the context of a carefully delineated network of hierarchical relations. As a counterpoint to these encounters between and among the many male characters, Tirso inserts into the primary action of the drama several scenes in which the Rey de Castilla (King of Spain) decides affairs of state and social well-being with various officials of his kingdom.

In one case, a scene in which the Spanish King and Don Gonzalo arrange for the marriage of Don Gonzalo's daughter, Doña Ana, to Don Juan punctuates the seduction of Tisbea, interrupting the chain of events. The effect of this and those other scenes in which the Rey de Castilla appears is to establish the King as the highest of mortal beings, as one who controls (albeit ineffectually) the lives of his subjects, as one who has the power to make and to remake the various marital matches by which he would create social harmony and stability. Yet, as in the opening scene of the *comedia* in which the *burlador* disobeys his uncle, Don Juan flaunts his disrespect for this most elevated of authorities, pausing to perpetrate his *burla* of Doña Ana and the Marqués before complying with the King's order, as relayed to Don Juan by his father, to leave Sevilla.

Don Juan's irreverence in the face of authority is not, then, surprising, particularly in view of the other events in the play and the nature of the action overall. Nevertheless, the way in which this authority reveals itself in *El burlador de Sevilla* and the dramatic world therein bears a close relationship to Don Juan's own linguistic facility. In contrast to Don Juan's empty performatives, his promises devoid of any intent to fulfill the letter of his word, the commands of the Kings of Naples and of Spain embody an obvious intent to impose their individual will on the events and lives under their jurisdiction. The royal edicts emanate from the putative central force in the drama and affect all under the rule of the Kings. That Don Juan parades his disrespect for these edicts and their bearers is significant at the level of plot. But because Don Juan disregards the force of the promises he makes (despite his open reliance on the representational aspects of language) *and* the authority embodied in the directives of others, the linguistic cast of the seductions carries over into all of Don Juan's dealings in the world of men.

The two lines of linguistic inquiry in *El burlador de Sevilla* outlined thus far (the one associated with the seductions proper and serving to reveal Don Juan as an actor, the other deriving from Don Juan's dealings with figures of worldly authority) converge and come into focus in Don Juan's encounters with the sepulchral Statue of the Comendador. Like the *burlador*'s exchanges with other male characters, his dealings with the Statue reveal the hierarchical ordering of the world. As the Statue of the Comendador tells Don Juan during his final terrestrial moments, he is an earthly agent of God: "Las maravillas de Dios / son, don Juan, investigables, / y así quiere que tus culpas / a manos de un muerto pagues" ["The marvels of God are provable, and He therefore wants you to pay for your faults at the hands of a dead man"] (lines 2746–49). This series of exchanges also succeeds in placing the *burlador* in a situation in which he must not only make but also keep a promise, since as Catalinón later explains it at the King's court, "Don Juan, del Comendador / haciendo burla, una tarde, / después de haberle quitado / las dos prendas que más valen, / tirando al bulto de piedra / la barba por ultrajarle, / a cenar le convidó" ["Don Juan was mocking the Commander one afternoon, after having taken from him the two things of greatest value. Pulling on his beard so as to outrage him, Don Juan invited him to dinner"] (lines 2827–33). The result of this *burla* is a reciprocal invitation that Don Juan, giving his word as a *caballero* or gentleman, promises to honor. In a recapitulation of all that has transpired between the *burlador* and his female victims, Don Juan promises the Statue—gives his word and his hand ("Bajo esta palabra y mano" [line 2442])—to dine at the Ulloa chapel.

At the same time, this encounter brings into focus the other skirmishes and encounters between Don Juan and the male characters of the drama. A representation of Doña Ana's father (in Oedipal terms, the "father" that Don Juan killed in order to possess the "mother") as well as an agent of God, the Statue functions as an overdetermined avatar of the Father. He thereby recalls the previous exchanges between fathers and sons, not just those between the *burlador* and Don Diego and Gaseno, the two other fathers in the drama, but those involving the other male figures. Don Pedro Tenorio also plays a protective role not unlike that of a real or a surrogate father. Even Anfriso can be included in this schema: he is described by Tisbea as "un pobre padre / de mis males testigo" ["a poor father who has witnessed my tragedy"] (lines 2198–99). That Anfriso is her suitor and will later become her husband does not obviate his function as a figure of paternal authority for Tisbea. In the meting out of divine justice, then, the Statue represents all of the various father-figures in the drama and functions as a symbolic father, in the role of what Jacques Lacan has called the "paternal metaphor" or the "name of the father."[18]

In *El burlador de Sevilla,* the Statue is both an agent of God's will, a supernatural *verbe de Dieu,* and a kind of synecdoche, representing as he does all of the father-figures in the *comedia.* Thus, he assumes the terrestrial role of the divine "figure of the Law." By holding Don Juan to a promise, the Statue tacitly holds him answerable for all of his promises; that Don Juan discovers a linguistic loophole in the form of intention does the *burlador* little good. The outcome of the meeting is fatal even though Don Juan assures the Statue that "A tu hija no ofendí, / que vio mis engaños antes" ["I did not offend your daughter; she saw through my deceit"] (lines 2757–58). Don Gonzalo dismisses this defense and any possible remorse with one key phrase: "No importa; que ya pusiste / tu intento" ["It makes no difference; your intent was clear"] (lines 2759–60). The *burlador* is not even given time to confess and thereby absolve himself of his sins. It is simply too late, "No hay lugar; ya acuerdas tarde" ["There is no time for this; you remember too late"] (line 2762).

The issue of Don Juan's intent is, of course, central to the linguistic

18. Carlos Feal also discusses *El burlador de Sevilla* in terms of the "name of the father" (22–24); Paul Julian Smith discusses it in broadly Lacanian terms (*Writing in the Margin* 146–56).

and contractual questions that we have been discussing, as is the Statue's symbolic role. Behind Don Juan's promises to his female victims there was no intent at all, or, rather, there was the intent *not* to honor the *appearance* of intent inherent in the performance of a promise. When Don Juan swears to fulfill his promise his intention is completely otherwise. Don Juan's sins against society are not so much sins of carnality as they are sins of linguistic perversion. In this regard the Marqués de la Mota is hardly any better than his friend and cohort. Moreover, Doña Ana's desire to betray the honor and word of her father is equally symptomatic of a widespread social problem. Don Juan's failure to keep his promises therefore threatens the very discursive texture of the social fabric in a society in which speech is the one essential means of making a contract: giving one's word constitutes no less than the commitment of individual honor to a point of common interest in a society in which a promise is more binding, more valuable, than any legal document.

To cite just one example taken from a *comedia* by a contemporary of Tirso, in *La Estrella de Sevilla* [The Star of Seville] a written contract is deemed virtually without value. The polemic here is against the written word; and the play displays a profound mistrust of the worldly usefulness of *papel*. Midway through the drama, two characters discuss a "contract" to be taken out on a third individual. But at the offer of a written contract, one of the two conspirators refuses on these grounds:

> ¡Yo cédula! ¡Yo papel!
> *tratadme con más llaneza,*
> que mas en vos que no en èl
> confia aqui mi nobleza.
>   Si vuestras palabras cobran
> valor que a los montes labra,
> y ellas cuanto dizen obran,
> dandome aqui la palabra,
> señor, los papeles sobran.
>   *A la palabra remito*
> *la cedula que me days,*
> *con que a vengaros me incito,*
> *porque donde vos estays*
> *es escusado lo escrito.*
>   Rompedlo, porque sin èl
> la muerte le solicita
> mejor, señor, que con èl;

que en parte desacredita
vuestra palabra el papel. (*Rompele.*)
   Sin papel, señor, aqui
nos obligamos los dos,
y prometemos ansi,
yo de vengaros a vos,
y vos de librarme a mi.
   Y si es assi, no ay que hazer
cedulas, que estorbo han sido. . . .
                 (lines 1558–83)

[Documents, papers, for me! Treat me more informally, since my nobility has greater trust in you than in paper. If your words possess enough value to move mountains, if they can do everything they say, then, my lord, papers are unnecessary if you give me your word. I remit to your word this document you give me, in which you incite me to avenge you, since, wherever you are, there is no need for writing. Tear it up, since, without it, death will pursue him better, my lord, than with it, and such a paper will discredit your word. (*He tears it up.*) Without paper, my lord, we both hereby commit ourselves and thusly promise: I to avenge you, and you to free me. And if it is thus, there is no need for documents, which have only been a nuisance. . . .]

The strong polemic against a written contract (*cédula, papel*) stems from the ways in which a piece of paper can contradict a man's word. Accordingly, the best way to make a contract is by means of mutual obligation, by promising. One places his faith not in a piece of paper, but in a person and his personal honor, in the force and validity of an action that an individual's words have in the world. Furthermore, the ambiguity of the word *papel* at work in *El burlador de Sevilla* is at work here as well. In *La Estrella de Sevilla,* Sancho elliptically refers to the types of roles played by individuals that contravene and contradict the authentic nature of their speech in what can be read as a lamentation of the proliferation of paper contracts *and* deceitful role-playing.[19] The distinction between personal honor and the written word as

19. See Elias L. Rivers on this aspect of *La Estrella de Sevilla.* See, too, Harlan Sturm and Sara Sturm, and Charles Oriel, all of whom consider writing and inscription in relation to honor in this drama, touching on the dual meaning of the word *papel* (paper, dramatic role).

contract cuts to the heart of what we might call the myth of honor. What is suggested, of course, is that honor as a code exists apart from individuals and society, that the code, in a sense, is like a Platonic form to which men are bound by means of social and personal obligation. In fact, honor as such inheres in the actions and words of men, and the code is then extracted from those manners of comportment. Honor is implied, then, in the ways in which individuals interact; it is articulated most openly when one speaks. At a second remove is the written word, which supplements the notion of honor implied in the making of an oral contract. What Don Juan does so skillfully is to play upon the different registers of honor—the implied, the spoken promise, the written word—at different moments as is most opportune for his particular pursuit. That he blurs the distinctions inherent in honor as a code, as derived from deeds and words, emphasizes both Don Juan's shrewd manipulation of language, the subtle distinctions between speech and writing, and the guile of his victims, who seem not to be aware of the implications of, if not the differences between, spoken and written words.

Emphasis on the spoken word and oral contracts derives in part perhaps from the relative illiteracy of the Spanish population (although the literacy rate in sixteenth- and early seventeenth-century Spain was, in fact, higher than has been thought).[20] But this emphasis probably derives as well from the power of the Church in Spanish society, from patristic theories of the sign, and from the importance of those theories for the religious doctrine associated with the sacraments. A sacrament—literally some sacred thing that is hidden or secret—is the sensible sign of Christ's love for and union with the Church. Paul says in Ephesians 5:25–26, "Christus dilexit Ecclesiam, et tradidit semetipsum por ea, ut illam sanctificaret, mundans eam lavacro aquae in verbo vitae" ["Christ loved the Church and gave himself up for her that he might sanctify her, cleansing her by the washing of water in the word of life"]. The role of the sacrament, similar to its presentation in Paul's formulation, entails both an action and the speaking of words in order to provide the possibility of grace and redemption. For Aquinas, this meant, "Dicendum quod sacramenta, sicut

20. In an early study, Richard L. Kagan says that "no more than 10 to 15 percent of the population could read and write. . . . Analphabetism remained the rule in most Spanish cities and towns well into the nineteenth century" (23, 27). More recent studies indicate that the literacy rate in sixteenth- and early seventeenth-century Spain could, in the case of men, have ranged as high as between 50 and 70 percent. See P. Berger; Marie-Christine Rodriguez and Bartolomé Bennassar; Claude Larquié; Juan Eloy Gelabert González; J. N. H. Lawrance; and Sara T. Nalle.

dictum est, adhibentur ad hominum sanctificationem sicut quaedam signa" ["As has been said, the function of sacraments is to act as a certain sign conducive to the sanctification of men"] (*The Sacraments* 3a.60.6). According to Augustine in *In Joannis Evangelium,* the sacrament is formed when "Accedit verbum ad elementum, et fit Sacramentum, etiam ipsum tanquam visibile verbum. . . . Nam et in ipso verbo, aliud est sonus transiens, aliud virtus manens" ["The word is conjoined to the element and the sacrament is made, itself becoming, as it were, a visible word. . . . For in that very word, one thing is the sound, which is transitory, another is the virtue, which remains"] (80, 3; col. 1840). Each of the sacraments, of which there are seven under the New Law, is composed of two parts, one of which is matter, called the element, the other of which is form, called the word. When the word is joined to the element, the sacrament is made. To translate this into the terminology with which we have been discussing *El burlador de Sevilla,* sacraments are a kind of performative, a complex action that takes place in language, in which words spoken during the course of the accompanying action and the action itself join to form a sensible or visible sign of the holy process. The word both empowers and embodies the sacrament, which, despite its oral and transitory nature, is powerful throughout all time.

The linguistic aspects of the sacramental rites are most apparent, and most pertinent for this discussion, in the sacrament of marriage. Matrimony is the only sacrament in which the two individuals directly involved act as the ministers of the sacramental rite. It is, then, a form of contractual agreement effected in language, one accomplished by a pair of individuals who act as instruments of Christ in the granting of their consent to a union that metaphorically embodies the living image of the unity of Christ and his Church. But matrimony also has worldly importance apart from the role it plays in religious and spiritual life and apart from the strictly biological function of reproduction that it both institutionalizes and monitors. As Augustine teaches in *De Sancta Virginitate,* "Habeant conjugia bonum suum, non quia filios procreant, sed quia honeste, quia licite, quia pudice, *quia socialiter procreant,* et procreatos pariter, salubriter, instanter educant, quia thori fidem invicem servant, quia sacramentum connubii non violant" ["Let marriage partners be regarded as good not because they produce children, but, rather, because they do so virtuously, as the law prescribes, and with modesty, because they procreate conjugally, and they rear their begotten in like manner, wholesomely and earnestly, because, between themselves, they preserve the sanctity of the marriage bed, and they do not dishonor the sacrament of marriage"] (12, 12; col. 401). The enactment of the marriage rite constitutes the performance of an oral contract that has a bearing on all of society in that it "procreates" at a social level as well. This sacramental rite is thereby reinscribed in day-to-day life as a part of conventional contracts and exchanges. Don Juan, by freely promising to many, without, in fact, intending to honor any of the promises, by perverting the linguistic basis of religious doctrine on the sensitive issue of the sacrament of marriage, thus contravenes and profanes not only those doctrines and sacraments but also menaces the very foundations of Spanish society.[21]

The sacramental nature of Don Juan's promises as well as their binding nature as a contract are shown most clearly in the scene in which the *burlador* seduces Aminta. Of all of the victims, Aminta is the most adept linguistically *and* theologically, shrewdly anticipating any possible loopholes on which Don Juan might later rely for excuses. She makes him swear not once but twice, and this after a discussion of the orthodoxy of annulling her nuptials with Batricio in order to take the *burlador* as a husband. But Don Juan is obviously not a man of his word; his promises are merely "sound, which is transient," in which there is no "virtue."

The chaos created by Don Juan—erotic and linguistic—is therefore justly punished. The sheer magnitude and number of his misdeeds render him dangerous, even fatal. There is, however, an element of scapegoating involved in the meting out of this just recompense.[22] As we have noted, Don Juan is hardly the only deceitful individual in the world portrayed in *El burlador de Sevilla,* a fact that Bruce W.

21. A similar point with regard to marriage as a social contract is made by Tony Tanner in his discussion of adultery in the "bourgeois novel" of the eighteenth and nineteenth centuries when he says, "By analogy we may say that if the marriage bond is rendered unstable—and that is the ultimate implication of adultery—then by extension nothing in society is truly 'bonded,' and the state of chaos . . . may recommence at the very center of the most civilized society. As though by some reverse mythical all-at-once-ness, society at its heart returns to that 'infamous promiscuity of things and women' from which man, by means above all of the idea of marriage, first emerged into true social humanity" (66). In fact, marriage as socially productive is a concept that antedates the bourgeois novel, at least in Spanish literature, even if it receives its most thorough and thoroughly modern assessment in novelistic fiction.

22. On scapegoating and the scapegoat mechanism in myth and ritual, see René Girard, *Violence and the Sacred; "To double business bound,"* especially "Violence and Representation in the Mythical Text" (178–98); and *The Scapegoat,* particularly "That Only One Man Should Die" (112–24). See also on this topic "Generative Scapegoating," in Robert G. Hamerton-Kelly, ed., *Violent Origins* (73–145). For a Girardian reading of scapegoating in *El burlador de Sevilla,* see Judith H. Arias; in Spanish society, see Timothy Mitchell, particularly the discussion of "Scapegoating as Popular Theatre" (109–15).

Wardropper succinctly sums up when he says that "Don Juan de-
ceives . . . in a deceit-full society" (*"El burlador de Sevilla"* 65). Even
though Don Juan is not and cannot be mistaken for the innocent victim
of sacrificial ritual, neither is he the only character in the *comedia*
deserving of punishment; he is not merely a perpetrator of evil, but also
a victim insofar as he pays for the sins and trangressions of others as
well as for his own misdeeds. In this way, his actions serve to unify
society against him, and his death restores unity to society itself. Finally, Catalinón's timely announcement of the *burlador's* more timely
demise allows the King to reassert his authority and to set the world
immediately to right by ordering everyone to marry: "¡Justo castigo del
cielo! / Y agora es bien que se casen / todos, pues la causa es muerta, /
vida de tantos desastres" ["A just punishment from heaven! And now it
is right that everyone should wed, since he who gave life to all of these
disasters, the cause, is dead"] (lines 2851–54).

The movement toward marriage en masse, toward the nuptials of
Octavio and Isabela, Tisbea and Anfriso, the Marqués and Doña Ana,
and the consummation of the marriage of Aminta and Batricio, is, of
course, a convention of Golden Age *comedias*. But despite the conventional nature of this final scene, we must note that, for all of the havoc
that he wreaked, Don Juan himself instigated this happy ending. As a
kind of destructive erotic force in the world, the *burlador* either chan-
nelled existing or incited new attractions, acting very much like a
seventeenth-century Cupid. Isabela, for instance, is so unsure of her
suitor that she must ask him to swear once more to uphold his promise
to marry her *after* he, or the man playing his part, has "enjoyed" her
favors. The other noblewoman in the drama, Doña Ana, finally gives
herself up to her lover, the Marqués, when it appears that she is to be
married by her father and the King to someone else: Don Juan. Tisbea,
a prime example of the *mujer esquiva* or disdainful or flighty woman
(McKendrick, *Woman and Society* 159), shuns all suitors only to fall
victim to her arrogant pride. By attempting to marry above herself, she
falls easy prey to Don Juan's promises. In this way, too, Aminta falls
into Don Juan's trap, although initially with some misgivings. If it
seems, then, that the *burlador* disrupts the harmony of an idyllic
world, destroys happy conjugal unions, the truth is otherwise. Only at
the end of the anarchical path stretching from Italy to Spain is matrimony resurrected as the symbol of social harmony. It is only after Don
Juan's perfidy that Octavio, the Marqués, the prideful Tisbea, and the
greedy Aminta set aside their individual desires and content themselves with their lot as a part of a holy union leading to some common
good: they become like others in their world.

Don Juan thereby serves a patriarchal social function in two senses. First, he unifies society against him and assumes a collective burden of guilt. Second, he engenders the conditions by which desire is directed toward matrimony in socially productive ways. Although Don Juan may not seem to play a positive role in the patriarchal world of *El burlador de Sevilla,* he does serve a significant social function by showing how love construed in terms of Christian matrimony can bring individuals into closer union with the deity and can thus benefit the common good of all mankind. Moreover, like his mythical forebear, Eros, or Cupid, Don Juan is a daemonic force in the world, the means by which Tirso's all too human souls are led to a sacramental union that will grant them spiritual immortality; Don Juan's failed promises are contradicted by the potential good of the four mutual promises made at the end of the drama. In this way, the inquiry into the uses, abuses, and ends of language is brought to a fitting conclusion. The character who relies on the written word for his cues is duly punished, and the rest of society reaffirms its sustained commitment to social order by means of oral contracts. It would not be misleading to identify Don Juan with Freud's Eros or "life instinct," as the force that, "by bringing about a more and more far-reaching combination of the particles into which living substance is dispersed, aims at complicating life and at the same time, of course, preserving it" (Freud, *The Ego and the Id, Standard Edition* 19:40). This is the point of Miguel de Unamuno's *El hermano Juan* as well. As Unamuno's Juan explains to his "victims," "Metí entre vosotros la discordia, pero para traer la reconciliación" ["I sowed discord among you, but all in order to bring about reconciliation"] (*Obras completas* 5:808). Thus, Juan concludes, "Mi destino no fué robar amores, no, no lo fué, sino que fué encenderlos y atizarlos para que otros se calentaran a su brasa. . . . Los antiguos, que fueron unos niños, me llamaron Cupido, el arquero" ["My purpose was not to steal love, no, that was not it. Rather, it was to incite love and to stoke the fires so that others could warm themselves near the embers. . . . The ancients, who were like children, called me Cupid, the archer"] (*Obras completas* 5:815).

The concept of seduction with which we began—either when it is construed traditionally in terms of sexual seduction or when it is read as an unproblematic structural device—therefore fails to apprehend and to interpret fully those linguistic dimensions of the drama that we have been discussing here. Rather, seduction is presented in *El burlador de Sevilla* in its more etymologically strict sense, as a "leading away," perhaps even a "leading astray" (Latin, *se- / ducere*), as a linguistic seduction dependent upon the worldly complexity of making promises. As such, the seductions in this *comedia* emphasize what is at stake in various aspects of speech. The dangers of breaches in a previously agreed-upon linguistic economy are nothing less than the collapse of social order. It seems to me that this is the point at which *El burlador de Sevilla* can be read in the context of ideas in Juan de la Cueva's *El infamador* and Ruiz de Alarcón's *La verdad sospechosa;* Leucino's defamations and Don García's lies affect society in ways similar to Don Juan's perversions of the promise. Tirso's *comedia* finds its rightful place in a literary culture obsessed with the relations between language and literature on the one hand and with reality on the other.

It is also important to see that the lesson of Tirso's *comedia* is not merely a moral one, but that it pertains as well to the crucial relationships between sign and referent and between word and deed so prominent in current discussions of literature. Indeed, I would suggest that the recent trends in criticism that radically separate literature from the world, or a word from its worldly referent, exercise the same type of seduction practiced by Don Juan in that such approaches rely on a rhetoric that is forceful but nonetheless skeptical of its worldly import. Tirso's play advocates nothing less than the fidelity of a performative action and proposes as inevitable the connection between literature and the world. The consequences of this assertion are significant for understanding the precise nature of a written text in a world of spoken language. Although Doña Ana's letter signifies both seduction and the making of a promise, it takes on its real meaning only when it is brought into the realm of the spoken word. A *papel* or dramatic role is meaningful only in its potential, and its meaningful nature remains merely potential until it is acted upon, just as, in fact, Don Juan acts upon the contents of Doña Ana's letter and acts within the parameters that it establishes.

Thus, the written text assumes a worldly force when it has been drawn into the world by the action and discourse it engenders, which in turn underscores the impact of Tirso's *comedia* in that it, too, transcends its status as a text only when it is performed; in this way the drama also constitutes a form of worldly action by embodying the honor of its author. The parallel between Don Juan's performance of the *papel* and the performance of *El burlador de Sevilla* is, however, something of a paradox. The *burlador*'s identification with and reliance on a textual basis discloses that which ought to remain concealed: that this representation of human action is simply that. The enactment of a text can only claim to be life*like,* not life itself. Don Juan's progress through the events of the drama reveals, first, his reliance on language and, second, how this language derives from a written, and also social, text. His punishment thereby absents from the final moments of the *comedia* the one character capable of disclosing and manipulating the mainsprings of the drama, the one character who exposes as illusory the notion that the other characters are not reading from *papeles* of their own, that they are real people. Don Juan, then, shows how, at least within the confines of the dramatic world, the concept of *true* speech is a mere illusion; it is always the actualization of a prior text, be it written or social.

Was Tirso, in fact, aware of these aspects of his *comedia?* Are the self-referential aspects of his drama actually part of the aesthetic plan of the work? These are questions that cannot be answered definitively. However, we ought to recall that Tirso was censured by the Board of Reformation of the Council of Castilla and was therefore aware of the dangers inherent in using language in a "secular" manner. It is also possible to point to moments in *El burlador de Sevilla* in which Tirso acknowledges his awareness of issues of language, literary tradition, and their possible social ends. First, the name of the fourth of Don Juan's victims, Aminta, is taken directly from the pastoral tradition, most likely from Torquato Tasso's *Aminta.* In this sixteenth-century Italian drama, Amor leaves the world of the gods to dwell a while with the shepherds; and he uses his wiles to unite Aminta with the disdainful Silvia. Tirso's use of the name recalls the Italian drama, even if his Aminta is female and not male, a typical Spanish alteration (see Arce 154–56); Juan de Jáuregui's Spanish translation of the text was published first in 1607 and again in 1618. More important in terms of this reference to *Aminta,* Tasso inscribes himself in his drama—a kind of courtly play in which various members of the entourage are discussed and represented—in the guise of Aminta's friend and adviser, Tirsi. Again, Thyrsus is a name from the pastoral tradition. Yet it is strangely close to the pseudonym of the Mercedarian friar who writes himself into his dramas using variations on the name, e.g. Tarso in *El vergonzoso en palacio,* or in the scene with the fishermen in *El burlador de Sevilla.* When Tisbea spots Don Juan and Catalinón foundering in the sea, she calls out to the *pescadores* for help: "Daré voces: ' ¡Tirseo, / Anfriso, Alfredo, hola!' " ["I will call out: Tirseo, Anfriso, Alfredo!"] (lines 509–10). This kind of self-inscription in the cases of Tasso and Tirso creates a curious sense of symmetry. The differences between Tasso and Tarso or Tirso and Tirsi are minor indeed, evocative of Don Juan's clever play on words, "que hay de amar a mar / una letra solamente."

Tirso, a name common to the pastoral tradition, is derived from classical sources: the thyrsus is a staff carried by devotees of Dionysus's cult that is covered by ivy and grapevines and is crowned with pine-cones. In the classical Greek tradition, Dionysus and dionysian rites represent not so much the unbridled sensuality that has been attributed to the god and his cult by our modern-day culture, but, rather, the means by which individuals can experience communion with the gods. Moreover, in a manner similar to Don Juan, Dionysus is not merely the god of religious communion, but also of the drama, of the dramatic moment itself. With respect to the thyrsus as a symbol in Euripides' *Bacchae,* Charles Segal has pointed out that the staff is ambiguous in nature: "Covered with ivy (lines 25, 709, 1055), able to open channels of life-sustaining fluids from the earth (702–11), it is yet a dangerous weapon, a 'missle' (*belos,* 25) that can inflict wounds" (*Dionysiac Poetics* 12).[23] Possessing both positive and negative connotations, the thyrsus is a symbol of nurturing and violent power, an ambiguity that is found in the figure of Dionysus as well as in Euripides' drama, of which Segal remarks:

> This god [Dionysus] theatrically stages his own triumph. His victorious procession as a civilizing force and as a savior from the East leaves behind as much chaos as coherence. He acts out on the stage the *hieros logos,* or holy tale, of a god defeating the enemies of order. . . . If the gods themselves spread disorder, the order we need to stay alive lies elsewhere. Perhaps, Euripides suggests, it lies in the work of art that contains but does not resolve the violence. The hero of the tragedy may be in some sense the shaping power of the poet that fashions the lucid form of the play. Euripides has given this play a highly formalized, traditional structure, marked by careful articulation of the parts, striking beauty of language, intricate strength and deliberate orderliness of design. All these counterbalance the random creativeness, and destructiveness, of the smiling god. (*Dionysiac Poetics* 346–47)[24]

23. The numbers in parentheses in the citation refer to the pertinent lines in the Greek text. See also Girard's discussion of Dionysus and Euripides in *Violence and the Sacred* 119–42.

24. In this context, and to anticipate another aspect of this discussion, it is significant that Friedrich Nietzsche says in *Ecce Homo,* in words that might be attributed to Don Juan, "I am a disciple of the philosopher Dionysus; I should prefer to be even a satyr to being a saint" (*Basic Writings of Nietzsche* 673).

The order and disorder sowed by Dionysus in the world of the *Bacchae* might be seen to bear a close resemblance to the type of chaos created by the *burlador;* in this sense the carefully structured *comedia* serves as counterpoint to the apparent violence of Don Juan's actions. Segal's description of Euripides, Dionysus, and the *Bacchae* is, then, an apt description of Tirso, his *burlador,* and *El burlador de Sevilla.* By raising the specter of violence and disorder in the *comedia,* Tirso encourages us to seek order elsewhere, perhaps in the socially productive unions with which he draws the drama to a close.

Indeed, as if in fulfillment of its ostensible polemic against Don Juan, *El burlador de Sevilla y convidado de piedra* ends, appropriately, with the graphic elimination of its protagonist (lines 2858–59). Not only is Don Juan excluded from the society in which he played a key role, the drama's eponymous hero is struck from the title, too. Yet if Don Juan is erased from the title of the drama in which he first appeared, he nevertheless returns to the stage in subsequent performances of *El burlador de Sevilla* and, more important, in subsequent versions of his story. To be sure, Tirso's *comedia* even anticipates this possibility of representation and rewriting, and with the same paradigm of the dramatic moment, Don Juan's perfidy as based on Doña Ana's letter. In relaying Doña Ana's message to the Marqués and in duping Batricio and Gaseno with the same text, Don Juan shows how one literary work can become a springboard for another, how an individual can rewrite the work of someone else into that of his own. The character who was punished for his linguistic excesses thereby offers himself as an example to others who would write his story by rewriting it as it was already written. Don Juan contrives, despite his death, to provide a model for repetition and revision; he is like a text that is constantly being reread, reinterpreted, and revised.

Don Juan Tenorio as *Refundición*

> *Je suis un homme-plume. Je sens par elle, à cause d'elle, par rapport à elle et beaucoup plus avec elle.*
> —*Gustave Flaubert, letter to Louise Collet, 1 February 1852*

Although issues of honor and seduction are omnipresent in the dramatic action of *El burlador de Sevilla,* in José Zorrilla's *Don Juan Tenorio* they are of much more limited explicit interest. This does not mean, however, that honor and seduction are not important to the concerns of the drama. Honor and seduction in *Don Juan Tenorio,* though not immediately and obviously significant, are operative at different levels and to varying degrees, extending from individual characters and their actions, to the author's intentions in undertaking the rewriting of an earlier drama, and even to the structure of the play itself. Honor and seduction prove crucial to the drama, revealing themselves in terms of the related notions of desire and dependency. Even though *Don Juan Tenorio,* a revision of *El burlador de Sevilla,* appears to claim a spontaneously self-generated origin, it nevertheless acknowledges its implicit dependency on its predecessors. The task at hand, then, is to try to disengage the seventeenth-century *comedia* from its nineteenth-century revision and to discover what dependency has to do with Don Juan, honor, and seduction.

The most interesting avenue into a full consideration of these problems is also one of the most indirect. It begins not with *Don Juan Tenorio,* but, rather, with the several pages that Zorrilla devotes to a polemical discussion of his most famous work in his mammoth literary autobiography, *Recuerdos del tiempo viejo* [Recollections of Times Past]. The essay, "Cuatro palabras sobre mi *Don Juan Tenorio*" [Four Words on my *Don Juan Tenorio*] is well known, often cited, and, for two reasons, somewhat controversial. First, because Zorrilla criticizes his own play in the face of its nearly universal popularity, he appears to be trying to discredit his masterpiece. Second, the playwright stands accused by critics of not revealing all of his sources for the drama, because he mentions only a few other Don Juan plays. Zorrilla anticipates the first point and says that "after thirty years, it's natural that an author would recognize the defects of a work" (1801). He goes on to say that he finds fault neither with the audience for enjoying the drama, nor with his publishers for not giving him a percentage of the considerable profits generated by the frequent publication and annual presentation of the play; his criticisms pertain solely to the play as such.[25] Zorrilla could not, however, have anticipated the second point. Although he acknowledges his familiarity with two other works treating Don Juan, Tirso's *El burlador de Sevilla y convidado de piedra* and Antonio de Zamora's *No hay plazo que no se cumpla ni deuda que no se*

25. Many have detected in Zorrilla's criticisms some bitterness, attributing it to his desire to "destroy" his play and the figure of Don Juan. Gladys Crescioni Neggers claims that "Even Zorrilla, the author who, according to the majority of critics, has most successfully elaborated the theme [of Don Juan], tried to destroy him with his attacks on him in *Recollections of Times Past*" (13). See also Salvador García Castañeda, Introducción, *Don Juan Tenorio* 35–41. On the subject of Zorrilla's plight and his attempted remedies, see Francisco Cervera y Jiménez-Alfaro.

pague, critics have endeavored to show that Zorrilla must have been, could have been, or was familiar with other versions as well. The usual choices for sources include Mérimée's *Les âmes du purgatoire* and the drama by Dumas *père, Don Juan de Marana ou la chute d'un ange.*[26]

These cavils aside, by far the most interesting aspect of "Cuatro palabras sobre mi *Don Juan Tenorio*" has little to do with issues of self-criticism and only indirectly to do with questions related to sources. There are, of course, minor reservations, along with some small expressions of satisfaction. For instance, Zorrilla is exceedingly proud of his creation of Doña Inés while he holds little fondness for his Don Juan, and he is bothered by the violation of the unity of time in the first act. But these observations pale in comparison with the paragraphs on the writing of *Don Juan Tenorio.* Here, truthfully or not, Zorrilla discloses his version of the inception of the drama. He goes on to say how, and to what extent, he intrudes upon the play. Instead of providing irrefutable information on sources or ammunition for those critics seeking to debunk either the originality of *Don Juan Tenorio* or Zorrilla, this brief essay offers a fascinating opportunity to witness an author's reconsideration of a particular work and, moreover, to explore the mechanisms by which he hoped his work would be read. Finally, implicit in this procedure as well is the designation of a number of authors with whom Zorrilla wishes to be compared, which raises, of course, the question of his honor and reputation as an author.

The essay begins with a brief description of the 1843–44 theater season in Madrid and then continues with a discussion of Zorrilla's *Don Juan Tenorio:*

> Carlos Latorre returned to Madrid in February of 1844 and he needed a new work. It fell to me, by rights, to provide him with it, but I didn't have anything in mind and time was of the essence: the theater was closing in April. I don't remember who gave me the idea of a recasting of *Don Juan Tenorio,* or if I, animated by the little effort the revision of *Las travesuras de Pantoja* had cost me, stumbled on the idea while leafing through Moreto's *comedias.* The fact is that—without any more informa-

26. Virtually nobody believes Zorrilla's account of his sources. Casalduero is typical of critics and scholars when he says of Zorrilla's sources: "The most important is Alexandre Dumas' *Don Juan de Marana ou la chute d'un ange,* but one must almost insist on Zamora's contribution" (*Contribución* 136). See also García Castañeda, Introducción, *Don Juan Tenorio* 24–34; Narciso Alonso Cortés 323–25; and Aniano Peña, Introducción 40–49. For a somewhat different view, see Weinstein 124–25.

tion or study than that of *El burlador de Sevilla,* by that ingenious friar, and Solís's poor revision, which until then had been
presented under the title of *No hay plazo que no se cumpla ni
deuda que no se pague* or *Convidado de piedra*—I committed
myself to write a Don Juan of my own making in twenty days.
(1799)

Zorrilla's account reveals both a carelessness in presentation (it appears as though Moreto were the "ingenious friar" who authored *El
burlador de Sevilla*) and a faulty memory (in fact, Zamora and not Solís
was the author of *No hay plazo que no se cumpla*). Significantly, he
stresses the pragmatically hasty writing and exclusively Spanish gene-
sis of his drama. Moreover, with his deprecatory reference to his
drama's eighteenth-century precursor, *No hay plazo,* he singles out
Tirso's play as the most influential of all other treatments of Don Juan.
Don Juan Tenorio is thereby not merely an adaptation of the Don Juan
character, but a recasting of *El burlador de Sevilla.*

The effectiveness of this strategic move is undercut, however, by
Zorrilla himself. He goes on to say that he began to work with "that
magnificent plot without knowing Molière's *Dom Juan,* or Father Da
Ponte's precious libretto, or, finally, anything of what those in Ger-
many, France, and Italy had written on the great idea of a sacrilegious
libertine as personified in one man: Don Juan" (1799–1800). Zorrilla,
with his mention of Molière and Da Ponte, sets himself up for a drub-
bing by scholars bent on proving that texts other than those by Tirso
and Zamora were used as sources for *Don Juan Tenorio,* since his
disclaimer does not appear to be free of equivocation. But the salient
point of this brief bibliography is that, like Mérimée in *Les âmes du
purgatoire,* he chooses to mention only Molière and Da Ponte by name,
two out of the many authors who had written about Don Juan. In
addition, this is a strangely motivated reference. Neither Molière nor
Da Ponte wrote his text without the benefit of another version, a
subtext. So Zorrilla's admission of a palimpsestic precursor, *El burlador de Sevilla,* is really nothing out of the ordinary, but the rule. Except, in the context of this paragraph in which Tirso, Molière, and Da
Ponte are given pride of place, it is unusual that an author would go to
such pains to offer a confused justification thirty years after the fact.

A clue to the reasoning behind and organization of this paragraph can
be found in Zorrilla's use of two key terms, *refundición,* or recasting or
revision, and *argumento* or plot. *Refundición* (from *refundir,* to recast) is
a metaphor that, as the *Diccionario de la Real Academia Española* tells
us, "means to comprehend, or to include," or, more specifically, "to give a

new form or shape to a creative work." In these terms, a *refundición* is literally a rewriting in which aspects of one literary text are reworked so as to admit the claims of both inclusion and originality within another text, which is to say, the *refundición* supposedly contains its precursor— the elements of plot and character—even as it stands apart from the earlier text.

This process of rewriting was especially common in Spain during the late eighteenth and early nineteenth centuries. Although *refundiciones* were assailed by various critics for their lack of originality and for the ways in which the original texts were distorted if not destroyed, they succeeded in keeping alive an active interest in a national theater, primarily for two reasons. First, the revisions could have been undertaken for aesthetic reasons, in order to bring Golden Age *comedias* into line with neo-classic dramatic precepts, specifically the so-called Aristotelian unities of time, place, and action. Second, there were practical considerations involved in undertaking the revision of another work: oftentimes the earlier drama's language and the exigencies of staging made its performance infeasible. In the process of rewriting a drama, the language could be updated and the various practical problems of staging could be dealt with, all without recourse to expensive scenery or special effects. Yet regardless of the reason for the *refundiciones,* the result was continued interest in the Golden Age, since seventeenth-century *comedias* were thereby fashioned into the stuff of the nineteenth century and made accessible to all. This means, of course, that the process of the *refundición* ideally constituted a critical and aesthetic reevaluation, not just a reworking but also a refurbishing of what had previously been judged outmoded or inappropriate.

There are other considerations as well, in many respects more pressing ones. Because of forceful government censorship, particularly during the "ominous decade" beginning in 1823, the steps involved in the creation of an original dramatic work (as opposed to a translation or *refundición*) were many and difficult. Furthermore, due to a general lack of authors' rights over their literary output, dramatists were virtually unable to realize a significant profit from their endeavors. In exchange for the time and effort expended on a drama an author received a lump sum and gained nothing from the subsequent publication, republications, and performances (see Paul Patrick Rogers). In Zorrilla's case, all rights to *Don Juan Tenorio* were sold to Manuel Delgado, a Madrid publisher, for 4200 *reales*. Even though the drama was later republished no fewer than fifteen times during his life, Zorrilla received nothing further. Despite, moreover, his efforts to recover something from Delgado later on—by appealing both on legal and on ethical grounds—Zorrilla's total recompense for his play remained those first 4200 *reales*. As Zorrilla bitterly notes in "Cuatro palabras," *"Don Juan Tenorio,* which produces thousands of *duros* and six days of diversion throughout Spain and the Spanish Americas, does not produce a single *real* for me" (1803).

Viewed, however, in terms of literary labor, *refundiciones* often paid better than original works *if* the issue of time is taken into account. In addition to the limitations of sources that he claims, Zorrilla admits that *refundiciones* require little effort, and, as a case in point, he mentions his revision of *Las travesuras de Pantoja,* which (and note the economic terms) had cost him little effort, and he likewise confesses that his *Don Juan Tenorio* was written in a mere twenty days. Zorrilla would probably concur, then, in the conclusion that *refundiciones* offer among other things two distinct advantages: they are historically important for keeping alive the tradition of the national theater and, more important, for permitting an author to become part of that tradition; and they are easily written.

Another telling aspect of this notion of the *refundición* has to do with Zorrilla's concept of dramatic filiation. He not only recognizes the advantages of the *refundición* when an author is pressed to produce a literary text, he also sees the relationship between the *comedia* and its offspring as a question of historical dependency. Of the success of his version of *Las travesuras de Pantoja, La mejor razón, la espada,* Zorrilla says, perhaps in a fit of false modesty, "there is no reason to praise me for it [the triumph], since anything worthwhile in the work is by Moreto, and not me" (1799). He attributes what is good and worthwhile in his revision to the original author and not to his own invention and thereby acknowledges that the extraordinary popularity of one work, of a revision, is contingent on the prior drama.

The nature of this process is made all the more explicit by Zorrilla's reference to "that magnificent *plot*" not to the *protagonist,* Don Juan. In this way, Zorrilla, like Mérimée and Byron, follows Horace's advice to the Pisos, "publica materies privati iuris erit" ["public matter shall be of a private right"], the end result of which is the creation of a common ground whereby two distant and distinct authors can be compared. Like Mérimée, whose *Les âmes de purgatoire* constitutes a claim to fame, setting him in the company of Molière and Mozart, and Byron, whose epigraph and opening stanzas to his "epic poem" serve notice of its intended literary and didactic import, Zorrilla turns his hand to a familiar "plot," Don Juan as found in the story of *El burlador de Sevilla,* which he adopts as a fulfillment of obligation.

As in other treatments of Don Juan in which an introduction or frame tale explains or even explains away literary precursors and precedents, Zorrilla's "Cuatro palabras" functions as a form of belated preface to the drama, articulating the author's thoughts on his own work. By focusing on *El burlador de Sevilla* as the preeminent subtext, Zorrilla creates a context in which to understand one of the most misunderstood of plays. This means that the narrative presentation of the writing of *Don Juan Tenorio* ought to be read as a theoretical tract in which Zorrilla's assumptions as to the nature and purpose of rewriting are outlined in order to suggest the means by which the text at hand can best be read. The issue thus raised by this essay is nothing less than the manner in which *Don Juan Tenorio* both contains and reorders *El burlador de Sevilla*.

However, the conventional point of departure in discussions of *El burlador de Sevilla* and *Don Juan Tenorio* has been to enumerate the differences between the two dramas. Indeed, Zorrilla's *refundición* has all too often been set in opposition to Tirso's play so that together the two dramas could be analyzed in terms of the social as opposed to the individual, religious orthodoxy as opposed to heterodoxy, and condemnation as opposed to salvation. It is nevertheless true, of course, that discussion of these oppositions is not entirely groundless, as the studies of Joaquín Casalduero (*Contribución* 133–49), Leo Weinstein (119–29), and Salvador García Castañeda (21–24) prove. *El burlador de Sevilla* does insist on the complicity of the social body in Don Juan's transgressions; and religious orthodoxy is prized, is indeed inevitable, at least to the extent that Don Juan's scapegoating is and can be the only solution to a world thrown into chaotic disorder (Parker, "The Spanish Drama of the Golden Age"; Wardropper, "*El burlador de Sevilla*"). The view that Zorrilla's version presents the struggles of an individual against the interests of a repressive and unyielding social hierarchy is equally apposite, as is the notion that the basic tenets of orthodox Catholicism are glossed over in order to reconcile salvation with the rights of an individual as construed in terms of Romantic ideologies (Mazzeo; Abrams; Romero; ter Horst, "Ritual Time"; Sebold 66–70). But no matter how useful these oppositions may be for heuristic purposes, this type of mechanical classification is unable to take into account the process by which Tirso's drama is rewritten because it views the two texts as existing in a static rather than a dynamic economy of literary exchange. Another, more successful, approach entails the identification of the precise point at which *Don Juan Tenorio* demonstrates its inclusion of and indebtedness to its precursor. Although questions of difference and similarity do enter into this type of discussion, the real issue is one of dependency, of how Zorrilla's drama depends on *El burlador de Sevilla* and how that dependency manifests itself.

Outwardly, the two dramas are dissimilar in the extreme. Tirso's complex and tightly focused drama is rewritten into a seemingly confusing collection of repetitive scenes of boasting and confrontation. The first part of *Don Juan Tenorio* opens in Buttarelli's inn, where a masked Don Juan writes a letter while his manservant, Ciutti, chats with the innkeeper. After entrusting the finished letter to his page, Don Juan leaves the inn, having ordered two bottles of wine to be set aside. This day marks the anniversary of a wager between Don Juan and his rival Don Luis made in order to prove which of them was capable of seducing more women and killing more men in a year's time. In this same act, Don Juan and Don Luis meet, remove their carnival masks and, after bantering and bragging of their adventures, get to the heart of the matter and tally up the count. Don Juan wins. But Don Luis spots a lacuna in Don Juan's list of victims, "una novicia / que esté para profesar" ["a novice on the eve of taking her vows"] (lines 669–70; 484), and another bet is on. Don Juan wagers that in the space of six days he can seduce both a novice and Don Luis's intended bride, Doña Ana de Pantoja. The penalty for the loser of this wager will be death. At the precise moment that the two rivals prepare to leave the inn, Don Juan and Don Luis are each taken prisoner, both of them having arranged to have the other locked up for the duration of the bet. Yet each escapes and later encounters the other at the house of Doña Ana, where Don Luis has hastened to protect his interest in the bet. Doña Ana assures her lover that she will be true and makes plans for a ten o'clock rendezvous with him. Immediately following this scene, Don Luis is again taken prisoner, this time by Don Juan's companions. Doña Ana's servant—after accepting a bribe—agrees to allow Don Juan to enter the house that evening in place of Don Luis. The outcome of the new wager has almost been decided.

Yet the letter that Don Juan was writing at the beginning of the play was, in fact, sent to a novice, Doña Inés de Ulloa, meaning that this lacuna was already being attended to when he made the bet with Don Luis. Indeed, with the help of her *dueña*, Brígida, who is also in his pay, Don Juan gains easy access to the novice's chambers in the convent at nine o'clock that same evening, since Brígida helps Doña Inés read Don Juan's letter, which was cleverly concealed in a prayer-book, and prepares her youthful charge for Don Juan's visit. For her part, Doña Inés is so emotionally overwrought by the prospect of seeing Don Juan that, upon his entrance into her chambers, she promptly faints. But even this fits into Don Juan's plans, since he escapes from the convent with the prostrate Doña Inés in his arms and Brígida close behind.

With Doña Inés safe in his villa on the outskirts of Sevilla, Don Juan finds enough time to seduce Doña Ana and then, around midnight, to woo the ex-novice, all before Don Luis and Don Gonzalo descend upon him, each demanding satisfaction, the one for the seduction of his fiancée, the other for the abduction of his daughter. Despite the fact that Don Juan begs the Comendador to permit him to marry Doña Inés (as arranged earlier by the two fathers), Don Gonzalo refuses and Don Juan must do battle with both Doña Inés's father and Doña Ana's lover, killing each of them in turn. He avoids capture by jumping from a balcony into the river below, escaping in the boat in which he arrived. The first part of the play closes with Doña Inés's heartfelt entreaty to her rescuers to spare Don Juan's life at any cost.

The first act of the second part of the drama opens with two scenes in which the sculptor of the Tenorio sepulchral pantheon speaks to the statues. Then, speaking with Don Juan (who has returned after five years of wandering in parts unknown), the sculptor recapitulates the action of the drama thus far: we learn that, except for Don Juan, all of the major characters have died, including Doña Inés. Don Juan contrives to remain in the pantheon and directs to the statue of Doña Inés a lengthy encomium in which he restates his deep and eternal love for her. At this point, Doña Inés's statue disappears and in its place materializes the "Shadow of Doña Inés." In the ensuing conversation, she warns Don Juan that he will shortly be fighting for his life, both in the real world and in the afterlife. Not only will his soul hang in the balance, but hers will as well: she has commended her soul to God in return for Don Juan's salvation. After the shadow disappears, two of Don Juan's friends, Centellas and Avellaneda, discover a fearful and half-crazed Don Juan in the pantheon. To prove to his mocking friends that he is as brave as ever, Don Juan rashly invites all of the statues in the pantheon to dinner and then, directing himself particularly to the Statue of the Comendador, he issues him a personal invitation. Of course, Don Gonzalo's statue acts on the invitation and in return offers one of his own. When Don Juan meets with the Comendador, he witnesses his own interment, the result, apparently, of his duel with Centellas and Avellaneda. When he takes the Statue's profferred hand, both he and the Statue of Don Gonzalo begin to descend to Hell together. But in this version of the story, Don Juan's last-minute avowal of religious faith is heard and Doña Inés's love saves him. The drama ends with this striking reversal as the souls of the two lovers rise toward heaven to the sound of celestial music.

This lengthy exposition of the plot of *Don Juan Tenorio* barely scratches the surface of the multitude of events and encounters in the play. Alongside the dramatic economy of language and action in *El burlador de Sevilla,* Zorrilla's eventful and swiftly paced *refundición* meanders, coming together as a coherent drama in the first part only when the contents of the written texts—first the lists and then the letter to Doña Inés—are revealed. Even though the second part of the play does not wander to the extent of the first, it nevertheless seems a sluggish conclusion in its lengthy expansion of a mere 475 lines of its subtext. It is difficult, furthermore, to detect obvious points of plot comparison between the two works beyond the inclusion and expansion of the double invitation. Tirso's four, carefully planned seductions are reduced to one not represented in the dramatic action of Zorrilla's play. As for Doña Inés, although she is abducted by Don Juan and exposed to his charms, this type of leading away (again, *se-* / *ducere*) hardly constitutes the same kind of conquest for which Tirso's *burlador* was justly infamous. Clearly, if the notion of Zorrilla's *Don Juan Tenorio* as a *refundición* of *El burlador de Sevilla* is to be sustained, some other means of "inclusion"—distinct from even a near-repetition of plot— must come into play.

In point of fact, *Don Juan Tenorio,* though not an overt repetition of its precursor, both includes *El burlador de Sevilla* and thematizes its inclusion thereof, making this process of rewriting into the stuff of drama. The entire first part of Zorrilla's drama turns on issues related to writing and rewriting; the continuing conflict between Don Juan and Don Luis, depicted most clearly during the second bet, is an outgrowth of just this sort of thematic interest. To be sure, the interest in writing is obvious in the opening scene, in which a masked Don Juan pens a letter. But there is yet another aspect to this scene that points both to the drama's filiation from its predecessor and to its incipient interest in writing.

Reminiscent of the early scenes in *El burlador de Sevilla,* in which Catalinón furnishes all pertinent information about his master, Zorrilla's version of the *gracioso,* Ciutti, answers Buttarelli's questions concerning the masked Don Juan. Unlike Catalinón, however, Ciutti does not give out his master's name:

BUTTARELLI.	¿A su servicio estás?
CIUTTI.	Ya ha un año.
BUTTARELLI.	¿Y qué tal te sale?
CIUTTI.	No hay prior que se me iguale;
	tengo cuanto quiero y más.

	Tiempo libre, bolsa llena,
	buenas mozas y buen vino.
BUTTARELLI.	¡Cuerpo de tal, qué destino!
CIUTTI.	Y todo ello a costa ajena.
BUTTARELLI.	¿Rico, eh?
CIUTTI.	Varea la plata.
BUTTARELLI.	¿Franco?
CIUTTI.	Como un estudiante.
BUTTARELLI.	¿Y noble?
CIUTTI.	Como un infante.
BUTTARELLI.	¿Y bravo?
CIUTTI.	Como un pirata.
BUTTARELLI.	¿Español?
CIUTTI.	Creo que sí.
BUTTARELLI.	¿Su nombre?
CIUTTI.	Lo ignoro en suma.
BUTTARELLI.	¡Bribón! ¿Y dónde va?
CIUTTI.	Aquí.
BUTTARELLI.	Largo plumea.
CIUTTI.	Es gran pluma.

(lines 17–32)

[BUTTARELLI.	How long have you served him?
CIUTTI.	A year now.
BUTTARELLI.	How does it suit you?
CIUTTI.	I am better off than a prior. I have all that I could want and then some! Time to myself, a full purse, fine women, good wine.
BUTTARELLI.	My God! What luck!
CIUTTI.	And all at his expense.
BUTTARELLI.	Rich, eh?
CIUTTI.	Spends money like confetti.
BUTTARELLI.	Straightforward?
CIUTTI.	Like a student.
BUTTARELLI.	Noble, I suppose?
CIUTTI.	Like a prince.
BUTTARELLI.	Brave?
CIUTTI.	A pirate.
BUTTARELLI.	A Spaniard?
CIUTTI.	I think so.
BUTTARELLI.	His name?
CIUTTI.	It slips my mind.

BUTTARELLI.   You dog! And he is going to . . . ?
CIUTTI.   Stay here.
BUTTARELLI.   Look at him scribble.
CIUTTI.   He is a mighty quill.

(472–73)]

Like Tirso's version, Zorrilla's drama toys with issues related to identification (name) and identity (personal characteristics and worldly possessions). Unlike Tirso's *burlador,* however, Zorrilla's Don Juan is not first identified either in terms of relation by blood or in terms of familial ties, but rather, in terms of qualities inhering in him as an individual. More to the point, he is identified as a writer and an *instrument* of writing; in a sense, the act of seduction is linked to writing by means of the phallic "pluma" or quill. The process by which the still-unidentified Don Juan is to be known is thus associated from the outset with writing in such a way that the individual is metaphorically cast as the author of his own nature.

This initial suggestion of the significance of writing for *Don Juan Tenorio* and the drama's protagonist is brought home even more forcefully in the scenes involving Don Juan and Don Luis. But even before Don Juan returns to center stage, the notion of rewriting is introduced by a coincidence in naming that will assert itself throughout the drama. Among the two rivals' cohorts who arrive at the inn to witness the outcome of the bet is Don Rafael de Avellaneda, whose name recalls probably the most famous—or infamous—author of a spurious continuation of a text in Spanish literature, Alonso Fernández de Avellaneda, author of the second part of the *Quijote*. But Avellaneda's extension of the *Quijote* is not the issue here. Rather, Cervantes himself took great pains to discredit the spurious continuation and to substitute one of his own, which is to say, Cervantes undertook to rewrite the extension of the original first part of his novel. The appearance of a character named Avellaneda thereby neatly refocuses the problems of writing and rewriting and does so in the context of naming, a problem to which the first part of *Don Juan Tenorio* next turns.

Once Don Juan and Don Luis appear on stage together, dependency becomes an issue of importance on many levels. In one manifestation of this concern (and surely in part as a function of his role as antagonist in the drama), Don Luis is portrayed as a weaker version of the Don Juan character. This weakness is not necessarily revealed in terms of physical characteristics or even in terms of a lack of brashness or bravery, but, rather, linguistically: Don Luis's speech is consistently couched in the contingent tenses of possibility and probability as opposed to Don

Juan's use of tenses of outright assertion. In another, the rivals depend on written accounts of their exploits to prove their claim to having won the bet. Although Don Juan is portrayed as both a more powerful individual and assertive character, his word finally is not in and of itself sufficient to back up his claim to the rightful possession of his name.

The notion of dependency as embodied in duplication and repetition carries over into the settling of the wager. Each of the rivals, in an attempt to prove that he has been more treacherous, proceeds to relate his adventures of the previous year. Yet except for minor deviations— such as the mention of Don Luis's imminent wedding to Doña Ana and those differences owing to the fact that Don Luis's enumeration follows Don Juan's—the entire speech of each character is nearly an exact repetition of that of his rival; the two stories correspond at every point. Furthermore, what has previously only seemed uncannily similar (their actions, speech, and gestures), is now transparently repetitious: both Don Juan and Don Luis seek adventures where there are wars; both announce their arrival and their willingness to take on anybody or anything; both keep meticulous records of their deeds in the form of lists.[27]

The fact that Don Juan and Don Luis have kept written accounts of their adventures constitutes not merely an interesting footnote to their rivalry but instead an important step in determining the winner of the wager. On the basis of what each has said, neither rival distinguishes himself so as to be able to claim to have won the bet. As Don Juan says of the situation, "La historia es tan semejante / que está en el fiel la balanza; / mas vamos a lo importante, / que es el guarismo a que alcanza / el papel: conque adelante" ["Your story is so like mine our scale stands even. But now let us proceed to the true weight of the matter: the value of our lists. On with it"] (lines 631–35; 483). In fact, the duplications do not end here. The stories are so similar to one another that even the manner in which they have been set down is the same:

> DON LUIS.   Aqui está el mío: mirad,
> por una línea apartados
> traigo los nombres sentados
> para mayor claridad.
>
> DON JUAN.   Del mismo modo arregladas
> mis cuentas traigo en el mío:

27. See Denah Lida on the lists in *Don Juan Tenorio*.

en dos líneas separadas,
los muertos en desafío,
y las mujeres burladas.
(lines 637–45)

[DON LUIS. Here's mine! Look: for the sake of clarity I placed
all the names on this side of the line.

DON JUAN. I kept my accounts by the very same method. One
column for the dead and another for the women.
(483)]

As this exchange demonstrates, the rivals have strayed from the recitation of their adventures to a discussion of the textual representation
of their deeds, and from there to a complete reliance on the two written accounts. The only way to calculate the winner of the bet is to
consult the written tally. What began as a contest between two men
becomes a confrontation between two texts in which *one version* of the
same story will be granted privilege over the other. Words take on
critical importance; they are more meaningful than the deeds they
supposedly represent.

Of course, the intention all along was to count up the number of men
killed and of women seduced by each man, to find out "quien haría en
un año, / con más fortuna, más daño" ["who could do more harm with
more luck in the course of one year"] (lines 80–81; 474). But because of
the similarities between the two stories, the only way to prove the
contention of each is to add up the numbers as they have already been
recorded in the lists, which means that the relationships among writing, identification, and identity are key in *Don Juan Tenorio*. Don Juan
and Don Luis both must have recourse to what they have *written* in
order to prove themselves to be what they have *said* they *are*. The
progression as it pertains to the masked character seen at the beginning of the play emphasizes what may be termed his textual dependency. Admittedly, Don Juan names himself, as well as—considering
the nature of the action—Don Luis, Don Gonzalo, and his father, Don
Diego. But his ability to stand as a distinct character in terms of action
and not by name alone is contingent upon a text and upon the greater
authority that he musters by means of his writing of that text. In turn,
what he writes derives its authority only by means of its comparison
with other written texts, which is, in a manner, similar to the way in
which the prescribed Horatian text would derive its significance from
the reworking of a familiar literary topos in *literary* form.

As it happens, Don Juan does win the bet he made with Don Luis, coming out ahead in both categories. Don Juan kills nine more men and seduces sixteen more women than Don Luis. Yet it is obvious that he has won only because he possessed the textual authority to support his claim: "Si lo dudáis," he tells Don Luis, "apuntados / los testigos ahí están" ["If you doubt it, the witnesses are listed here"] (lines 657–58; 483). Don Juan evinces a superiority that is both numerical and discursive, a superiority that transcends all of the many open similarities between his story and Don Luis's, between his list and that of his rival. Without the lists, Don Juan, Don Luis, or anyone else for that matter, would have been hard-pressed to name the winner of the bet. With his list, Don Juan has proven that he indeed was singularly able.

The emphasis on identification as opposed to identity has the effect of suppressing the name of the single most important text treating Don Juan, *El burlador de Sevilla,* the title of which could easily have been conferred on the winner of the wager. This would have followed directly upon Tirso, as the name *burlador* is given to Don Juan by others precisely because of what he does.[28] Yet *El burlador de Sevilla does* seem to be present, if only as a touchstone of the character Don Juan and not as either an openly acknowledged predecessor or an obvious palimpsest. In particular it appears to exercise much influence on the opening scenes of the drama. One notable point of contact between the *comedia* and its nineteenth-century revision pertains to the second half of the Tirsian title . . . *y convidado de piedra* [. . . and the Stone Guest]. In response to the stolid presence of Don Gonzalo and Don Diego in the inn, each there to witness the settling of the bet, Buttarelli remarks, "¡Vaya un par de hombres de piedra!" ["What a pair of stone men!"] (line 251; 477). This reference points, however, not to Don Juan, but to the Statue. In much the same way that Tirso erased his protagonist

28. The passage in question from *El burlador de Sevilla* reads:

CATALINÓN.   fuera bien se pregonara:
                « Guárdense todos de un hombre
                que a las mujeres engaña,
                y es el burlador de España ».
DON JUAN.   Tú me has dado gentil nombre.
                    (lines 1485–89)

[CATALINÓN.   It would be good if they were to proclaim: "Let all protect themselves from a man who tricks women, the Trickster of Spain."
DON JUAN.   You have given me a charming name.]

from the title of his drama—Batricio bringing the *comedia* to a close
(lines 2858–59), not only excluding Don Juan from society but also
from the title of the work to which he initially gave his name—Zorrilla
emphasizes the *similarities* between the fathers in the two dramas and
the *differences* between the *burlador* and Don Juan.

This type of veiled allusion is part and parcel of a larger program of
difference between both characters and dramas presented in terms of
dependency. It is, moreover, in force throughout the first part of *Don
Juan Tenorio*. But dependency is not merely apparent here as the standard dramatic ploy of foregrounding the protagonist, even though this
is one way in which it manifests itself early in the drama. In the
exchange involving the lists, the point is, rather, to demonstrate the
contingency of the rivals' speech, the way it depends on a textual basis.
Instead of hinting at this sort of textual basis, as did Tirso, Zorrilla
brings it to the forefront of his drama, but with a significant difference.
Whereas the *burlador* intercepts *papeles*, which can be both missives
and dramatic roles, and (mis)represents them, Don Juan and Don Luis
write their own. In the context of *Don Juan Tenorio*, the rivals are,
quite literally, self-made men, yet men whose identities are nonetheless contingent on the type of text backing them.

If Don Juan and his rival Don Luis appear to be self-made individuals, clearly Don Gonzalo de Ulloa, the Comendador, Don Diego Tenorio,
and Doña Ana de Pantoja are characters in *El burlador de Sevilla,*
characters whose roles have been written prior to the inception of
Zorrilla's Don Juan play. In both dramas, Don Gonzalo is the father
who comes to his daughter's aid and who is consequently slain; he later
reappears in the guise of the Statue. Don Diego, Don Juan's father, is
forced in each drama to admit to the dissolute nature of his son. Doña
Ana, originally Don Gonzalo's daughter, is, despite minor changes, one
of Don Juan's victims in each drama, since the situation of her seduction neatly parallels that of Tirso's Doña Ana de Ulloa. In Tirso's play
the price of Don Juan's *burla* or trick was her father's life, in Zorrilla's
drama it is the life of her fiancé. In every instance the characters' roles
are well defined and Zorrilla remains faithful to Tirso's prescription.
But Zorrilla also creates his own characters, including Buttarelli, Lu-
cía, Brígida, and Doña Inés, casting the various roles in such a way
that Don Juan appears as the controlling figure of the new dramatis
personae. Of these four new characters, the first three are brought into
Don Juan's sphere of influence by accepting his money and by playing
a role in his various schemes while the last receives her *papel*, the
letter, directly from her lover.

The sixty-four lines of the love-letter contain several allusions to traditional topoi which are then taken up in subsequent scenes.[29] Yet of all of the traditional images and ideas embodied in this letter, by far the most significant is that of the *alma* or soul. The novice's altruistic act of pledging her soul culminates a kind of extended meditation on the nature of transcendent Christian love, which both is initiated by and derives from the *papel* written by Don Juan. No less than five times does the word *alma* occur in the letter, and it always does so in the context of Doña Inés herself (lines 1644, 1666–67, 1692, 1725; 502–3). It comes as no surprise, then, that Doña Inés should see and portray herself in terms of this commingling of souls ("alma de mi alma" ["soul of my soul"]); it is even less surprising, given her sacrifice, that God, according to Doña Inés, should warn her that she should make sure that Don Juan does not take her soul from her tomb (3008–13; 524).

The notion of this commingling of souls and uniting of destinies as presented here is nothing new. Yet it serves to underline the cardinal importance of the letter—and all texts—in *Don Juan Tenorio* and in Don Juan's story, indeed, the complicity of narration and literature in the very act of seduction,[30] which is to say, it points to what René Girard has referred to as mimetic desire. One *locus classicus* of this aspect of seduction is to be found in Dante's *Divina Commedia,* Canto 5 of the *Inferno,* where Francesca relates the sad course of her love for Paolo. The scenario begins in a general sense when Francesca attributes much of her past to Love and his powers; it continues with an instance of mimetic desire when Francesca tells how "amore" taught her and Paolo of "the dubious desires" (lines 100, 120). While reading of Lancelot and Guinevere, Paolo and Francesca begin to act as the two lovers do in the book: when Lancelot and Guinevere kiss, so do Paolo and Francesca. The passion of the two lovers who read together ends by leading them to the second circle of the Inferno where Dante finds them. The oneness enjoyed or suffered by Francesca and Paolo stems from their reading of the Arthurian lovers. According to Francesca, it is a union engendered by a text, progressing from reading to an enact-

29. The letter and its significance in *Don Juan Tenorio* are discussed by Gustavo Pérez Firmat 3–15; although my analysis is similar to that of Pérez Firmat, we do not always arrive at the same conclusions.

30. In his discussion of Balzac's *Sarrasine,* Roland Barthes describes the narrative situation, the exchange between the narrator and a beautiful woman, as a bargain in which seduction appears as an *act* of narration: "if you give yourself to me, I will tell you a story: tit for tat: a moment of love in exchange for a good story" (86). Barbara Johnson extends this observation into a more general principle, "Story-telling, as Barthes points out, is thus not an innocent, neutral activity, but rather part of a bargain, an act of seduction" (7).

ment of the actions described therein. As Francesca succinctly states, "Galeotto fu 'l libro e chi lo scrisse" ["A Gallehault was the book and he who wrote it"] (line 137). The "Galeotto" or pimp is both the author of the book (or the action described in the book) and, in Girardian terms, because the book engenders an action, the author of the fate of Francesca and Paolo as well (see Poggioli; and Girard, *"To double business bound"* 1–8).

In terms of Don Juan and Doña Inés, this commingling of souls picks up various threads found in *El burlador de Sevilla,* specifically the notion of the daemonic Don Juan and that of the reading of a narrative scenario in a letter, fashioning of these different materials the mutual dependency of Don Juan and Doña Inés. Doña Inés, "soul of my soul," becomes the soul of love, the Psyche of Eros, the manner in which, in a skewing of Platonic and Christian doctrine, Zorrilla's Don Juan can reconcile himself with God. The joining of the two souls and destinies (lines 1662–63; 502) means that the spiritual future of each is dependent on the other. Not only does Doña Inés save Don Juan's soul, but Don Juan saves the soul of Doña Inés. In this sense, Zorrilla's Don Juan is a *daemon,* too; his testimony to Doña Inés's love for him is the deciding factor in the fate of each. The fact that Don Juan repents— "¡Señor, ten piedad de mí!" ["God, have mercy on me!"] (line 3769; 537)—overrides the Statue's grim sentence, "Ya es tarde" ["It is too late!"] (line 3770; 537). Doña Inés's investment of her soul is repaid in kind.

Like the inception of love between Francesca and Paolo, Doña Inés's love for Don Juan derives from reading, in this case not of a book, but of the letter sent to her by Don Juan:

> ¡Ay! ¿Qué filtro envenenado
> me dan en este papel,
> que el corazón desgarrado
> me estoy sintiendo con él?
> ¿Qué sentimientos dormidos
> son los que revela en mí?
> ¿Qué impulsos jamás sentidos?
> ¿Qué luz que hasta hoy nunca vi?
> ¿Qué es lo que engendra en mi alma
> tan nuevo y profundo afán?
> (lines 1732–41)

[Oh! What poisonous filter is hidden in these words? It tears my heart apart! What hidden, sleeping thoughts these words reveal

in me. What strange feelings they arouse. They cast a light upon
me unlike any I have ever seen before. What has sown my soul
with such new and deep desire? (503)]

Once disseminated by Don Juan's *papel,* the poisonous filter takes hold
of the novice and she begins to repeat the content of the letter, to learn
her *papel* or dramatic role: "¡Ah! Bien dice: juntó el cielo / los destinos
de los dos, / y en mi alma engendró este anhelo / fatal" ["Oh, he spoke
true! Heaven joined our destinies and engendered in my soul this fatal
longing"] (lines 1748–51; 503). Don Juan's letter is not, then, just a
point from which poetic and dramatic coherence originate but also the
means by which Doña Inés completes her brief *cursus* in the *ars
amatoria.* The letter is the text from which her actions in the drama
derive, that which provides her with her *papel,* or role. Thus, the Don
Juan of *Don Juan Tenorio* writes not only his own role, the list or *papel,*
but writes other roles as well, demonstrating in the process the power
of men's words with respect to female resolve. To restate the remark of
Dante's Francesca, "Don Juan fu 'l libro e chi lo scrisse" ["Don Juan
was the book and he who wrote it"].

Despite its late appearance in the play, and despite the fact that it is a
secondary text in terms of Don Juan's identity, the letter sent to Doña
Inés is of primary importance for understanding the temporal ordering
of the drama, and, in turn, the role played by *El burlador de Sevilla* in
regard to the dependency of *Don Juan Tenorio* on its precursor. The
papel is actually read in the third scene of the third act, roughly midway through the first part of the play, but it is being written as the
drama opens. The effect of this lapse between the writing and the
reading of the letter (into which the comparison of the lists is inserted)
is to divide past actions from future developments, to create a dramatic
parenthesis into which the past is interpolated. This means, of course,
that Don Juan intended to abduct Doña Inés *before* he met with Don
Luis to settle their bet. Doña Inés enters into Don Juan's second wager
with his rival, but more to the point, the second wager with Don Luis
already enters into Don Juan's future plans. As Robert ter Horst points
out, the novice is Don Juan's "fundamental goal" ("Ritual Time" 82).

   The division between the past and future plans, as well as the ellipti-
cal presentation of the letter that points up these differences, fits into a
linear pattern of increasingly obsessive passion ("pasión insensata"),
one that is best described by Don Juan himself: "Empezó [esta pasión
insensata] por una apuesta, / siguió por un devaneo, / engendró luego
un deseo, / y hoy me quema el corazón" ["It began (this obsessive

passion) with a bet and grew into a frenzy which later engendered a desire—and now my heart is consumed with fire"] (lines 1310–13; 496). Construed in terms of strict diachrony, *Don Juan Tenorio* begins with a wager, follows with a recapitulation of that first bet, and continues with the inception of another bet that corresponds to Don Juan's growing desire. This desire finally becomes overwhelming in its force, burning Don Juan's heart. But with which wager, the first or the second, does *Don Juan Tenorio* really begin? Linearity notwithstanding, the division between the first and second bets, the reading and discussion of the *papel,* marks the point at which the two key figures, Tirso's *burlador* and Zorrilla's Don Juan, begin to differ. Only the list of misdeeds allows the protagonist of *Don Juan Tenorio* to be identified as *a* Don Juan at all. Without a legendary past, which is to say, without Don Juan's literary past as embodied in the list, Don Juan is just one more Romantic roué who finds true love and, determined to secure the object of his adoration, infringes upon various social conventions much to the delight of his cohorts. On the other hand, with a past history of seductions and slayings as recorded in the list, Don Juan becomes *a* Don Juan; and Don Juan and Zorrilla implicitly acknowledge the filiation from Tirso's *burlador.* The circularity of the first part of *Don Juan Tenorio* thus features the pertinent information of the past, *El burlador de Sevilla,* in order to render the future drama intelligible, doing so by means of incorporating entire an earlier text that both explains the past (and past texts) and engenders the future of the drama (as well as the drama itself). Yet even as the prior text is included in the *refundición,* it is rewritten by the other text that constitutes the basis for a new series of actions: Don Juan's letter to Doña Inés, and, by extension, *Don Juan Tenorio.*

Don Juan's *papel,* as distinct from the *papel* sent to Doña Inés, is therefore in essence *El burlador de Sevilla.* The act of inclusion, the symbolic incorporation of *El burlador de Sevilla* in the form of the list, permits Zorrilla to invoke the literary past necessary for the virtually iconic character that he will (re)write into existence. Moreover, by organizing the opening acts of his drama around issues of repetition and doubling, Zorrilla stages the exact situation of *Don Juan Tenorio* with respect to Tirso's *comedia:* two similar if not identical texts are compared, one is found inferior, and the author of that text (Don Luis) is duly punished.[31] The first wager forces the staging of a textual con-

31. On doubling and parallelism in *Don Juan Tenorio* see George P. Mansour. See also Pérez Firmat 16–31. Another approach to the question of repetition is that of David T. Gies ("Don Juan contra Don Juan").

frontation between dramas and the characters of those dramas (Don Diego, Don Gonzalo, and Doña Ana from the *comedia,* with Don Luis as an antagonizing force, on the one hand; Don Juan and Doña Inés as well as the servants as Zorrilla's creations, on the other). The second wager stages the systematic elimination of the avatars of *El burlador de Sevilla.* Indeed, the second wager itself assumes the guise of a doubling. When Don Luis proposes that his rival seduce a novice, Don Juan doubles the terms of the bet: "¡Bah! Pues yo os complaceré / doblemente, porque os digo / que a la novicia uniré / la dama de algún amigo / que para casarse esté" ["Bah! I'll be glad to oblige, and doubly so. For along with the novice I'll throw in the bride of a friend who's about to marry"] (lines 671–75; 484). As the curtain falls on the end of the first part of the play, Tirso's characters have ceased to pose an impediment to Zorrilla's rewriting. Both Don Luis and Don Gonzalo are dead, Doña Ana is dishonored, and Don Diego has been repudiated. When the second part of the play takes up the action some five years later with all of the principal characters gone except Don Juan, only the Statue of the Comendador, originally Tirso's character, and the shadow of Doña Inés, the residual effect of Zorrilla's character, remain to enter into a kind of spiritual duel to determine by whom, and for which dramatist, Don Juan is to be claimed. The outcome should come as no surprise. Don Juan's salvation is predicted as early as the tallying of the lists. He not only wins the first wager numerically, by killing thirty-two men to Don Luis's twenty-three, but by an inversion of his rival's accomplishment. This numerical inversion in terms of the dead thereby anticipates Zorrilla's inverse solution to his protagonist: Zorrilla shows how even Don Juan can be made immortal.

Don Juan's dramatic immortality is patently Zorrilla's immortality, too, and Zorrilla is hardly unaware of its significance, that it derives from his revision of a canonical text. Moreover, the power of revision and its importance for assessing the relative literary merits of an author were not lost on Zorrilla's contemporaries. Two reviews of *Don Juan Tenorio* demonstrate a keen awareness of precisely these issues. In one of the first critical reactions to the drama following the premiere, we read of the relative success of Zorrilla's drama. According to this assessment, the reasons for success are to be found in Zorrilla's artistry. With this, the review moves from a discussion of the poetry of the drama to the personal success of the author:

> On Thursday night in the Teatro de la Cruz, *Don Juan Tenorio,*
> an original drama in verse, premiered for the benefit of Carlos

Latorre. It was an undertaking worthy of Zorrilla, who presented to the theater a Don Juan whose conduct was as dissolute as it was chivalric, a character already portrayed by Lope de Vega, Tirso de Molina, Zamora, Molière, Balzac, Dumas, and the immortal Byron. (*El Corresponsal* 31 March 1844)

This same tendency is found in the review of the drama in *El Dómine Lucas*. In fact, this second review seems to have been based on the first, as some phrases are practically identical:

This work places its author at the level of the great geniuses who have distinguished themselves in the nations most advanced in literary terms. Lope de Vega, Tirso de Molina, Zamora, Corneille, Molière, Balzac, Dumas, Byron, all of these colossal geniuses have painted in brilliant colors a Don Juan whose conduct was as dissolute as it was chivalric; and Zorrilla's greatest triumph is in having rivaled his predecessors with dignity and without copying them; in fact, he bests them on many occasions. (*El Dómine Lucas* 1 May 1844)

Zorrilla is here seen as the *rival* of his precursors, and as a successful rival at that. The drama becomes the means by which Zorrilla takes on—and triumphs over—other authors. *Don Juan Tenorio* is Zorrilla's "title of nobility," is a claim to a place in the pantheon of literary immortals.[32]

The opening scene of *Don Juan Tenorio* in which the masked and seated Don Juan, the "gran pluma" or "mighty quill," writes what turns out to be a missive to Doña Inés, ought to present us not only

---

32. This aspect of the drama and of Zorrilla's relation to it figures prominently in Pérez Firmat's recent study in which he suggests that the temporal distortions in the play—including the 200-minute hours—can be explained by Bloom's notion of the anxiety of influence and the rhetorical trope of metalepsis. As tempting as Pérez Firmat's analysis of the reversability of time in *Don Juan Tenorio* is, I would suggest that Bloom's concept of *daemonization* is a much more appropriate category for this analysis of Zorrilla's "anxiety of influence." According to Bloom in *The Anxiety of Influence,* "*Daemonization* or the Counter-Sublime is a war between Pride and Pride, and momentarily the power of newness wins. . . . *Daemonization,* like all mythification of the fathers, is an individuating moment purchased by withdrawal from the self, at the high price of dehumanization" (101, 109). Finally, this *daemonization* is, in Bloom's words, a "mythification of the fathers," which both allows the new poet to stand as an individual even as the predecessor, by losing his originality, becomes demonstrably less distinct.

with a glimpse of Don Juan but also with the image of Zorrilla. In fact, Zorrilla says of this scene:

> That now-famous quatrain came to me when I was trying to present my character as quickly as possible, as if fearing that he would escape me: "How the damned are shouting. May I be struck by lightning if I don't shut their mouths as soon as I've finished this letter!" ["¡Cuál gritan esos malditos! / Pero, mal rayo me parta, / si en concluyendo mi carta / no pagan caros sus gritos"]. Let the truth be said in peace and God's grace. When this quatrain was written, it was more as if I were speaking than Don Juan. . . . The most palpable proof that I was speaking and not Don Juan is that the characters waiting on stage—more for me than for him—were Ciutti, the Italian waiter that Jústiz, Allo, and I had had in the Café del Turco in Seville, and Girolamo Buttarelli, the innkeeper who had put me up in 1842 on Carmen Street. (1800)

Beginning with the first scene of the drama, in which the very act of writing is portrayed, we can read—and we have read, as did Zorrilla— the author of this passage into the subsequent conflicts surrounding Don Juan *and* into the final moments of salvation. By his own admission, Zorrilla implicitly presides over, and partakes of, the salvation of Doña Inés and Don Juan and thereby engenders his own literary immortality.

Seduction is thus very much a part of *Don Juan Tenorio* even if it does not initially appear to be so. Seduction is operative here as the alluringly seductive *authorial* immortality already conferred on Tirso. Although not so specific or obvious as Mérimée's disclaimer, Zorrilla's drama, when read in conjunction with his "Cuatro palabras," is none- theless explicit in its intention to revise the literary landscape, to replace a statue with a shrine to love, which is to say, to Love's powers and to immorality. As for honor, it too, as we have seen, is involved in *Don Juan Tenorio,* particularly in the way that Zorrilla honors himself with his literary monument. There is, in fact, another character in the drama who, like Don Juan, represents Zorrilla. This time, however, the representation of the author has nothing to do with the triumph of one individual over another, but rather with the triumph of the artist over his single most meaningful rival: time.

As the second part of the play opens, the sculptor of the sepulchral statues is in the Tenorio pantheon, and he addresses his creations. This monologue constitutes an extended consideration of artistic glory and immortality:

> ¡Ah! Mármoles que mis manos
> pulieron con tanto afán,
> mañana os contemplarán
> los absortos sevillanos;
> y al mirar de este panteón
> las gigantes proporciones,
> tendrán las generaciones
> la nuestra en veneración.
> Mas yendo y viniendo días,
> se hundirán unas tras otras,
> mientra en pie estaréis vosotras,
> póstumas memorias mías.
> ¡Oh! frutos de mis desvelos,
> peñas a quien yo animé
> y por quienes arrostré
> la intemperie de los cielos;
> el que forma y ser os dio,
> va ya a perderos de vista;
> ¡velad mi gloria de artista,
> pues viviréis más que yo!
>   (lines 2656–75)

[Oh, my marble beauties, carved so lovingly with these hands. When Seville comes tomorrow, wide-eyed, to contemplate your grand proportions and the beauty of this pantheon, our age will earn the veneration of generations to come. Days will come and go, men will come and go while you still stand, my posthumous memories. Oh, children of my labor, stones I brought to life and for which I was at the mercy of the heavens. He who gave you form and being is now going to lose sight of you. Watch over my artistic glory. You will live longer than I. (519)]

A typically Romantic creative genius, the Escultor depicts himself as a little god who creates and gives life to the statues, all the while defying the undeniably greater forces at work in the world. Moreover, the statues will bear forth the glory of the sculptor, will grant him the possibility of artistic fame and immortality. Zorrilla also uses the Escultor to advance a subtle polemic relative to compensation for artistic endeav-

ors. When Don Juan attempts to slip him something for the statues—
"Pues bien merece algo más / un retrato tan maestro. / Tomad" ["Such a
likeness deserves something more. Here"] (lines 2866–68; 522)—the
Sculptor replies, "Mirad que están bien pagadas" ["But they are well
paid for"] (line 2872; 522). If, as I suggest, the Escultor represents
Zorrilla, then we ought to understand this brief exchange in terms of
the relative status of authors in early nineteenth-century Spain (see
Ciplijauskaité, *El poeta* 9–66). The monuments of the statues correspond, therefore, to the document that is *Don Juan Tenorio;* the pantheon of the dead is the gallery of great authors.

The notion of the *panteón* or pantheon as a type of literary cemetery
is not peculiar to Zorrilla's *Don Juan Tenorio.* Indeed, the pantheon of
the Tenorios in Zorrilla's *Don Juan,* the family cemetery, has as its
origin in the drama two prior manifestations, the one literary, the
other literal. To begin with the literary "source," in one of his *cuadros
de costumbres* or portraits of local color, "El *album*" [The Album], Mariano José de Larra discusses the early nineteenth-century fad of the
album in high society. According to Larra, an album is a book of blank
pages that belongs to a woman; in this book, distinguished men inscribe themselves: "if he is a poet, he prints some verses, if he is a
painter, a sketch, a musician, a composition, etc." Almost all of the
inscriptions have to do with the owner of the album, which means,
according to Larra, that the inscriptions are "different fountains in
which a single Narcissus looks at himself and is reflected" (84). Different scraps of verse, different sketches or musical compositions all treat
the same theme, the woman who owns the album: they are all versions
of the same story. This leads Larra to assert:

> an album, therefore, becomes a *pantheon* where a portion of nota-
> ble men come to be interred as a sort of advance loan to posterity.
> In spite of the fact that not every man who merits being found in
> an album is equally meritorious in future times . . . an album
> frequently becomes a sort of pantheon, a cemetery, where fools
> and wits are interred side by side . . . (84–85)

If the album is a pantheon in which those who are notable find themselves inscribed, rather, interred, then the Tenorio pantheon becomes a
representation of a cultural repository of past glories. That Don Juan
must return to the pantheon in order to obtain his salvation is only
proper: because he was resurrected from death, he and his author must
return to that point of origin in order to find their immortality.

To write in the terms proposed by Larra's album is to write from the pantheon of the dead, from the cemetery, to write from the perspective of death. And this is quite literally the case if we recall that Zorrilla was catapulted to immediate literary renown when he read an elegy in a cemetery on the occasion of Larra's interment in February 1837. In other words, Zorrilla's own literary career began where another's ended, in a cemetery, in a pantheon, that led him to his own inscription in the pantheon of Don Juan, now in the guise of the Esculter. With respect to *Don Juan Tenorio,* a repetition in which repetition figures prominently, Zorrilla is, therefore, doubly inscribed, doubly immortal, in that traces of the author are to be found both in Don Juan and the sculptor. *Don Juan Tenorio* as a drama is thus one more link in an ongoing chain, the reinterpretation of another document, of the original letter.

Although it is currently fashionable to speak of never-ending texts, of infinite regression and *mise en abîme,* and although one could say that, by reference, Zorrilla's *Don Juan Tenorio* necessarily and endlessly recreates *El burlador de Sevilla* with every reading and performance, that type of intepretive indeterminacy is the easy way out of the consideration and comparison undertaken here. More to the point, the repetitions and doublings in *Don Juan Tenorio* require the re-creation on the part of the audience, including the scholar and critic, of a restricted field of allusion and literary history that is in fact literary, that takes into account authors and texts as mutually dependent entities. In the case of Zorrilla's *refundición,* the nineteenth-century revision both brings its precursor up to date and situates itself and its author in close proximity to one of Spanish literature's canonical texts. *Don Juan Tenorio* should be seen, therefore, as what it purports to be, as an extension of both Zorrilla and *El burlador de Sevilla,* and as perhaps the *comedia*'s most flattering interpretation. If we were to complete the scheme, the force of *Don Juan Tenorio* would encompass Tirso, too, would indeed form a common ground, a *res communis,* for the encounter of two authors, and, of course, for their critics as well. The seductive powers of *Don Juan Tenorio* are such that it remains the quintessential example of Spanish Romantic play, the text to which historians of nineteenth-century Peninsular literature inevitably turn and to which later authors respond.[33] All pay homage—adversarial or otherwise—to the drama as a worthy predecessor in the canon.

33. But see Gies ("Don Juan contra Don Juan," "*Don Juan Tenorio,*" and "José Zorrilla"), who remarks, "I don't share the general opinion that *Don Juan Tenorio* is the Romantic drama par excellence" ("*Don Juan Tenorio*" 3 n. 1).

El nuevo Don Juan and the Itinerary of the Letter

> *Cartas, relaciones, cartas:*
> *tarjetas postales, sueños,*
> *fragmentos de la ternura,*
> *proyectados en el cielo,*
> *lanzados de sangre a sangre*
> *y de deseo a deseo.*
> —*Miguel Hernández*, "Carta"
>
> "*Yo soy carta viva.*"
> —*Adelardo López de Ayala*, El nuevo Don Juan

In terms of text and commentary, of a literary work and literary responses, *Don Juan Tenorio* was as provocative as *El burlador de Sevilla*. Unlike Zorrilla, who portrayed Don Juan in a favorable, even sympathetic, light, a number of late nineteenth-century authors and commentators—including Adelardo López de Ayala, Francisco Pi y Margall, Felipe Picatoste y Rodríguez, and Manuel de la Revilla y Moreno—viewed the character in an obviously negative way. There is little doubt that Zorrilla's idealization and glorification of the seducer as well as the subsequent popularity of *Don Juan Tenorio* were in large part responsible for this negative reaction. Although the general public was admiring, journalists, critics, and other authors were extremely harsh in their assessments. Opinions regarding Don Juan thus fell into two distinct categories. There were those—usually literary critics— who viewed the character with suspicion and dislike, and those— usually the public at large—who saw in Don Juan the positive, quintessential expression of the Spanish soul.[34]

Francisco Pi y Margall remarks in his introduction to Tirso de Molina's *¿Tan largo me lo fiáis . . . ?*:

> Zorrilla falsifies the character of Don Juan. . . . I would have something more to say if, instead of limiting myself to examining the character of Don Juan, I were to offer a critique of the whole drama, where I almost dare to say that there are more errors than things to admire, although there are many of the latter. . . . I understand that Zorrilla, with his *Don Juan Tenorio*, has better succeeded in satisfying the exigencies of the public

---

34. For a more detailed consideration of the popularity of Zorrilla's drama, see my "Nostalgia and the Popularity of *Don Juan Tenorio*." For a contrasting view, see Timothy Mitchell's discussion of the drama in *Violence and Piety* 169–89.

than those of art; he is well served by his brilliant gifts. What a pity that he did not think more about satisfying the exigencies of art, rather than those of the public! (lx, lxv–lxvi)

Alongside this assertion of the "falsification" of Don Juan's character as perpetrated by Zorrilla, consider Felipe Picatoste's comments, which clearly follow from those of Pi y Margall and which emphasize the contradictory nature of Don Juan and the drama. According to Picatoste:

> No poet has falsified the character of Don Juan more; no one has presented him as more suspect, more incomprehensible, more irresolute, more variable. . . . The public is constantly in doubt: it is convinced only that Don Juan is a rake. Moreover, Don Juan repents in a moment, and then is saved, a denouement without justification. . . . Thus, this drama sums up all of the modifications that the character of Don Juan has suffered . . . causing the traditional type to lose his primordial signification, which does not mean that we deny the innumerable things to admire with which the work is adorned. (184–85)

Note the strange modulation, the severe criticisms offset by the vague references to the "things to admire" in *Don Juan Tenorio*. Instead of appealing to questions of dramatic form, poetic taste, or religious orthodoxy, as had other critics of the drama, Pi y Margall and Picatoste accuse Zorrilla of "falsifying" Don Juan, of turning the character into something he is not. The popularity of the drama, a given never questioned, remains somewhat puzzling to both of these authors.

These aesthetic questions were refocused in this same period in an explicitly moral consideration of the drama, one that steers clear of vituperation but that nevertheless calls into question Don Juan's salvation. Echoing Pi y Margall and Picatoste, Manuel de la Revilla asks, "What has Zorrilla done to the character of Don Juan Tenorio?" He answers his own question: "It was not enough for him to break openly with tradition, saving Don Juan at the end, but it seemed necessary to falsify him completely. Don Juan is, above all, a great character, but Zorrilla's protagonist is barely a character at all; rather, he is a strange bunch of inexplicable contradictions." But falsification is not the only issue, as Revilla demonstrates:

> that an unbridled libertine, seducer, violent assassin, bully, traitor, perverted son, disloyal friend, and no gentleman (for the Don Juan of Zorrilla is all this), that he would challenge his victims

once they were dead, and that, once the hour of atonement arrives, one moment of repentance provoked out of fear and the influence of a woman in love would be enough so that such an impure soul could obtain salvation while the victims remain condemned, in the eyes of morality, whatever this might be, this is absurd, irritating, and impious.

Not only does Zorrilla falsify Don Juan, but the author himself is morally suspect: "a drama of this type is subtitled religious and it is presented as a special function on All Saints and All Souls Days" (451–52). The quasi-religious character of the annual performances of Zorrilla's *Don Juan Tenorio,* to say nothing of the author's *mis*representation of the *burlador,* is roundly condemned. Zorrilla has masked the insidious nature of his protagonist, and it is up to subsequent authors and commentators to reveal Don Juan for what he really is.

There were literary responses to Zorrilla's drama as well, the most strident and sophisticated of which is to be found in Adelardo López de Ayala's *alta comedia* (comedy of manners), *El nuevo Don Juan.* From the perspective of our own century, the *alta comedia,* which developed in response to the excesses of Spanish Romantic drama, is, in the words of Francisco Ruiz Ramón, "a type of theater in which the essential aim is to express an ideology, which then subordinates conflicts and characters, such that the most important aspect of the drama is the answers and not the questions, because the author has solved everything before writing his work, a work that was written precisely as a response." Despite Ruiz Ramón's cynical presentation and his peculiar notion of ideology, the didactic aims of the *alta comedia* are precisely those he mentions. The plays were meant both to provide answers and to "unmask the enemies and . . . to upset the good conscience of bourgeois society, insofar as this was possible" (449–50). Set in the mundane world of nineteenth-century Spain, the dramas attempted not only to reveal but also to offer remedies for the foibles and excesses of the theatergoing public. Don Juan, due to the presentation in *Don Juan Tenorio* and the drama's enormous success, was closely scrutinized.

   The action of *El nuevo Don Juan,* which develops in less than twenty-four hours, is easily summarized. Diego is preparing to leave Madrid on a business trip to Alicante. The trip should last only two or three days, but he is still uneasy, since he has noticed that Juan de Alvarado, a known philanderer, has been following his wife Elena. Although Elena assures Diego of her irreproachable conduct and abiding love, all of Diego's fears are borne out when Juan contrives to enter their home.

During the course of his brief conversation with Elena, Juan manages to obtain, by manipulating linguistic conventions and common courtesies, an open invitation to visit the house when he pleases. Juan, at Diego's behest, proceeds to make prompt use of this standing invitation. It turns out, in fact, that Diego was right about Juan's motives, but mistaken about those of his wife. In the ensuing action of the drama, Elena conducts herself honorably, protecting herself and her friend Paulina not only from Juan, but also from Diego's friend Segundo, the play's "second" Don Juan figure. As the drama draws to a close, Elena admonishes Paulina, who had hoped to reform and to marry Juan, "Nada esperes de un Don Juan" ["Do not hope for anything from a Don Juan"]; and she reassures Diego, "¡Nada temas de tu Elena!" ["Do not worry about your Elena!"] (3:264).

The drama's dual focus is most explicit in these last two lines. Weaving two threads together—each of which were clearly drawn from literary antecedents—Ayala foregrounds the role of the woman in Don Juan's story ("¡Nada temas de tu Elena!") even as he develops a strong polemic against Don Juan himself ("Nada esperes de un Don Juan"). From Don Juan's role as a seducer derives a somewhat different series of events than those discussed thus far, but it is nonetheless a series related to the traditional story. To give only one example, like Doña Inés in *Don Juan Tenorio*, Paulina sets out to save an errant seducer and extols the mutual benefits to be derived from such an action:

> Y cuando pienso que yo
> casi niña, y sin más armas
> que mi ternura, consigo
> que un hombre venza sus malas
> costumbres y entre en la senda
> del bien . . . Entonces doy gracias
> a Dios, que me hace instrumento
> de obra tan buena, y se arrasan
> mis ojos, y . . . yo procuro
> ser mejor. Si alguna falta
> sorprendo en mí, "¡Si él me viese!",
> me digo, y para evitarla
> siempre imagino que estoy
> delante de sus miradas . . .
> ¡Qué bello es ser la esperanza
> de un hombre!
>
> (3:211)

[And when I think that I, almost a child and without any more arms than my tenderness, might ensure that a man vanquishes his bad habits and enters on the pathway of goodness. . . . Then I give thanks to God, who has made me the instrument of such goodness, and my eyes well up with tears, and . . . I try to be better. If I discover any fault in myself, I say to myself, "If he were to see me!" And in order to avoid that, I always imagine that I am before his eyes. . . . How beautiful it is to be the hope of a man!]

Yet this plan of action does not run true according to the course set by Doña Inés's love for Don Juan. Instead, Ayala rejects the Romantic solution and uses this one situation to demonstrate the losses that are incurred whenever trust is placed in a figure like Don Juan: "Nada esperes de un Don Juan."

Immediate correspondences in plot aside—and there are many of them—by far the most important development in Don Juan's story to be found in *El nuevo Don Juan* is the textual aspect of the drama and the ways that this both serves Ayala's ends and recalls elements of *El burlador de Sevilla* and *Don Juan Tenorio*. Beginning with the first scene of the play, writing, this time in the form of inscription, is self-consciously thematized. The relationship between Diego and Elena is portrayed in terms of inscription whereby a woman wears her love for her husband written on her face ("el amor de mi marido lo llevo escrito en la cara" [3:201]). Recalling Tirso's Doña Ana, who wrote the *papel* or missive to the Marqués, Elena displays her affection for her husband as a written mark of possession. The moral line of inquiry initiated by this metaphor is brought to a fitting end, then, with Elena's reassuring remark to her fearful husband, "¡Nada temas de tu Elena!"

Between Elena's mention of the inscription and the end of the drama, several other issues related to writing come to the fore, always in the context of various male characters in the drama. Except for early references to a letter from Elena's mother, which never arrives, the authors are always men, specifically Diego, Juan, and Segundo. The most important of these involves Juan, who, following immediately upon the scene in which Elena announces that she wears Diego's love written on her face, presents himself at her door. He says that he brings a letter from Elena's mother. In fact, it turns out that Juan is a "living letter" and that the letter he supposedly brings to Elena from her mother is not from her mother at all. As the "letter" makes clear in the letter of introduction that he leaves with Elena, Juan only uses Elena's mother as a pretext for meeting the new object of his desire:

Digna concha de tal perla
será su madre: convengo;
mas yo, señora, no tengo
el honor de conocerla.
Sólo a usted he conocido;
con su trato quiero honrarme,
y usted no puede negarme
que su casa me ha ofrecido.
Gracias. Honor tan ansiado,
estimando como debo,
irá a ponerse de nuevo
a sus pies, JUAN DE ALVARADO.
(3:207)

[I agree that your mother must be a shell worthy of such a pearl.
But I, señora, do not have the honor of knowing her. I have only
met you, and I hope to honor myself with your friendship. You
cannot deny that you have offered me your home. Thank you.
Such a desirable honor, which I justly esteem, will once again
bring to worship at your feet, JUAN DE ALVARADO.]

Once again, a Don Juan prepares his way by writing a letter. This time,
however, he neither interprets a *papel* nor serves as a pen, but instead
arrives as the missive itself: "Yo soy carta viva" ["I am a living letter"]
(3:204). What began with Tirso as a suggestion of the *burlador*'s essentially theatrical nature and continued in Zorrilla's Don Juan in the
guise of the master author and daemonic ephebe here reaches the point
of the total textualization of Juan de Alvarado. No longer just a literary
character, he is an ambulatory metaphor for the text of which he is a
part.

Fully aware of his own nature, Juan shrewdly prepares for his next
meeting with Elena as well as for a likely confrontation with her jealous husband. Although Diego has set up a trick of his own—in which
his neighbors and even Elena will take part—Juan holds the trump
card. Suspecting some type of "ambush," Juan brings with him an old
love letter that Diego sent years ago to a former *novia* or fiancée named
Paz. Sent without a date, the missive seems to be like new ("sin fecha;
escrita parece / hoy mismo" [3:217]). Juan writes letters and is en-
meshed in the web of seduction, and even Diego is tainted by his past
deeds. But only Juan is a living letter, one that is presently able to
manipulate the scenario to his own advantage. After fending off Elena
and refusing her coy advances—contrived by Diego to reveal the in-

truder's true nature—Juan produces Diego's letter as an act of "friend-ship." Like Juan's "living letter," this letter also has its desired effect on Elena, just as, presumably, it did previously on Doña Paz. Elena, taken aback by the unsuspected turn of events, quietly accepts the "proof" of her husband's perfidy. But when Diego tries to explain his innocence, she reproaches him and flees to her bedroom, where she faints. Ayala thus twists the scenes of Doña Inés's seduction by Don Juan Tenorio, casting them in terms of an exchange of letters; he makes of them the basis for a domestic crisis, which inscribes Diego in a subtext of marital infidelities and establishes the tensions out of which the rest of the drama develops.

Given this densely textual environment, it comes as no surprise that Juan is the author of a volume of poetry and that this volume comes into Elena's possession. But Elena is no fool. She realizes what the book of poems means, that it could prove to be her undoing if the poems were allowed to do their intended work:

> Mientras cae en el garlito
> su autor, los versos leeré.
> (*Coge el libro.*)
> Y cómo miente sabré
> de palabra y por escrito.
> ¡Qué bien el pérfido amante
> encuaderna sus mentiras!
> (*Abre el libro.*)
> "¡Quisiera ser el aire que respiras
> para entrar en tu pecho a cada instante!"
> ¡Qué sutil!
>
> (3:241)

[While the author falls into the trap, I will read his verses. (*She takes the book.*) And I will find out how he lies by spoken and written words. How well the perfidious lover binds up his lies! (*She opens the book.*) "I desire to be the air you breath so as to enter your bosom at every instant!" How subtle!]

Understanding that Juan is a skillful liar, as were the Don Juans before him, Elena resists his verse, but she does so even as she acknowl-edges its power, having been forewarned of its effectiveness. As one of her friends informs her, "a sus versos debe / el amor de una gallarda / condesita" ["he owes the love of a charming young countess to his poetry"] (3:204). This offhand remark confirms that the book of verse is to serve the same function as the letter to Doña Inés; in the brief couplet that she reads, we can detect the filterlike effect of the verse-letter written by Zorrilla's Don Juan, by now the obvious trademark of the textual Don Juan that we have been discussing. Still, there is no doubt whatsoever that Elena recognizes Juan for what he is, a "perfidious lover" who binds his lies in the form of a book.

As is perhaps to be expected in a drama in which so much emphasis is placed on letters and letter-writing, Juan's undoing is the result of yet another letter. Believing that Elena is in love with him and that she wants to contrive by means of Juan's courting of Paulina a cover for their affair, Juan writes Elena a brief note in which he tells her that he understands her plans: "Comprendo el plan y lo sigo, / entreteniendo a Paulina" ["I understand the plan and will follow it by playing along with Paulina"] (3:262). But Elena quickly resolves the situation and the action of the drama by showing this *papel* or letter, which reveals the true nature of Juan's *papel* or role, to Paulina, who finally realizes that "No es tan fácil de un malvado / hacer un hombre de bien" ["It is not so easy to make a good man out of an evil one"] (3:262). This realization sets the stage for the final words of the drama and, with the repetition of this lesson, makes plain Ayala's didactic intent. Don Juan is a destructive force in society, whether single or married. Juan is a confirmed *calavera* or rake, and Segundo, his married counterpart, is no better. Marriage, within this system of honor, offers no guarantee, no protection from dishonor. But then again, within this system, only women are expected to be monogamous; men are to some extent exempt from the strictures of holy matrimony, at least insofar as convention, if not to say doctrine, indicates. The only remedy for this state of affairs, as in Tirso's rendering, is recognition and expulsion. There is no possibility for redemption and salvation in Ayala's presentation. Zorrilla's romanticized expectation of Don Juan's reform is, by comparison, impossibly unrealistic.

Ayala's own pessimism proves, however, to be his undoing, since the end of the drama suggests the salutary effects on society of someone like Juan. Clearly, Juan and Segundo are beyond redemption, but what of Diego? Throughout the drama Diego contrasts what he was when he wrote the letter to Paz with the man he now believes himself to be, implying that he is somehow different. If he has changed, then this change would seem to disprove Elena's admonition, "Nada esperes de un Don Juan." Or, as Diego himself admits in an aside, "yo soy un gran libertino, / sin sospecharlo siquiera" ["I am a great libertine, without even realizing it"] (3:225). Yet this question is resolved, as is the domestic discord, by Juan himself. Through the elimination of Juan and the "correspondencia" with Paz—a correspondence all the more charged given the fact that Juan has recently seduced Paz, too—domestic harmony is restored to the household of Diego and Elena. Juan's intrusion forces Diego to realize that his jealous fears are groundless; and the relieved husband can freely admit to his wife, "Y consolaste mi afán" ["You eased my suspicions"] (3:264). Even in Ayala's version of Don Juan's story, Juan plays a positive role in this resolution: like Tirso's *burlador,* Juan de Alvarado reinforces existing social bonds by reaffirming the viability and significance of the union of two adults. Despite Ayala's *explicit* condemnation of Don Juan, there is a moment when his text provides an *implicit* example of how Don Juan functions in patriarchal society as the means by which the circulation of the woman is closely regulated. Moreover, *El nuevo Don Juan* functions in relation to its predecessors as did Zorrilla's *Don Juan Tenorio.* Although Ayala writes within a specific tradition, he also writes against that tradition so as to distinguish himself from other authors. In an anonymous review of the premiere of the drama, Ayala's success is stated in precisely these terms: "*The New Don Juan,* as the title of this drama indicates, is not the trickster of Seville or the Don Juan Tenorio that we all know. He is one of the many pirates that navigates through the Court, that stands around every afternoon in the Puerta del Dasino, that then strolls along the source of the Castellana, that frequents the fashionable salons, busy trying to find some game to hunt" (*El Diario Español: político y literario* 14 May 1863). By creating a Don Juan that is both a Don Juan and a figure distinct from prior literary manifestations, Ayala, like Zorrilla and Tirso before him, has succeeded in creating a place for himself in the *álbum,* in the literary pantheon. As a figure, then, Don Juan appears to be negative and is often presented as such; as a force in patriarchal society and culture, however, he plays an undeniably positive role.

One issue with respect to *El nuevo Don Juan* and its treatment of Don Juan's story remains for discussion: the itinerary of the letter. Despite the fact that the *papel* addressed to Doña Paz and presented to Elena by Juan comes to a curious end in *El nuevo Don Juan,* its fate is no more odd than those of the letters in either *El burlador de Sevilla* or *Don Juan Tenorio.* The peculiarity of this fate both suggests Ayala's perspicacity in his presentation of Don Juan and emphasizes the appropriately punitive measures to be taken against the *burlador.* Once Juan de Alvarado explains that he received the letter from a vengeful Paz and that he fully believed that Diego was still seeing her, he offers to dispose of the offending missive:

DIEGO. ¡Ah! Dame, suelta . . .
ELENA. ¿Qué te he de dar?
DIEGO.   Ese escrito
del diablo.
ELENA.   ¡Ah! Sí . . .
(*Se registra el bolsillo: lo saca y se lo da.*)
JUAN.   Yo quisiera . . .
DIEGO. ¿Qué, Don Juan?
JUAN.   Tener el gusto
de reducirlo a pavesa
por mi mano; ya que he sido
instrumento . . .
(*Coge una vela.*)
ELENA.   No lo leas.
(*A Diego, que va a abrirlo.*)
DIEGO.   ¿Yo? . . . Quémelo usted.
(*Se lo da a Juan, que lo quema.*)
                      (3:231)

[DIEGO: Ah! Give it to me, let go . . .
ELENA. What do you want?
DIEGO. That letter from the devil.
ELENA. Oh. Of course . . .
(*She checks her pocket, takes out the letter, and gives it to him.*)
JUAN. I wonder . . .
DIEGO. What, Don Juan?
JUAN. If I might have the pleasure of reducing it to ashes with my own hand, since I was the instrument . . .
(*He takes a candle.*)
ELENA. Do not read it.
(*To Diego, who is about to open it.*)
DIEGO. Me? Burn it yourself.
(*He gives it to Juan, who burns it.*)]

Fire, then, is not totally absent from this version of the letter's journey in Don Juan's story. Instead of consuming one character or another, Don Juan or Don Gonzalo, it consumes the diabolical letter ("ese escrito / del *diablo*"), fulfilling the logical trajectory of the plots of its predecessors. The burning of this letter also repeats, in fact, aspects of the situation in the two earlier dramas we have discussed. Tirso's *burlador* presumably still carries the *papel* of Doña Ana that he intercepted; in *Don Juan Tenorio,* it is the Comendador who discovers the letter sent to

Doña Inés and who carries it with him to his death at the hands of Don Juan. This suggests that there is some obvious relation between possession of the letter and death in Don Juan, between the text and the outcome of the drama (remember, however, that this stands in contrast to the correspondence between writing a literary work treating Don Juan and the immortality of an author).

In Tirso's version, the polemic regarding language centered on types of authentic performatives, verbal and written contracts, and on how these pertain to the linguistic nature of honor. With some ambivalence, *El burlador de Sevilla* seems to side with the authenticity of the nonreiterable uniqueness of the performative utterance, the priority of speech over writing. But this ambivalence as embodied in Doña Ana's letter and its subsequent uses in the *comedia* also serves to enact the dramatic event per se, to reveal the essential theatricality of Don Juan and the distinctive nature of drama. In this version, the drama shows itself to be a pretense of worldy action derived from a written text, the force of which is dependent on the subsequent actions it engenders in the real world. Thus, *El burlador de Sevilla* both acknowledges its textual base, the prior existence of a dramatic performance as a dramatic text, even as it champions the power and validity of the spoken word in society generally.

The question of the text, far from being left out of either Zorrilla's *Don Juan Tenorio* or Ayala's new Don Juan, is almost grotesquely exaggerated in terms of the literary and textual characteristics of the protagonists. Both Zorrilla and Ayala celebrate Don Juan's textuality, his dependency on and essence as a text, only to punish the bearer of *the* text, the letter. Furthermore, in the case of Zorrilla, Don Juan explicitly serves as the means by which the author advances his career; in other words, he serves as the text by which an author achieves literary and worldly renown.

Thus, punishment and the letter go hand in hand in those instances in which misuse and misreading are both found. In Tirso's and Ayala's handling, the *burlador* and Juan de Alvarado each misrepresent the importance and meaning of a letter that they have in some way dislodged or detoured from its appropriate place or destination. The transparency of the letters' meaning—the transparency of meaning in light of the intended readers, the Marqués and Doña Paz—is clouded by their misappropriation. Likewise, in *Don Juan Tenorio,* Don Gonzalo finds the letter where it has slipped from his daughter's hand only to read in it not of Don Juan's love for Doña Inés but instead of what he perceives as his own dishonor. These dramas demonstrate, then, how letters do indeed mean different things to different people, as do literary texts. But in the context of these three dramas, there is an argument for the inviolability of literary intent and meaning: those who intrude upon, misinterpret, or misrepresent the contents of a letter are duly punished. The consistency of this presentation of the letter, when considered in conjunction with alterations in plot, points therefore to an incipient desire to stage the ongoing representation of a permanently inviolable text, a text in which meaning is absolutely univocal. As Franco Tonelli remarks of Molière's *Dom Juan,* "at one level Don Juan's function is to embody theatricality and/or theatre itself, but, at another level the personage embodies as well Molière's own dramatic will to theatrical authority" (460); therefore, the drama "creates an aesthetic space that is protective of the artist, of Molière and of Don Juan" (464). Yet the forces of Don Juan as a function of a dramatic text and as a literary character are constantly at odds one with another. Such interpretive inviolability as proposed by these dramas is precisely what Don Juan, who constantly rewrites and re-presents *papeles,* will not permit.

This is perhaps the moment to broach, at least provisionally, the question of meaning in relation to Don Juan and his story, beginning with the embedded texts in the various works, the letters. But what, in fact, is a letter? And what does a letter mean? Perhaps a fitting starting-place for this consideration is with a text composed of letters, with the question of an epistolary novel. Tzetvan Todorov addresses precisely this issue in a study of Laclos's *Les liaisons dangereuses.* He suggests that, in terms of the novel, the letters have a double meaning:

> On the one hand, they mean what the sentences that constitute them mean, and each letter says something different from the other. On the other hand, they possess a connotation, identical in the mind of all, which is that of the "letter" as a social phenomenon, and this connotation is in addition, or even in opposition, to the literal message of each letter. What is this connotation? In *Les Liaisons dangereuses,* it is three-fold. First of all, the letter signifies news, or more precisely, the possibility of a change in the preceding situation. . . . A second connotation common to all the letters is that one is on intimate terms with whom one corresponds. This is why Valmont and Danceny each try to establish a correspondence with the woman they pursue; it is also why Mme de Volanges is so shocked when she discovers Danceny's letters in her daughter's desk. . . . Finally, the third connotation of the letter is one of authenticity. As opposed to the spoken word, the letter asserts a sure proof. (115–16)

In terms of Don Juan and the texts that we have discussed, each of Todorov's "connotations"—news, intimacy, authenticity—is, in some way, applicable. With respect to the first point, Doña Ana's letter to the Marqués in *El burlador de Sevilla* does indeed signify a change in her situation, the fact that she is now to marry Don Juan. Moreover, her letter also implies (and promises) that there exists (or will exist) a special intimacy between the two cousins, as it does when Don Juan shows the missive to Aminta's husband Batricio. In this latter instance, the "proof" found by Batricio in the letter authenticates Don Juan's claim, and this despite the polemic in the *comedia* against written contracts.

In *Don Juan Tenorio*, Don Juan's letter to Doña Inés points to a change in the nature of his desire, creates an intimate bond between the author and the reader of the missive, and, finally, lends credence, at least in the eyes of Doña Inés, to Don Juan's professed love. Though not a letter, Don Juan's list authenticates his claims, is, in Todorov's words, "sure proof." Likewise, in *El nuevo Don Juan,* the "correspondence" between the various characters implies intimacy and furnishes proof, whether or not reliable, of transgressions. Therefore, the letters in these three texts suggest a means by which these dramas might be understood.

More to the point, what do the letters mean? This is a somewhat trickier question, as the exchange between and among Jacques Lacan, Jacques Derrida, Barbara Johnson, and John T. Irwin over Poe's "The Purloined Letter" indicates. Todorov says that letters have a double meaning, one literal, the other social and cultural. Lacan is not so immediately comprehensible. In his seminar, Lacan remarks that "we are simply dealing with a letter which has been diverted from its path; one whose course has been *prolonged* (etymologically, the word of the title), or, to revert to the language of the post office, a *letter in sufferance [lettre en souffrance,* literally, an undelivered letter]" (59). The issue for Lacan appears not to be necessarily one of meaning, at least not initially. He concludes, however, "the sender, we tell you, receives from the receiver, his own message in reverse form. Thus it is that what the 'purloined letter,' nay, the 'letter in sufferance' [undelivered letter] means is that a letter always arrives at its destination" (72).

If Lacan is typically recondite, Johnson's gloss of this passage is, fortunately, excellent; it forms, moreover, an integral part of her consideration of Poe, Lacan, and Derrida. Johnson begins the conclusion of her essay with this commentary on the letter and its destination:

> Everyone who has held the letter—or even beheld it— including the narrator, has ended up having the letter addressed

to *him* as its destination. The reader is comprehended by the letter: there is no *place* from which he can stand back and observe *it*. Not that the letter's meaning is subjective rather than objective, but that the letter is precisely that which subverts the polarity subjective/objective, that which makes subjectivity into something whose position in a structure is situated by an object's passage through it. The letter's destination is thus *wherever it is read:* the place it assigns to the reader as his own partiality. Its destination is not a place, decided *a priori* by the sender, because the receiver *is* the sender, and the receiver is whoever receives the letter, including nobody. When Derrida says that a letter *can* miss its destination and be disseminated, he reads "destination" as a place that pre-exists the letter's movement. But if, as Lacan shows, the letter's destination is not its literal addressee, nor even whoever possesses it, but whoever is possessed *by* it, then the very *disagreement* over the meaning of "reaching the destination" is an *illustration* of the nonobjective nature of that "destination." (144–45)

The point here is, I think, that the question of the letter's destination in "The Purloined Letter" is a moot issue, since the letter is, in fact, read not just by the person to whom it is addressed, but by others as well, all of whom find meaning therein. In this sense, the letter "means" in different ways because every reader finds his or her reflection in the text, is constrained to read in a certain way, is seduced—or in Johnson's words, "possessed"—by the letter.

Johnson goes on to point out that the sentence "a letter always arrives at its destination" suggests various readings, and that, furthermore, the meaning of the letter is not any particular reading, but *all* of them, that all "*repeat* the letter in its way of reading the act of reading. Far from giving us the 'Seminar' 's final truth, these last words *enact* the impossibility of any ultimate analytical metalanguage" (145–46). If the reader of the letter finds in it his or her own message, if the letter possesses the reader, then the act of reading is in some way a repetition of the strategies posed by the letter itself. This means that the meaning of the letter is indeterminable; it is undecidable. As Johnson puts it, "What is undecidable is whether a thing is decidable or not" (146; see Irwin 1176–80).

Indecision is, of course, at the heart of the types of issues being discussed in terms of Don Juan. For example, Don Juan's fate is undecidable, as one author after another attempts to resurrect Don Juan and to rewrite the end of his story, to provide the definitive solution to Don Juan's role and impact on society. Moreover, this indeterminacy is operative in the criticism pertaining to Don Juan as well, as the multiple critical approximations of Don Juan would seem to demonstrate. If the letters in the different versions of Don Juan's story that we have discussed postulate a permanently inviolable text, if the dramatic texts themselves posit stable meaning, the truth of the matter is apparently otherwise. All of these texts—the letters, the literary texts, the critical works—are at some level contradictory. The meaning of Don Juan would seem to reside, then, in this oscillation between decidability and undecidability.

The opposition in this discussion between decidability and undecidability parallels the opposition in treatments of Don Juan between condemnation and salvation. If Don Juan does not, finally, *really* repent, then he is, according to Catholic doctrine, justifiably condemned. But if, as Zorrilla's Don Juan says, "es verdad / que un punto de contrición / da a un alma la salvación / de toda una eternidad" ["it is true that a single act of contrition assures the soul's salvation for all of eternity"] (lines 3762–65; 537), then Don Juan must be allowed to repent and thereby to save himself and Doña Inés. But repentence is probably not the issue here; it makes no difference in social terms if Don Juan admits to and is forgiven his sins. He has *already* sown the seeds of discontent that bear fruit in the form of renewed social commitments. Repentence is not, therefore, the central question with respect to Don Juan. To insist on undecidability as a critical category in this instance is to refuse to sit in judgment over Don Juan. For Jean Rousset, it is to hesitate between a yes and a no (5), or, in Carlos Feal's terms, to resurrect Don Juan as the symbol of an imminent egalitarian social order (5).

This is the response suggested as characteristic by Kierkegaard in *Either/Or*. Whereas he claims in Victor Eremita's preface that "these papers come to no conclusion" (1:14), such hesitation or oscillation is consistent in responses to seduction. In "Silhouettes," the section preceding "The Seducer's Diary," "A" tells of a young woman's contradictory feelings and feeble attempts at judgment:

> A young girl, of course, is not a jurist, but it by no means follows that she cannot pass judgment, and yet this young girl's judgment will always be such that although at first glance it is a judgment, it also contains something more that shows that it is no judgment, and also shows that the very next moment a completely opposite judgment may be passed. "He was no deceiver. . . ." "He was a deceiver, an abominable person. . . ." "No,

he was no deceiver. He did not love me anymore; that is why he left me, but that, after all, was no deception. . . ." "Yes, now I see it; now I no longer doubt—he was a deceiver. . . ." "Yes, he was a deceiver. . . ." "He was no deceiver. . . ." The interrogation she will never finish, nor the judgment, either—the interrogation, because there are always interruptions; the judgment, because it is only a feeling. Once this movement begins, it can go on as long as it pleases, and there is no end in sight. Only by a break can it be brought to a halt—that is, by her cutting short this whole movement of thought; but this cannot happen, for the will is continually in service of reflection, which energizes the momentary passion. (1:185–88)

According to "A," neither interrogation nor judgment will ever be completed, precisely because they are, like Don Juan, never-ending processes. This indecision would seem to indicate that the meaning of Don Juan—and the meaning of the texts of which he is a part—is itself contradictory and incomplete, that interpretations are inconclusive, that Don Juan and the letters are undecidable.

In fact, the letter in Don Juan *does* mean something, in that these letters in particular and the texts of which they are a part in general signal seduction. But in the case of Don Juan, seduction is a masquerade. It is the means by which society "leads away" so as, in the end, to lead women back into the fold of patriarchal culture and to induce them to accept their appropriate role in relation to their male other. That Don Juan's beneficial social function in patriarchy is concealed behind the mask of disorder points to the complicity of these literary texts in the articulation and preservation of the status quo. Even in *Don Juan Tenorio,* in which the individual concerns with salvation and immortality are so pressing as to overwhelm the specific social content of Don Juan's story, Doña Inés is, as we have seen, seduced by Don Juan's letter and drawn into playing a prescribed role in relation to him. As contemporary psychoanalytic theories of women and femininity suggest, and as I shall disuss in the following chapter, women exist in Don Juan's world as what Luce Irigaray refers to as a "sexual imaginary . . . a more or less obliging prop for the enactment of man's fantasies" (*This Sex* 25). As the means of Don Juan's salvation, Doña Inés has come to accept herself as the imaginary on which Don Juan has projected his fantasies of salvation, as does Paulina in relation to Juan de Alvarado. He serves to draw the woman into the passion of patriarchy and serves as the paradigm by which desire is articulated in society, as the subtext for relations between men and women, as a literary and social text in which the latter are seduced by the former into fulfilling a specific role.

This consideration of honor and seduction, beginning with Tirso's *El burlador de Sevilla,* has demonstrated the extent to which seduction can, in fact, be linguistic in nature. We see, moreover, that seduction can function in a beneficial way in patriarchal society. The relation of honor to seduction is, however, somewhat more tenuous even though both are linked to questions of language. In the cases of the *burlador,* Zorrilla's Don Juan, and Ayala's Juan de Alvarado, these characters seemingly pervert the code of honor in the pursuit of their objects of desire. Honor, which is obtained by an author in the creation of a text, is, within the literary work itself, called into question by the characters involved in the various seductions. Yet, if seduction serves to uphold the patriarchal order, it cannot be seen to subvert the concept of honor. In other words, seduction must stand in some positive relationship to individual honor as it is constituted in language.

Once again, language becomes the focus of the discussion, first, as it embodies honor in society and bears it forth in a text; second, as it is involved in seduction; and, third, as it serves to structure and control social relations. Indeed, as Shoshana Felman has shown, it is possible to formulate a typology of Don Juan in which language becomes the common ground between and among various seductive figures and texts. Yet—and in the context of *El nuevo Don Juan*—it is important to note that Felman's theory operates not at the level of society, but, rather, at the level of the individual and individual text, which means that the ideological implications of Don Juan are left aside. I would suggest that it is when Don Juan becomes a recognizable psychological type—and recall Elena's penultimate injunction: "Nada esperes de *un* Don Juan" ["Do not hope for anything from *a* Don Juan"]—that the ideological implications become both more apparent and, paradoxically, more insidious. We turn, then, to the psychological text par excellence of the late nineteenth and early twentieth centuries, the novel, in order to understand the links between and among honor, seduction, and language as they relate to Don Juan and to his role in society. We turn from considerations of authorial interest in the dramatic Don Juan to his effects on the reader of those novelistic texts in which the *burlador* figures. Because it is difficult, if not impossible, to determine the nature of spectators' response to a dramatic "text," by dealing with works of fiction, we shall be better able to judge the effects of the narrative on individual readers, to try to judge the complex role played by Don Juan in narrative seduction.

Don Juan and the Reader:
The Psychology of Seduction

The concept of honor that is so apparent in the early dramatic versions of Don Juan's story continues to be important as we move into a consideration of the psychological aspects of Don Juan and seduction as found in novelistic treatments and the ways that these are indicative of a recognizable psychological type. There are, of course, Spanish novels that are specific retellings of Don Juan's story, much like Dumas's *Don Juan de Marana ou la chute d'un ange,* fictions that both recount and reshape the *materia prima,* for instance, Manuel Fernández y González's *Don Juan Tenorio* (1862). More interesting as regards the psychology of Don Juan, however, are those works in which the story or a specific version of the story functions as a prominent subtext or literary context for the novelistic action. In these works the primary action of the novel develops apart from the palimpsest even as the subtext contributes to the psychological depth of the literary characters in a mirroring of fictions similar to that found in the relationship between the two volumes of Cervantes's *Don Quijote;* the psychological presentation anticipates if not parallels the function of seduction and the role of women valued by society. Moreover, the reader of novels in which the story of Don Juan functions as a subtext, albeit openly acknowledged as such, must play an important role in the process of the fiction, must bring to bear an understanding of Don Juan and his role in literary texts and society.

The presence of Don Juan in novelistic fiction brings with it unexpected consequences. For example, one novel in which the story of Don

Juan figures in an important, if ironically disfigured, way is Benito Pérez Galdós's *Doña Perfecta* (1876), which has as its protagonist not a male libertine but the staunchly conservative and devoutly orthodox Perfecta Rey, who agrees to marry her daughter, Rosario, to her brother's son, José Rey, or in his diminutive, Pepe.[1] Pepe, a thirty-four-year-old engineer, arrives in Orbajosa from Sevilla and is immediately taken with his cousin. Doña Perfecta, however, has second thoughts about the match and conspires with her cronies, including the local priest and bishop, to make her nephew's life increasingly difficult and unpleasant in order to force him to leave Orbajosa and to abandon the original plan. So frustrated is Pepe that he begins to plot to abduct Rosario from her mother's home; he then appears to come to his senses, deciding to try to pursue legal means of obtaining his desired union with his cousin. But when he attempts to meet Rosario in order to tell her of his plans, he is, apparently, shot to death at Doña Perfecta's orders. As a result of this denouement, Rosario goes mad and is institutionalized, while Doña Perfecta dedicates herself to sponsoring religious functions at the local cathedral.

There are several indications in the novel that we are to read it as an ironic distortion of Zorrilla's *Don Juan Tenorio*. First, Galdós's Don Juan, Pepe, is from Sevilla and is the son of Don Juan Rey (which might be a play on Byron's *Don Juan,* in which the father of the Byronic hero is Don José); also, Pepe assaults tradition in Orbajosa, in this case by representing progressive ideological tendencies of nineteenth-century Spain. Second, the Comendador has been transformed into Doña Perfecta, who acts as the figure of the Law in the novel, going so far as to control *all* of the powerful male figures within her reach. There is even a character, Don Juan Tafetán, who is identi-

---

1. Ignacio-Javier López has studied the character of Don Juan in Galdós's novels—although not in *Doña Perfecta*—as well as in the novelistic fiction of other late nineteenth- and early twentieth-century Spanish authors as he traces the "degradation" of the character. In fact, López's study recapitulates many of the dynamics related to the criticism discussed in the first chapter of this study and appears to respond to Otto Rank's summary observation of the history of the figure, that it "seems that as the subject matter has grown older, so also has the depiction of the aging Don Juan grown in popularity among the poets. Such descriptions make it clear that an impulse toward devaluation is a consequence of the psychological problem of the aging Don Juan, and this devaluation increasingly wins the upper hand. The devaluation involves not only the mere humanizing of the hero, but rather reaches a point of involuntary ridicule that finally falls into conscious caricature" (Rank 111). In the end, the distinction made by López between fiction and reality turns out to be the traditional *literary* distinction between fiction and the merely human or the individual unbound by social, historical, economic, and political restrictions.

fied as the local Tenorio, at least so he says: "cuando andaba derechito
y espigado por la poca pesadumbre de los años, había sido un Tenorio
formidable. Oírle contar sus conquistas era cosa de morirse de risa,
porque hay Tenorios de Tenorios, aquél fue de los más originales"
["when he walked tall and gracefully, without the weight of many
years, he had been a formidable Don Juan. One would die laughing to
hear him speak of his conquests, because there are Don Juans and then
there are Don Juans; and he was one of the most original"] (451–52).
Finally, Rosario is imprisoned in her room by her mother in order to
keep her away from Pepe, meaning that, in a manner reminiscent of
Zorrilla's drama, he must plot to rescue her from the "convent" in
which she is being held against her will.

Yet it is at the level of the language used by Galdós that we can most
easily detect the influence of *Don Juan Tenorio* in *Doña Perfecta*. For
example, when Pepe tells his aunt that he and his cousin have been
secretly meeting and have promised to wed one another, the heroine of
the novel quotes from Zorrilla's drama:

> —La he visto anoche, y me ha jurado ante el Cristo de la capilla
> que sería mi mujer.
> —*¡Oh escándalo y libertinaje . . . !* Pero ¿qué es esto? ¡Dios mío,
> qué deshonra! —exclamó doña Perfecta, comprimiéndose otra
> vez con ambas manos la cabeza y dando algunos pasos por la
> habitación—. ¿Rosario salió anoche de su cuarto?
> —*Salió para verme. Ya era tiempo.* (474; my emphasis)

> ["I saw her last night and she swore to me before the Christ in
> the chapel that she would be my wife."
> "*Oh! Scandal and licentiousness!* But what is this! My God!
> What dishonor," Doña Perfecta exclaimed, holding her head
> with both hands while pacing back and forth. "Rosario left her
> room last night?"
> "*She left to see me. It was time.*"]

When Doña Perfecta reacts to Pepe's news, she uses the very words that
serve as a subtitle to one of the acts of *Don Juan Tenorio*, "Libertinaje y
escándalo" ["Licentiousness and scandal"]. By practically citing in this
way from Zorrilla's drama, by using the words of the subtitle to the first
act of the play, Galdós refers not to one specific moment, but to the
scenes of naming and unmasking, the lists, and mirroring. Furthermore, by implicating the first act of the drama, Galdós also recuperates
the deeds included in the lists. We are to understand, then, that, like

the Comendador, Doña Perfecta reads the relationship between Pepe and Rosario as one of seduction and dishonor, and that she has not heeded the most important of her nephew's words: "me ha jurado ante el Cristo de la capilla que sería mi mujer" ["she swore to me before the Christ in the chapel that she would be my wife"]. Because part of the defamation of Pepe's honor involved characterizing him as an atheist, or, worse yet, a "spiritist," Doña Perfecta fails to perceive the degree to which Pepe's progressive leanings nevertheless respond to aspects of traditional Catholic doctrine, not merely at the level of rhetoric, in the sense of clichés, but at the level of the symbol. The vow made by Pepe and Rosario before the statue of Christ and the fact that Pepe frames his commitment to Rosario in terms of "Society" and God—"Porque hay Sociedad, porque hay conciencia, porque hay Dios . . . digo y repito que me casaré con ella" ["Because there is such a thing as Society, because there is such a thing as conscience, because there is a God . . . I say and I repeat that I will marry her"] (473)—indicate that Pepe must be seen as part and parcel of a culture in which social progress is *always* linked to a Catholic past, meaning that women, as the end of *Doña Perfecta* would seem to prove, are not, in fact, implicated in that progressive tendency.

Equally significant in this context is Pepe's remark "Salió para verme. Ya era tiempo" ["She left to see me. It was time"]. In an ironic recasting of the Comendador's response to Don Juan's act of contrition in both *El burlador de Sevilla* [The Trickster of Seville] and *Don Juan Tenorio*, "Ya es tarde" ["It is too late"], the moment has arrived in *Doña Perfecta* for some type of change, or at least Pepe thinks it has. Yet, as the end of the novel indicates, and as Pepe seems to realize when he later writes to his father, Don Juan, it is *always* too late. The individual can never seem to escape from the belatedness of repenting. Pepe writes: "¡Cuánto siento que no estuviera usted a mi lado para apartarme de este camino! Ya es tarde. Las pasiones no tienen espera. Son impacientes y piden su presa a gritos y con la convulsión de una espantosa sed moral" ["How sorry I am that you were not at my side to draw me away from this path! It is too late. Passions cannot wait. They are impatient and ask for their prey with the shouts and convulsions of a frightening moral thirst"] (501). That Pepe himself repents and decides not to succumb to the violence around him is of little good. It is indeed too late for him to alter his destiny as the innocent victim of a sacrificial rite.

The importance for this novel of Don Juan's story in general and *Don Juan Tenorio* in particular has to do with the ways in which desire is inhibited and controlled. Marriage, even in the progressive nineteenth century, serves the interests of the family, is a union leading to a common social good. In this regard, women can be equally as oppressive as men, if not more so. The widowed Doña Perfecta becomes the symbolic, if marginalized, "name of the father." Thus, progressive political and social movements aside, the woman is destined to a life of isolation, as the situations of *all* of the women in *Doña Perfecta* demonstrate. Of course, Galdós, here and elsewhere in his novels, tends to a dark view of women; in fact, he tends towards punishing women, as in *La desheredada* (1881) and *La de Bringas* (1884), in which the female protagonists' aspirations condemn them to poverty and prostitution, or in *Tristana* (1892), in which the woman is physically maimed, married to the wrong man, and finally becomes a tabula rasa, having lost her ambition and memory.

An equally pessimistic vision of woman is to be found in other novels of this period, including those that are written in or that draw on the tradition of Don Juan. In what follows, I shall explore the dynamics of the psychology of Don Juan and his effects on those around him, particularly women, in several novels in which the presentation ranges from direly negative, as in Clarín's *La Regenta* [The Judge's Wife] (1884–85), or suspiciously optimistic, as in the case of Jacinto Octavio Picón's *Dulce y sabrosa* [Sweet and Savory] (1891), to patently ethical, as in Azorín's *Don Juan* (1922) and *Doña Inés* (1925). Despite the ostensible divergence of opinion with regard to Don Juan as a type—as both a psychological type and a social force—there is, as we shall see, a remarkable consistency underlying the assumptions, the aims, and the results of this series of novelistic representations, particularly in their effects and demands on their readers.

Don Juan Tenorio in *La Regenta*

> *C'est pourtant pour cet homme, que j'ay cru si différent du reste des hommes, que je me trouve, commes les autres femmes, étant si eloignée de leur ressembler.*
>
> —*Madame de Lafayette*, La Princesse de Clèves

Clarín's *La Regenta* deals with a young woman, Ana Ozores, who is trapped in the provincial world of Vetusta. As we learn in a lengthy flashback, although she perceives herself to be different from those around her, Ana is forced to conform to conventional expectations and to take a husband, in part for financial reasons, since the noble house of

Ozores has fallen on hard times. The least offensive to her of the various suitors is a wealthy, retired provincial judge or *regente,* Víctor Quintanar, who is many years Ana's senior. Once confined in a marriage that is more like the relationship between a daughter and her father, Ana begins to seek some type of meaning or fulfillment in the world around her. In an ironic twist on her name, and on Don Víctor's capacity to provide her with direction (*regir,* to guide; *regente,* one who guides), Ana senses that she is without purpose. Two options offer themselves, the one spiritual yet strangely erotic, in the guise of her confessor, the canon theologian Fermín de Pas; the other carnal, in the guise of the local Don Juan, Alvaro Mesía. As Ana becomes aware of the sexual nature of Don Fermín's desires, she repudiates him. At this point, Don Alvaro's fortunes wax and Ana falls passionately in love. Eventually, however, Don Víctor finds out about his wife's adultery— by means of Don Fermín's machinations—and, acting like a Golden Age hero, the husband challenges his rival to a duel. Against all odds, the cowardly Don Alvaro fatally wounds Don Víctor (by puncturing his bladder; the husband dies of peritonitis) and leaves Vetusta for Madrid, abandoning Ana, who is shunned by her former friends. As the novel draws to a close Ana is being cared for by Frígilis, a friend of her husband; when she tries to reconcile herself with Don Fermín, he, too, rejects her in a fit of impetuous anger.

Various critics have remarked on the importance of Zorrilla's *Don Juan Tenorio* for Clarín's *La Regenta,* since the drama forms part of the thematic material (by way of the manipulation of characterization and event) as well as part of the novel's diegetic development (by way of the presentation of the play in the sixteenth chapter). For Ricardo Gullón, "the theater scene is so relevant that I am in favor of calling it decisive" (176). Frank Durand goes somewhat further, reading *La Regenta* as a "distorted reflection of Zorrilla's play" ("Characterization in *La Regenta*" 91), while Robert M. Jackson rejects the negative implications of Durand's statement and finds instead a positive correlation between literature and life, the "fictional" and "real" worlds of the novel. For Jackson, the introduction of *Don Juan Tenorio* into the body of *La Regenta* allows Clarín to "distinguish ironically between literature and life." Moreover, this process of inclusion shows how "Clarín has successfully adopted Cervantes' use of literature within literature to establish separate planes of fictional reality"; thus, "Clarín has opened the door for Ana Ozores to become something of an autonomous character, standing a shade closer to 'reality' than her counterpart on stage, Doña Inés" (227, 227, 223). Continuing along this line, Germán Gullón suggests that the dense literariness of the novel affects the presentation of the characters, because "the literariness plays a significant role, and it allows the author to avoid the task of profiling certain characters in greater detail" (183). In sum, the parallels between the novel and the drama permit the development of a psychological depth in the characters and the sense that they are somehow "real."

All of these critics are correct in their assumptions, Ricardo Gullón for saying that the theater scene is "decisive"; Durand for seeing *La Regenta* as a "distortion" of *Don Juan Tenorio;* Jackson, along with Roberto G. Sánchez, for noting the importance of the distinctions between literature and life; and Germán Gullón for pointing out the economy in characterization. As Alvaro Mesía says to himself in one of the numerous examples of *style indirect libre* in the novel, "¡Si el *Don Juan* de Zorrilla ya sólo servía para hacer parodias . . . !" ["Really, by now Zorrilla's *Don Juan Tenorio* was only good for parodying"] (2:49; 377). The irony implicit in this statement, of course, is the poverty of Mesía's own "parody" of Don Juan, a poverty that both characterizes him for the reader and types him for the rest of the novel. However much he ridicules the play, Vetusta's Don Juan is indebted to his fictional predecessor; that Mesía is aging, even aware of his own physical limitations, points to further ironic discrepancies between the "fictional" Don Juan and the "real" Don Alvaro.[2] Indeed, the "distortion" of *Don Juan Tenorio* in the main action of *La Regenta* emphasizes much of the irony. Yet the differences between the fictional and the real are not just demonstrated throughout the novel, they are consistently remarked upon as well, by the narrator and by the characters themselves (see Rutherford 43–48). Zorrilla's drama therefore brings these ironic references into focus: Ana's flirtation with Mesía finds a literary antecedent; the many remarks about Don Alvaro's *donjuanismo* are given a

2. In this regard, see Elizabeth Sánchez. Ignacio-Javier López has an entirely different reading of the relationship between Zorrilla's *Don Juan Tenorio* and Clarín's Don Alvaro. López remarks that "Mesía is not a parody of Don Juan . . . he is the result of an ironic reflection that makes evident the degradation of the novelistic character with respect to the mythical model proposed by the narrator. Nevertheless, the denouement [of the novel] shows that said model is not valid. . . . Mesía triumphs at the end of the novel. . . . Mesía's triumph calls for the restatement of the model evoked by the narrator and, in this way, the irony that the narrator uses in his description of the Don Juan ends up by demonstrating that the similarity between Mesía and Don Juan is deceptive and that the comparison between the two is not valid" (101–2). López's emphasis on Mesía's "triumph" is perplexing, as he seems to imply a contrast with Don Juan's failure. Yet, in Zorrilla's *Don Juan Tenorio,* Don Juan does not fail. Indeed, he is successful: he is saved. Within the framework of the realist program, is it not possible to assert that Don Alvaro is saved? Moreover, are we not confronted by the same phenomenon of a woman's sacrifice for the good of a man?

concrete referent; and one possible outcome of the novelistic conflict is portrayed.

Although I am essentially in agreement with the broad outlines of these critical treatments of *La Regenta,* I am nonetheless skeptical that the relationship between the dramatic and novelistic texts has to do simply with matters of individual psychology or, as Clarín himself would have it, as an instance of literary homage to Zorrilla. In defending himself against an accusation of plagiarism, Clarín remarks:

> While answering a letter from the great poet Zorrilla, I told him that I was going to show my great admiration for his *Don Juan Tenorio* in a long chapter in my first novel. And so I did. But there's more. The idea of painting the effect that Zorrilla's *Don Juan Tenorio* when seen for the first time produces in souls of a certain poetic temper in the fullness of youth was not mine . . . but I didn't take it from Flaubert. . . . I took it from reality. The worthy young wife of a famous painter saw *Don Juan Tenorio* for the first time once she was married, and a friend of mine, Félix Aramburu, himself a poet and a famous writer on Penal Law, was the one who observed the interesting admiration, both sympathetic and significant, that the lady experienced and wanted to share with the rest of the audience, who were incapable of appreciating all of the brilliant freshness of Zorrilla's drama, which they knew by memory. ("Mis plagios" 1235)

For Clarín, the sixteenth chapter of *La Regenta* constitutes not an instance of plagiarism, but a type of literary homage, and his defense indicates the extent to which he viewed Zorrilla's drama as important for his novel.[3] Yet Clarín does not seem to realize what is at stake in the inclusion of *Don Juan Tenorio.* This visceral response to the drama turns up in subsequent critical treatments of the relationship between the dramatic and the novelistic texts, for instance, in the work of Roberto G. Sánchez, who views Zorrilla's drama as a "work so theatrical and innocent and, at the same time, so human" (175). Instead, I believe that the influence of *Don Juan Tenorio* on and its presence in the novel

3. See also the appreciative article Clarín wrote following Zorrilla's death in which he remarks, "*Don Juan Tenorio* is not inferior to anything. I admire the *Cantos del Trovador,* I admire many other poems by Zorrilla, but none more than the *suggestive* Don Juan, who *filters* into the cell and into the soul of Doña Inés and who wins her heart on the banks of the Guadalquivir, and who wins the hearts of us all" ("El teatro de Zorrilla" 119).

are far from benign; Don Juan as a type is a much more malevolently patriarchal, yet necessary, force in society than is usually acknowledged. Consequently, *Don Juan Tenorio*—as a drama of masculine desire that subsumes the feminine—represents a much more insidious presence in Clarín's novel.

Before entering into a fuller discussion of the novel, however, we ought to consider aspects of what is known as "femininity" and "the feminine," both as these concepts are viewed by Clarín and as they have been treated in psychoanalytic terms. By drawing on psychoanalytic concepts of gender, social organization, and the constitution of the individual subject, I shall show the structural and social significance of the inclusion of *Don Juan Tenorio* in *La Regenta*. This notion of the structural importance of the concept of woman and the role of the representation of the performance of *Don Juan Tenorio* will eventually allow us to consider another text and type of desire involved in *La Regenta:* that of Santa Teresa. Finally, these psychoanalytic approximations will help explicate the patriarchal aspects of Clarín's novel as it draws on *Don Juan Tenorio* and will demonstrate a way in which to refute what has recently been identified as the text's undecidability, a notion that must be discounted given the very specific slant of the narrative presentation.

Throughout the course of his writings on human psychology and sexual difference, Sigmund Freud addressed the question of femininity and "the feminine"—the seminal question "What does a woman want?"— with varying degrees of specificity and success. His definitive response to these issues is considered to be the relatively late text of the thirty-third "introductory" lecture, "Femininity" (1933 [1932]).[4] In this essay, Freud broaches once again the ineffable essence of woman and reiterates his theory of the innate bisexuality of all individuals before they suffer the crisis that is the Oedipus complex, which is to say, his theory that little girls are really little boys. All the while, Freud maintains that women are basically inferior, asserting that they have "little sense of justice," are "weaker in their social interests" and are less able to sublimate "their social instincts than men." In conclusion, Freud la-

---

4. See the essay of 1931, "Feminine Sexuality," *Standard Edition* 21: 225–43. In his biography of Freud, Ernest Jones remarks: "There is no doubt that Freud found the psychology of women more enigmatic than that of men. He once said to Marie Bonaparte: 'The great question that has never been answered and which I have not yet been able to answer, despite my thirty years of research into the feminine soul, is "What does a woman want?" ["Was will das Weib?"]' " (2:421).

ments the "incomplete and fragmentary" nature of his comments; he suggests, "If you want to know more about femininity, enquire from your own experiences of life, or turn to the poets, or wait until science can give you deeper and more coherent information" ("Femininity," *Standard Edition* 22:134, 135).

Freud's remarks on women are, indeed, provocative, and they have, with reason, given rise to considerable commentary in the recent re-reading of Freudian texts undertaken by psychoanalysts and feminists alike.[5] There is, however, yet another aspect of the lecture on feminin-ity that deserves comment, specifically, Freud's reference to "the po-ets." Given the origins of Freud's thought in the nineteenth century, particularly in the philosophic and literary traditions, the most strik-ing aspect of these remarks is the congruity between the psychoana-lyst's interest and viewpoints and those of nineteenth-century novel-ists. What are *Anna Karenina, Madame Bovary, Effi Briest,* and *La Regenta,* to cite the four examples suggested by Biruté Ciplijauskaité in *La mujer insatisfecha,* if not considerations of and answers to the question "What does a woman want?" In other words, the subject that Freud was to explore in the "scientific" terms of psychoanalysis, novel-ists in the realist tradition were exploring in the language of fiction.

In point of fact, it is somewhat difficult to pin down Freud's concep-tion of femininity or to find in his work a single answer to the riddle that is woman. But this is not to say that the question is unanswerable. As Juliet Mitchell puts it, "All answers to the question, including 'the mother' are false; she simply *wants*" (Introduction, *Feminine Sexuality* 24). Thus, the female subject does not merely desire her mother in some type of pre-Oedipal yearning, nor is her desire explicable in terms of a desire to possess the masculine—and patriarchal—power of the phallus in the guise of a child. Rather, woman, because of the biological fact of being female, of being "castrated," constantly desires, is an absence that cannot be converted into a presence or wholeness. In Luce Irigaray's words, the woman's "lot is that of 'lack,' 'atrophy' (of the

5. In this regard, see Lacan's *Le Séminaire de Jacques Lacan. Livre XX: Encore (1972–1973),* which is partially translated in Juliet Mitchell and Jacqueline Rose, eds., *Feminine Sexuality* 137–48. See also Luce Irigaray's highly critical reading of "Feminin-ity" in *Speculum* and her reconsideration in *This Sex;* Sarah Kofman's implicit and at times explicit response in her judicious reading of Freud; Elizabeth L. Berg's consider-ation of Irigaray and Kofman; and Juliet Mitchell's knowledgeable and comprehensive, if somewhat orthodox, study of the question in *Psychoanalysis and Feminism.* See Julia Kristeva's non-Lacanian version of femininity and motherhood ("Motherhood") as well as the theoretical appropriation of Kristeva's work by Drucilla Cornell and Adam Thurschwell.

sexual organ), and 'penis envy,' the penis being the only sexual organ of recognized value. Thus she attempts by every means available to appropriate the organ for herself: through her somewhat servile love of the father-husband capable of giving her one, through her desire for a child-penis, preferably a boy, through access to the cultural values still reserved by right to males alone and therefore always masculine, *and so on*" (*This Sex* 23–24; my emphasis). The female subject will, then, after her passage through the Oedipus complex, *desire* in the sense that she always desires to have the phallus, to establish identity in relation to patriarchal power, in contrast to the male subject, who will struggle to *represent* the phallus, to incarnate the power that inherently accrues to him in a patriarchal society.

Freud's discussion of femininity has served as the point of departure for Jacques Lacan's discussions of women and femininity, and Lacan's formulation of the linguistic aspects of psychoanalysis develops the notions of woman and femininity in ways useful for literary analysis. Because, for Lacan, men and women exist only as signifiers of and in language, they must necessarily identify themselves as masculine or feminine, which is not to say as men or women (*Encore* 36). At this moment of identification, a relationship is established between the individual and society, a relationship that has to do with patriarchal power—symbolized by the phallus—and an authority that manifests itself in language. Lacan says, therefore:

> when any speaking being whatever lines up under the banner of women it is by being constituted as not all [*pas-tout*] that they are placed within the phallic function. It is this that defines the . . . the what?—the woman precisely, except that *The* woman can only be written with the *The* crossed through. There is no such thing as *The* woman, where the definite article stands for the universal. There is no such thing as *The* woman since of her essence—having already risked the term, why think twice about it?—of her essence, she is not all [*pas toute*]. . . . There is woman only as excluded by the nature of things, which is the nature of words.

Because woman is the antithesis of masculine presence and patriarchal power, she is a nonexistent being, outside of language. Once woman is viewed as a not-all, Lacan can assert that, "from the side of the man . . . the whole of his realisation in the sexual relation comes down to fantasy" (Mitchell and Rose, *Feminine Sexuality* 144, 157). This means that woman—as an absence—becomes part of the dream of men, she exists only as an object on which fantasies of masculine desire are projected, as what Irigaray refers to in terms of a "sexual imaginary . . . a more or less obliging prop for the enactment of man's fantasies" (*This Sex* 25). In this sense, woman "has, in relation to what the phallic function designates concerning *jouissance,* a supplementary *jouissance*" that is, for Lacan, "beyond the phallus" and pertains to the woman alone (Mitchell and Rose, *Feminine Sexuality* 144–45).

The quintessential expression of the unknowable pleasure that is associated with the woman is to be found in mystic desire as it is experienced by women *and* by men; as Lacan says, "there are men who are just as good as women." In the ambit of Hispanic culture, two such exemplars of mystic desire are San Juan de la Cruz and Santa Teresa, both of whom Lacan mentions, especially the latter in the context of Bernini's statue of "Santa Teresa in Ecstasy," which follows closely on Simone de Beauvoir's account of mystic desire and sexual pleasure in terms of Santa Teresa in *The Second Sex.* Beauvoir comments that the "writings [of Santa Teresa] hardly leave room for doubt, and they justify Bernini's statue, which shows us the saint swooning in an excess of supreme voluptuousness" (747). According to Lacan, the distinctive feature of this nonphallic *jouissance* is the combination of sexual experience with the lack of sexual knowledge: "You only have to look at Bernini's statue in Rome to understand immediately that she's coming. And what is her *jouissance,* her *coming* from? It is clear that the essential testimony of the mystics is that they are experiencing it but know nothing about it" (Mitchell and Rose, *Feminine Sexuality* 147).

For Lacan, then, the riddle of female sexuality rests on this not knowing and not being able to know or to prove conclusively. What is not seen, is not, and woman, because she is anatomically incomplete and destined to live out her insufficiency, is, therefore, "not-all"; likewise, the *jouissance* of the woman is "beyond the phallus." And this leads us back to the "fact" that woman is constituted as a "lack," as an absence that cannot be explained. Freud asks, "What does a woman want?" Lacan answers with another question, "Who knows?"

To these perspectives on the question of woman, we can add those of Don Saturnino Bermúdez, who, in the thirteenth chapter of *La Regenta,* remarks of yet another rebuff by Obdulia, "¡Así eran las mujeres! ¡así era singularmente aquella mujer! ¿Para qué amarlas? ¿Para qué perseguir el ideal del amor? O mejor dicho, ¿para qué amar a las mujeres vivas, de carne y hueso? Mejor era soñar, seguir soñando" ["Such was Woman! Such, in particular, was this woman! Wherefore love women? Wherefore pursue the ideal of love? Or rather, wherefore love real women, women of flesh and blood? Better far to dream—to continue dreaming"] (1:503; 298). Clarín himself voices a similarly perplexed, if not to say misogynistic, view when he says, "With respect to woman, I only know that I know nothing, and that the same is true of the rest of men. . . . And this can be explained thus: in my opinion, woman represents the predominance of the unconscious in humanity. Woman is *natura naturans,* and there's no reason to inquire further" (*"La mujer"*). Indeed, Carolyn Richmond comments that Clarín's early opinions on women reflect "a highly conservative and traditional notion—we would call it a *prejudice* today—regarding what this being so different from man that was woman ought and ought not to do" ("Las ideas de Leopoldo Alas" 529). Of Clarín's representations of women, Richmond remarks, "the attitude adopted by Leopoldo Alas toward woman—the *other*—continues to be characterized by a basic lack of confidence and a condescension—if not to say contempt—at the heart of which one perceives not only an incomprehension of woman but also the consequences of the profound sadness of a lonely man" ("En torno al vacío" 343).

Because of these convergences in thought, between the psychoanalytic and the literary, the literary implications of the psychoanalytic perspectives on the question of woman are profound. If the nineteenth-century novel treats in detail the question of feminine desire, centers the novelistic discourse around woman, how is it that a woman, a "not-all," serves as the protagonist of a literary novel? In other words, if woman does not exist in language, how can a novel purport to treat a "lack"? This, then, is the crucial question to be answered with respect to *La Regenta,* a novel in which the central character is so clearly and so pressingly—in Lacan's terminology as otherwise—a "not-all." The answer to the question "What does woman want?" as it is posed by Clarín in terms of Ana Ozores is painfully obvious, and it has, in terms of the literary narrative of *La Regenta,* a dual aspect, one regarding the characters, the other regarding the novel as a whole. The absence that is woman is filled with the presence that is man and patriarchal desire at the same time that Ana's "wants" are supposedly fulfilled by Fermín de Pas and Alvaro Mesía, which is to say, *La Regenta* is filled with *Don Juan Tenorio.*

Let us begin discussion of the novel with a consideration of narrative form. *La Regenta* is divided into two parts, each consisting of fifteen chapters. In the first part, the action takes place in a span of three days; in the second part, over the course of three years. The temporal structure is systematic and orderly: the first scene of the first volume occurs in October in Vetusta's cathedral and deals with Celedonio, one of the acolytes; and the last scene of the second part of the novel takes place three years later, again in October in the cathedral where Celedonio kisses the unconscious Ana Ozores (see Durand, "Structural Unity"; Alarcos Llorach; and Rutherford 56–58).

The division of the novel into two parts and its temporal organization are complemented by various aspects of the plot, particularly the cluster of chapters at the center of the text. A dinner at the home of the Vegallanas in the thirteenth chapter delineates and summarizes the relationships between and among the characters as they have been presented so far. Ana is present with her husband, Víctor Quintanar, along with the two men who are pursuing her, Alvaro Mesía and Fermín de Pas. Throughout this chapter, we witness the play of desire between Ana and her two suitors, the implicit—and at times explicit—rivalry between the two men, as well as the total ignorance of the situation on the part of Don Víctor. A corresponding moment in the second part of the novel occurs in the sixteenth chapter, in which all of the principal characters, except for Don Fermín, attend a performance of *Don Juan Tenorio*. Because of its central placement in the novel, *Don Juan Tenorio* explicates the previous action, foreshadows the subsequent developments, and helps to explain the psychological nature of Clarín's many characters. Just as the performance of Zorrilla's drama foreshadows the outcome of *La Regenta,* the dinner reiterates the main points of the preceding chapters.[6]

It would be a mistake, however, to emphasize the structural importance of this cluster of chapters at the midpoint of the text at the expense of the generalized presence of desire and of Don Juan—including what he represents—throughout the novel. For example, the performance of the drama in the sixteenth chapter is the first explicit reference to Zorrilla's *Don Juan Tenorio,* but far from the first reference to Don Juan Tenorio, the literary character, either by the narrator or the characters in the novel (see Brent 105–9). Indeed, Don Juan is first mentioned in the third chapter in an antonomastic reference to the young men of Vetusta, "los más atrevidos Tenorios, famosos por sus temeridades, bajaban ante ella [Ana] los ojos, y su hermosura se adoraba en silencio. Tal vez, muchos la amaban, pero nadie se lo decía . . ." ["The most forward Tenorios, famous for their temerity, low-

---

6. A good discussion of these scenes can be found in María del Carmen Bobes Naves 45–51. Foreshadowing has also been a major topic in critical treatments of *La Regenta.* See Miriam Wagner Rice, "The Meaning of Metaphor" and "Metaphorical Foreshadowing"; Noël M. Valis, "Order and Meaning"; Edith Rogers; and Stephanie Sieburth, "Interpreting *La Regenta*" and *Reading* La Regenta.

ered their eyes before her (Ana), and adored her beauty in silence. Perhaps many men loved her, but none told her of his love . . ."] (1:182–83; 78). The subtle use of free indirect discourse here as throughout the novel, along with the allusive suspension points in this passage, allows for this comment to be attributed to Ana herself, as opposed to the narrator; and the sentence that follows, with its anxious accretion and modification of details, does nothing to dispel the illusion that we as readers are directly privy to La Regenta's innermost thoughts, even though the moment seems to end with the narrator's own voice:

> Aquel mismo don Alvaro que tenía fama de atreverse a todo y conseguirlo todo, la quería, la adoraba sin duda alguna, estaba segura; más de dos años hacía que ella lo había conocido; pero él no había hablado más que con los ojos, donde Ana fingía no adivinar una pasión que era crimen.
> Verdad era en estos últimos meses, sobre todo desde algunas semanas a esta parte, se mostraba más atrevido . . . hasta algo imprudente, él que era la prudencia misma, y sólo por esto digno de que ella no se irritara contra su infame intento . . . pero ya sabría contenerle; sí, ella le pondría a raya helándole con una mirada . . . Y pensando en convertir en carámbano a don Alvaro Mesía, mientras él se obstinaba en ser de fuego, se quedó dormida dulcemente. (1:183)

> [Don Alvaro himself, who had a reputation for never flinching from adventure and for never failing in one, loved her, adored her, without any doubt, of that she was certain—she had known it for more than two years, although he had never said anything, except with his eyes, where she pretended not to notice a passion which was a crime.
> It was true that these last few months, particularly during recent weeks, he had been more audacious—and even somewhat imprudent, he who was prudence itself, and who for this reason alone merited her not being outraged by his infamous enterprise—but she would know how to contain his ardor when the time came. Yes, she would put him back into line, freezing him with a look. And so, pondering on her conversion of Don Alvaro Mesía into an icicle while he insisted upon being of fire, she slipped sweetly into sleep. (78)]

This first, seemingly casual, observation reveals the essential trajectory of Ana's train of thought, as well as the trajectory of the novel itself, from Tenorios as a general class to the most important Don Juan of all, "Don Alvaro himself." Moreover, Ana is not unaware of Don Alvaro's interest in and intentions toward her. She actually seems to derive sensual pleasure from the thought, from the possibility of "containing his ardor," going so far as to convert his passion into a frigidly phallic icicle. It appears, then, that Ana anticipates the performance of *Don Juan Tenorio,* and that, perhaps without realizing it, she senses that her future includes some involvement with Vetusta's Don Juan.

Yet there is some confusion in the novel as to whether or not a person similar to the dramatic Don Juan does or even can, in fact, exist. Moreover, if he does exist, to what extent are his powers similar to those of his literary predecessor? On the one hand, Ripamilán, the archpriest, counsels Ana to forget any idea that she might have of becoming a nun, particularly as a means of escaping her inevitable destiny as a "married woman," because "Todo eso de hacerse monja sin vocación, estaba bien para el teatro; pero en el mundo no había Manriques ni Tenorios que escalasen conventos, a Dios gracias" ["That business about taking the veil without any vocation was all very well in the theatre, but in the world there were no Manriques or Tenorios climbing into convents, thank God"] (1:241; 118). On the other hand, Pepe Ronzal, in the first explicit linking by another character in the novel of the romantic protagonist with his novelistic avatar, opines that "ese señor don Juan Tenorio [Mesía] puede llamar a otra puerta, que la Regenta es una fortaleza inexpugnable" ["that Don Juan Tenorio (Mesía) can go knocking on another door, because the judge's wife is an impregnable fortress"] (1:277; 141). Whereas one character denies the possibility that a Don Juan might exist in the real world, another not only affirms his existence, but designates his epigone. Still, among these Vetustans, the one thing that is never called into question is Ana Ozores's virtue. She is untouchable, beyond the seductive charms of any local Don Juan. As the narrator slyly informs us immediately prior to the first mention of Don Juan's name (and in an allusion to Fray Luis de León's treatise on women, *La perfecta casada* [The Perfect Wife]), "en Vetusta decir la Regenta era decir la perfecta casada" ["in Vetusta, to say the judge's wife was to say the perfect wife"] (1:182; 78).[7] Therefore, although there exists the possibility of seduction in

---

7. The same process of allusion and confirmation—in which the narrator makes an oblique reference that is subsequently confirmed by a character—is at work here, too. The narrator ironically refers to Fray Luis de León's *La perfecta casada,* and this allusion is affirmed by Ana herself when she later remarks in a letter to Don Fermín of her marital responsibilities, "En esto he mejorado mucho; porque fray Luis de León me

Vetusta, because there exists a seducer in Don Alvaro, the seduction of Ana exists as an *im*possibility. Or, at least in the case of La Regenta, Don Alvaro is denied much of the power and influence with which others would endow him.

But it is important to see that these comments represent only one side of the issue. There are other characters, including Don Alvaro himself, who see the situation in terms directly opposed to these early opinions. Mesía, for instance, considers himself "the extempore Don Juan" (1:295; 153). Furthermore, he has no doubt whatsoever that he will succeed in seducing Ana Ozores, since "tan mujer era la Regenta como las demás" ["the judge's wife was a woman like any other"] (1:294; 153). More important, the seduction could not fail provided that "la Regenta podía . . . creer que el Tenorio de Vetusta había dejado de serlo para convertirse en fino, constante y platónico amador de su gentileza" ["she were able . . . to think that the Don Juan of Vetusta had stopped being a Don Juan and had turned into a true, constant and platonic lover of her charm"] (1:296; 154–55). Others in Mesía's circle of friends and acquaintances are equally interested in the success of Don Alvaro's adventure. Echoing Mesía's own thought, Obdulia observes in the all-important sixteenth chapter, "La Regenta, ¡bah! la Regenta será como todas . . . Las demás somos tan buenas como ella" ["The judge's wife! Bah!—I'm quite sure the judge's wife is the same as other women. The rest of us are just as good as her"] (2:34; 367). For her part, Visitación aids and abets her former lover, Don Alvaro, in every conceivable way so as to ensure that she does not have to "renunciar al placer de ver a su amiga caer donde ella había caído; por lo menos verla padecer con la tentación" ["renounce the pleasure of seeing her friend fall where she herself had fallen, or at least seeing her tormented by temptation"] (2:15; 355). Whereas one group of Vetustans endows Ana with an individuality expressed as moral purity, another sees her as similar to—and as similarly amoral as—all other women.

There are, then, two distinct schools of thought in the novel on the

---

enseñó en su *Perfecta casada* que en cada estado la obligación es diferente; en el mío mi esposo merecía más de lo que yo le daba, pero advertida por el sabio poeta y por usted, ya voy poniendo más esmero en cuidar a mi Quintanar" ["In this respect I have made much improvement, for Fray Luis de León has shown me in his *Perfect Wife* that one's obligations vary according to one's state; my husband deserves more than I used to give him, but following the wise poet's and your own counsel I now take more care to cherish my Quintanar"] (2:195–96; 477). Again, Ana begins to see herself in the terms proposed by others in the text. On the effects of reading in *La Regenta* see Benigno Sánchez-Eppler. On the power of literature not only to mirror but also to determine social realities, see Nancy Armstrong.

Don Juan question, on the possibility of there being a local Don Juan and on Ana's susceptibility to the charms of Don Alvaro. This uncertainty exists, however, only in the world of the characters of *La Regenta*. The narrator, prior to the sixteenth chapter, confirms Ana's initial intuition by referring to Mesía as "the Tenorio" (1:235; 114) during the fateful first contact between La Regenta and her future lover, fleeting to be sure, as he is leaving town on the stagecoach and their eyes briefly meet. There is no question as to the nature or the telos of Ana's involvement with Don Alvaro. From La Regenta's first musings on the local young men as Don Juans to the narrator's overt and unambiguous reference to Don Alvaro as a Tenorio, from the Vetustans' general realization of Mesía's desire to possess Ana to the desire of Don Alvaro's friends and former lovers to help him in his conquest, everything and everybody in *La Regenta,* including the narrator—and, almost absurdly, Don Victor, who threatens Ana, "si me apuras, le mando a Paco o al mismísimo Mesía, el Tenorio, el simpático Tenorio, que te enamoren" ["if you push me, I shall send Paco or even Mesía, that Don Juan, our charming Don Juan, to woo you"] (1:383; 215)—all conspire toward the heroine's downfall. As the narrative presentation makes clear, there will be a seduction and it will parallel, in some sense, the paradigmatic seduction found in *Don Juan Tenorio.* It is, therefore, a slight misstatement of fact to emphasize the degree of foreshadowing that takes place in the sixteenth chapter. Zorrilla's drama serves as an explicit subtext throughout the novel, not just from the sixteenth chapter on, and a decision has already been made with respect to the fact of seduction and the victim. What happens in the sixteenth chapter, then, is that the victim herself realizes and implicitly acquiesces to what is already apparent to almost everyone else.

These overt references to Don Juan and *Don Juan Tenorio* are not the only indications of the relationship between the play and the novel. Much more subtle, and insidious, are those points in *La Regenta* at which the narrator draws on the language of Zorrilla's drama and introduces it into, and as, his own narration. Most conspicuous, of course, are those references to Zorrilla's Doña Inés and to her seduction by Don Juan, a seduction that takes place, curiously enough, while the would-be seducer is absent. As we have seen, in *Don Juan Tenorio* desire is awakened in the virginal Doña Inés when Don Juan manages to send to her in the convent a prayer book in which he has concealed a letter. With her reading of this epistle, the novice sees and in turn portrays herself in terms of a commingling of souls. In fact, Doña Inés becomes the means of Don Juan's salvation. She has come to accept herself as, in the words of Irigaray, the imaginary on which Don Juan has projected his fantasies. This commingling of souls picks up various threads of literary tradition as it fashions out of these materials the mutual dependency of the seducer and the seduced. Like the inception of love between Francesca and Paolo, Doña Inés's love for Don Juan is, in René Girard's terms, mediated by the letter concealed in the devotionary; and it acts upon her like a poisonous filter or love potion.

Clearly, in *La Regenta* the incorporation of *Don Juan Tenorio* constitutes an important moment of external mediation: it is at that point that Ana begins to interpret her situation in terms of the drama.[8] Yet there are other analogous moments of the disseminating power of seduction as found in *Don Juan Tenorio* that refer back to the play. In one instance, when Ana is wandering through her garden during the evening hours, she realizes that Mesía is on the other side of the wall. He finally screws up his courage to call out to her, the "demon of seduction" prodding this timid Tenorio to act, but Ana has fled in realization of what is at stake and of the potential—and actual—power that Don Alvaro has over her: "Sí, sentía ella que don Alvaro se infiltraba, se infiltraba en las almas, se infiltraba por las piedras; en aquella casa todo se iba llenando de él, temía verle aparecer pronto" ["Yes, she felt as if Don Alvaro were a filter, as if he could filter through walls and even into souls. Everything in the house was filling up with him, and she was afraid that she might suddenly see him appear again"] (1:381; 213).

The power of infiltration, the power of masculine presence to fill the feminine "house," turns up again in the sixteenth chapter while Vetusta is at the theater watching *Don Juan Tenorio,* and here the similarities between Zorrilla's Doña Inés, Dante's Francesca and Paolo, and Clarín's Ana are far from gratuitous.[9] La Regenta is enraptured by the drama and carefully observes the action and the actors:

8. Sobejano, in the introduction to his edition of the novel, makes use of Girard's discussion of mimetic desire, but Sobejano sees Santa Teresa as the model for Ana Ozores: "Santa Teresa is the model for Ana *in* the story as well as the model that, in many respects, Alas took *for* his protagonist." Sobejano points out that this is a case of external mediation. He goes on to say that "internal mediation, on the other hand, does not exist [in the novel]" (Introducción, *La Regenta* 1:51). As we shall see, Santa Teresa is a significant model in the novel for the mediation of desire, but essentially a failed model. Moreover, Sobejano is plainly mistaken when he says that there is no example of internally mediated desire in the novel, though he is right to the extent that internal mediation does not occur in the case of Ana.

9. Ignacio-Javier López also discusses filters in his *Caballero de novela* 96–98.

clavados los ojos en la hija del Comendador, olvidada de todo lo que estaba fuera de la escena, bebió [Ana] con ansiedad toda la poesía de aquella celda casta en que se estaba filtrando el amor por las paredes. "¡Pero esto es divino!", dijo volviéndose hacia su marido, mientras pasaba la lengua por los labios secos. La carta de don Juan escondida en el libro devoto, leída con voz temblorosa primero, con terror supersticioso después, por doña Inés, mientras Brígida acercaba su bujía al papel; la proximidad casi sobrenatural de Tenorio, el espanto que sus hechizos supuestos producen en la novicia que ya cree sentirlos, todo, todo lo que pasaba allí y lo que ella adivinaba, producía en Ana un efecto de magia poética, y le costaba trabajo contener las lágrimas que se le agolpaban a los ojos.

"¡Ay! sí, el amor era aquello, un filtro, una atmósfera de fuego, una locura mística; huir de él era imposible; imposible gozar mayor ventura que saborearle con todos sus venenos. Ana se comparaba con la hija del Comendador; el caserón de los Ozores era su convento, su marido la regla estrecha de hastío y frialdad en que ya había profesado ocho años hacía . . . y don Juan . . . ¡don Juan aquel Mesía que también se filtraba por las paredes, aparecía por milagro y llenaba el aire con su presencia!" (2:47–48)

[With her eyes riveted on the novice, oblivious of everything but what was happening on the stage, she anxiously drank in the poetry of the chaste cell into which love was filtering through the walls. "But this is divine!" she said, turning to her husband, as she ran her tongue over her dry lips. Don Juan's letter, hidden in the book of devotion, read at first in a trembling voice and then with superstitious fear, as Brígida the go-between holds a candle close to the piece of paper; his almost supernatural nearness; the terror which his supposed sorcery awakes in the novice, who already thinks she can feel its effects; everything, everything that took place there and that Ana imagined was poetic magic to her, and it was with difficulty that she held back the tears which were pressing at her eyes.

'Oh!, yes, that was love: a philtre, fire, mystical madness. It was impossible to run away from it, impossible to enjoy greater fortune than to savour it, poisonous as it was. Ana compared herself with the novice. Ozores Mansion was her convent, her husband the rigid rule of boredom and coldness in which she had professed a full eight years before; and Don Juan—Don Juan was Mesía, who also filtered through the walls, made miraculous appearances and filled the air with his presence!' (376–77)]

Note the extreme care with which Clarín has calibrated the representation of this central moment, the latent sensuality that bursts forth from Ana as she fills herself, rather, "drinks in" the poetry of the drama, licking her lips in delight, savoring the poison that she knows the drama to be. Note as well the reappearance of the love potion, the fact that it is mentioned three times in this citation, first in the context of Doña Inés's cell, next in terms of the drama, then in the way that Don Alvaro filters "through the walls," just as earlier he had seemed capable of infiltrating the grounds of the Ozores mansion, which now becomes the convent in which Doña Inés reads of Don Juan's love for her. Finally, Ana's complicity in this moment is suggested by her own desire to perceive herself in, and to read herself into, this scenario; Clarín stresses the parallels between what La Regenta actually sees and what she *wants to see.* Just as in the case of Dante's Paolo and Francesca, and in that of Zorrilla's Doña Inés, actions and words are predicated on a literary antecedent, desire is mediated by a literary text, by a textual model that has been present all along. Thus, in his presentation of this key scene in *Don Juan Tenorio,* Clarín has underscored the duality of seduction, in its religious and carnal aspects (by returning Don Juan's missive, which moves from hand to hand and reader to reader in the drama, to its starting point, placing it once again in the pages of the devotionary); and the dangers inherent in the act of reading. To be sure, reading might be dangerous in that it can seduce an individual from one path or course of action to another. But, in the context of *Don Juan Tenorio* and *La Regenta,* reading and interpretation, even if loosely construed in terms of watching a drama, draw women more deeply into the web of patriarchy. Far from containing Don Alvaro's ardor as was suggested earlier in the novel, Ana revels in the poison disseminated by the drama and by Don Alvaro's desire for her.

The complicity of *Don Juan Tenorio* in the act of seduction is understood, however, only by the narrator, who uses this scene in the sixteenth chapter to belittle Mesía, to show how ridiculous is this Don Juan. But this is not to say that Don Alvaro is without attractions. Despite the fact that he is not the dashing and daring Don Juan of *El burlador de Sevilla* and *Don Juan Tenorio,* that he is past his prime— "Cuarenta años y alguno más contaba el presidente del Casino" ["The president of the Gentlemen's Club was somewhat over forty years old"]

(1:289; 149)—Mesía is nevertheless the complete gentleman, and his effect on women reflects this. He is so charming that "a aquel hombre se le podía perdonar todo. ¡Qué tacto! ¡qué prudencia! ¡qué discreción!" ["one could forgive that man for absolutely anything. Such tact! Such prudence! Such discretion!"]. He appeals even to the most chaste of women; "Entre monjas podría vivir este hombre sin que hubiera miedo de un escándalo" ["he could live in a nunnery without fear of scandal"] (1:311; 164).

Don Alvaro *is* seductive, *is* an "electrical love machine" (1:358; 198), but he is not merely that. He uses his seductive charms for political ends. Seduction is not, therefore, the final goal in Mesía's game; power is what Mesía truly desires, and he is willing to "seduce" women and men alike. Not only is he the president of the Casino and the leader of the Dynastic Liberal Party in Vetusta, Mesía runs the affairs of the conservative party as well, since the Marqués de Vegallana, who is the head of the most reactionary political party in Vetusta, leaves all of the work to a protégé, in this case, Don Alvaro. Though the Marqués likes to think that he is in charge of political matters, everything that is proposed can be traced back to Mesía. Don Alvaro is content with the appearance that the Marqués runs conservative politics in Vetusta. What Don Alvaro craves, therefore, is not recognition, which would upset his plans, but power, plain and simple.

In fact, Mesía is a ruthless and patient seducer who plays several games at the same time. Ana, the biggest fish in the pond that is Vetusta, has taken up two years of his time: "¡Dos años hacía que ella debía de creerle enamorado de sus prendas! Sí, dos años llevaba de prudente sigiloso culto externo, casi siempre mudo, sin más elocuencia que la de los ojos" ["For two years now she must have believed him to be enamoured of her sterling qualities! Yes, he had already devoted two years to the external worship of the judge's wife—worship which was prudent and discreet and nearly always silent, its only eloquence being the eloquence of the eyes"] (1:295; 154). But La Regenta is small fry for Mesía, as is Vetusta. His real goal is Madrid, where he has been seducing the wife of a minister: "La señora del personaje de Madrid era de las que exigían años" ["The wife of the personage from Madrid was one of those women who took years"] (1:295; 153–54). So persistent is Don Alvaro that he pursues the "ministra" one summer while away from Vetusta, provoking Ana's jealousy. Indeed, Mesía uses this information, disseminated through Visita, to incite Ana's desire: " 'Don Alvaro había vencido la virtud de la *ministra,* había sido su amante todo el verano en Palomares . . . y después se había burlado de ella, no había querido seguirla a Madrid' " [" 'Don Alvaro had conquered the virtue of the minister's wife, he had been her lover throughout the summer in Palomares . . . and then he had mocked her, he hadn't followed her to Madrid' "] (2:303; 550). The irony of this story is that Don Alvaro, when he abandons Ana at the end of the novel, goes to Madrid, leaving Vetusta to whisper about "sus amores *reanudados* con la *Ministra* de Palomares" ["his renewed affair with the minister's wife from Palomares"] (2:526; 708). To be sure, Don Alvaro possesses seductive charm, but his interest is always focused on something *beyond* the woman in question. This Don Juan is, then, *explicitly* an agent who functions *within* society, if for his own benefit. After all, the scandalous aspect of Ana's affair with Don Alvaro was not the affair itself. Rather, Ana's indiscretion and the fact that Don Alvaro and Don Víctor entered into a duel constitute the scandal: "Vetusta había perdido dos de sus personajes más importantes . . . por culpa de Ana y su torpeza" ["Vetusta had lost two of its most important personages—all because of Ana and her blundering"] (2:526; 708).

Zorrilla's *Don Juan Tenorio* supports, therefore, Don Alvaro's quest to conquer La Regenta. Despite the fact that Mesía senses in the drama "a powerful rival" (2:45; 375), it is as she watches the events in the drama—and, she imagines, her own life—unfold before her, that Ana gradually reconciles herself to the role that she is to play in the drama that is life in Vetusta. Moreover, Ana's extreme anxiety at the possible disapproval of her confessor, Don Fermín, serves as a counterpoint to her delight in Zorrilla's drama; she knows that to attend the theater during various religious holidays is forbidden. If de Pas would have prevented La Regenta from attending the performance of *Don Juan Tenorio*, then Don Alvaro's rival is not to be found in any text, but, rather, in the guise of Ana's confessor.

This, then, is the internal mediation in the novel, the way that Don Alvaro's desire for La Regenta, and his quest for power, mirrors de Pas's own far from spiritual yearnings. So complete is the rivalry between the men in the form of this internal mediation, the narrative itself emphasizes the many manifest similarities between the two. Whereas Don Alvaro craves political power and uses women to that end, Don Fermín seeks to extend his empire by means of the authority of the Church. Given the differences in their respective domains, the Magistral is still conscious of his appearance and its effect; he is as seductive in his way as Don Alvaro. Yet there is a marked difference between the two men in this regard. De Pas, at the age of 35 (1:106; 29), is in his prime. Furthermore, he conceals beneath his ecclesiastical robes a physique of immense athletic power and masculine beauty. In a description of voluptuous and narcissistic detail, virtually a photograph taken while the Magistral is shaving, the narrator informs us:

> Estaba desnudo de medio cuerpo para arriba. El cuello robusto parecía más fuerte ahora por la tensión a que le obligaba la violencia de la postura, al inclinarse sobre el lavabo de mármol blanco. Los brazos cubiertos de vello negro ensortijado, lo mismo que el pecho alto y fuerte, parecían de un atleta. El Magistral miraba con tristeza sus músculos de acero, de una fuerza inútil. Era muy blanco y fino el cutis, que una emoción cualquiera teñía de color rosa. Por consejo de don Robustiano, el médico, de Pas hacía gimnasia con pesos de muchas libras; era un Hércules. . . .
> Mientras estaba lavándose, desnudo de la cintura arriba, don Fermín se acordaba de sus proezas en el juego de bolos, allá en la aldea, cuando aprovechaba vacaciones del seminario para ser medio salvaje corriendo por breñas y vericuetos; el mozo fuerte y velludo que tenía enfrente, en el espejo, le parecía un *otro yo* que se había perdido, que había quedado en los montes, desnudo, cubierto de pelo como el rey de Babilonia, pero libre, feliz. . . . Le asustaba tal espectáculo, le llevaba muy lejos de sus pensamientos de ahora, y se apresuró a vestirse. En cuanto se abrochó el alzacuello, el Magistral volvió a ser la imagen de la mansedumbre cristiana, fuerte, pero espiritual, humilde . . . (1:409–10)

[He was naked from the waist up. His powerful neck seemed even more powerful now, because of the strain put upon it by his tensed position as he leaned over the white marble wash basin. His arms, like his broad, powerful chest, were covered with fine black curly hair; they were the arms of an athlete. The canon looked sadly at his muscles of steel, charged with useless power. His complexion was pale and delicate, the slightest emotion tinging it rose-colour. On the advice of Don Robustiano, the doctor, De Pas exercised with heavy weights; he was a Hercules. . . .

As Don Fermín washed, he recalled his prowess at skittles, back in his home village, where he had always made the most of the opportunities offered by holidays from the seminary to go half savage, running through rocky scrub in the high hills. The brawny, hairy young fellow before him in the mirror somehow seemed like a lost *alter ego* which had stayed behind in those hills—naked, as hairy as the King of Babylon, yet free, happy. He was alarmed by this sight, which carried his thoughts far away, and he dressed hurriedly. As soon as the canon had buttoned up his collar he was once again the image of Christian meekness, strong yet spiritual and humble. (232–33)]

As this extensive citation demonstrates, Don Fermín is a massive contradiction who suffers from his self-perceived alterity, and it is these contradictions that motivate his role in the novel. In spite of his apparently self-effacing humility, his Christian meekness, de Pas is covertly masculine. Although like Hercules, the traditional mediating figure and hero of Olympian patriarchy, in terms of his physical strength, de Pas is powerful *and* impotent. The narrator's modification and qualification of the descriptions as well as his insistence on the Magistral's semi-nudity heighten the erotic presentation of this man of the cloth. Alongside the rather clinical description and putative self-presentation of Don Alvaro, Don Fermín stands marked as a figure of sensual potency.

In a classic example of Freudian sublimation, once in ecclesiastical garb de Pas's energies are devoted to the cultivation of his flock and the manipulation of his immediate superior, the Bishop of Vetusta. In a virtually sacred repetition of Mesía's lay authority, the Magistral's power is presented in terms of spiritual and personal prisoners: "Vetusta era su pasión y su presa. Mientras los demás le tenían por sabio teólogo, filósofo y jurisconsulto, él estimaba sobre todas su ciencia de Vetusta. La conocía palmo a palmo, por dentro y por fuera, por el alma y por el cuerpo, había escudriñado los rincones de las conciencias y los rincones de las casas. Lo que sentía en presencia de la heroica ciudad era gula" ["Vetusta was his passion and his prey. Although others thought of him as a wise theologian, philosopher and lawyer, he himself prized above all other branches of knowledge his knowledge of Vetusta. He knew it inch by inch, inside and out, soul and body; he had examined the corners of consciences and the corners of houses. What he felt in the presence of the heroic city was gluttony"] (1:105; 28). With respect to the Bishop, "El [de Pas] era el amo del amo. Tenía el Obispo en una garra, prisionero voluntario que ni se daba cuenta de sus prisiones" ["He (de Pas) was the master's master: he held the bishop in an iron grip, a voluntary prisoner who did not even notice his shackles"] (1:107; 29). Again, this power of manipulation is not exercised as an end in and of itself. It is, in fact, a *business* with economic aspects, and it is presented as such throughout the novel.

Above all, the Magistral's mother, Doña Paula, views her son as one among many investments, investments that include land, houses in the countryside, usurious loans, and a store specializing in religious paraphernalia, La Cruz Roja [The Red Cross], from which all the churches in the diocese are required to make their purchases. These business interests are, of course, carefully concealed from Vetusta, but there is still talk and considerable resentment (1:389–96, 565–72; 219–223, 343–47). Yet of all of these *tangible* assets, the most important is Don Fermín himself; and it is an *intangible* asset with which the Magistral is endowed that is the most valuable of all: his way with words, both inside and outside of the cathedral. He "seduces" wealthy young women into convents, convinces wealthy men to support the works of the Church, instructs girls in the catechism. More important, unlike those who use sophisticated rhetorical strategies in the pulpit and who thereby confuse the Vetustans, de Pas "no era cómico, ni trágico, ni épico" ["was not a comedian, or a tragedian, or even a reciter of epics"] (1:449; 260). Instead, "Si en los asuntos dogmáticos buscaba el auxilio de *la sana razón, en los temas de moral iba siempre a parar a la utilidad. La salvación era un negocio, el gran negocio de la vida. Parecía un Bastiat del púlpito. 'El interés y la caridad son una misma cosa. Ser bueno es *entenderla*' "* ["When dealing with dogma he sought the aid of sound reason, but in moral matters he always had recourse to utility. Salvation was a transaction—the great transaction of life. He was the Bastiat of the pulpit. 'Self-interest and charity are one and the same thing. To be virtuous you merely have to understand charity' "] (1:452; 262).

With an emphasis on logic, a colloquial style, and a direct message, the Magistral succeeds in communicating his spiritual values to Vetusta. For him religion is a business, the business of salvation, especially as it then translates into monetary profit. Like the French liberal economist Frédéric Bastiat to whom the narrator refers, de Pas sees religious life in the economic terms of investment and dividend, capital and interest. His investment of time and energy is repaid not in the spiritual terms of salvation or even redemption, but rather, money, always in service to his mother's desire for more:

> Fermo, además de su hijo era su *capital, una fábrica de dinero.* Ella le habría hecho hombre, *a costa de* sacrificios, de vergüenzas de que él no sabía ni la mitad, de vigilias, de sudoreo, *de cálculos,* de paciencia, de energía y de pecados sórdidos; por consiguiente *no pedía mucho si pedía intereses* al resultado de sus esfuerzos al Provisor de Vetusta. El mundo era su hijo . . . pero su hijo era de ella, *debía cobrar los réditos de su capital, y si la fábrica se paraba o se descomponía, podía reclamar daños y perjuicios, tenía derecho a exigir que Fermo continuase la produciendo.* (1:547; my emphasis)

[Fermo, as well as being her son, was her *investment, her mint*. She had made a man of him through self-sacrifice, shameful deeds, half of which he knew nothing about, sleepless nights, sweat, *calculation,* patience, astuteness, energy and sordid sins. *She was not, then, asking for too much if she asked* the result of all her efforts, the vicar-general of Vetusta, *for her interest*. The world belonged to her son . . . but her son belonged to her, *she had a right to charge interest on her capital. And if the mint stopped working or broke down it was her prerogative to claim for damages; she had a right to demand that Fermo maintained production*. (330–31; my emphasis)]

This extraordinary paragraph makes abundantly clear that Fermín is an investment, a money-making proposition, for the Church *and* for his mother. Indeed, we could go so far as to say that religion *is* a business, that *the* religion in Vetusta is one of power and money: "En aquella casa [del Magistral] el recuento de la moneda era un culto. Desde niño se había acostumbrado don Fermín a la seriedad religiosa con que se trataban los asuntos de dinero" ["In the Magistral's home, the counting of the takings was a cult. Ever since his childhood, Fermín had been accustomed to seeing money matters treated with religious seriousness"] (1:564; 342).

Don Alvaro and Don Fermín function in the novel as mirror images of greed, the one in the domain of the secular, the other in that of the sacred. Once they take as the object of their desire La Regenta, they come into conflict and become rivals. So obvious is this conflict, various characters remark on it, much to de Pas's chagrin. As he explains to Ana in the second volume, "Ayer ese hombre [Mesía] estaba borracho . . . él y otros pasaron delante de mi casa . . . a las tres de la madrugada. . . . Orgaz le llamaba a gritos: '¡Alvaro! ¡Alvaro! aquí vive . . . tu rival . . .' eso decía, tu rival . . . ¡la calumnia ha llegado hasta ahí . . . !'" ["Yesterday that man (Mesía) was drunk. He and others walked past my house at three o'clock in the morning. Orgaz was shouting to him: 'Alvaro! Alvaro! This is where your rival lives.' That was what he said, your rival—the calumny has gone that far"] (2:289; 541). But it is not a question of calumny, and de Pas knows it: the realization of this rivalry occurs earlier in the novel, in the thirteenth chapter in such a way that it delineates the path of the internal mediation.

Following upon an initial comparison of the two men by Ana, Clarín mentions Don Alvaro's general fear, then the magistral's growing awareness of the rivalry: "Don Alvaro ya miraba al Provisor con prevención, ya le temía; el Provisor no sospechaba que don Alvaro pudiera ser el enemigo tentador de la Regenta. . . . Cuando le vio con Anita en la ventana, conversando tan distraídos de los demás, sintió don Fermín un malestar que fue creciendo mientras tuvo que esperar su presencia" ["Don Alvaro was already beginning to distrust and even fear the vicar-general. But the vicar-general did not suspect that Don Alvaro might be the enemy who was tempting the judge's wife. . . . Yet when Don Fermín saw Don Alvaro by the dining room window deep in conversation with Anita, and saw both of them so oblivious to everybody else, he was seized by an anxiety which grew while he waited for them to appear in the salon"] (1:491; 289). The uneasiness on the part of the two men continues, until finally the rivals and the object of their desire silently confront one another: " '¡Qué diablos es esto!' pensó de Pas; y entonces precisamente fue cuando se encontró con los ojos de don Alvaro; fue una mirada que se convirtió, al chocar, en un desafío; una mirada de esas que dan bofetadas; nadie lo notó más que ellos y la Regenta" [" 'What the devil is this!' thought De Pas. It was at this moment that he met Don Alvaro's look which, as it hit him, became a challenge—the kind of look which slaps a man in the face. Nobody noticed it but the judge's wife and the two gentlemen"] (1:508; 302).

This brief encounter is followed by a lengthy dilation by Ana on what she has just witnessed, a consideration that is brought up short by the piercing screams of Obdulia, who is caught suspended above the ground in the basketlike seat of a wooden swing. First, Víctor and two younger men try to rescue Obdulia from her predicament. Next, Don Alvaro steps into the fray, virtually sure of his success. He too fails to free Obdulia. It then falls to de Pas to try, while Don Alvaro and his friends idly watch, waiting for the priest to make a fool of himself. But Don Fermín succeeds in rescuing Obdulia *and* in appearing elegantly masculine before the onlookers. Mesía's failure becomes de Pas's triumph.

The usurpation of masculine power by the apparently effeminate priest, clothed as he is in the feminine skirts prescribed by the Church (1:409–10, 514; 232–33, 307), confirms an earlier moment in this thirteenth chapter when Don Alvaro reflects on his own usurpation of the priest's role as confessor. Part of the perverse pleasure that Mesía takes in seduction is to demand that his lovers stop going to confession and, furthermore, that they "confess" to him (1:493; 291). There is a point, then, at which the roles played by Mesía and de Pas, the dandy and the priest, are virtually acknowledged as interchangeable: the one is comparable to the other, carefully modeled on his rival, which means that, in Don Fermín and Don Alvaro, there are not one but two Don Juans.[10]

In fact, the schema proposed by Girard's theory of mimetic desire is somewhat more complex than the two triangles (Don Alvaro–Ana–*Don Juan Tenorio,* Don Alvaro–Ana–Don Fermín, both hinging on La Regenta) would seem to suggest. Even though de Pas recognizes that he possesses a rival in Mesía, as do others in the novel, he too, believes himself to be rivaled, and seriously so, by a literary text and model of desire that extends beyond the boundaries of knowledge set by patriarchy, the spiritual desire of Santa Teresa. As she becomes more involved in spiritual questions, Ana returns, at Don Fermín's suggestion, to her predilection for reading the works of the mystics. But Ana becomes much too fervent in her readings and in her slavish desire to imitate the saint: "Deseaba encontrar semejanzas, aunque fuesen remotas, entre la vida de Santa Teresa y la suya, aplicar a las circunstancias en que ella se veía los pensamientos que la mística dedicaba a las vicisitudes de su historia. El espíritu de imitación se apoderaba de la lectora, sin darse ella de cuenta de tamaño atrevimiento" ["She wanted to find similarities, even though they might be remote ones, between St. Teresa's life and her own, trying to apply to the circumstances in which she found herself the mystic's thoughts about the vicissitudes of existence. The spirit of imitation was taking hold of Ana; she did not realize how presumptuous she was being"] (2:191; 474). Finally, de Pas begins to feel threatened because "La Regenta habló de Santa Teresa con entusiasmo de idólatra; el Magistral aprobaba su admiración, pero con menos calor que empleaba al hablar de ellos, de su amistad, y de la piedad acendrada que veía ahora en Anita. Don Fermín tenía celos de la Santa de Avila" ["The judge's wife talked about St. Teresa with all the enthusiasm of an idolatress; and the canon approved her admiration, but with less warmth than when he spoke of the two of them, of their friendship, and of the pure piety which he could now discern in her"] (2:207; 484–85).

De Pas fears, of course, that, as Ana becomes more involved in the

10. Moraima de Semprún Donahue makes this point. Ignacio-Javier López, on the other hand, sees only one avatar of Don Juan in the novel, Don Alvaro, although he does admit that Mesía and de Pas are similarly diabolical (99–100). Regarding the rivalry between Don Fermín and Don Alvaro, Biruté Ciplijauskaité comments, "Clarín brings the civil and ecclesiastical powers face to face . . . showing that in both cases it is less a question of the conquest of a woman than of dictatorship in the city. The ideological and the purely political are combined, as are the economic and the moral" (*La mujer insatisfecha* 56).

mystics and mystic contemplation, she will begin to draw away from her confessor, to become self-sufficient in her desire. This is similar to Lacan's discussion of mystic desire as feminine desire par excellence; because she is the recipient of the unmediated Logos, Santa Teresa is "beyond the phallus," literally, beyond the rational knowledge of sexual experience. Desire that takes place outside of the realm of the masculine, beyond the control of men, apparently excludes the power of patriarchy. In this sense, Santa Teresa—as a model of desire as embodied in a literary text—constitutes a much more serious threat to either of the two men who desire La Regenta than does *Don Juan Tenorio,* which, as we have seen, stages by means of seduction the ongoing possession of women by men, of the feminine by the masculine. Yet, as Clarín goes to great lengths to demonstrate, Ana's devotion to Santa Teresa ineluctably draws her closer to her confessor and spiritual seducer, just as *Don Juan Tenorio* aids and abets Mesía's aims.

It would appear, then, that two types of desire—the one masculine as represented by *Don Juan Tenorio,* the other feminine yet seemingly far superior to its masculine other as it is embodied in Santa Teresa—are in direct competition. If we were to consider the novel in terms of the triangular relationships of mimetic desire, in addition to the two examples of external mediation (the one involving Don Alvaro, which is predicated on *Don Juan Tenorio;* the other involving Don Fermín, which takes as its model Santa Teresa's desire for a mystic spiritual union), there is the internal mediation, which is constituted as the rivalry between the priest and the local Don Juan. Moreover, there is an articulation of the mediation of desire itself, between the masculine, phallic desire found in *Don Juan Tenorio* and the feminine, nonphallic *jouissance* of Santa Teresa.

The power of the opposition between the masculine and the feminine, Don Juan and Santa Teresa, delineates the two extremes of desire in *La Regenta.* Ana's initiation into the *jouissance* or pleasure of mystic contemplation occurs early in the novel, prior to her first contact with Don Alvaro or to her marriage to Don Víctor. Yet, in direct contrast to Francesca and Doña Inés, it is not the writing of a masculine other, of a Galeotto, that induces her rapture. Rather, it is her own poetry, her own voice, that brings her closer to a mystical union with the Logos. In a retrospective presentation of a scenario that approximates an erotically mystic moment, the young Ana climbs a nearby hill and, in the fullness of the experience of the natural world around her, senses a divine presence that inspires her to write: "Cuando todavía el pensamiento seguía dictando a borbotones, tuvo la mano que renunciar a seguirle, porque el lápiz ya no podía escribir; los ojos de Ana no veían las letras ni el papel, estaban llenos de lágrimas" ["Her mind was still pouring forth words, when her hand had to decline to follow because the pencil could write no more. Ana's eyes saw neither letters nor paper, they were full of tears"] (1:210; 96).

So overcome is Ana that she falls ill. At this point, Ana's poetry creates a small scandal in Vetusta. To write is "una cosa hombruna" ["a mannish thing"] (1:232; 112), and "en una mujer hermosa es imperdonable el vicio de escribir" ["in a beautiful woman, writing is an unpardonable vice"] (1:234; 113). Indeed, we could say that the distinction between Santa Teresa and Don Juan is one of self-inscription as opposed to being inscribed, since it is, once again, a question of roles: "las mujeres deben ocuparse en más dulces tareas; las musas no escriben, inspiran" ["women should occupy themselves in gentler tasks, the Muses don't write, they inspire"] (1:232; 112). Furthermore, Ana's ecstatic response to the writing of poetry corresponds to her attacks of hysteria; the mystic experience she undergoes is curiously similar to what is referred to throughout the novel as Ana's "illness," which, oddly enough, is attributed by Visitación to the desires of men:

> ¡Cómo se ríe cuando está en el ataque! Tiene los ojos llenos de lágrimas, y en la boca unos pliegues tentadores, y dentro de la remonísima garganta suenan unos ruidos, unos ayes, unas quejas subterráneas; parece que allá dentro se lamenta el amor siempre callado y en prisiones. . . . Cualquiera diría que en los ataques tiene pesadillas, y que rabia de celos o se muere de amor. . . . Ese estúpido de don Víctor con sus pájaros y sus comedias . . . no es un hombre. Todo esto es una injusticia; el mundo no debía ser así. Y no es así. Sois los hombres los que habéis inventado toda esa farsa. (1:331)

> [How she laughs when she's having an attack! Her eyes fill with tears, and she puckers her lips in the most enticing way, and from that lovely, lovely throat of hers come such sounds, such cries, like underground laments—it's as if Love, always kept down and in chains, were moaning away in there. . . . During her attacks you'd think she was having nightmares, and going mad with desire, or dying of love. That idiot Don Víctor with his birds and his plays . . . he isn't a man at all. It's all so unfair, life shouldn't be like that. And it isn't like that. All this farce is just an invention of you men. (179)]

Mystic ecstacy *or* hysterical attacks, woman is destined to play a role in the "farse" invented by men.[11] Thus, the function of woman, as an inspiration, is to exist as the necessary yet secondary element in an equation involving three terms: to exist between two men, between families, between an author and the literary text. Woman is always the projection of masculine desire and in service to that desire.

The subordinate position of women notwithstanding, Ana Ozores *is* La Regenta, the protagonist of Clarín's novel. To return to our initial question, How can a novel deal with a "lack" that is necessary but not essential in the rigorously masculine and patriarchal world portrayed here? Because she exists as a demonstration of the extent to which the distinctions between the masculine and the feminine, the carnal and the spiritual, the options offered by Don Alvaro and Don Fermín, are corrupted by the overwhelming power of social organization in which *all* desire in the novel is masculine. The inclusion of *Don Juan Tenorio* as a subtext for *La Regenta* makes this all the more clear. The feminine cannot but be subsumed by the masculine, in much the same way that Don Fermín taints the aura of spirituality that surrounds him with the poison of his own urgent sexuality.

   Indeed, de Pas's role as a seducer, as a Don Juan figure in the novel, should not be underestimated. In a social and ideological sense, his situation within the hierarchy of the Church signals his crucial function as one who regulates and oversees the social roles of various individuals, particularly since the Magistral is confessor to a number of Vetusta's most prominent female citizens. But *all* of Don Fermín's dealings with women are directed toward drawing them into the social fabric of patriarchal society even as they are tinged with hints of erotic energy. For example, when he tutors the young girls in the catechism, de Pas reveals both their role as woman to them and his own possessive voluptuousness in regard to one of the students to the novel's readers: "Era la obediencia ciega de la mujer, hablando; el símbolo del fana-

---

11. Similar sentiments can be found in Clarín's *Su único hijo*. The director of an opera company, Mochi, controls his female star, Serafina, and serves much as her pimp; the narrator comments, "Always serene, always smiling, but ferocious and cruel at heart, Mochi made his friend [Serafina] understand that the tolerance of the master would continue, and that it was indispensable for balancing the company's budget" (*Su único hijo* 123). Likewise, in her musings on her husband Bonis's conduct, Emma recalls that social organization itself is the invention of men: "Suddenly she recalled some of the theories . . . that marriage was conventional and that jealousy and honor were conventional, things that were invented by men to organize what they called society and the State" (214–15).

tismo sentimental, la iniciación del *eterno femenino* en la eterna idola-
tría. El Magistral, con la boca abierta, sin sonreír ya, con las agujas de
las pupilas erizadas, devoraba a miradas aquella arrogante amazona
de la religión" ["What was speaking there was the blind obedience of
woman: the symbol of sentimental fanaticism, the initiation of the
eternal feminine into eternal idolatry. The canon-theologian's face was
serious again, his mouth was open, his pupils were sharp as needles.
He was devouring with his gaze that arrogant amazon of religion"] (2:
202–3; 482). As Lou Charnon-Deutsch points out in her extremely
perceptive discussion of *La Regenta*, "for all its appearances, the catechism class is not a rite of initiation into a man's world, the world
described in the first two chapters of the novel, but rather instruction
in the art of mediocre, monotonous speech and male idolatry" (83–84).
In other words, the catechism does not *empower* a woman by giving her
speech, by allowing her to enter into the world of men; it is a means of
instructing her in her subordinate role in patriarchal society.

Even more telling are the relationships between de Pas and the
characters in the novel named Teresa, specifically his servant-girl
Teresina, with whom it seems that he maintains covert sexual relations, and Rosa Carraspique, or Sor Teresa, a young woman who has
entered the convent under his tutelage. On the one hand, Teresina
supplies de Pas with a carnal version of Santa Teresa. She satisfies
various sensual whims, such as when, with Doña Paula away collect-
ing rents and debts in the country, the Magistral and Teresina share
breakfast: "Don Fermín, risueño, mojaba un bizcocho en chocolate;
Teresa acercaba el rostro al amo, separando el cuerpo de la mesa;
abría la boca de labios finos y muy rojos, con gesto cómico sacaba más
de lo preciso la lengua, húmeda y colorada; en ella depositaba el
bizcocho don Fermín, con dientes de perlas lo partía la criada, y el
señorito se comía la otra mitad. Y así todas las mañanas" ["Don
Fermín smiled and dipped a sponge finger into the hot chocolate.
Teresa brought her face close to her master, moving her body away
from the table as she did so, and parted her delicate, scarlet lips.
Then, with a comical gesture, she stuck out her moist red tongue
rather more than was necessary, and upon it Don Fermín placed the
sponge finger. The servant girl bit into it with teeth of pearl, and the
master ate the other half. This was what happened every morning"]
(2:231; 501). It is important to observe in passing that the servant-girl
is here called Teresa and not by her diminutive, which is more com-
monly used throughout the novel. Also, the physical contact between
the priest and the servant-girl is *suggested* but not explicitly *described*. But most significant, of course, is the mere fact of this coyly

sexual type of tease and that it is an ongoing aspect of the relationship between the Magistral and Teresina.

On the other hand, Sor Teresa fulfills a spiritual role in relation to
Don Fermín. The effect of this is to show how the supposedly feminine
model of desire as represented by Santa Teresa is indeed subsumed and
controlled by the desire of men. There is, therefore, in the world of *La
Regenta,* no feminine model of desire that stands apart from the masculine other. Everything is contingent on masculine models of desire
whereby the feminine exists only as a projection of the desires of men.
In this context, Santa Teresa inevitably becomes like Don Juan's Doña
Inés, the text of seduction and salvation, which is most evident in the
cluster of chapters in the second phase of the novel that deal first, with
the deaths of Sor Teresa and Santos Barinaga, and second, with the
conversion of the local atheist Pompeyo Guimarán and with Ana's
participation in the Good Friday procession.

Because Sor Teresa dies from an illness contracted in the convent
that she entered at de Pas's behest, her death is universally attributed
to him by the Vetustans, who discuss "la *influencia deletérea* del Magistral y . . . la muerte de sor Teresa" ["the canon-theologian's deleterious influence and Sister Teresa's death"], going so far as to remark that
Don Fermín is "un vampiro espiritual, que chupa la sangre de nuestras
hijas" ["a spiritual vampire, sucking our daughters' blood"] (2:239;
506). To this stain on his honor must be added de Pas's *perceived* role in
the death of Santos Barinaga. Prior to the arrival of the Magistral and
his mother in Vetusta, Barinaga owned a shop supplying religious
items to the local churches. Forced out of business by competition from
La Cruz Roja, so impoverished and embittered is Barinaga, he dies
outside the doctrine of the Church and must be interred without ceremony. Though Barinaga was not himself important in the world of
Vetusta, his death seems to confirm the general disrepute into which de
Pas has fallen: "Aquel pobre don Santos había muerto como un perro
por culpa del Provisor, había renegado de la religión por culpa del
Provisor, había muerto de hambre y sin sacramentos por culpa del
Provisor" ["That poor man Don Santos had died like a dog, and it was
the vicar-general's fault; he had renounced religion, and it was the
vicar-general's fault; he had died of hunger and without the sacraments, and it was the vicar-general's fault"] (2:267; 526). Don Fermín
becomes an "assassin" (2:258; 520).

The deaths of these two characters in the twenty-second chapter
constitute a serious blow to the prestige and influence of the Magistral.
But this does not mean that he has been vanquished by Vetusta. In the
twenty-sixth chapter, de Pas succeeds in reclaiming his position, forc-

ing his enemies to admit that "¡El papel Provisor sube!" ["The vicar-
general's stock is rising!"] (2:349; 583). Reflecting the fact that he is a
business, Don Fermín's stock rises when Pompeyo Guimarán converts
to the faith on his deathbed, insisting that he will confess only "con
ayuda del señor Don Fermín; tengo motivos poderosos para exigir esto,
son voces de mi conciencia" ["with the help of Señor don Fermín. I have
powerful reasons for demanding this, the voice of my conscience"]
(2:346; 580).

More significant, however, is the Magistral's success in persuading
La Regenta to take part in the Good Friday procession. Dressed in a
simple purple tunic, Ana will march, in an imitation of Santa Teresa
who founded the Discalced Carmelites, barefoot through the streets of
Vetusta. This in itself scandalizes the town—and creates no end of
embarrassment for Don Víctor—but in an erotic key. While Ana walks
behind a statue of the Virgin, the entire town "se la devoraba con los
ojos" ["devoured her with their eyes"]; and "Obdulia estaba pálida de
emoción. Se moría de envidia. '¡El pueblo entero pendiente de los pasos,
de los movimientos, del traje de Ana, de su color, de sus gestos . . . ! ¡Y
venía descalza! ¡Los pies blanquísimos, desnudos, admirados y compa-
decidos por multitud inmensa!' Esto era para la de Fandiño el bello
ideal de la coquetería" ["Obdulia was pale with emotion and dying of
envy. 'The eyes of the whole town riveted on Ana's steps, her movements, her clothes, her colour, the look on her face! And she was barefoot! Her feet, naked and as white as white, admired and pitied by the
immense crowd!' For Obdulia Fandiño this was the perfect ideal of
coquetry"] (2:360–61; 590). As for Don Fermín, the degradation of Ana
becomes the exaltation of the Magistral and of his power:

> iba [Ana] pregonando su gloria. . . . "El era el amo de todo
> aquello. El, a pesar de las calumnias de sus enemigos había
> convertido al gran ateo de Vetusta haciéndole morir en el seno
> de la Iglesia; él llevaba allí, a su lado, prisionera con cadenas
> invisibles a la señora más admirada por su hermosura y gran-
> deza de alma en toda Vetusta. . . . él descalzaba los más floridos
> pies del pueblo y los arrastraba por el lodo . . . allí estaban,
> asomando a veces debajo de aquel terciopelo morado, entre el
> fango . . ." (2:367)

> [she (Ana) was there to proclaim his glory. . . . "He was the mas-
> ter of all that. He, in spite of his enemies' slander, had converted
> the great atheist of Vetusta and made him die in the bosom of
> the church; and now he was leading forth, as his prisoner in

invisible chains, the lady who was most admired in all Vetusta
for her beauty and her spiritual superiority. . . . he bared the
most select pair of feet in town and dragged them through the
mire—there they were, showing now and then beneath that
purple velvet, in the slime." (595)]

In Santa Teresa, then, Ana finds yet another means by which she is
drawn into playing a role in the world of men.[12] In a contrary sense,
when Ana *does* stop reading the works of the mystics, de Pas senses
that his influence over La Regenta is waning (2:434; 640). Finally, Ana
gives up the good fight and, as if fulfilling Obdulia's prophecy that "la
Regenta será como todas" ["I'm quite sure the judge's wife is the same
as other women"], she admits, "Mi salud . . . exige que yo sea como
todas" ["My health . . . demands that I be like other women"] (2:420;
630). Indeed, throughout the novel Ana has been trying to become
"like" other women. First, she attempts to become like Don Fermín's
beatas. Ana, "resuelta a huir de los extremos, a ser *como todo el mundo,*
insistió en seguir a las *demás beatas* en todos sus pasos" ["determined
to avoid extremes, to be the same as everybody else, she persisted in
following in the footsteps of all the other religious fanatics"] (2:140;
440). Later, of course, she succumbs to Don Alvaro and becomes like
Visitación and Obdulia, who safely remarks at the novel's end, "Todas
somos iguales" ["All we women are the same"] (2:525; 707) when Ana
realizes that "La visión de Dios . . . Santa Teresa . . . Todo aquello
había pasado para no volver" ["The vision of God, St Teresa . . . all that
had passed away never to return"] (2:532; 712).

Ultimately, all that is visionary in *La Regenta,* all that would accrue
to woman, man notwithstanding, is systematically purged during the
course of the novel. Throughout, Ana is subjected to the perversely
proprietary scrutiny of men, as when Celedonio spies on her in the
garden of her home from the cathedral tower in imitation of de Pas
(1:104–5, 2:102; 28, 415), which confirms that to exist in this world is to
exist within the purview of the phallus, be it the law of the Father or
the spyglass of the Magistral. If Ana Ozores, at the beginning of the
text and in the recapitulation of her life in the opening chapters, carries within her the possibility of some type of self-sustaining or redemp-
tive force—in psychoanalytic terms, the possibility of a mystical

12. See Valis's discussion of Santa Teresa and Ana's mysticism, in which emphasis is
placed on the sickly nature of such desire (*The Decadent Vision* 97–102). This is clearly
another example in the novel of the privileging of masculine desire over feminine
jouissance.

jouissance—by the time that Clarín's narration draws to a close, La Regenta has been reduced to silence and to the ultimate marginality accorded women by a patriarchal society. She cannot exist even in relation to the masculine other, because she is dependent on the hybrid Frígilis, whose human fragility allows for him to care for her, social values aside.

Clarín has thus answered the question "What does a woman want?" even less sympathetically than Lacan. Instead of a metaphorical shrug of the shoulders, the flippant equivalent of "Who knows?" Clarín answers with the monumentally yet classically ambiguous "Who cares?" Both question *and* answer, interrogative *and* statement of fact, *La Regenta* addresses the status of woman and her desires in nineteenth-century Spanish society and demonstrates the extent to which an escape from the strictures of patriarchy is unpracticable. Even worse is the way in which the feminine is first explicitly excluded and then implicitly condemned. Unlike the protagonists of *Anna Karenina, Effi Briest,* and *Madame Bovary,* La Regenta experiences only a social death, and is therefore denied any possibility of the escape that is implied in the (pseudo)heroic deaths of her literary companions. With respect to Emma, Charnon-Deutsch astutely comments on how woman is consigned to a life of abject marginality:[13]

> Although predictably she is in a state of collapse, she does not die like Emma Bovary or the pornographic heroine. Instead she merely ceases to exist as a thinking person. No books, thoughts of religion or hell, no communication with the outside world, not even the consolation of confession is afforded her. She calls to mind the pitiful Isidora [of *La desheredada*], another famous fallen idol, but Ana is even more ostracized than Galdós's Isidora. Her doctor has ordered her to avoid all trauma, all thinking. So in this regard as well, Ana is forced at last to become a woman like any other, stripped of the superior consciousness for which she was admired or loathed, and doomed to a feminine somnolence. (119–20)

13. Others have seen in *La Regenta* a critique of the inferior status of women. Antonio Vilanova, for example, says that "it seems evident that one of the problems that Leopoldo Alas intends to denounce is the monstrous injustice by which a woman of healthy and normal sensuality—whose extraordinary beauty is coveted and desired by all and who is married in the flower of youth to a decrepit old man who treats her as if he were her father—is condemned by religious faith and social morals to a total sexual and affective frustration, which places her physical and mental health at grave risk and which will lead her toward true attacks of hysteria and, in some cases, to the edge of insanity" (82).

To be sure, the marginality of the protagonist and heroine of the novel as it is effected by the narrator and author of *La Regenta* corresponds to the marginalizing and patriarchal tendencies of the psychoanalytic theories of Freud and Lacan as well as to the anthropological and literary theories, broadly speaking, of René Girard (see Moi). In this way, novelistic discourse of the nineteenth century, psychoanalysis as an outgrowth of nineteenth-century culture and thought, and Girard's theories, as examples of a twentieth-century extrapolation of these two traditions, reveal themselves to be firmly entrenched in the patriarchy of Western culture. Luce Irigaray says of Freud and his theories of women:

> Now Freud is describing an actual state of affairs. He does not invent female sexuality, nor male sexuality either for that matter. As a "man of science," he merely accounts for them. The problem is that he fails to investigate the historical factors governing the data with which he is dealing. And, for example, that he takes female sexuality as he sees it and accepts it as a *norm*. That he interprets women's sufferings, their symptoms, their dissatisfactions, in terms of their individual histories, without questioning the relationship of their "pathology" to a certain state of society, of culture. As a result, he generally ends up resubmitting women to the dominant discourse of the father, to the law of the father, while silencing their demands. (*This Sex* 70)

I would suggest that there are significant parallels between and among Freud, Clarín, and the others discussed here. Clarín acts much as Irigaray says that Freud acts, indeed much as Don Juan acts: Clarín ends up resubmitting Ana to the dominant discourse of the father, to the law of the father, while silencing her demands.

We could say that Ana Ozores attempts to become, in Jacques Derrida's terms, an affirmative woman, one who negates both falsehood and truth, in fact, one who negates all such oppositions to arrive at affirming the possibility of both presence and absence, possession and lack, the active and the passive (*Spurs* 97–100, passim). For Sarah Kofman, this is the "third woman," neither hysteric nor narcissist like the "first" and "second" women, but an incarnation of the refusal of Freudian bisexuality, an incarnation of undecidability.[14] In this sense,

14. See as well Berg's insightful discussion of the "third woman" in her essay on Kofman and Irigaray (18–20). See also Kristeva, and Cornell and Thurschwell. Labanyi appears to suggest something similar to the "third woman" when she speaks of Ana in

Ana is the protagonist, and the *only* protagonist, of *La Regenta*. She stands at the center of the text, being fulfilled, of course, by seduction and *Don Juan Tenorio*, being filled by the desire that circulates around her, being inscribed in the drama that is life in Vetusta. Yet, and more important, Ana serves not only as a receptacle, but also as an enclosure, the definitive form of the novel that Clarín wrote. She is at one and the same time excess and lack, presence and absence, that which fills and is filled. Because she is La Regenta and *La Regenta,* because she reflects and refracts the personalities and the texts of the personalities contained in the novel, because she serves as the focal point for a variety of narrative strategies, she reveals herself—and the novel—to be surprisingly modern: her indecision becomes her "lack" of choice, becomes what some would call the elusive undecidability of the text.

Is it possible, however, to sustain the notion of undecidability in terms of *La Regenta* given the overwhelming condemnation of the novel's protagonist? I think not. Undecidability is, in effect, a philosophical term drawn into the arena of literary criticism as a means of refusing to make a decision with respect to literary meaning. Literary applications of the term itself derive in large part from Derrida's use, which in turn draws on Gödel's use of the term in his studies of "metamathematics." As Michael Ryan puts it in an attempt to reconcile Derridean deconstruction with nondoctrinaire Marxism, "what allows any complex system to be complete also seems to render it incomplete in one move." In other words, "the system is necessarily 'undecidable' because it generates elements that can be proved both to belong to the system and not to belong at the same time. The axiomatic system is necessarily incomplete." This means that to search for the *one* principle that will define a system is to discover that the "master" principle is itself part of the selfsame system, which "simply generates another metalevel, which requires accounting for an infinite regress" (17).

In the most extreme and extensive instance of reading *La Regenta* as an ambiguous or undecidable novel, Stephanie Sieburth remarks that "structural coherence, taken to an extreme, can produce ambiguity rather than clarity, and that, countering the text's remarkable process of ordering, there is an equally strong tendency toward what might be called 'entropy of meaning.' " For Sieburth, this "entropy of meaning" stems from the fact that *La Regenta* is "a presentation of multiple

---

terms of confusion and as a hybrid. Undecidability has been an important recent topic in critical discussion of the novel; in particular, see Valis's "Order and Meaning," and Sieburth, "Interpreting *La Regenta*" and *Reading* La Regenta.

versions of its own plot, of its reading and of its writing," all of which means that the novel functions as a sort of *mise en abîme*. Although, according to Sieburth, a *mise en abîme* can allow for moments of clarity, the effect in *La Regenta* is otherwise, since the "narration tends to break down into a mass of fragments which may be juxtaposed with one another, and question each other. The *mise en abîme* undermines the unity of the text." Finally, every "segment of the text may be read on a linear part of this plot, or as a reflection or quotation of another segment. . . . *La Regenta*'s greatness, then, arises from the double motivation of each of its elements, and from the balance achieved between the mimetic and self-reflexive tendencies of the text, which allow neither reading to overpower the other" ("Interpreting *La Regenta*" 275, 282, 291).[15]

What in philosophical discussions becomes an issue of "truth" or the "ground" of the philosophical question itself is here refocused as an opposition between mimesis and self-reflexivity, which is not to say that questions of representation are insignificant. In fact, and as Tobin Siebers incisively notes, "Linguistic undecidability really amounts to a Romantic strategy to confront what is perceived to be the differentiating capabilities of literature and language. It tries to turn a dangerous element into one that is self-reflexive and self-destructive in the hope that what is violent and threatening in language will define itself without any effort on our part" (*The Ethics of Criticism* 39). In this way, literary undecidability becomes ethically and morally suspect; it constitutes a kind of critical *méconnaissance,* a motivated misrecognition of the profound moral implications of literature and language in society.

I have been suggesting that *La Regenta* is "undecidable" only as long as meaning is held in abeyance. But is, in fact, the meaning ambiguous? In the final paragraphs of the novel, La Regenta approaches the Magistral's confessionary and waits for him to call her. Instead of hearing Ana, however, Don Fermín bolts from the confessionary, gestures threateningly toward La Regenta and then rushes from the chapel, whereupon she falls to the marble floor in a faint. Celedonio, the effeminate acolyte from the first chapter of the novel finds her when he goes to close the chapel:

> Celedonio sintió un deseo miserable, una perversión de la perversión de su lascivia: y por gozar un placer extraño, o por

15. These issues are treated extensively in Sieburth's *Reading* La Regenta, of which the article "Interpreting *La Regenta*" is just a part.

probar si lo gozaba, inclinó el rostro asqueroso sobre el de la Regenta y le besó los labios.

Ana volvió a la vida rasgando las nieblas de un delirio que la causaba náuseas.

Había creído sentir sobre la boca el vientre viscoso y frío de un sapo. (2:537)

[A wretched desire stirred in Celedonio: a perversion of his perverted lust. To enjoy a strange pleasure, or perhaps to discover whether he would enjoy it, he bent over and brought his vile face close to the face of the judge's wife and kissed her mouth.

Ana returned to life, overcome by nausea and tearing at the mists of delirium.

She had thought that she had felt on her lips the cold and slimy belly of a toad. (715)]

The horrifying image with which the novel ends leaves little doubt as to Ana's status in the text.[16] From serving as the "obliging prop" for Don Fermín's and Don Alvaro's fantasies, from allowing herself to be degraded by her two suitors both spiritually and morally, Ana becomes the perfect object of masculine desire: alive yet unconscious, she serves as an object of sensual experimentation for the repulsive Celedonio. Far from being ambiguous or undecidable, *La Regenta* is explicitly condemnatory of Ana's role in Vetusta. To be sure, *no* woman is presented in this text in a positive sense, but the process by which La Regenta is made to be like the other women corresponds to the pattern discernible in the dramas treating Don Juan and his exploits. The "lessons" that Ana Ozores "learns" have precisely to do with *how* she functions in society, *how* she fulfills, and must go about fulfilling, the desires of the men around her.

In terms of psychological presentation in the novel, then, the shift of focus from the seducer to the seduced openly demonstrates the deleterious effects that desire has on women in patriarchal society. But this shift in focus does nothing to obviate the positive benefits that accrue to seducers as individuals and to society as a whole. As is the case, for example, in *El burlador de Sevilla,* desire is acceptable and operative only in the domain of men. Ana's imploring of Don Alvaro that he swear eternal love—"Para siempre, Alvaro, para siempre, júramelo"

16. On the last sentence of the novel see Valis, "Sobre la última frase." On the reference to the toad, see John W. Kronik.

["For ever, Alvaro, for ever, swear it"] (2:449; 651)—goes against the pattern of masculine desire: in *La Regenta,* women pass from man to man in response to the desires of men. Although it is possible to read the novel as a bitter condemnation of patriarchal society, it is, I think, a mistake to do so given the harsh treatment accorded Ana. *La Regenta* is, therefore, layered yet unequivocal in its meaning: woman must indeed be a prop for the fantasies of men, and, in the end, nothing more.

With respect to questions of honor, seduction, and language as they relate to Don Juan and to his role in society, *La Regenta* clearly articulates the ways in which masculine desire exploits women not merely for its own pleasure but for material gain and power as well. In this sense, seduction as a kind of linguistic facility or gift serves as a tool in what can be called the "will to power," particularly since language serves as the arbiter of all of these relationships. Even if this type of seduction most obviously benefits the individual, within a market-oriented economy and patriarchal culture the individual "will to power" is construed as *socially* beneficial. *La Regenta* presents us, therefore, with a dark vision of the world, with the potentially destructive nature of the seduction of words, with the insidious force of individual honor and desire when they act in concert with social ends. Although we as readers might be able to reject some of the conclusions at which the novel seems to arrive, the narrative presentation is absolute. The options available to those who would recuperate *La Regenta* as an open work, ambiguous in its meaning, are few.

The Psychology of Forbidden Fruit in *Dulce y sabrosa*

> *Flérida, para mí dulce y sabrosa*
> *más que la fruta del cercado ajeno . . .*
> —*Garcilaso de la Vega,* Egloga III

> *rara es la fruta que llega a los labios de su legítimo poseedor sin que la hayan picoteado los pájaros.*
> —*Jacinto Octavio Picón,* Dulce y sabrosa

Clarín's contemporary Jacinto Octavio Picón wrote several works that might be considered in the tradition of Don Juan's story, among them *Juan Vulgar* (1885), which is studied in this context by Ignacio-Javier López (67–71), and *Juanita Tenorio* (1910). Yet it is Picón's *Dulce y sabrosa*—described by Emilia Pardo Bazán as "an extensive

commentary on Ovid's *Ars amandis* [*sic*]" (54)—that most openly derives from and comments on the tradition and nature of the *burlador* or
trickster. Neither a retelling of Don Juan's story nor a novel that relies
on earlier texts for specific aspects of character and plot, *Dulce y
sabrosa* moves at least one step beyond previous works and offers a
portrayal of a bourgeois seducer who, in a sense, leaves his donjuanesque past behind him. This is not to say, however, that Picón's
Don Juan succeeds in moving beyond the confines of the character as
traditionally conceived. Despite the charming presentation of the relationship between this bourgeois Don Juan and his principal victim,
Cristeta Moreruela, there is indeed a darker side to the novel, albeit
one that tends to remain in the shadow of the wit and style of the
narration.

The comments of two of Picón's recent critics reveal the ambivalence
at work here. According to Gonzalo Sobejano:

> The manner in which the story is told is charming, but it consti-
> tutes a negative testimony as to the type of society in which such
> cases of seduction and abandonment occur. In that society,
> woman is, for the fancier of virgins, a coveted fruit that is bitten
> into and, once bitten, no longer excites desire until it reappears
> in another's garden. Woman has to win her man by deploying a
> humiliating strategy. Cristeta is, therefore, another victim of
> her society. (Introducción, *Dulce y sabrosa* 28–29)

Yet Sobejano sums up his assessment of *Dulce y sabrosa* by noting that
it is "a rather amusing narration" (57); and he ends his introduction to
the novel by citing parts of some of the negative nineteenth-century
reviews that stressed the immoral nature of Picón's best-known work
(57–58). Likewise, Noël M. Valis remarks of Picón's novels in general
that "the reality masked by his stylistic charms is far more bitter and
harsh than one might at first reading discern"; and of *Dulce y sabrosa*
in particular, she asks, while reflecting on the end of the novel, "Is this
simply nineteenth- (and twentieth-) century male domination of the
historically submissive female? In one sense, probably so. Yet given the
time and place, one couldn't have expected any less from Picón; and as
it is, we've gotten much more." But, playing on the notion of "sweet and
savory" fruit, Valis also characterizes *Dulce y sabrosa* as "a delectable
work" (*The Novels of Jacinto Octavio Picón* 11, 165, 142).

The ambivalence apparent in the comments of these critics—the
acknowledgment of the quality of the novel and the concomitant admission of certain darker aspects of the text—is what makes *Dulce y*

sabrosa such an interesting work in an examination of Don Juan. It is precisely in the discrepancy between "stylistic charms" and the "bitter and harsh reality" that the real message of Picón's novel is to be found, perhaps not Picón's message, but the implicit message that the text bears. Although not so startlingly violent as Galdós's *Doña Perfecta* or so openly dystopian as Clarín's *La Regenta, Dulce y sabrosa* presents us with crucial insights into the psychology of Don Juan and his effects on women, and these observations coincide with those found in the other literary texts studied thus far. In my own analysis of *Dulce y sabrosa,* I shall follow the lead of previous critics, especially Sobejano and Valis, but I shall also try to bring into greater relief the message that Don Juan inevitably bears. I shall focus on the play of masculine and feminine differences in the novel, and on various concepts and phrases that recur with haunting regularity. In this way, I shall demonstrate the skill with which Picón worked *with* and *within* the traditional story of Don Juan as well as the inexorable recapitulation of all that the *burlador* represents.

Like *La Regenta, Dulce y sabrosa* is an attempt to come to grips with the enigma that is woman, particularly as she functions in response to male desire. In an extensive dream sequence near the end of the novel, Don Juan formulates the question as follows: "Entre tantas [distintas mujeres], ¿cuál es la dispensadora de la dicha, cuál la verdadera mujer? ¡Nadie lo sabrá nunca!" ["Among all these different women, which administers happiness, which is the real woman? Nobody will ever know!"] (339). Put in these terms, the masculine dilemma becomes clear: when there are so many women and types of women, it is difficult, impossible even, to choose between and among them all. Don Juan's response to this dilemma is entirely to be expected. Why should men have to choose?

By means of a lengthy flashback, Picón's novel tells the story of the relationship between Juan de Todellas and Cristeta Moreruela, he a wealthy seducer of all types of women, she an orphan, raised by her lower-class aunt and uncle, who becomes a showgirl in a second-rate theater. Although assailed by many potential suitors, the beautiful Cristeta does not succumb to any of them. None offer the one thing essential to her conception of a relationship, love: "instintivamente consideraba su hermosura complemento de su corazón: quien no poseyese éste, no disfrutaría de aquélla" ["she instinctively considered her beauty to be a complement to her heart: whoever did not possess the latter would not enjoy the former"] (103). Eventually, it is Don Juan who manages to convince Cristeta that he is sincere in his attentions, and she lets herself fall in love with him. The situation plays itself out as Don Juan's seductions usually do: Don Juan gets what he wants and he abandons Cristeta, though not without some remorse and guilt on his part. As recompense, he leaves Cristeta a check for 5,000 pesetas.

Rather than end his story here, Picón begins at this point; and he writes a different novel, showing how the abandoned woman reconquers her Don Juan. Cristeta takes the money and uses it to create an elaborate fiction designed to make her former lover believe that she is now either the wife or lover of a man named Martínez and that she has a small son that might or might not be the child of Don Juan. The strategy is obvious. Believing Cristeta to be forbidden fruit, Don Juan will want to possess her again; and he does. So skillfully does Cristeta construct this elaborate drama and so carefully does she play her part—almost as if she were performing in a drama (Valis, *The Novels of Jacinto Octavio Picón* 159–64)—that Don Juan is driven to distraction. Finally, because he simply cannot bear the thought that she does not love and belong to him alone, he goes so far as to offer to marry Cristeta when she reveals her intricate plan of reconquest. But Cristeta realizes the one "true" law of love, that only forbidden fruit is desirable, and she refuses Don Juan's offer. As the novel ends, Don Juan and Cristeta reach a kind of stalemate. They are reconciled but still at odds: "Callaron, cambiando dos miradas que hacían inútil toda protesta de sinceridad. En la imaginación de ambos surgió la misma idea, formulada en sentido contrario. El pensó: 'Será mi mujer'; y ella se dijo: 'Si me caso le pierdo' " ["They fell silent, exchanging glances that rendered pointless all protests of sincerity. He thought, 'She will be my wife'; and she said to herself, 'If I marry him, I will lose him' "] (349).

Even though this is not a retelling of the traditional story of Don Juan, Picón demonstrates an ample and perspicacious knowledge of the literature treating the *burlador*. *Dulce y sabrosa* is shot through with oblique as well as obvious references to prior literary manifestations of the topic.[17] There are, for example, general references to Don Juan, as when the narrator calls Todellas a "decadent Tenorio" (267). Moreover, there are allusions to specific works, to Tirso's *El burlador de Sevilla,* in the play on the myth of Cupid and Psyche—"¡Luz, luz, quiero verte la cara!" ["Light! Light! I want to see your face!"] (176)— and the strange graphic representation of this myth (276) and in the

17. In fact, Picón wrote a study of the theater of Adelardo López de Ayala in which he discussed, among other works, *El nuevo Don Juan,* which he described as an "inferior work . . . due to the choice of the subject" (*Ayala: estudio biográfico* 31).

references to belatedness (253–54) as well as in the invocation of the *burlador*'s motto par excellence, "¡Quien tal hizo, que tal pague!" ["You shall reap as you sow"] (182). With respect to Zorrilla's *Don Juan Tenorio,* Don Juan's seduction of Cristeta takes place on a sofa (162), an open reference to Zorrilla's renowned scenario in which Doña Inés is seduced; Cristeta gives Don Juan one night to consider their future together—"Toda la noche, te queda toda la noche; ¡piénsalo bien!" ["All night, you have all night. Think it over carefully!"] (332)—recalling Doña Inés's words to Don Juan (lines 3021–23; 524); and Don Juan's dream (335–40) seems to be presented as if through the filter of Zorrilla's drama. Picón goes so far as to describe Don Juan de Todellas's development as a character in terms of these two theatrical works, remarking that "ya no era el temible Burlador de Sevilla, que seduce, logra y desprecia, sino el Tenorio apasionado que se rinde a doña Inés" ["he was no longer the fearful Trickster of Seville, who seduces, possesses, and scorns, but the passionate Don Juan who submits himself to Doña Inés"] (301). Even Clarín's *La Regenta* seems to be evoked, in the long conversation between Don Juan and Cristeta while on individual balconies (130, 133) and in the description of Cristeta's confession of the deception of her lover (347).

There are more complex references as well, among them the description of the kisses between Don Juan and Cristeta, and of those between Don Quintín (Cristeta's uncle by marriage) and his chiseling lover Carola. Twice in reference to Don Juan and Cristeta and once in regard to Don Quintín and Carolina the narrator cites a line from one of Gustavo Adolfo Bécquer's *Rimas.* When Don Juan seduces Cristeta, the narrator says of their first mutual kiss, "Sonó un beso digno del Paraíso" ["A kiss worthy of Paradise was heard"] (163), a phrase that is taken from Bécquer's "Rima XXIX" and that turns up in the dilation on the representation of sex in literature when Picón describes various aspects of love and again when he comments on the affair between Don Quintín and Carola (166, 205). A nineteenth-century retelling of Dante's story of Paolo and Francesca in which the moral implications of the scene have been stripped away, Bécquer's poem reiterates the seductive powers of literature, narrating how the Arthurian lovers' kiss provoked that of Dante's sinners and that of Bécquer and an unnamed woman. In the context of *Dulce y sabrosa* this allusion is exceptionally rich. Picón not only explicitly refers to Dante and Bécquer but to an entire tradition of amatory literature as well as to the seductive power of texts in *Don Juan Tenorio* and *La Regenta.*

These references are, however, but a slight indication of Picón's vast knowledge of the literature pertaining to Don Juan. The description of

Don Juan de Todellas with which *Dulce y sabrosa* opens demonstrates how fine is Picón's familiarity with the topic. The narrator begins by presenting us with his version of Don Juan, "caballero madrileño y contemporáneo nuestro, cuya manía consiste en cortejar y seducir el mayor número posible de mujeres" ["a gentleman from Madrid and our contemporary, whose mania consisted of courting and seducing the greatest possible number of women"] (69). Don Juan's surname is, of course, significant, and doubly so, because "no cabe duda de que Todellas es corruptela y contracción de *Todas-Ellas,* alias o apodo que debió de usar alguno de sus ascendientes" ["there is no doubt that Todellas is a corruption or contraction of 'Todas-Ellas,' 'All-of-Them,' an alias or nickname that one of his forefathers must have used"] (70). Not only does his name identify him, it contains within it the sign that this Don Juan is one of a long line of seducers. Indeed, "él se precia de contar entre sus abuelos al célebre Mañara, y si no dice lo mismo de Tenorio, es por no estar demostrado que en realidad haya existido" ["he boasted of including the celebrated Mañara among his grandfathers, and if he didn't say the same thing about Don Juan Tenorio, it was because it hasn't been proved that he really existed"] (70); and his role in society is precisely that of his predecessors: "No es un seductor vulgar, ni un calavera vicioso, ni un malvado, sino un hombre en-amoradizo que se siente impulsado hacia *ellas,* para iniciarles en los deliciosos misterios del amor, semejante a los creyentes fanáticos, que a toda costa pretenden inculcar al prójimo su fe" ["He is not a common seducer, nor a vicious libertine, nor an evil-doer, but a man constantly falling in love who feels himself impelled toward them, *women,* so as to initiate them into the delicious mysteries of love, like those fanatic believers who, at all cost, try to inculcate in their fellow man their own faith"] (70–71).[18] In other words, Don Juan introduces women to the pleasures of love and teaches women how to act in love in relation to men. As José Ortega y Gasset puts it in terms of Don Juan in general— and in a manner applicable to Picón's version of the *burlador*—"The donjuanesque delight is to be found in witnessing time and again that marvelous scene of feminine transfiguration, that pathetic instant in which the larva becomes, in honor of a man, a butterfly. Once the scene is concluded, the cold grimace returns to the lips of Don Juan, and, leaving the butterfly to burn its recently unfolded wings in the sun, he

18. Miguel de Mañara (1627–79), a historically verifiable figure who lived in Sevilla, is sometimes mentioned in conjunction with the *burlador*. Mérimée drew on the legend for his *Les âmes du purgatoire* as did José de Espronceda for *El estudiante de Salamanca.* On the relation between Don Juan and Miguel de Mañara, see Leo Weinstein 104–18.

turns to another chrysalis" ("Divagación ante el retrato de la marquesa de Santillana," *Obras completas* 2:693). Don Juan is not, therefore, merely a social but also a developmental principle in the world in which he lives.

Of more substantial issues, such as personal beliefs, the narrator says that "Don Juan es deísta, pues dice que sólo la Divinidad pudo concebir y crear la belleza femenina: y es bastante buen cristiano, recordando que Cristo absolvía a las pecadoras y perdonaba a las adúlteras" ["Don Juan is a deist, since he says that only the Divinity could have conceived of and created feminine beauty; and he is a good enough Christian, recalling that Christ absolved sinful women and pardoned adulteresses"] (76). Of course, only women are presented as sinners and adulterers. More to the point, Don Juan is no atheist; he considers himself to be a Christian, which is not to say that he is not somewhat "pagan." Rather than a crucifix at the head of his bed, he has a statue of Eros, who holds a torch in his hands. The narrator explains Don Juan's justification of this touch by saying that, "no pudiendo hallar imagen auténtica del Dios omnipotente, y parecíéndole un poco tristes los crucifijos, ha colocado en su lugar aquella representación del amor, que es la delicia y mantenimiento del mundo" ["not being able to find an authentic image of omnipotent God, and since crucifixes seem a little sad to him, he has hung in its place a portrait of love, which is the delight and sustenance of the world"] (76). Linking together Christianity and Eros, Don Juan dedicates himself to the religion and the art of love, viewing himself as integral to the proper functioning of the way of the world.

The narrator becomes coy when it comes to discussing Don Juan's appearance, and it is here that he introduces a key distinction that will be maintained throughout *Dulce y sabrosa:* "En cuanto al retrato de las prendas físicas de don Juan . . . mejor es no hacerlo; a los lectores poco ha de importarles la omisión, y en cuanto a las lectoras, preferible es que cada una se le figure y finja con arreglo al tipo que más agrade. Baste decir que es simpático, y, aunque sin afeminación ni *dandysmo,* cuidadoso de su persona" ["As for a portrait of Don Juan's physical qualities, it is better to say nothing; for male readers, such an omission will be of little importance, and, as for female readers, it is to be preferred that each one think and imagine him as the type she finds most pleasing. It is enough to say that he is likeable, and, even though not effeminate or a dandy, that he is careful of his appearance"] (76). In a novel that treats the difficult relations between men and women, difference is inscribed in terms of the implied readers, too. In fact, it is asserted that women and men expect different things from a text, need different types of cues. In the case of Don Juan, male readers will not need or want to know what he looks like, and female readers are left to their own fantasies.

In the second chapter, however, in which Cristeta is introduced, the narrator's descriptive strategy is completely otherwise. The chapter heading reads, "En que, para satisfacción del lector, aparece una mujer bonita" ["In which, for the satisfaction of the male reader, a pretty woman appears"] (79). Are these male readers left to imagine what this beautiful woman looks like? Of course not. She is described in lush detail, described as seen by Don Juan as he examines her from head to foot. Next to the narrator's reservation with respect to Don Juan's appearance, this prolix description of Cristeta is all the more significant, particularly because it is a woman *as seen by* a man that is being described here. Don Juan is taking voluptuous possession of Cristeta, albeit visually; we, as readers, are implicitly included in the act. If there is any doubt as to the nature of Don Juan's gaze, the narrator dispels it with references to Cristeta's curvaceous figure, her breasts and thighs as modeled by her clothing. Furthermore, Don Juan does not stop with Cristeta's clothing: he begins to undress her until he can see her in that precise "instant" at which he will be able to judge her ripeness. In this process, woman becomes an object for male scrutiny, and male readers vicariously become Don Juans.

The distinction between the expectations and desires of male and female readers, especially as that distinction translates into the type of narrative presentation employed, is important, since both Cristeta and Don Juan are avid readers. In Cristeta's case, she reads dramas, particularly romantic dramas. These literary texts condition her expectations of reality, above all the reality of the world of the theater of which she is eager to become a part. Once she starts to work as a singer, the narrator tells us about this subculture, contrasting Cristeta's fine illusions with drab reality. He describes the later of the four shows put on during any given day as follows:

> El público que frecuentaba la tercera y cuarta función se componía casi exclusivamente de hombres aficionados a comprar hecho el amor, y de pecadoras elegantes. A última hora se ponían las piezas y zarzuelitas más verdes, y cual si esto les sirviese de aperitivo, era de ver cómo a la salida muchos caballeros, o vestidos de tales, esperaban en la calle la salida de bailarines, coristas y figurantas: por fin, cuando terminado el espectáculo comenzaba la puerta del escenario a vomitar mujeres envueltas en mantones y con toquillas de estambre a la cabeza, cada hom-

bre se llevaba su prójima, que solía ser ajena; alguna, envidiada
de las demás, subía en coche, y ya formadas las parejas, que a
veces en realidad eran tercetos, todos se iban contentos; ellas
haciéndose conquistadas, y ellos imaginando triunfo lo que, a lo
más, era compra. (96)

[The audience that frequented the third and fourth shows was
composed almost exclusively of men who were aficionados of
buying love already prepared, and of elegant, sinful women.
During the last hour the raciest pieces and operettas were presented, and, as if these served as an aperitif, it was a sight at the
end of the evening to see how many gentlemen, or men dressed
as gentlemen, waited in the street for the dancers, chorines, and
extras. Finally, when the show had finished and the stage door
began to vomit women wrapped up in shawls and scarves, each
man took up with his better half, who was usually someone
else's, too. One of the women, envied by the rest, would climb
into a carriage; and now that the couples—in reality, sometimes
threesomes—were formed, everybody left happy. The women
had been conquered and the men imagined a triumph in what
was, in fact, a purchase.]

In the narrator's depiction, the theater, far from being a temple to
beauty and art, becomes a market in which women are bought; and the
crudely gustatory and physical nature of the description alongside the
suggestion of odd numerical combinations only augments the sordid
aura surrounding this world.

The passage just cited confirms what is suggested in the title of the
novel, that, as is traditional in literary treatments of sexual topics,
eating will function as a metaphor for, or prelude to, a sexual relationship. So it is that Cristeta finds that the men in the audience "se la
comían con los ojos" ["ate her with their eyes"] (101), a phrase that is
found elsewhere in the novel (107, 215, 233). Yet she is shrewd enough
to observe the other women around her and to realize that only rarely
are they anything more than a single course, and at times not even
that, but merely a table servant:

A poco de ingresar en el teatro observó Cristeta que a cuantas
compañeras suyas pecaban y se envilecían por codicia, les salía
errado el cálculo. Hoy se entregaban a un calavera rico, mañana
a un señorito achulado, tal noche a un marido ajeno, tal otra a
un pollancón estúpido; y total, alguna cena, algún traje, desem-

peñar a costa de uno lo que había de lucir con otro, y a la postre el rostro ajado y la juventud malbaratada: vida de moza mesonera, trajín constante, pocas propinas y vejez mendiga. (104)

[Shortly after beginning to work in the theater, Cristeta observed that, for all of her fellow showgirls who sinned and degraded themselves with greed, the reckoning came out wrong. Today they would give themselves to a rich cad, tomorrow to a vulgar little señor, that evening to some woman's husband, another night to a stupid dandy. In sum, a little supper, some clothes, get out of hock at the expense of one fellow what was to be worn with another, and, in the end, by the time for dessert, a wrinkled face and misspent youth. In other words, the life of a tavern keeper: constant hustle and bustle, but a few tips, and the old age of a beggar.]

Not surprisingly, every illusion Cristeta has about the theater and about actresses—that they are women "perpetuamente ocupadas en ser grandes señoras, reinas y hasta diosas" ["perpetually occupied in being great ladies, queens, and even goddesses"] (90)—gives way to a much more realistic notion of the theatrical world. Finally, Cristeta admits that "el teatro y el arte que ella se había fingido leyendo dramas y comedias . . . no eran el arte y el teatro que la realidad le presentaba" ["the theater and the art that she had imagined while reading dramas and comedies . . . were not the art and the theater that the real world offered her"] (126). In terms remarkably similar to Ana Ozores's view of things in *La Regenta*, Cristeta "soñó con una vida toda poesía y encanto, y tropezó con una existencia llena de vulgaridad y desilusión" ["dreamed of a life full of poetry and enchantment, and she found an existence full of vulgarity and disillusionment"] (126). Literature leads Cristeta to expect one thing where she finds something completely different.

For his part, Don Juan is familiar, of course, with amatory literature; references are made to his reading of canonical texts, for example, Dante. But his real interest is in reading *women*. In a reaffirmation of Cristeta's status as an object in the novel, as a piece of fruit to be savored, Don Juan, before abandoning his lover, sees Cristeta as a *book*:

Cristeta era el mejor libro de amor que él había leído, el volumen cuyas páginas le proporcionaron goces a la vez más intensos y más plácidos, el más original y nuevo, pues era texto escrito con

admirable ingenuidad, y ejemplar por nadie manoseado: ¡ni
siquiera tenía cortadas las hojas! ¡Qué prólogo tan deleitoso y
lleno de promesas! ¡Qué capítulos tan impregnados de sincera
pasión! ¡Cómo, párrafo tras párrafo, había ido viendo al amor
quedar victorioso de la castidad! . . . Quién leyese luego todo
aquello, ¿sería capaz de apreciarlo? (172)

[Cristeta was the best book of love that he had read, the volume
whose pages had given him pleasures that were, at one and the
same time, intense and peaceful, the most original and newest
book, as the text was written with admirable ingenuity, and this
copy had not been handled by anyone else: the pages weren't
even cut! What a delightful prologue, so full of promises! What
chapters, so impregnated with sincere passion! How was it that,
paragraph after paragraph, he had continued to see love triumph over chastity! . . . Would whoever read the book next be
capable of appreciating it?]

The graphic sexual allegory of a reader taking possession of a book,
cutting the pages and beginning to read, leaves little to the imagination. So insistent is the image of Cristeta as a book that Don Juan
thinks in those terms again after he has left her when he realizes that
he wishes to "reanudar la lectura del poema estúpidamente interrum-
pido" ["renew his reading of the poem that was stupidly abandoned"]
(227). And Cristeta accepts this designation when she asks Don Juan,
somewhat disingenuously, "¿Es decir, que mi obligación era quedarme
toda la vida esperando a que se antojase volver a acordarte de mí, como
se queda un libro en un estante, hasta que su dueño tenga capricho de
volverlo a leer?" ["Which is to say that my obligation was to remain
waiting for a lifetime until it occurred to you to remember me, like a
book on a shelf, which waits until its owner, on a whim, decides to
reread it?"] (296).

Worse than being a screen for the projection of masculine fantasies,
woman, here Cristeta, becomes an object capable of speaking of one
thing only, and only when a man wants to "read" her. This instructively recalls Plato's discussions of written texts in the *Phaedrus*. On
the one hand, "written words . . . seem to talk to you as though they
were intelligent, but if you ask them anything about what they say,
from a desire to be instructed, they go on telling you just the same
thing forever." On the other hand, this composition, written and bound
as a book, "drifts all over the place, getting into the hands not only of

those who understand it, but equally of those who have no business with it; it doesn't know how to address the right people, and not address the wrong. And when it is ill-treated and unfairly abused it always needs its parent to come to its help, being unable to defend or help itself" (275d, e; Hamilton and Cairns 521).[19] Woman, inscrutable, is either silent or says "the same thing forever." She might or might not be understood, is liable to be "ill-treated and unfairly abused" and to have no recourse or protection. Fruit *or* book *or* woman, once enjoyed, all can be set aside, because their use is exhausted, their meaning, limited.

This view of woman as a mere piece of fruit or a book is disturbing, and it is so pervasive in *Dulce y sabrosa* that we must ask what stance the narrator takes on the issue.[20] Clearly, with respect to his male readers, his representation stresses those aspects of the female characters that he thinks men will find titillating. From the outset of the presentation of the female characters, the narrator has linked his gaze to Don Juan's in granting the seducer's perspective the privileged point of view, as in the second chapter when he describes Don Juan's walk in the Retiro: "La temperatura era grata y el paseo estaba muy lucido, como si aquella tarde se hubiesen citado allí las madrileñas más lindas y elegantes, al contrario de otros días, en que parece que se congregan las cursis y feas para amargar*nos* la vida, atormentar*nos* los ojos y hacer*nos* dudar del Todopoderoso" ["The temperature was pleasant and the walk was splendid, as if on that afternoon all of the most beautiful and elegant women in Madrid had arranged to meet there, as opposed to other days, when it seems that the pretentious and ugly women congregate there so as to make life bitter for *us*, to torment *our* eyes, and to make *us* doubt in God"] (80; my emphasis). Don Juan is not the only man interested in women in the novel, in their appearance and effect, as the inclusive pronoun *nos* (us) indicates. The narrator himself is very much involved in this world and seems to side with Don Juan where vulgar and homely women are concerned.

With respect to his female readers, the narrator appears to be offering a cautionary tale and an example of how true love might work in

19. Jacques Derrida's commentary on this dialogue is interesting, particularly in terms of the discussion of the "logos" and the "orphan," which is the written word ("Plato's Pharmacy").

20. This would seem to suggest that literature itself is of slight value, a view to which I doubt Picón would subscribe. However, there are a number of conflicting assessments and valuations in Picón's statements and in his novels, leading one to suspect that almost *any* single position is open to, if not interpretation, speculation.

this world if not in another. He situates Don Juan's and Cristeta's relationship in terms both of Adam and Eve and of future lovers, mentioning the inevitable repetition of words of love, "aquel estupendo y delicioso dúo que por primera vez tuvieron Adán y Eva, y que probablemente sostendrán, pareciéndoles original, el postrer hombre y la última mujer que quedan sobre el haz de la tierra" ["that stupendous and delicious duet begun by Adam and Eve, which will probably be heard from—and thought original by—the last man and woman to remain on the face of the earth"] (131). Yet if the narrator is offering a cautionary tale as to the eternal battle of men and women, the tone he takes in apostrophes directed toward the female readers is, at best, condescending, and, at worse, ironic. Of the first time that Don Juan and Cristeta murmur the night away on the respective balconies of their adjoining rooms, the narrator remarks in a mockingly chivalrous aside, "Sabed, ¡oh tímidas y pudorosas doncellas merecedoras del blanco azahar! que la puerta de comunicación no se abrió aquella noche" ["Know, oh timid and virtuous maidens worthy of the white orange-blossom, that the door between their two rooms did not open that night!"] (131).

Even more telling in this regard is a comparison of the narrator's thoughts on women with those of Don Juan. Don Juan, trying to divine Cristeta's present situation and how she comported herself after he abandoned her, reflects, "Lo cierto era que él [don Juan] había tenido sucesor, y la existencia del niño demostraba que el reemplazo fue rapidísimo. Nunca pudo recordarse con más oportunidad aquello de 'a rey muerto, rey puesto.' ¡Al fin, mujer! Tanta promesa, tanto juramento, y luego . . . Todas son iguales' " ["The fact is that Don Juan must have had a successor, and the existence of the child showed that the replacement was exceptionally quick. Never had he recalled with greater timeliness the adage 'Off with the old and on with the new.' 'When all is said and done: woman! So many promises, so many oaths, and then . . . They're all alike' "] (218). The narrator has this to say about women:

> es que la mujer, por sensual y materialista que sea, tiene en los instantes de dolor una pureza de sentimientos que rara vez brilla en el hombre. (185)

> La mujer es poco dada a pensar; mas cuando piensa despacio, ¡pobre del hombre! (187)

> ¿Dónde mayor alegría para una mujer lista que entrar en pacto contra un hombre? (267)

[woman, however sensual and materialistic she might be, possesses in instants of pain a purity of sentiment that rarely
shines forth in man.

Woman is little given to thought; but when she ponders something carefully, the poor man!

Where is there greater happiness for a smart woman than to
enter into a plot against a man?]

Sensual and materialistic, not given to thinking, conniving: that is
how the narrator describes women in general. Of Cristeta in particular,
the narrator notes that she is "romántica, como casi todas las mujeres
españolas" ["romantic, like almost all Spanish women"] (103). Discussing the battle of wits between Don Juan and Cristeta, he notes of a
possible "chance" meeting between the two: "Hermoso día, pero el piso
demasiado húmedo. Don Juan piensa: 'No irá,' y se queda en casa
leyendo. Cristeta sale. Al fin mujer. Paseo en balde" ["A lovely day, but
the ground is too damp. Don Juan thinks: 'She won't come,' and he
stays at home reading. Cristeta goes out. When all is said and done:
woman. A walk in vain"] (224).

Thus, in his presentation of what Valis describes as "the eternal
quandary of relations between men and women" (*The Novels of Jacinto
Octavio Picón* 166), the narrator, perhaps unavoidably, echoes his Don
Juan and sides with his own kind. But he does so in a way that is both
patronizing and condescending, using language that allows for a confusion of viewpoint. Moreover, I would suggest that there is something in
the very nature of the presentation that insistently upholds the otherness of women as inevitable and that allies the narrator even more
closely with Don Juan and Picón's novel in toto with Don Juan's role in
society.[21] Before considering this aspect of *Dulce y sabrosa,* however, we
ought to look at the narrative counterpoint to the relations between
Don Juan and Cristeta, the bitterly humorous—and fiercely cruel—
presentation of the affair between Cristeta's uncle Don Quintín and
Carola, an aging chorus girl.

21. In this regard it is pertinent to ask whether the narrator's attitude can be attributed to Picón. Despite the fact that Sobejano refers to Picón as being "profeminist"
(Introducción, *Dulce y sabrosa* 27), the author of *Dulce y sabrosa* certainly appeared to be
otherwise. When queried as to his thoughts on the possibility of Emilia Pardo Bazán
taking a chair in the Spanish Royal Academy, Picón tersely said that "women cannot
form part of the Academy [because], first and foremost, we would feel inhibited; we
wouldn't be able to talk freely. . . . There's the lack of freedom in expression—and many
other reasons that oppose such a thing!" (quoted in Valis, *The Novels of Jacinto Octavio
Picón* 202 n. 31).

There is ample evidence in the novel that Don Quintín has been some-what of a lower-class version of Don Juan throughout his life. As Don Quintín is about to become trapped in a flirtation of Don Juan's cre-ation, the narrator rhapsodizes of Don Quintín's amorous past:

> ¡Oh, memoria, qué dulces recuerdos trajiste! ¡Oh, fantasía, cómo los poetizaste! Mozuela que allá en el pobre lugarejo le esperabas en el pajar; sabrosa luna de miel con [su esposa] Frasquita; cocinerilla vencida en la trastienda, en una sofocante siesta de verano; dichosas y felices aventuras, ¡cómo y con qué fuerza surgisteis en la imaginación del estanquero [don Quintín], po-blándola de halagadoras reminiscencias que le inspiraron deseos de nuevos triunfos! (118)

> [Oh, memory, what sweet recollections you brought! Oh, fantasy, how you poeticized them! The young thing there in that humble place awaited you in the hayloft; the savory honeymoon with (his wife) Frasquita; the little cook conquered in the back room of the shop during a suffocating siesta one summer; joyful and happy affairs: how and with what force you surged forth in the imagination of the tobacconist (Don Quintín), peopling it with flattering reminiscences that inspired in him a desire for new triumphs!]

Now in his twilight years, Don Quintín yearns for the opportunity to embark on new amorous conquests.

To be sure, there is some doubt as to whether or not Don Quintín will be able to sustain a steady diet of renewed sexual vitality. After his wife Frasquita has caught him in the flirtation arranged by Don Juan, she bitterly reproaches him in a telling metaphor that again links sex with food: "¡No puedes con la comida en casa, y querías ir de fonda!" ["You can't manage to eat the food given you at home, yet you wanted to go out to eat!"] (147). He who turns down food "at home" obviously ought not to be able to "go out to eat"; Doña Frasquita's words haunt Don Quintín as he sets out in search of one of the chorus girls he knew when Cristeta worked in a theater in Madrid. Yet, with his first good meal under his belt, Don Quintín later decides that, "aunque fuese de tarde en tarde, podía comer de fonda" ["even if it were only from time to time, he could go out to eat"] (156).

The operative distinction here is, of course, between the quality of the food available at home and that available when going out to eat, a difference that the narrator underscores in sexual terms when he details the various meals that Don Quintín provides his wife and his lover:

> En el estanco [en casa] no se comía más que sopa, cocido, ensalada, y de postre fruta, cuando por barata hasta los soldados podían comprarla. La tacañería de Quintín suprimió los buñuelos de Todos los Santos, el besugo de Nochebuena y los panecillos de San Antón; en cambio para su daifa, pavo y perniles se le antojaban poco. . . . Su mayor delicia consistía en obsequiarla [a Carola] con merengues, que luego ambos comían a medias, mordiéndolos al mismo tiempo por opuestos extremos, hasta que, tropezándose las culpables bocas, sonaban escandalosos besos. (205)

> [In the shop (at home), they ate nothing more than soup, stew, salad, and, for dessert, fruit, when it was so cheap that even soldiers could buy it. Don Quintín's stinginess precluded doughnuts on All Saints, sea bream on Christmas Eve, and rolls for Saint Anthony. Yet, for his mistress, turkey and ham struck him as too little. . . . His greatest pleasure consisted of offering her (Carola) meringues, of which they each ate half, biting into them at the same time at opposite ends until, when the guilty mouths touched, scandalous kisses were heard"]

Stingy at home, a sensual spendthrift with Carola, Don Quintín suddenly develops a healthy appetite *and* a taste for sweets. In fact, "a consecuencia de las cenas, y particularmente de los postres, el infeliz no tenía cabeza para nada" ["as a consequence of the suppers, and particularly the desserts, the unhappy man did not have a head for anything"] (204).

These same distinctions are to be found in the respective descriptions of the wife and the mistress. First Carola, the mistress: "Era mujer de cuarenta y tantos años, gruesa, ex-guapa, en buen estado de conservación, aunque algo ajada. . . . Vestía bata flotante de percal claro; no debía de llevar corsé, porque se le notaba el temblor de las carnes libres" ["She was a woman of some forty years, stout, ex-beauty, in a good state of conservation, if somewhat aged. . . . She usually wore a loose robe of threadbare percale; she must not have worn a corset, since the trembling of loose flesh was noticeable"] (150). If a little past her prime, the narrator nevertheless concedes that Carola is well preserved; and as far as Don Quintín is concerned, "Carola no era mujer: era un serrallo" ["Carola was not a woman: she was a concubine"] (194). Doña Frasquita, on the occasion of disrupting Don Quintín's last meal with Carola, is described thus:

Era alta, flaca, barbipeluda, huesosa, sin pecho, recta de caderas; la figura espantable, los ademanes ridículamente trágicos. Venía toda vestida de oscuro, con largo velo a la cabeza, de suerte que, por su traje y catadura, parecía una de aquellas entre brujas y dueñas calderonianas que hace doscientos años servían para arredrar galanes, vigilar mozas y asustar chiquillos. (327)

[She was tall, skinny, bony, with a hairy chin, no bosom or hips; her figure was frightening, her gestures ridiculously tragic. She was dressed totally in black, with a long veil on her head, so that, in her dress and bearing, she seemed like one of those Calderonian characters of 200 years ago, half witch, half *dueña,* that frightened away suitors, watched over young women, and scared children.]

The contrast between the two women could not be more dramatically stark. Who wouldn't prefer Carola to Doña Frasquita, going out to eat to eating at home?

These scenes between Don Quintín and Carola offer a significant counterpoint to the relationship between Don Juan and Cristeta, especially given the catch-phrase "¡No puedes con la comida en casa, y querías ir de fonda!" ["You can't manage to eat the food given you at home, yet you wanted to go out to eat!"]. The opposition between *casa* and *fonda* is one that turns up elsewhere in the novel and eventually forces a reconsideration of the conclusion of *Dulce y sabrosa.* When Don Quintín tries to find out for Cristeta if Don Juan has returned to Madrid, or when he might, he learns that "se plantará aquí [Don Juan] sin avisar, como siempre; luego come unos días de fonda hasta que puede venir Mónica, su cocinera" ["Don Juan will settle here without any warning, as always; then he'll go out to eat for a few days, until Mónica, his cook, can come back"] (200). In other words, Don Juan "goes out to eat," too, as we already knew: the seduction of Cristeta took place in the coastal town of Santurroriaga in the *Fonda de España.* That Cristeta gives herself to Don Juan in a *fonda* or inn raises the question of whether or not Don Juan ever eats "at home," or if he will ever truly *want* to get married and to settle down to a steady diet of home cooking. Perhaps Cristeta is right, therefore, to refuse to marry Don Juan. Yet, by refusing to marry her erstwhile lover, Cristeta becomes, in a sense, *unheim-*

lich, the Freudian uncanny, which is almost, but not quite, *heimlich,* or "homely," familiar.²²

This tendency to cast what is desirable as other, and what is possessed as all too familiar and, thus, undesirable, is, of course, the point of the novel. So pervasive and inevitable is this logic that an entire network of relations fits into this scheme of things: the all too *heimlich* Frasquita, the unknown and desirable Carola, "eating at home," "going out to eat," a schema in which the *unheimlich* always leads the individual home again. In this regard, it is interesting to note that, when Don Juan once again seeks to seduce Cristeta, he is so beside himself that even the delectable food prepared by his cook Mónica fails to tempt him (304–9): what Don Juan cannot get by going out to eat ("de fonda") he does not want at home ("de casa"). Yet this problem of the forbidden fruit also forms the crux of *Dulce y sabrosa* because it raises the specter of how—or if—we are ever to get beyond the otherness that plagues sexual and social relations, the contrary nature that lies at the heart of desire, to arrive at some type of equilibrium.

Certainly the conclusion of the novel suggests that no real equilibrium is possible. When Don Juan offers to marry Cristeta despite the manifest differences in class—and remember that Cristeta herself knows that to think of marriage "sería bobada: don Juan no había de casarse con una comiquilla" ["would be stupid: Don Juan wouldn't marry a showgirl"] (127)—she replies, "¡Eso . . . jamás!" ["That! Never!"] (348). She goes on to sum up the problem in this way, abnegating herself in the process:

> Lo que yo quiero no es tu libertad, sino tu cariño. ¿Casarnos? ¿Para qué? ¿Para darte por seca y rigurosa obligación lo que por

22. In his essay "The Uncanny" (*Standard Edition* 17:217–52), Freud says that "*heimlich* is a word the meaning of which develops in the direction of ambivalence, until it finally coincides with its opposite, *unheimlich. Unheimlich* is in some way or other a subspecies of *heimlich*" (*Standard Edition* 17:226). Bound up with an involuntary repetition, "the uncanny is that class of the frightening which leads back to what is known of old and long familiar" (*Standard Edition* 17:220), which means that the "uncanny is in reality nothing new or alien, but something which is familiar and old-established in the mind and which has become alienated from it only through the process of repression" (*Standard Edition* 17:241). Curiously, Freud links the uncanny with male fear of women, which does tie in, in a psychological sense, with Don Juan's ongoing seduction of women: "It often happens that neurotic men declare that they feel there is something uncanny about the female genital organs. This *unheimlich* place, however, is the entrance to the former *Heim* [home] of all human beings, to the place where each one of us lived once upon a time and in the beginning" (*Standard Edition* 17:246).

libre y complacido albedrío quiero que sea tuyo? ¿Para mermar a la pasión el encanto de la espontaneidad? ¿Por ventura serán entonces más cariñosos tus besos, más prietos tus abrazos? ¿Tendremos mayor firmeza en la confianza ni más brava abnegación en la desgracia? ¿Qué ceremonia, qué rito, qué fórmula ha puesto el Señor por cima de este anhelo con que mi pensamiento quiere volar para hacer nido en tu alma?

. . . .

¿Llevar tu nombre? Bajando está siempre de mi pensamiento a mis labios; mío es aunque no quieras, y al dormirme siento que se me asoma a la boca para guardarte todo el aliento de mi vida. ¡No! tú, libre como el aire; yo esclava, quieta, callada y mansa como el agua eternamente enamorada del cielo que, aun sin darse cuenta de ello, igual refleja los alegres arreboles del alba que las tristes nubes de la tempestad. (348–49)

[What I want isn't your freedom, but your love. Us, marry? For what? So as to give you as a hard and fast obligation what I would have be yours through the happiness of free will? So as to sap the joy of spontaneity from our passion? Will your kisses then, by chance, be more loving, your embraces more firm? Will we be any more secure in our trust or any more ferocious in our abnegation in disgrace? What ceremony, what ritual, what formula has our Maker placed above the longing with which my thoughts wish to fly to you and to nest in your soul?

. . . .

Bear your name? It is always falling from my thoughts to my lips. It is mine, whether you want it to be or not. And when I fall asleep, I feel as if it rests in my mouth, so I can save all of the breath of my life for you. No! You, free as the air. I will be a slave, calm, quiet, and meek, like the water that is eternally enamored of the sun, who, without even realizing it, reflects both the joyful rosiness of dawn and the sad clouds of the storm.]

Don Juan and Cristeta can be together without possessing each other, can continually experience their love spontaneously. But even this is not a solution to the dilemma of relations between the two lovers. As the novel draws to a close, the lovers lapse into silence, each formulating their view, their *contrary* view, of the future. Don Juan is certain that Cristeta will be his wife; Cristeta, fully cognizant of the risk inherent in marriage, is certain that she will lose him. Each is caught up in the relationship in such a way that possession becomes crucial, yet impossible in any binding sense: they are each, therefore, only as good as their word, as what they withhold.

In her burning desire to be with Don Juan, Cristeta becomes a slave, a mere reflection of her lover. She forgoes all legitimate claims that a woman might have over a man she can call her husband, as she recognizes, principally that of his name. The opposition here is clear: there *is* a difference between love and marriage. As Carmen Martín Gaite puts it in terms of the eighteenth century, love "was the domain of passion, of lies, of storms"; marriage is that of

> temperance and virtue. Marriage was made to appear to a woman as holy and beneficial, and she would choose it without vacillating. But it was not possible to confuse the one (love) with the other (marriage): the two were irreconcilable. Love was the desire for freedom, escape, burning passion; marriage, submission, moderation, virtue. Love, in a word, was opposed to virtue. (183)

But Cristeta seems to have things confused. By giving up marriage for freedom and love, she ends up being submissive yet virtuous. To put it another way, Don Juan gets everything that he wants and needs, including his freedom and the passion of love; Cristeta gets—Don Juan, and, at the same time, becomes like a wife, virtuous and submissive. Moreover, if she obtains her goal, she also becomes like one other character in the novel: Carola. Cristeta is absolutely dependent on Don Juan. Even if she has not proven herself to be as endlessly avaricious and self-interested as the chorus girl, she nonetheless schemes in much the same way that Carola does. True, Carola wants only money, while Cristeta wants love. Yet, in the end, both are forced to do the same thing to earn their daily bread. The two women may no longer work in theaters, but, as Cristeta's cleverly managed drama demonstrates, they continue to play predetermined roles in the drama of men, to *entertain* those they depend on for economic support. The relationship between Don Quintín and Carola is not simply a humorous counterpoint to that between Don Juan and Cristeta. It is the darker mirror of the forces involved in the economy of relations between men and women in which it is the *burlador* who seduces the women into accepting that, in the end as in the beginning, men call the shots.[23]

23. Geraldine M. Scanlon points out that, ostensibly, single women had freedoms similar to those of men (123) while married women possessed relatively no rights whatsoever (126). Moreover, seduction "was only punished by the law for rape." Yet punishment

Thus, women can never give themselves over to men completely; they must always withhold something so as to remain unknown, mysterious (Valis, *The Novels of Jacinto Octavio Picón* 166). Unlike Eve, woman cannot let her Adam possess the forbidden fruit or he will never again want to taste it. If this were the only message of *Dulce y sabrosa,* it would be a banal one indeed. But the success with which Picón is able to articulate this disturbing truth while disarming his readers by the sheer elegance and humor of the narration suggests that there is something else involved here. As has been pointed out in other contexts, Don Juan as a social figure aids and abets the aims of patriarchal society and culture by seducing women into fulfilling a specific function in relation to men. He ensures that all women are alike. In this light, Picón is exceptionally perceptive when he says of Don Juan de Todellas that he is "a man constantly falling in love who feels himself impelled toward them, *women,* so as to initiate them into the delicious mysteries of love." Like Clarín's Fermín de Pas, who is responsible for instructing the young girls in Vetusta in the catechism (2:202; 482), Don Juan initiates women into love, is the Catullian bird that pecks the fruit before it arrives at its legitimate destination.

In a similar manner, Picón's novel initiates women into the concerns of men with respect to love. Maintaining the distinction between male and female readers, though only implicitly, Picón advocates in the preface to his book something like "art for art's sake."[24] He begins with a hypothetical situation, creating an ambience of ennui and malaise: "Figúrate, lector, que vuelves a tu casa mohino y aburrido, lacio el cuerpo, acibarado el ánimo por la desengañada labor del día. Cae la tarde; el amigo a quien esperas, no viene; la mujer querida está lejos, y aún no te llaman para comer" ["Imagine, dear (male) reader, that you return home melancholy and bored, your body is exhausted, your soul, embittered by the disappointing labors of the day. Late afternoon falls, the friend for whom you wait doesn't show up, your beloved wife is far away, and they still haven't called you for dinner"] (67). For whom are these pages ostensibly written? For a man, obviously, given the details

---

for "carnal relations between a man and young woman from 12 to 23 years of age, achieved by the abuse of confidence or by deceit" (134), ranged from one to six months in prison, as opposed to six years for monetary fraud involving sums greater than 2,500 pesetas.

24. Valis rightly says that we "should not be deceived" by Picón's apparent stance: "the novelist's claims to literary frivolity, real enough in his style and elegant wit, are continually undermined by a half-hidden, sometimes open, intent to instruct and inform. A serious moral purpose is always at the heart of the writer's work" (*The Novels of Jacinto Octavio Picón* 143).

of language and situation. In contrast to the available facts of reader-ship discussed by Peter B. Goldman and to the apostrophes in *Dulce y sabrosa* directed toward women, this is a novel by a man and is written for men. In keeping with the tenor of his opening words, Picón closes the preface with a general question and a pointed answer:

> ¿A quién le faltan en la vida días negros, estériles para el trabajo, en que la soledad trae de la mano a la melancolía?
>
> Contra ellos está escrito este libro, que, entre desconfiado y medroso, dejo pasar de mis manos a las tuyas. Recíbelo, no como novela que mueve a pensar, sino como juguete novelesco, contra-veneno del tedio y engañifa de las horas. (67)

> [Who doesn't have such dark days, worthless in terms of work, in which solitude brings melancholy?
>
> Against those, this book is written, which somewhere between wary and afraid, I let pass from my hands to yours. Take it, not as a novel that will move you to thought, but as a novelistic toy, an antidote for tedium and a way to fill time.]

Dulce y sabrosa is intended not to provoke thought but pleasure; it is a novelistic toy, a cure for boredom. From this opening page the situation of the reader is obvious: if your woman is far away and unable to entertain you, pick up a book, which is, of course, consistent with the presentation of Cristeta in the novel.

It is important to see that this is the message only for the *male* readers. For *female* readers, *Dulce y sabrosa* is, as Pardo Bazán percep-tively remarks, an extended commentary on Ovid's *Ars amatoria*. But the novel is not merely a commentary, it is, in and of itself, a seductive and instructive treatise on the nature of feminine wiles, on the vaga-ries of women's fashion as it appeals to men, on the need to be beauti-ful, submissive, and tantalizing. Written humorously, but not in the key of humor, Picón's novel initiates its female readers into the intrica-cies of love, so that they might better understand how to please men.

Although acute in its psychological presentation of relations be-tween men and women, *Dulce y sabrosa* also advocates the continued value of the status quo.[25] Indeed, if a tract for "free love," love without the restrictions of society, *Dulce y sabrosa* is as bleak in its outlook as *La Regenta*. To Don Juan's question, "¿Y el mundo, la sociedad y las

---

25. Hazel Gold addresses this issue, remarking on the "ideological collapse" of an author who is trying to fix in time a historical moment that is undoing itself.

gentes?" ["And the world, society, people?"], Cristeta replies with more questions: "¿Ahora te preocupas por eso? ¿Te cuidabas de ello al perseguir casadas? Los que acaso me disculparan adúltera, me rechazarán amante . . . ¡Ya lo sé! Pero ¿a quién consagro yo mi existencia, a ti o al prójimo?" ["You worry about this now? Did you worry about it when you pursued married women? Those that might forgive me for being an adulteress will reject me for being a mistress, as I well know. But, to whom ought I to devote my life, to you or to your fellow man?"] (349). Once Cristeta has compounded her otherness with social marginality, she has failed to heed the warnings implied in the romantic literature she so avidly read, in which women were always ready to be ravished, "esos que, según los casos, terminan en muerte violenta, o boda y perdón de padre bondadoso" ["those that, according to the situation, end with a violent death or with a wedding and the pardon of a generous father"] (90). Neither married nor dead, Cristeta becomes like Ana Ozores, perhaps not at the end of *Dulce y sabrosa,* but probably at some point in her hypothetical "future."[26] Cristeta's triumph is, then, a Pyrrhic victory in that she will have to continue to scheme and to manipulate, will have to continue to be "dulce y sabrosa" or "sweet and savory"; she must function as the novel *Dulce y sabrosa,* "not as a novel that will move you to thought, but as a novelistic toy, an antidote for tedium and a way to fill time." She now not only belongs to Don Juan de Todellas, she has become like all of them ("todas ellas"). She has learned her lessons well and is now not the "perfect *wife,*" but the perfect consort.

The ambivalence that characterizes critical assessments of *Dulce y sabrosa*—operative in the comments of Sobejano and Valis—is actually an astutely sensitive reaction to a complex literary text. Picón's novel is, in Valis's apt word, "delectable," a pleasure to read given its narrative wit and psychological complexity. But this critical ambivalence is a product not of an ambivalent message as found in the text itself, it is the *pleasurable* reading of the text, not the *insidious* one. Masked by the narrative charm is a vision as destitute of optimism as Clarín's, one in which man and woman are destined to repeat endlessly the words—and the problems—of love as first expressed by Adam and Eve. But because Cristeta has learned her lessons well, by the end of the novel she no longer seems to be a "muchacha plebeya elegantizada

26. Nelly Clémessy's reading of the conclusion of *Dulce y sabrosa* is diametrically opposed to mine. She remarks that the "optimistic denouement, resolutely open to a happy future, ends a love story that is impregnated with *joie de vivre*" (187).

de repente, sino hija de grandes, hecha desde niña a todos los refina-
mientos del lujo" ["plebeian girl suddenly made elegant, but the daughter of nobles, accustomed from childhood to all of the refinements of
luxury"] (292). After reading *Dulce y sabrosa,* any other woman could
become the same: indeed, Picón even includes prices along with the
minute descriptions of clothing (84).

It is not my intention here either to belittle Picón's achievement in
Dulce y sabrosa or to take him to task for presenting his version of Don
Juan's story as he has. As Barbara Johnson notes, sexual difference
and literature are probably inexorably linked; to fault Picón for what is
a social and cultural problem would therefore be naive. Johnson says:

> If human beings were not divided into two biological sexes, there
> would probably be no need for literature. And if literature could
> truly say what the relations between the sexes are, we would
> doubtless not need much of it then, either. Somehow, however, it
> is not simply a question of literature's ability to say or not to say
> the truth of sexuality. For from the moment literature begins to
> try to set things straight on that score, literature itself becomes
> inextricable from the sexuality it seeks to comprehend. It is not
> the life of sexuality that literature cannot capture; it is litera-
> ture that inhabits the very heart of what makes sexuality so
> problematic for us speaking animals. Literature is not only a
> thwarted investigator but also an incorrigible perpetrator of the
> problem of sexuality. (13)

Picón, even if profeminist, cannot help it if *Dulce y sabrosa* as a novel
exercises the same seductive charm as its hero Don Juan. The novel's
verbal grace is like that of the *burlador.* It seems to be merely a light
romantic novel in order to accomplish its social purpose of indoctrination; in this sense, the novel itself becomes like a piece of tantalizingly
forbidden fruit. In the end, some fruit is forbidden, some apples are
more rotten than others, and some only just begin to lose their blush.

Ethical Ends in *Don Juan* and *Doña Inés*

we know a life dissolving
in its past, and a future passing back into its life.
We build a bridge of waves over the waves, & drift on.
—David St. John, "Four O'Clock in Summer: Hope"

el autor de estas líneas leyó el Oráculo manual, *de Baltasar Gracián, y se
sorprendió al encontrar una estrecha afinidad entre la idea que se tenía
de Nietzsche y la filosofía de Gracián. La afinidad estribaba, princi-
palmente, en la exaltación de la impasibilidad y de la dureza. "¡Sed
duros!", decía Nietzsche. "¡No perezcáis de desdicha ajena!", voceaba
Gracián. (Entre paréntesis, ¡qué absurda, qué inhumana esta exaltación
de la dureza! Y nosotros, los que en 1900 la propugnábamos, ¡cómo
no veíamos en el ardor y la soltura de la juventud que la vida, la
experiencia, nos había de llevar hacia la indulgencia y la piedad, la
dulce, la amorosa piedad!)*

—Azorín, *"El auge de Gracián"*

The various Don Juans discussed thus far have had in common not just
their interest in seduction and their linguistic gifts, but also their
relative youth. Tirso's *burlador* or trickster is presented as a gallant
young nobleman; Zorrilla's Don Juan is likewise young, as appears to
be López de Ayala's Juan de Alvarado. With *La Regenta* and *Dulce y
sabrosa* we begin to see the effects of time and the toll of age: Fermín de
Pas has lost many of the illusions of his youth; Alvaro Mesía is clearly
past his prime; Juan de Todellas begins to fret over what he sees as his
incipient and solitary dotage. Yet, with the exception of Tirso and,
perhaps, López de Ayala, these authors only suggest the possible outcome of Don Juan's supposedly misspent youth. Either he moves on to
other conquests and, eventually, his retribution, or, sensing the en-
croachment of time, he settles down. What then?

This is the question broached by Azorín in what ought to be read as a
novelistic diptych, *Don Juan* and *Doña Inés (Historia de amor)* [Doña
Inés (A History of Love)]. In these two novels, Azorín suggests what is
the ethical and socially productive outcome of the types of scenarios of
seduction presented by other authors. Although others write earlier of
aging Don Juans, for example, Théophile Gautier in *La comédie de la
mort* (1838) and Guerra Junquiero in *A morte de Don João* (1874),
Azorín, in continuing Don Juan's story, in writing of the *end,* and not
the *beginning,* of the life of a seducer, reinscribes Don Juan's beneficial
social function in positive, not negative or even ambivalent, terms. He
offers a broadly spiritual model by which society can perpetuate itself
and its timeless values by means of individual acts of charity.

It would be a mistake to emphasize the philosophical dimensions of
Azorín's novels to the exclusion of their humorous, indeed openly
parodic, aspects, as Robert C. Spires has most recently demonstrated in
terms of *Doña Inés* (74–90). In fact, in the early decades of the twentieth century a number of works appear that contribute to what Ignacio-
Javier López terms the "degradation" of Don Juan, among them Ramón

del Valle Inclán's prose *Sonatas* (1902–5) and his drama *Los cuernos de don Friolera* (1921), to say nothing of Ramón Pérez de Ayala's *Tigre Juan* and *El curandero de su honra* (1926). Yet, despite the evident humor and in some cases obvious disparaging of Don Juan, there is a lingering sense of fondness and sympathy, which does lead once more to the underlying seriousness of almost any enterprise associated with the figure of the *burlador,* however he is portrayed.

To some extent, Azorín's sympathetic portrayal of Don Juan can be read as characteristic of the attitude of the Generation of '98 toward the *burlador.* As José María Martínez Cachero remarks of Tirso's condemnation in *El burlador de Sevilla,* "the condemnation of Don Juan seemed to be too extreme to the men of the Generation of 1898, as did Zorrilla's granting of salvation. It would be difficult to find any righteous individuals who would understand the latter. Neither Paradise nor the Inferno. Purgatory is best. And earthly existence could be a type of Purgatory. The best thing, therefore, would be to rescue Don Juan, to put him on his feet once again, and to return him to the world" (*Las novelas de Azorín* 176). Yet, once Don Juan is again made part of everyday life, the question remains: what then? Azorín's answer as presented in *Don Juan* and *Doña Inés* draws, I believe, on the philosophy of Friedrich Nietzsche, not only on the concept of the *Übermensch* or superman, which is, of course, explicitly linked to Don Juan in Shaw's *Man and Superman* (1901–3), but on the notions of the will to power and the eternal return.

Azorín's relationship to Nietzsche's thought, although lengthy and complex, need not concern us here (see Sobejano, *Nietzsche en España* 105–7, 395–419, passim); and Nietzsche's ideas are well enough known to need little exposition. It would, however, be useful for a consideration of Azorín's novels to have in mind specific points with respect to the will to power and the eternal return, particularly as they relate to questions of ethics. Moreover—and as a means of using these notions in a discussion of *Don Juan* and *Doña Inés*—a distinction, via Kierkegaard, must be made in the nature of repetition itself. If a philosophical excursus seems to draw us away from novelistic representations of Don Juan, the truth, in fact, is otherwise. Because the *burlador* is such an integral figure in Western literature and patriarchal social culture, a consideration of Nietzsche's will to power and the eternal return will actually focus more sharply many of the underlying ideological functions of this character and social force.

For Nietzsche, the will to power can be identified with a "striving for distinction" that "keeps a constant eye on the next man and wants to know what his feelings are." Interest in the other, the next man (and in Nietzsche, it is always a man, a distinction I shall preserve in this discussion), is not simply a form of empathy, but, rather, manifests itself as a desire "to perceive or divine how the next man outwardly or inwardly *suffers* from us, how he loses control over himself and surrenders to the impressions our hand or even merely the sight of us makes upon him" (*Daybreak* 68). In this sense, the striving for distinction is a desire to dominate the "next man," even if this type of domination is indirect, intuited, or merely dreamed. This, of course, is the negative aspect of Nietzsche's thought that is, if initially embraced by Azorín, later repudiated when he invokes "la piedad, la dulce, amorosa piedad" ["piety, sweet, loving piety"], a quality that is somewhat ironically attributed to God in *Doña Inés,* albeit in the form of "serene piety" (*Obras completas* 4:807). Yet Nietzsche confesses in *Ecce Homo* that his "humanity does *not* consist in feeling with men how they are, but in *enduring* that I feel with them. My humanity is a continual self-overcoming." The will to power is not necessarily to be understood as an act of domination in the manner of dominating others, but as an act of self-empowerment that can, indeed, be generalized to the extent that Nietzsche remarks, somewhat immodestly, on his "task of preparing a moment of the highest self-examination for humanity, a *great noon* when it looks back and far forward, when it emerges from the dominion of accidents and priests and poses, as a whole, the question Why? and For What?" (*Basic Writings of Nietzsche* 689, 747). Viewed in this light, the will to power becomes the means by which an individual releases himself from the chains of destiny and asserts his own priority over his world and his actions in that world.

It is here, in that "great noon," that the importance of the eternal return is to be found. In *Thus Spoke Zarathustra,* Nietzsche presents the notion of the eternal return in a parable. Traveling with a "dwarf," "the spirit of gravity, my devil and archenemy" (156), Zarathustra wends his way on a solitary, steep path. When the dwarf chances to jump off his shoulder, Zarathustra makes a startling discovery in the form of a gateway standing where they had stopped, a gateway he baptizes as "Moment" and at which he divines the meeting of two paths that stretch backward and forward to eternity, paths that appear to be contradictory. But, he asks,

> are not all things knotted together so firmly that this moment draws after it *all* that is to come? Therefore—itself too? For whatever can walk—in this long lane out *there* too, it *must* walk once more.

And this slow spider, which crawls in the moonlight, and this moonlight itself, and I and you in the gateway whispering together, whispering of eternal things—must not all of us have been there before? And return and walk in that other lane, out there, before us, in this long dreadful lane—must we not eternally return? (*Thus Spoke Zarathustra* 158)

By posing the notion of the eternal return as a question—"must we not eternally return?"—Nietzsche also raises the issue of the will. One must assent to the inevitability of an answer in the affirmative, and repetition thereby ineluctably draws the individual into the ongoing authority of destiny. To put it another way, there appears to be a paradox constantly at work in the twin notions of the will to power and the eternal return.

In a recent reconsideration of Nietzsche in the light of contemporary literary theory (and particularly the work of René Girard), Tobin Siebers resolves this paradox by stressing the *ethical* nature of the positions taken by the philosopher. With respect to the will to power Siebers explains:

It is the power by which the self effects its own change. The summit of this development arrives with Zarathustra, who counsels people to stand firmly in themselves. Nietzsche associates the will to power with the inexhaustible procreative power of life, which nevertheless strives, like Freud's *Todestrieb,* to discharge itself. (*The Ethics of Criticism* 136)[27]

Consideration of this assessment of Nietzsche's will to power in the light of the previous discussions of Don Juan leads to several pertinent points of contact. Siebers's account could be read almost as an allegory of the *burlador* and his role in and effects on society. Most significant, though, is the reference to Freud and to the contrary yet complementary instincts of life and death, integration and dispersal, as they are involved in repetition (the clearest formulation of which is found in Freud's *Beyond the Pleasure Principle* [*Standard Edition* 18:1–64]). What is Don Juan if not that primal force willing and able to destroy and to disintegrate himself in order to bring about a more productive ordering of patriarchal society, to reinforce the values of patriarchy?

In this regard, the repetitive nature of Don Juan—of his actions and

27. In this regard, see also Norman O. Brown 107–8; Herbert Marcuse 118–24; and Walter Kaufmann.

of the many versions of his story—comes into play, which brings us to
Nietzsche's theory of the eternal return. Siebers says:

> The doctrine of the eternal return portrays each moment as a
> gateway where the past and future meet in a decision of the
> present. It is therefore more than a theory to redeem the past. It
> places the weight of decision on each moment. . . . The eternal
> return represents the will as the force that orients understand-
> ing not toward a mythical past, here seen as the world of resent-
> ment and revenge, but toward an ethical future. . . . Most impor-
> tant, to think the eternal return is to overcome the contempt of
> the human. (139–40)

With the present moment designated as the point at which an ethical
move toward the future can be made, as the point at which the past can
both return and be improved upon, the possibility for change within a
continuum of stability is thus envisioned.

The formulation of this point is indeed similar to Azorín's, although
there is a definite shift from a pessimistic to an optimistic vision of
repetition in the writings of Nietzsche's Spanish disciple. In the largely
autobiographical *La voluntad* [Will] (1902), the protagonist's teacher
Yuste laments, "Todo es igual, todo monótono, todo cambia en la apari-
encia y se repite en el fondo a través de las edades. . . . la Humanidad es
un círculo, es una serie de catástrofes que se suceden idénticas, iguales.
Esta civilización europea, de que tan orgulloso nos mostramos, desapa-
recerá como aquella civilización romana . . ." ["Everything is the same,
everything monotonous. Everything changes in appearance and in the
final analysis repeats itself throughout the ages. . . . Humanity is a
circle, a series of catastrophes that follow each other in succession,
identically, the same. This European civilization, of which we show
ourselves to be so proud, will disappear like the Roman civilization . . ."] (*Obras completas* 1:887). There is no hint, no allusion, to
change or to the role of the individual in this pessimistic view of human
history. Yet, in a later version of the eternal return as expressed in a
virtually untranslatable play on idiomatic turns of phrase, Azorín is
somewhat more optimistic in his outlook: " 'Vivir—escribe el poeta—
es *ver pasar*.' Sí; vivir es ver pasar: ver pasar en lo alto de las nubes.
Mejor diríamos: vivir es *ver volver*. Es ver volver todo un retorno per-
durable, eterno; ver volver todo—angustias, alegrías, esperanzas—,
como esas nubes que son siempre distintas y siempre las mismas, como
esas nubes fugaces e inmuntables" [" 'Living—writes the poet—is *seeing happen*.' Yes, living is seeing happen: seeing what happens at the

height of the clouds. We would do better to say: living is *seeing return*. It is seeing everything return in an eternal, unending return; seeing everything return—agonies, happinesses, hopes—like these clouds, that are always different and always the same, like these transient and immutable clouds"] (*Obras completas* 2:705).[28] Allowing for the existence of happiness and hope alongside anguish, Azorín links the eternal return to the diverse yet constant movements of the clouds. However indirectly, he also posits an individual perspective by asserting this return as a function of sight, which is, of course, involved with literary creation.[29]

If the paradoxical nature of the eternal return—change in stasis—seems both more paradoxical and vexing than before, it might be helpful to formulate these notions in the terms proposed earlier in the nineteenth century by Kierkegaard in *Repetition,* the distinction that he makes between *recollection* and *repetition,* which involves the individual in the struggle to repeat, not merely to recollect. For Kierkegaard, "what is recollected has been, is repeated backwards, whereas repetition properly so called is recollected forwards," which is to say, to recollect involves the individual in a reliving of the past, while repetition draws him into the future. The importance of these ideas becomes clear when the specifically moral aspects of the distinction are considered. Within the essay itself, Kierkegaard asserts, and proceeds to demonstrate, that "repetition, therefore, if it is possible, makes a person happy, whereas recollection makes him unhappy" (*Fear and Trembling, Repetition* 131). And, in explanation of his intent in *Repetition,* Kierkegaard says that the "concept Repetition, when it is employed in the sphere of individual freedom, has a history, in the fact that freedom passes through several stages in order to attain itself" (quoted in Lowrie xvi). First, freedom is defined as pleasure, second, as shrewdness, each of which "falls into despair." Finally, "freedom breaks forth in its highest form, in which it is defined in relation to itself. . . . Now the highest interest of freedom is to bring about repetition, and it fears

28. Yet another way of translating this is as follows: " 'To live—writes the poet—is *to see everything pass by.*' Yes, to live is to see everything pass by: to see everything pass by at the height of the clouds. We would do better to say: to live is *to see everything return.* It is to see everything return in an eternal, unending return: to see everything return—agonies, happinesses, hopes—like these clouds that are always different and always the same, like these fleet and immutable clouds." The dynamic at work here seems to be the coming and going of everything in the world and the absolute remove of the speaker.

29. On Azorín's thoughts on time and repetition see Carlos Clavería; Pedro Laín-Entralgo; Miguel Enguídanos; Marguerite C. Rand; José María Maravall; Jorge García Gómez; and Leon Livingstone 15–43.

only lest change might have the power to alter its eternal nature"
(quoted in Lowrie xvii). In these terms, recollection means that man
must despair of ever escaping from the past; repetition, on the other
hand, offers man the possibility of moving into the future, toward
happiness, toward freedom, *and* toward the true repetition, which is
expressed as a type of religious movement. In its broad outlines, then,
Kierkegaard's notion of repetition anticipates many of Nietzsche's own
ideas—cryptic to be sure—on the nature of the eternal return.

The distinction between recollection and repetition not only emphasizes the role of the individual and of individual will as forces of change
in an essentially static world, it also goes to the heart of the issues we
have been discussing, both with regard to Don Juan and the weight of
literary tradition and with respect to critical recuperations of the inherent meaning of Don Juan's story. Azorín is aware of the role of repetition in the rewriting of Don Juan's story; the epigraph to his *Don Juan*
ironically underscores an author's dilemma. Taken from Racine's
Bérénice, the citation reads, ". . . toute l'invention consiste à faire
quelque chose de rien" ["every invention consists of making something
from nothing"]. Perhaps it should read, in the case of Don Juan, "something from everything." In any case, in literary terms, merely to retell
the story as found in Tirso's *El burlador de Sevilla* or Zorrilla's *Don
Juan Tenorio* would be to recollect the past, to fail to overcome the
necessity and inevitability of the eternal return, to fail in a self-
overcoming.[30] To reshape the material of the past, however, implies an
individual will dedicated to the labor of repetition. Thus, what Azorín
found implied in earlier versions of Don Juan's story, the positive function of the *burlador* in patriarchal society as inscribed in a literary
text, becomes the explicit topic of the novels in which he struggles with
the burden of literary tradition. What Nietzsche's thought, via Azorín,
brings to an interpretation of Don Juan applies equally well to the
authors that write of the *burlador.*

Before examining *Don Juan* and *Doña Inés* in detail, we ought to consider Azorín's ideas on the novel. As some critics would have it,
Azorín's novelistic texts are more like essays in form, or worse, they
lack any logic of form whatsoever. Commenting on the two novels to be

---

30. José María Martínez Cachero voices something similar when he remarks, "Azorín
proposes treating in novelistic form a subject that he borrows. To repeat with adding
something more would result in a waste of time and would suppose a manifest incapacity
in a writer; to add some detail of secondary importance would not improve things" (*Las
novelas de Azorín* 175).

discussed here, José María Valverde contends, "With the name of Don Juan and with the presence of a nun and of a Don Gonzalo, one perceives [in *Don Juan*] an allusion to the Don Juan theme, but it is hard to see a plot in this series of images without explicit connections. . . . [In *Doña Inés*] the action—rather, the plot, since there is barely any action—is somewhat more visible than in *Don Juan,* but in an evasive and lifeless form" (341, 346). G. G. Brown is even more extreme and severe in his remarks, claiming that *Don Juan* "has no plot, no interest in individual character, no ideological content, and is merely a further series of descriptions, anecdotes from the past and present, and glimpses of some inhabitants of a small Castilian town. . . . *Doña Inés,* whose title suggests that it, too, will have something to do with the legend [of Don Juan] . . . is again a series of static fragments strung together in incongruous fashion" (54–55).

Azorín would probably concur with his critics' notion of his view of novelistic form, if not with their negative assessments. According to the author of *Don Juan* and *Doña Inés,* in a novel, which is a representation of life in the real world,

> no debe haber fábula . . . ; la vida no tiene fábula; es diversa, multiforme, ondulante, contradictoria . . . todo menos simétrica, geométrica, rígida, como aparece en las novelas. . . . Y por eso, los Goncourt, que son los que, a mi entender, se han acertado más al desideratum, no dan *una vida,* sino fragmentos, sensaciones separadas. . . . Y así el personaje, entre dos de estos fragmentos, hará su vida habitual, que no importa al artista, y éste no se verá forzado, como en la novela del antiguo régimen, a contarnos tilde por tilde, desde por la mañana hasta por la noche, las obras y los milagros de su protagonista . . . , cosa absurda, puesto que *toda* la vida no se puede encajar en un volumen, y bastante haremos si damos diez, veinte, cuarenta sensaciones. . . . (*Obras completas* 1:863–64; ellipses in the original)

> [there ought not to be a plot . . . life doesn't have any plot; it's varied, multiform, undulant, contradictory . . . everything but symmetrical, geometrical, rigid, as it appears in novels. . . . That's why the Goncourts—who, to my mind, have best understood the desideratum—don't give a life, but fragments, separate sensations . . . And therefore the character, in between these fragments, lives his regular life, which is not important to the artist, who will no longer see himself forced, as in the novel of the old style, to tell us every detail, from morning until night,

> the works and miracles of his protagonist . . . something absurd, since *all* of a life cannot be enclosed in one volume, and it's enough if we create ten, twenty or forty sensations. . . . (*Obras completas* 1:863–64; ellipses in the original)]

Interested in "separate sensations," Azorín suggests that the artist, the novelist, shapes raw material into a number of isolated moments in the interstices of which the protagonist continues to live. Still, this conception leaves us with *isolated moments,* fragments that seem, at least according to Valverde and Brown, without relationship to one another, without any type of form.

In fact, it could be argued that Azorín's novels are reasonably conventional in terms of form as well as character and plot. As regards form, in the case of *Don Juan,* the novel is loosely chiastic in structure; grouped around the nearly central nineteenth chapter, which deals with an act of individual charity, are continuing and contrasting themes and characters. For example, the eighteenth chapter tells of the failure of a new provincial governor (who is also a poet), of how he loses his job when he upholds what he believes to be just action as opposed to the written law of the land. Chapter 20 continues this line of inquiry with a presentation of the next governor, who believes *only* in the law as found in the legal codes. Similarly, chapters 16 and 22 deal with children, first with a teacher who tries to provide his pupils with pleasant memories by teaching them about nature, then with a mother's memories of her son's childhood and her hopes for his future. *Doña Inés* responds to a different formal principle. Its fifty-two chapters, without the added fillip of a prologue, correspond to the weeks in a calendar year. Given, first, the manner in which Azorín draws out the narrative—using the chapter titles to allude to this process: "XLIX: ¿Epílogo? No; todavía no" ["XLIX: Epilogue? No, not yet"]; "LI: Tampoco es esto epílogo" ["LI: This is not an epilogue, either"]; "LII: Epílogo" ["LII: Epilogue"] (*Obras completas* 4:839, 844, 846)—in order to arrive at the number fifty-two, and second, the overt interest in the topics of time and repetition in the novel, it is plausible to consider this text a work that necessarily repeats itself in a cyclical manner, as do the hours in a day, the weeks in a year.

Character and plot are equally important in these two novels, although it is in this respect that Valverde and Brown reveal their particular blind spot as readers. I have already suggested that *Don Juan* and *Doña Inés* are relatively conventional as novels; I should add that they are *conventional novels* presented in an *unconventional way.* Azorín leaves it to his readers to discover the moments between the "sensations," the "regular life," to spin the thread that will eventually turn the individual chapters into a string, with a beginning and an end, that forms a circle. In other words, by writing in a specific tradition, that of Don Juan, Azorín—like Zorrilla or Clarín and Picón—is able to invoke a history for his protagonists, a history that is meaningful, however, only for those readers familiar with the many versions of Don Juan's story *and* with the workings of narrative fiction. If Picón assumes that the reader of his text is a man who will share the viewpoint of his narrator, Azorín goes much further: he requires the collusion of the reader in the creation of his novels.[31] The reader of *Don Juan* and *Doña Inés* must provide the novels with their internal logic, the connecting tissue that makes of the "separate sensations" a coherent and, finally, a cohesive narrative body. In terms of the distinctions drawn earlier, it is the responsibility of the reader to take part in the repetition, and not just the recollection, of Don Juan and his story by discovering the ethical aspects so delicately rendered by Azorín. In so doing, the reader will implicitly acquiesce to many, if not all, of the ideological assumptions expressed in the fiction.

Because my focus for the discussion of *Don Juan* and *Doña Inés* will in part be on the role of the reader in the creation of the fiction, I shall initially treat the two parts of this novelistic diptych separately. *Don Juan* is of particular interest with respect to the relation of individual will to written law on the one hand and social justice on the other, especially as these relate to various social institutions. *Doña Inés* offers the means by which to consider the role of the individual in the process of the eternal return, the role of will in the decision to recollect or to repeat. By dealing with these texts within the framework of Nietzsche's thought as it illuminates Don Juan and pertains to the types of issues discussed thus far, we shall see the *logical* conclusion to the scenario of seduction, particularly in its novelistic guise: Ana Ozores is shunned by society; Fermín de Pas's career is stalled in Vetusta; Alvaro Mesía moves on to Madrid; Juan de Todellas finds a solution for his fear of growing old alone; Cristeta Moreruela defies social conventions to become Juan's concubine. What then?

Azorín's *Don Juan* tells the story of Don Juan de Prados y Ramos, who, the narrator informs us in the first sentence of the first chapter, "es un hombre como todos los hombres" ["is a man like every other man"] (*Obras completas* 4:219). If not so reluctant to relate the particulars of appearance as was Picón's narrator, Azorín offers little that would

31. Roland Barthes makes a similar distinction between the "readerly" (*lisible*) and the "writerly" (*scriptible*) text in *S/Z*.

allow us as readers to distinguish this Don Juan from any other, or any other man for that matter. The protagonist is virtually anonymous in his manner of self-presentation, since, "Cuando nos separamos de él, no podemos decir de qué manera iba vestido" ["When we leave him, we cannot say how he was dressed"] (*Obras completas* 4:219). Over the course of thirty-nine brief chapters and an epilogue, this Don Juan meets with friends and acquaintances of all classes, including the *maestre* Don Gonzalo, the *maestre*'s wife and daughter, Angela and Jeannette, as well as Angela's sister, Sor Natividad, and a host of others. Moreover, the narrator, who figures openly in the narrative (if only as a voice and not an identifiable character), tells us of local history and current events in the small, unnamed city in which the action takes place. There is, then, a full story to be found here: plot, characters, and action.

There is also, *pace* Brown, an ideological point of view taken in the novel, which is apparent as early as the prologue and which openly reappears in the corresponding framing moment, the epilogue. *Don Juan* begins abruptly with a reference to the protagonist only to break off this initial train of thought with a legend that provides Azorín with a religious *and* literary context for his story: "Don Juan del Prado y Ramos era un gran pecador. Un día adoleció gravemente . . . En el siglo XIII, un poeta, Gonzalo de Berceo, escribe los *Milagros de Nuestra Señora*" ["Don Juan del Prado y Ramos was a great sinner. One day he fell gravely ill . . . In the thirteenth century, a poet, Gonzalo de Berceo, wrote the *Miracles of Our Lady*"] (*Obras completas* 4:217; ellipsis in the original). The narrator then tells of a sinfully sensual monk. Despite repeated attempts at reform, the monk continues to partake of earthly delights. When Saint Peter—the patron saint of the monk's monastery—intervenes with God on the monk's behalf, it is to no avail. Then the Virgin appeals to God, who finally relents. The moral of this story leads to the novel: "Don Juan del Prado y Ramos no llegó a morir; pero su espíritu salió de la grave enfermedad profundamente transformado" ["Don Juan del Prado y Ramos did not die; but his spirit emerged from the grave illness profoundly transformed"] (*Obras completas* 4:218).

With the epilogue, the spiritual nature of the religious overtones is again apparent. The worldly Don Juan del Prado y Ramos has become Hermano Juan, a poor man who renounces all worldly goods in order to concentrate on matters less than mundane: "Mi pensamiento está en lo futuro, y no en el pasado; mi pensamiento está en la bondad de los hombres, y no en sus maldades" ["My thoughts are of the future and not the past; my thoughts are of the generosity of men, and not their wrongdoings"]. The wonders of the world have been replaced by those of "la fe de las almas ingenuas y la esperanza que nunca acaba" ["the faith of ingenuous souls and the hope that never ends"]. Finally, referring to love, Hermano Juan says, "El amor que conozco es el amor más alto. Es la piedad por todo" ["The love I know is the highest love of all. It is pity (compassion, piety) for everything"] (*Obras completas* 4:275–76). The carnal love that is mentioned with regard to the monk in the prologue and that is traditionally associated with Don Juan gives way to "piedad," precisely the mixture of spiritual piety and pity invoked by Azorín in his reflections on Nietzsche and Gracián. Don Juan del Prado y Ramos, sinner, has, as Martínez Cachero suggested, been made to live through the Purgatory of earthly life, has been returned to the world, redeemed, and reclaimed for humanity. Azorín has completed the trajectory of Don Juan's story by drawing the *burlador* into the flock and leading him back to the fold.

In a word, Don Juan has been converted, or so it seems. As William James puts it in *The Varieties of Religious Experience:* "To be converted, to be regenerated, to receive grace, to experience religion, to gain an assurance, are so many phrases which denote the process, gradual or sudden, by which a self hitherto divided, and consciously wrong inferior, and unhappy, becomes unified and consciously right superior and happy, in consequence of its firmer hold upon religious realities" (157). James posits a "moral change," divinely instigated or not, from one conscious state of unhappiness to a conscious state of fulfillment. The nature of the change—gradual or sudden—is unimportant; the fact of change, and of awareness, is key to the process of conversion. Referring to conversion as an "affective experience which, to avoid ambiguity, should, I think, be called the state of assurance," James sets forth four characteristics pertaining to regeneration: (1) "the loss of all worry, the sense that all is ultimately well with one, the peace, the harmony, the *willingness to be*, even though the outer conditions should remain the same. . . . A passion of willingness, of acquiescence, of admiration is the glowing centre of this state of mind"; (2) "the sense of perceiving mysteries not known before"; (3) "the objective change which the world often appears to undergo. 'An appearance of newness beautifies every object' "; (4) "the ecstasy of happiness produced" (201–2, 206).

By the end of the novel, Don Juan del Prado y Ramos, now Hermano Juan, displays the four marks mentioned by James as characteristic of conversion. Hermano Juan appears confident yet humble, acquiescent; he opens himself to the future; the physical world undergoes a perceptible change; he is possessed of the calm ecstasy of the greatest kind of love. The profound and profoundly transforming illness suffered by

Don Juan's "spirit" seems to have brought about the former *burlador*'s conversion, the weaving of this errant thread into the fabric of society.

There is, however, another way of looking at the question of conversion as found in the novel. Is it really accurate to say that Don Juan has been converted? Or should Azorín's spiritual and ethical solution be read as the logical and necessary outcome of Don Juan's story, not just as it is presented in Azorín's *Don Juan* but as a broadly literary and cultural phenomenon? In the thirty-nine chapters between the prologue and the epilogue, what, if anything, occurs that would lend credence to the notion of conversion, to the spiritual reawakening of Don Juan and the embracing of a religious humanism? In fact, the presentation in the novel of what might be called religious matters is consistently tinged with a less than doctrinaire and at times frankly decadent sensuality, which threatens to taint the putative spirituality of the world portrayed therein. In the description of the anonymous small city in which the action of the novel is set, the narrator goes into great detail about the religious life of the region. The fourth chapter, "Censo de población" [Census of the population], is almost entirely given over to an enumeration of those directly and indirectly involved in the day-to-day life of the Church. After listing the various distinctive groups and classes, the narrator goes on to discuss the monasteries and, especially, the convents. Of the latter, we learn that there are four; of these four, the wealthiest convent, San Pablo, that of the Hieronymites, is the one of most interest to the narrator, both for historical reasons and because Sor Natividad is the abbess.

Two chapters are devoted to a discussion of the history of the convent of San Pablo. These chapters relate the conflict in the sixteenth century between the local bishop, Don García de Illán, and the nuns. It seems that, following upon the Council of Trent, the bishop instituted reforms intended to bring an end to "la vida . . . placentera y alegre" ["the amusing and happy life"] of the convents: "Las monjas entraban y salían a su talante. No estaba prescrita la clausura. Se celebraban en los conventos fiestas profanas y divertidos saraos" ["The nuns came and went as they wished. Enclosure was not prescribed. Profane parties and pleasurable soirées were held in the convent"] (*Obras completas* 4:225). Although the three other convents in the city acceded to the new restrictions, the nuns in the convent of San Pablo refused, incurring the wrath not only of Don García de Illán (whose name ironically recalls that of the wily necromancer of the eleventh exemplum of Don Juan Manuel's *El conde Lucanor*) but of various popes. With every recourse to appeal exhausted, the nuns finally gave in; "pero de la antigua y libre vida siempre quedó en el convento un rezago de laxitud y profanidad" ["but a trace of the laxity and profanity of the old, free life always remained in the convent"] (*Obras completas* 2:226).

It should come as no surprise that the abbess who now presides over the convent of San Pablo is also somewhat lax herself. Sor Natividad is first presented while she is with her sister Angela and her niece Jeannette. This first glimpse of the nun is, for the most part, relatively objective in its perspective. Still, the narrator's gaze is unmistakably masculine. The details emphasized in the description are sensually carnal. In a manner similar to the presentation of Picón's Cristeta—and, moreover, in a manner similar to the strange mixture of carnality and spirituality in Clarín's Fermín de Pas—the body of the nun is perceived beneath her white habit.[32] But the narrator does not stop with the merely tantalizing perception of curves through Sor Natividad's clothing. His gaze intrudes on the nun in her cell: "Cuando llega el momento del reposo, sor Natividad se va despojando de sus ropas. Se esparce por la alcoba un vago y sensual aroma. Los movimientos de sor Natividad son lentos, pausados; sus manos blancas van, con suavidad, despojando el esbelto cuerpo de los hábitos exteriores. Un instante se detiene sor Natividad. ¿Ha contemplado su busto sólido, firme, en un espejo? La ropa de batista es sutil y blanquísima" ["When the moment for rest arrives, Sor Natividad begins to undress. A vague, sensual aroma spreads through the room. Sor Natividad's movements are slow, deliberate; her white hands move smoothly to remove the outer habits from her slender body. Sor Natividad pauses for an instant. Has she contemplated her solid, firm bust in the mirror? Her fine batiste clothing is perfectly white"] (*Obras completas* 4:228). In a moment of self-contemplation similar in nature, but not in effect, to that of Don Fermín in *La Regenta,* Sor Natividad reveals her latent sensuality in a passage that reveals the essentially voyeuristic nature of the narrative. Yet what was openly, in the case of the Magistral, a moment of self-contemplation is here made to seem only vaguely narcissistic. By framing the moment as a question—"¿Ha contemplado su busto sólido, firme, en un espejo?" ["Has she contemplated her solid, firm bust in the mirror?"]—rather than in Clarín's language of direct assertion—"el mozo fuerte y velludo que tenía [de Pas] enfrente, en el espejo, le parecía un *otro yo*" ["The brawny, hairy young fellow before him in the mirror seemed like an *alter ego*"] (*La Regenta* 1:410; 232)—Azorín's narrator leaves Sor Natividad's spiritual nature open to conjecture.

---

32. On the relationship between Clarín and Azorín see Martínez Cachero, " 'Clarín' y 'Azorín,' " and "Cuando José Martínez Ruiz empezaba"; Valverde 34–35, 40–54; Manuel María Pérez López; and Antonio Ramos-Gascón.

This is not to say, of course, that the Abbess's sensuality is left undecided. In a pair of chapters entitled "Una terrible tentación . . ." [A Terrible Temptation . . .] and ". . . Y una tentación celestial" [. . . And a Celestial Temptation], in scenes that seem to draw, again, on *La Regenta,* first the eighteen-year-old Jeannette, then Sor Natividad, tempt Don Juan. In the first instance, Jeannette is the temptress, Don Juan the tempted. In what could be read as a continuation of the first description of Sor Natividad,

> Se detiene [Jeannette] frente a un ancho espejo. Calla un momento, pensativa. Avanza un poco el busto y se contempla la línea ondulante—deliciosamente ondulante—del torso. Da dos pasos erguida. Se levanta luego la falda hasta la rodilla y permanece absorta ante la pierna sólida, llena, de un contorno elegante, ceñida por la tersa y transparente seda. El pie—encerrado en brillante charol—se posa firme en el suelo. Las piernas mantienen el cuerpo esbelto, con una carnosa y sólida redondez en el busto. (*Obras completas* 4:259)

> [She pauses before a large mirror. She falls silent for a moment, pensive. She moves her bust forward a little and contemplates the undulant line—deliciously undulant—of her torso. She takes two steps, erect. She then lifts her skirt to the knee and remains absorbed by the solid leg, which is shapely, with an elegant turn, encased in the glossy, transparent silk. Her foot—enclosed in brilliant patent leather—rests firmly on the floor. Her legs support her slender body, the fleshy, solid roundness of her bust.]

None of these self-absorbed yet flirtatious gestures escapes Don Juan. If in the past these scenes of sensual confrontation between the young girl and her admirer resolved themselves innocently, this particular exchange is charged with significance: "Ahora Jeannette pone el libro que está leyendo en manos de don Juan y le dice, con un gesto de inocencia: —Señor caballero, explíqueme usted esta poesía de amor; yo no la entiendo" ["Now Jeannette puts the book that she is reading in Don Juan's hands and says to him, with a gesture of innocence, 'My dear sir, explain to me this love poetry. I don't understand it' "] (*Obras completas* 4:259). Once again, a text becomes the site of seduction; this time, however, Don Juan del Prado y Ramos is, like Byron's Juan, passive.

This same passivity characterizes the "celestial temptation" found in the next chapter. As in the earlier presentation of the abbess, her physical, not spiritual, nature is emphasized:

> De cuando en cuando, sor Natividad se inclina o se ladea para coger una flor: bajo la blanca estameña se marca la curva elegante de la cadera, se acusa la rotundidad armoniosa del seno . . . Al avanzar un paso, la larga túnica se ha prendido entre el ramaje. Al descubierto han quedado las piernas. Ceñida por fina seda blanca, se veía iniciarse desde el tobillo el ensanche de la graciosa curva carnosa y llena. ¿Se ha dado cuenta de ello sor Natividad? Ha transcurrido un momento. Al cabo, con un movimiento tranquilo de la mano, sor Natividad ha bajado la túnica. (*Obras completas* 4:260; ellipsis in the original)

> [From time to time Sor Natividad bends or leans to pick a flower: the elegant curve of her hip is outlined beneath the white serge, the harmonious fullness of her breasts is emphasized. . . . When she takes a step forward, her long tunic catches in the branches. Her legs are revealed. Encased in the fine white silk, the ankle leads toward gracefully fleshy and full curves. Does Sor Natividad realize what has happened? A moment passes. Finally, with a calm movement of the hand, Sor Natividad lowers the tunic.]

In a virtual repetition of the prior chapter involving Jeanette, Sor Natividad, knowingly or not, reveals her body to Don Juan. The presentation—with the striking use of words like "ceñida," "seda," and "carnosa" and the focus on the nun's breasts—both echoes that of the previous chapter and, with Don Juan's presence, confirms the narrator's perspective in the first glimpse of Sor Natividad. The question that was earlier left unanswered, itself almost repeated in the description of Jeannette, is tacitly answered in the twentieth chapter. The allusive suspension points ("la rotundidad armoniosa del seno . . ." ["the harmonious fullness of her breasts . . ."]), which ought to leave the other details to the reader's imagination, are checked by the onward rush of the narration, Sor Natividad's step forward. And the more recent question is, indeed, answered by the abbess's discreet gesture of modesty and the subsequent exchange: "—Hermosa—ha contestado don Juan, contemplando la delicada tracería de piedra. Y luego, lentamente, bajando la vista y posándola en los ojos de sor Natividad: —Verdaderamente . . . hermosa. Dos rosas, tan rojas como las rosas del jardín, han surgido en la cara de sor Natividad. Ha tosido nerviosamente sor Natividad y se ha inclinado sobre un rosal" [" 'Beautiful,'

Don Juan replies, contemplating the delicate stone tracery. And then, slowly, lowering his glance and resting it on Sor Natividad's eyes, 'Truly . . . beautiful.' Two roses, as red as those in the garden, blossom in Sor Natividad's face. She coughs nervously and bends over a rose bush"] (*Obras completas* 4:261; ellipsis in the original).

    These two contiguous scenes of temptation inversely mirror the situation in *La Regenta*. Instead of two Don Juans, Don Alvaro and Don Fermín, there is simply Don Juan del Prado y Ramos. Instead of the solitary Ana Ozores onto whom are projected the carnal and spiritual fantasies of her suitors, Azorín offers Jeannette and Sor Natividad. In the end, however, the spiritual domain is again invaded by the carnal, and it is Don Juan who moves freely between the world of the convent and the drawing room, who brings out, or, as it were, articulates, the sensuality in Sor Natividad. In fact, in the presentation of Sor Natividad's encounter with Don Juan, her sensuality seems most natural. When she blushes, her cheeks are two roses and her proximity to the rosebush itself furthers the association of the abbess with the beauty— and sensuality—of the natural world.[33]

    The manner of the presentation of these two scenes involving Sor Natividad, Jeannette, and Don Juan suggests in a positive way what has previously—misleadingly—been asserted as negative, the carnal aspects of spirituality, which are, of course, part and parcel of mystic desire. Whereas in *La Regenta* Ana's interest in mysticism was viewed with nothing short of horror by those around her, in *Don Juan* Sor Natividad's obvious sensual pleasure in herself and her self-consciously modest yet nevertheless coy act of blushing before Don Juan restore to the spiritual domain a sensuality, derived from the intrusion of the masculine, that is presented as if it were natural, inevitable. Moreover, as if in response to the remark regarding Clarín's Don Alvaro—that

---

    33. In this regard, it is important to note that these same symbols of natural sensuality, the red roses and the rosebush, are present in the "poor" convent, that of the Capuchins of the Passion, and by means of juxtaposition, that the nuns are associated with the flowers. The nuns stand out against the white walls as they walk through the corridors as do the red roses growing in the interior courtyard, an implicit comparison highlighted by the similarity of the verbs. Again, there is a note of sensuality in this religious enclosure. Consider, too, the other significant reference to a red rose in chapters 35 and 36, which deal with a flower given to Don Juan by Jeannette. One explanation for this emphasis on the rose can be found in Gregorio Marañón's late discussion of Don Juan, in which he comments that the burlador's popularity will continue to flourish, "like the roses from the rosebush that the real Don Juan, Don Miguel de Mañara, planted there in Seville, several centuries ago. These roses still bear every spring the same color of sinful flesh and the same intoxicating aroma as when Mañara offered them to his lovers" (*Obras completas* 10:546–47).

"Entre monjas podría vivir . . . sin que hubiera miedo de escándalo" ["He could live in a nunnery without fear of scandal"] (*La Regenta* 1:311; 164)—Azorín's Don Juan enters the convent without creating any scandal whatsoever, which is not to say that he is not seductive or that the nun is unaware of her attraction for him. In other words, the spiritual world is seen to possess a natural, latent physicality, and Don Juan no longer represents a threat to nubile young women and beautiful nuns. To the contrary, when La Tía turns a young girl who must be "the niece" out of her home for something involving a "señorito," it is Don Juan who sees the girl leave the house with a suitcase and a bird in a cage, surely symbolic of her situation. While the girl is seated on her luggage, crying, Don Juan passes by and casually drops some "blue bank notes" in "the niece's" lap. Although perhaps ironic, it is also meaningful that it is Don Juan who witnesses the departure and who offers his charity: he is not only the cause of her downfall—the "señorito" has obviously acted like a Don Juan—but also the means by which "the niece" will survive.

Significantly, however, Don Juan's "temptation" occurs prior to what must be seen as the moment of his conversion, which means that this version of the *burlador* ceases to represent a supposed menace to society and social harmony *before* his spirit was "profoundly transformed." Thus, Don Juan is not, in fact, and never is, the threat he might seem. Indeed, in Azorín's rendering, Don Juan del Prado y Ramos's putative conversion comes about when he acts to better society by means of a charitable act that entails his destitution, and, hence, leads to the Hermano Juan of the end of the novel. Rather than a conversion, James's process "by which a self hitherto divided and consciously wrong inferior, and unhappy, becomes unified and consciously right, superior and happy," rather than the "profound tranformation" ironically mentioned in the prologue to the novel, Azorín's Don Juan fulfills his destiny as a literary character by providing for the renewal of the cycle of which he is a part.

At some point after his "temptation," Don Juan is walking in the mountains above the city when he sees a young boy carrying a load of wood on his back. The child's bare feet are bleeding and his burden is so heavy that he must struggle to raise his head to look at Don Juan. Moved by the sight of the boy, Don Juan takes the child on his knees and cleans the wounded feet. The boy, initially shy, becomes calmer and "entonces el niño le coge la mano a don Juan y se la va besando en silencio. ¿Qué le pasa al buen caballero que no puede hablar?" ["then the child takes Don Juan's hand and kisses it in silence. What has happened to the good gentleman who cannot speak?"] (*Obras completas*

4:263). This individual act of charity recalls others in the novel, all
involving children: the teacher who takes his pupils into the mountains, who says, "Yo quiero . . . que estos niños tengan un recuerdo
grato en la vida" ["I want . . . these children to have a happy memory in
their lives"] (*Obras Completas* 4:238); the new governor, the poet, who
is so irate at what he finds in the orphanage, "niños . . . escuálidos,
famélicos . . . vestidos de andrajos" ["squalid, starving children . . .
dressed in rags"] (*Obras completas* 4:241), that he loses his temper and
his appointment; the colonel of the Guardia Civil, both of whose children have died, who gives a young boy, a prisoner, additional food to eat.

   In a sense, these individual acts of charity are without effect, since,
relatively speaking, nothing changes. Yet, after Don Juan's encounter
with the barefoot boy, an enormous amount of money is left to the small
city, supposedly by Don Antonio Cano Olivares, to be used for the
construction of "unas espléndidas escuelas . . . dotadas de pensiones
para los niños pobres" ["some splendid schools . . . endowed with grants
for poor children"] (*Obras completas* 4:264). We are to infer that it is
Don Juan who endows the city with the money for the schools, surely in
part as a reaction and a response to the plight of the barefoot boy. Don
Juan has acted in a manner calculated to alter the future by helping
those who will inherit the present; his charity is profoundly humane,
recalling the Nietzsche who remarks that "humanity does *not* consist
in feeling with men how they are, but in *enduring* that I feel with
them. My humanity is a continual self-overcoming." Don Juan's gift,
which impoverishes him, is the token of his self-overcoming—not
conversion—and the symbol of his endurance. His thoughts at the end
of the novel are firmly focused on the future that he has created and for
which he has provided, not on the past that he has lived.

Leaving aside for the moment the question of conversion, in the light
of these demonstrations of social and personal ethics, *Don Juan* reveals itself to be a profoundly humanistic text. Neither especially orthodox in its embracing of Christian doctrine nor openly dogmatic in
its advocacy of individual charity, Azorín's novel nevertheless presents
the reader with an answer to the problematic social issues found in the
nameless and therefore ostensibly universal "small city." Rather than
spiritual and social anarchy—which are envisioned in the novel by
both the Bishop and the President—what we find are spontaneous acts
of generosity that transform society in such a way that the basic tenets
of patriarchal social culture remain in place. This means that Don
Juan's place in society is never questioned, his morality is never suspect; Azorín shows how "every other man" is indeed good, depending

on the social role he is destined to fulfill. As Kierkegaard's "B" says in *Either/Or,* "the ethical . . . is that whereby a person becomes what he becomes. It does not want to make the individual into someone else but into the individual himself; it does not want to destroy the esthetic but to transfigure it. For a person to live ethically it is necessary that he become conscious of himself, so thoroughly that no accidental element escapes him. The ethical does not want to wipe out this concretion but sees in it its task, sees the material with which it is to build and that which it is to build" (253). In the terms proposed by Nietzsche in *The Wanderer and his Shadow,* Don Juan has succeeded in his self-overcoming, in overcoming his "passions," which might account for his "transformation":

> The man who has overcome his passions has entered into posses-sion of the most fruitful soil, like the colonist who has become lord over the bogs and forests. To sow the seeds of spiritual good works on the soil of the vanquished passions is the next and most urgent task. The conquest itself is a means, not an end: if it be not so regarded, all kinds of weeds and devil's crop quickly spring up upon fertile soil that has been cleared, and soon the growth is all wilder and more luxuriant than before. (224–25)

If Azorín's *Don Juan* is, in fact, a conventional novel—in that there are characters, plot, a traditional narrative form, and a definite ideo-logical point of view—the author has left to the reader the task of repeating the text in its entirety. Yet the novel is indeed incomplete: it is one-sided in its portrayal of social relations and the effects of Don Juan on society. Although we see how Don Juan affects both Jeannette and Sor Natividad, the results of his attractions to and flirtations with various women are never divulged. Thus, we must turn to *Doña Inés* for the other half of the story, as well as for an answer to the question regarding conversion.

Set in 1840, the action of *Doña Inés* (*Historia de amor*) begins in Ma-drid but quickly moves to Segovia until the final two chapters, which are set in Buenos Aires. Ostensibly a sentimental novel treating affairs of the heart, while in fact a thoroughgoing parody of sentimental con-ventions (see Spires), *Doña Inés* plays on techniques associated with twentieth-century narrative in order to draw the reader more closely into the fiction. As the novel begins, a single woman, the wealthy Doña Inés de Silva, receives what must be a letter of farewell from her lover Don Juan. Depressed, she travels to Segovia, where her aunt and uncle—Tía Pompilia and Tío Pablo—still live. The two are living contrasts in approaches to time and represent two divergent forces at work in Doña Inés; married to one another yet living apart, Tía Pompilia, for whom "nada a su alrededor ha de estar inmutable" ["nothing around her is to remain immutable"] (*Obras completas* 4:763), pursues her social interests while Tío Pablo, for whom all must remain the same, writes in solitude and meditates on the nature of time and human existence.

In Segovia, Doña Inés hears of a young poet Diego Lodares, who is known in Segovia as Diego el de Garcillán and who is having an affair with Plácida, Doña Inés's maid. When Doña Inés and Diego meet by chance they are both struck by Cupid's arrow, "una flecha—invisible— [que] ha partido de corazón a corazón" ["an arrow—invisible—that split each heart"] (*Obras completas* 4:789), and they each become increasingly obsessed until yet another chance meeting in the cathedral where Diego kisses Doña Inés and she gives herself over to him "con una repentina y profunda laxitud" ["with a sudden and profound laxity"] (*Obras completas* 4:815), precisely Sor Natividad's state of being in *Don Juan*. All of Segovia finds out about this brief encounter and the subsequent affair, and Diego is called to account for his actions before Don Santiago Benayas, the local political authority, who chastises the poet merely for passing the boundaries of good taste in some of his published verse. With a final admonition to respect established aesthetic norms—"A la Musa, señor Lodares, se la solicita discretamente y no se la violenta. ¡Y vaya usted con Dios, amigo Diego!" ["The Muse, Señor Lodares, is solicited discreetly, and is not forced. And God be with you, Diego, my friend!"] (*Obras completas* 4:833)—Diego is let off the hook. Doña Inés, on the other hand, feels that she must somehow make amends. In a letter to her uncle, she gives gifts of money to her servants and friends, provides for her relatives, and then orders that her estate be liquidated. In the final chapters of the novel, a number of years have passed; Tío Pablo dies, and we see Doña Inés in Buenos Aires, where she has founded at her own expense a boarding school for poor children. Old and infirm, Doña Inés "no puede ya salir de su aposento. . . . El corazón la angustia. Su mano blanca se posa en sus labios y envía un beso, cuatro besos, muchos besos a los niños del jardín. Y acaso en el jardín, bajo el venerable y amado ombú, cobijado en su sombra, apartado del bullicio, hay un niño—otro futuro poeta—, un niño huraño y silencioso, con un libro en la mano" ["can no longer leave her room. . . . Her heart troubles her. Her white hand rests on her lips and she sends a kiss, four kisses, many kisses to the children in the garden. And perhaps in that same garden, sheltered in the shade of a venerable and beloved ombú tree, apart from the bustle, is another child—another future poet—a shy, silent child with a book in his hand"] (*Obras completas* 4:847).

The final words of the novel allude to Diego el de Garcillán and to the structuring principle of the narrative: repetition. Indeed, *Doña Inés* is elaborately organized around the possibility of repetition and change, around the way situations present themselves time and again and are somehow altered by individual will. As the novel opens, the extremely distant narrative voice brings us closer to the block of homes in Madrid where Doña Inés lives, behind the walls of which "está lo anodino. Lo anodino, es decir, lo idéntico a sí mismo a lo largo del tiempo; lo inalterable—dentro de lo uniforme—en la eternidad" ["is the ordinary. The ordinary, which is to say, that which is self-identical throughout time; that which is inalterable—within that which is uniform—in eternity"] (*Obras completas* 4:740). In words that echo Yuste's lament in *La voluntad*, the narrator prepares us for the events that follow. Once inside Doña Inés's home he details certain of the furnishings, daguerreotypes and lithographs, one of which is a picture of Buenos Aires. Emphasizing yet again the repetitive nature of life, the narrator points out that this is the lithograph that Doña Inés inevitably contemplates while she waits to hear from Don Juan, which links her seduction with Latin America in an anticipation of the end of the novel. Moreover, it turns out that Diego Lodares, although from Garcillán, actually grew up in Argentina, where his parents moved when he was twelve. In Argentina, Diego spent most of his time reading rather than working, usually in the shade of an *ombú* tree, which is the symbol of "la tradición poética y sentimental del gaucho" ["the sentimental and poetic tradition of the gaucho"] (*Obras completas* 4:776). At the end of *Doña Inés,* then, the heroine has founded a home where, perhaps, another young boy, a poet, might grow up. In an act of individual charity analogous to that found in *Don Juan,* one identical to that of Don Juan de Prados y Ramos, Azorín's protagonist has allowed for history to repeat itself.

This is not the only element of repetition in the novel. The story of Doña Inés and Diego is a recapitulation of a similar scenario involving Doña Inés's fifteenth-century ancestor Doña Beatriz González de Tendilla, whose history Tío Pablo is writing. Doña Beatriz, the wife of Don Esteban de Silva, is the aging protagonist of a tale of star-crossed lovers. Enamored of a beautiful troubadour who presents himself at the de Silva palace, Doña Beatriz devotes herself to the young man, who reciprocates her love, spending his days in Doña Beatriz's chamber where she caresses and combs his long blond hair until he disappears, never to be seen again. Despondent at the loss of her lover, Doña Inés nevertheless goes through the motions of preparing for a grand feast declared by her husband. When she opens a box holding her jewels to find locks of long blond hair (placed there, we are to infer, by Don Esteban, who has killed the troubadour), Doña Beatriz faints, then goes mad and lives out her days in isolation.

There are several aspects of the story of Doña Beatriz that are echoed in Doña Inés's own situation. Doña Inés strongly resembles her forebear, and Diego is a modern troubadour and shares the blue eyes and the beautiful golden locks of his fifteenth-century predecessor. But there are points at which the two accounts diverge, too, which means that we must account for both repetition and difference. The broad outlines of the story of Doña Beatriz are repeated in that of Doña Inés with the exception that the latter *acts* to avoid the fate of the former. In Leon Livingstone's words, "Doña Inés, abandoned by Don Juan, does not find herself in the same terrifying situation as Doña Beatriz, whose husband discovers her infidelity; and the bloody denouement of the first version of the story is not duplicated in the second. Azorín's use of this idea is not so much a 'return' as a 'repetition'" (*Tema y forma* 127).[34] To put this in the terminology proposed by Kierkegaard's theory of repetition, Doña Inés's encounter with Diego does not simply recollect that of Doña Beatriz's involvement with the troubadour, it repeats the situation, demonstrating in the process how an individual can alter that repetition to include change by acting within the parameters previously established. Thus, rather than succumbing to grief, an egoistic and solipsistic gesture, Doña Inés devotes herself to the future in the guise of the school for the poor children.

There is a suggestion in *Doña Inés* that this charitable gesture is involved in the creation of a new civilization. Included in the chapters that prolong the novel, the coy references to epilogues, is the fiftieth chapter, entitled "Hacia una nueva civilización" [Toward a New Civilization]. In this chapter, in which a profoundly disillusioned history of Europe is intercalated, the question of the future of civilization is posed in the unattributable voice of *style indirect libre*. At loose ends after the departure of Doña Inés, Tío Pablo (in whom some have seen Azorín) finds himself profoundly tired. In response to the question "¿Hacia dónde caminaba la humanidad?" ["Where was humanity going?"], the novel responds with a brief history of incipient socialism, bringing the

34. See also Julián Marías; Martínez Cachero, *Las novelas de Azorín* 188–202; Manuel Durán; José B. Vidal; Thomas C. Meehan; and Kathleen M. Glenn 69–94.

narration up to 1849, at which point Tío Pablo dies, asking the same question: "¿Hacia dónde camina la humanidad?" ["Where is humanity going?"]. This time we find an answer, however cryptic:

> La civilización basada en el derecho romano está agotada. Siglos antes o siglos después, al fin vendrá la muerte de la civilización actual. Hacia una nueva civilización caminaba la Humanidad. Virtualmente, el Derecho Romano estaba ya muerto. Se sentía don Pablo profundamente triste. . . . Se caminaba acaso hacia un período de caos y de barbarie. *Natura non rompe sua legge,* había escrito uno de los maestros de don Pablo, Leonardo de Vinci. La naturaleza no rompe sus leyes. Haga lo que haga la Humanidad, sea cuerdo o loco el hombre, sean ordenadas o anárquicas las sociedades humanas, al cabo, después de la barbarie, la Humanidad recomenzará lentamente su trabajo de civilización. El hombre es un animal de inteligencia y de orden; la inteligencia y el orden, en el transcurso de los siglos, a través de catástrofes y de horribles caos, acaban por imponerse. Y esto sucedería ahora; se caminaba hacia una nueva civilización. "¡Adiós, Europa!— repetía don Pablo en los últimos meses de su vida—. ¡Adiós, Acueducto y todo lo que tú representas! ¡Adiós, Imperio romano!" (*Obras completas* 4:841–43)

[This civilization based on Roman law is exhausted. In a few or in many centuries the death of the present civilization will come. Humanity was moving toward a new civilization. Roman law was now virtually dead. Don Pablo felt profoundly sad. . . . Humanity moved toward a new period of chaos and barbarity. *Natura non rompe sua legge,* one of Don Pablo's teachers, Leonardo da Vinci, had written. Nature does not break its own laws. Whatever Humanity may do, whether or not man is sane or crazy, whether or not human societies are ordered or anarchical, finally, after the barbarity, Humanity will begin its work of civilization anew. Man is an animal of intelligence and order, and throughout the centuries, in catastrophes and horrible chaos, he ends up imposing his will. And that would probably happen now. Humanity moved toward a new civilization. "Goodbye, Europe!" Don Pablo repeated during the last months of his life. "Goodbye, Aqueduct and all that you represent! Goodbye, Roman Empire!"]

In a lengthy speculation on the nature of change, which is linked to the evolutionary processes of humanity in its struggle toward civilization, the narrative claims to find itself at a crucial moment of historical rupture. Humanity is subordinated to a superior will that ensures continuity throughout the cataclysms of chaos and order, a view of humanity that comes close to that of Galileo, cited by Tío Pablo several chapters earlier: " 'Tra gli uomini è la potestà di operare, ma non egualmente participata da tutti: e non è dubbio che la potenza d'un imperadore è maggiore assai che quella d'una persona privata; ma e questa e quella è nulla in comparazione dell'onnipotenza divina' " ["All men are capable of working, but not all men are equally capable; there is no doubt that the power of an emperor is greater than that of a private citizen. But neither of these is anything when compared to Divine Omnipotence"]. Relativizing the notion of *individual* will, the capacity for inducing change, Tío Pablo, via Galileo, posits the existence of a supreme—and supremely omnipotent—*divine* will. But he never advocates submission, nor does he fear or wish to forestall change: "No sentía los terrores que pudieran sentir sus amigos y conocidos. El agotamiento de una civilización era para él un hecho ineludible. Hubiera, sí, querido ver algo de la nueva y lejanísima organización social" ["He did not experience the terror that his friends and acquaintances might have experienced. The exhaustion of civilization was, for him, an unavoidable fact. Yes, he would have liked to have seen something of that new and distant social organization"] (*Obras completas* 4:843). Serenely beyond such fears, Tío Pablo becomes the perfect observer of the perfect mechanism known as civilization.

There is, however, yet another aspect to this question pertaining to the future of civilization. What is posed as a question in the fiftieth chapter is rendered as a statement in the title of that same chapter. This rubric functions in at least three ways: first, as an anticipation of the questions found in the chapter, second, as a possible commentary on Tío Pablo's death, and third, as a description of Doña Inés's journey to the New World, indeed, to a new civilization. In fact, this chapter interrupts, as it were, the narrative flow from Doña Inés's letter of farewell in chapter XLIX to the brief vignette of her trip "desde Europa hacia el Nuevo Mundo" ["from Europe to the New World"] (*Obras completas* 4:845). In this sense, Tío Pablo's musings, in which a moment of historical rupture was suggested, are contradicted by Doña Inés's act of profound humanity. As was the case of Diego el de Garcillán, what sets sail from Spain and Europe for the New World inevitably returns, be it in the form of the person who originally departed or in the form of life nurtured in the shade of the *ombú*. Civilization does not end, although Tío Pablo does envision the death of the present civilization. Rather, it evolves, changes within a constancy of form, as Doña Inés lived the story of Doña Beatriz, changing a violent end for one of altruistic generosity: "Del pasado venimos al presente; del presente habremos de caminar hacia el porvenir" ["from the past we come to the present; from the present we will have to move toward the future"] (*Obras completas* 4:770). If not so powerful as "divine omnipotence," the individual is nevertheless capable of exercising a will that alters that which is to come.

This view of the possibility of change and of the individual's effecting that change complements a perspective that is espoused in similar terms in *Don Juan*. In the earlier novel, Jeannette's father Don Gonzalo asks, "¿Qué será de París dentro de doscientos años? No lo sabemos. ¿Hacia adónde va la Humanidad? Nadie puede decirlo. Entre tanto, gocemos del minuto presente. *Sub lege libertas.* La mayor suma de libertad, dentro de la ley. Dentro de unas pocas leyes limitadas a garantizar la seguridad del ciudadano" ["What will have become of Paris in two hundred years? We do not know. Where is Humanity going? Nobody can say. In the meantime, let's enjoy the present. *Sub lege libertas.* The greatest degree of liberty within the law. Within those few laws limited to guaranteeing the security of the citizen"] (*Obras completas* 4:256). Anticipating Tío Pablo's musings, Don Gonzalo speculates on the future, but only to posit his own individual freedoms in the form of a *carpe diem*. The "liberty" advocated in the Latin "*Sub lege libertas*" found in *Don Juan* is contradicted in *Doña Inés* by the Italian "*Natura non rompe sua legge.*" Whereas one individual seeks for those freedoms guaranteed him by the law, another submits himself to the laws of nature, which promise an inevitable flux.

But are the two maxims incompatible? Within the fictional world of *Don Juan* and *Doña Inés* they are, in fact, the obverse and reverse of the same coin. Freedom is advocated by and prescribed for man: *Sub lege libertas;* the laws of nature—like Freud's biology—are immutable for woman: *Natura non rompe sua legge.* In the first novel of this diptych, Don Juan del Prado y Ramos comes to his act of charity *after* "ha amado mucho y todas las mujeres se le rendían" ["he has loved a great deal and every woman surrendered herself to him"] (*Obras completas* 4:276). He possesses the freedom to evolve with time. In the second novel, Doña Inés, as a consequence of being abandoned by Don Juan and of her flirtation with Diego el de Garcillán, leaves behind all her worldly possessions and devotes herself to the future. Don Juan del Prado y Ramos is, indeed, free within the laws of patriarchy to seduce; Doña Inés de Silva acts within the laws of nature to fulfill her destiny as a woman, as one who is seduced and who nurtures, who provides for the future of man.[35] If Don Juan's act of charity is identical in *form* to that of Doña Inés, if both use their money to create homes and schools for the poor, the *substance* of the two acts is different. Don Juan's anonymous donation comes as the culmination of his life; he has enjoyed wealth and worldy fulfillment prior to his self-overcoming. Doña Inés, however, comes to the New World and to found the school almost as an act of atonement for her complicity in seduction. Don Juan becomes Hermano Juan and lives in spiritual tranquility and plenitude. Doña Inés fulfills symbolically her biological function of motherhood and becomes "Mamá Inés," living in sufferance, as revealed by her physical appearance: "La cara está pálida; anchas y profundas son las sombras de los ojos. Las arrugas de la faz son hondas. . . . No puede ya salir de su aposento la anciana fundadora del soberbio colegio. Es muy viejecita y está enferma. El corazón la angustia" ["Her face is pale; there are wide and deep shadows under her eyes. The wrinkles in her face are deep, too. . . . The elderly founder of the splendid school can no longer leave her room. She is very old and is sick. Her heart troubles her"] (*Obras completas* 4:847).

The novelistic diptych of *Don Juan* and *Doña Inés* presents the reader with the completion of the *burlador*'s story as a history of self-overcoming in which the individual acts of charity are seen as the logical and ethical culminations of seduction. What is for the man a scenario of freedom and pleasure is for the woman a drama of self-denial. After all, Diego el de Garcillán is a poet *and* a functionary of government; his role in the scandal that is the kiss is tolerated by Segovia. In fact, so complete are these relations of complicity, the interplay of religion, government, and social law in seduction, Diego's sobriquet "el de Garcillán," which refers to a village in the province of Segovia, sounds strangely close to the name of the sixteenth-century bishop Don García de Illán: laxity, compliance, and the "greatest degree of liberty within the law." If the individual must undertake acts of charity in order to alleviate suffering and to enable society to move continually and inexorably toward the fulfillment of civilization, humanity, now seen as patriarchy, nevertheless exerts its authority as the law.

35. María Doménica Pieropán's "feminist" reading of *Doña Inés* comes to a conclusion opposed to my own. She sees Doña Inés as finding a nonpatriarchal kind of fulfillment at the end of the novel and as asserting a feminine independence, indeed, as escaping from her creator: "Obtaining not only personal realization but also social integration, Inés seems to have usurped the author-ity [Pieropán's spelling] of her creator: the Inés who travels and founds a school contradicts the Azorinian philosophy of the eternal return, showing that, indeed, there are heroes, there are legendary acts, there are extraordinary developments of personality" (239).

Don Juan's "tranformation" is not, then, a conversion, religious or otherwise, but, rather, a kind of Nietzschean redemption. The *burlador* is not "divided, and consciously wrong inferior, and unhappy"; the world in which Don Juan lives is itself fragmented and out of joint and he therefore brings unity to that which is incomplete. In "On Redemption," Nietzsche writes:

> "I walk among men as among fragments of the future—that future which I envisage. And this is all my creating and striving, that I create and carry together into One what is fragment and riddle and dreadful accident. And how could I bear to be a man if man were not also a creator and guesser of riddles and redeemer of accidents?
>
> "To redeem those who lived in the past and to turn every 'it was' into 'thus I willed it'—that alone should I call redemption." (*Thus Spoke Zarathustra* 139)

A principle of order, repetition, and redemption, Don Juan both converts others *and* restores harmony and unity to a world in need of stability and continuity. In this sense, Don Juan *is* the humanity of which Tío Pablo speaks. The character Don Juan and these two novels of which he is a part evince a calm and even a satisfaction unexpected in stories involving the *burlador* as they move toward the inevitable acceptance of individual responsibility and charity. If we see Azorín's novels as a fitting conclusion to disorder and chaos, the *whole* of Don Juan's social role and the force of his latent humanism—though patriarchal, to be sure—become apparent.

In one of his considerations of Don Juan, Gregorio Marañón says, "Practically speaking, Don Juan, once old, can follow one of these three paths: either he gets married; or he persists in being a Don Juan, replacing his corporal decay with technical artistry; or he can devote himself to religion. Husband, dirty old man, or friar: this is how he will end up" ("La vejez de don Juan" [Don Juan's Old Age], *Obras completas* 1:440). For his part, Unamuno remarks that "Don Juan, after the years of his ardent youth have passed, usually marries and becomes a respectable member of the bourgeoisie, full of complaints and prejudices, recalcitrant, even neo-conservative" ("Sobre don Juan Tenorio," *Obras completas* 3:329). Azorín seems closer to Marañón in his assessment of Don Juan, is much more moderate in his approach to Don Juan's progression through time; but he *is* insistent on the *burlador*'s conventionality, on his necessary role as a social force. In the guise of spirituality,

Don Juan becomes Marañón's friar or Unamuno's Hermano Juan. Anonymous, like every man, he converts others to his religion, as, in the case of *Doña Inés,* Doña Beatriz's descendant is impelled toward the act of charity with which the novel closes. Very much in the tradition of his spiritual and intellectual mentor Nietzsche, Azorín discovers within the tradition of which he is a part the means of undoing and furthering that same tradition *without* the nihilism characteristic of Nietzschean paradigms. Clarín's Ana Ozores finds herself to be like other women, and the gallant Don Juan de Todellas teaches Cristeta—and Picón's female readers—how to be "dulce y sabrosa" or "sweet and savory"; Azorín shows his readers how this version of the *burlador* and one of his "victims" find within themselves a spiritual form of humanity that contributes to the continuity of Western civilization.

The ethical impulse detected in Azorín's *Don Juan* and *Doña Inés* discovers those traces of Don Juan's function as a positive social force and foregrounds them in the extension of the traditional story of the *burlador.* Azorín answers the question that is Don Juan not with hesitation—not by opting for the undecidable—but in the affirmative, in an affirmation of society's structure, order, and potential civilization. This is not to suggest that Azorín's position is absolute in its espousal of social hierarchies. As the emphasis on individual acts of charity demonstrates, Azorín stakes out moral ground somewhere between what is referred to in *Don Juan* as "Justice" and "the Law."

In fact, this point is articulated in a conversation between Pozas and the "presidente de la Audiencia" (president of the Court) Don Francisco de Bénegas. Pozas asserts that it is possible to separate "Justice" from "the Law," whereas Don Francisco maintains that, with this division, "quedarían alterados, subvertidos, derruídos los fundamentos del orden social" ["the foundations of social order would end up altered, subverted, destroyed"]. The problem, of course, has to do with nothing less than the foundations of society itself; as the Presidente asks, "si usted prescinde de la Ley, ¿en dónde va usted a asentar los fundamentos del orden social?" ["if you do away with the Law, on what are you going to lay the foundations of social order?"]. This question, though logical, is never explicitly answered in either *Don Juan* or *Doña Inés*. When Pozas attempts to respond, saying, "Yo asiento los fundamentos del orden social . . ." ["I lay the foundations of social order . . ."], Don Francisco abruptly cuts him off: "¡No, no! ¡Si ni puede decir usted nada! Si usted suprime la Ley, viene el caos, la anarquía . . ." ["No! No! You can't say anything! If you suppress the Law, chaos will come, anarchy . . ."] (*Obras completas* 4:238–39; ellipses in the original). The order imposed by the law is opposed to the disorder of anarchy, just as the spiritual laxity of the nuns was contained by the bishop Don García de Illán. The function of the law is to contain those elements that threaten to undermine social harmony and well-being, a point that is emphasized at the end of the exchange between Pozas and the Presidente:

> Caía la tarde. Caminaba detrás un mendigo y los ha alcanzado [a los hombres]; era un pobre caminante, andrajoso, con las melenas y las barbas largas; llevaba a la espalda un fardelito con ropa. El vagabundo ha pedido limosna a los caballeros; y como no se la dieron, se ha alejado, murmurando reproches y dando con el cayado en el suelo.
>
> Don Francisco se ha detenido, ha mirado con un gesto de severa reconvención a Pozas, y luego, señalando al mendigo, ha exclamado:
> —¡Ahí tiene usted! (*Obras completas* 4:239–40)

> [Evening was falling. A beggar walked behind the men and caught up with them. He was a poor tramp, dressed in rags, with long hair and a beard. On his back he carried a small pack with clothes. The vagabond asks the gentlemen for some alms; and because they gave him nothing, he has wandered off, murmuring reproaches and beating his staff on the ground.
>
> Don Francisco stops, looks with a gesture of severe reprimand at Pozas, and then, pointing to the beggar, exclaims, "There you have it!"]

The beggar does not incite the men to charity but instead serves to prove the point made regarding social order. Government protects the status quo and keeps the poor at bay; the law, ostensibly linked to justice, has no place for those unlike Don Francisco, Pozas, or the "new" governor.

If there is no place in the worlds of *Don Juan* and *Doña Inés* for anarchy, there is likewise no place for the miserly and miserable upholding of laws that do not serve all of the people. What is seen as absolute at the level of social reality and society's laws is subsequently modified—but not contradicted—at the level of the individual. Azorín thereby suggests that it rests with the individual, in an affirmative sort of "will to power," in a self-overcoming, to strengthen the foundations of society by means of individual acts of potentially collective benefit. The *burlador* initiates—with seduction—the reaffirmation of social bonds; Azorín's "everyman" brings the story of seduction to an end with individual acts of charity that further the collective aims of civilization in what Nietzsche might have called "a moment of the highest self-examination for humanity, a *great noon* when it looks back and far forward, when it emerges from the dominion of accidents and priests and poses, as whole, the question Why? and For What?"

The four novels studied here have given a clear sense of the ways in which seduction—by means of language—works in both a literary and a social sense. To a greater or lesser extent, seduction reveals itself to be intimately related to patriarchal social ends, and the novelistic presentation conspires with Don Juan in the aims of seduction. In the case of *La Regenta,* Ana Ozores was punished for trying to be more than what she was, a woman; and she was truly punished in that she was forced to live out her life in a vacuum. As Susan Kirkpatrick says of the female protagonist of Fernán Caballero's [Cecilia Boehl] *La gaviota* [The Sea Gull] (1849), an earlier novel in which the aspirations of an ambitious woman are considered:

> Retributive justice in this novel does not allow María to die of her illness but instead decrees that she end up where she belongs—in her native village, married to the barber she once scorned, keeping house, bearing and raising children as she should have done all along. Thus denying her protagonist the stature a tragic death might have bestowed upon her, Boehl purposefully dismantles the Romantic paradigm that glorifies the overreacher even in his defeat. In contrast to the dignity of a Romantic death, María's destiny is pictured as a comic hell. (267)

In truth, María is treated better than is Ana; Clarín's protagonist *wanted* children, hoped, if momentarily, to discover fulfillment in that way. In a reductive sense, then, it is possible to read *La Regenta* as a cautionary tale with an easily understood moral. The result of seduction is that women are all the same, regardless of where they start out. To cite Kirkpatrick on *La gaviota* yet again, "if woman's 'exalted place' is not accepted willingly, then it is imposed anyway as a penalty" (267).

Although Picón's Cristeta does not suffer a fate similar to that of La Regenta, by the end of *Dulce y sabrosa* she too has been rendered like other women. If she is smart enough to realize that marriage is a trap, she is nevertheless entrapped in a system that will exploit her. In essence, she becomes Juan de Todellas's mother, in a manner similar to Azorín's Doña Inés, who becomes Mamá Inés. Seduction, then, ensures the role of women in relation to men; and these novels exercise that same type of seduction by drawing the reader into the fiction and demonstrating the "inevitability" of their conclusions.

This conclusion is consonant with Nancy Armstrong's view of seduction in the English domestic novel. Armstrong claims:

> The communication situation established by seduction is one where the female subject desires to be what the other desires her to be. To relinquish the power of self-definition is the whole objective of seduction. . . . But if the woman relinquishes the power to discover a self that she believes society to consider to be her true self, then the distinction between seduction and education is rhetorical. (204–5)

By understanding novelistic fiction as an educational process that exercises a political and ideological force, Armstrong shows how literature functions as a type of seduction. In this sense, the collusion of the reader in the elaboration of Don Juan's story becomes one more means by which patriachal society continues its hegemony. Once seduction is seen as a part of social life, as virtually a female *rite de passage,* the reader must acquiesce to the validity of seduction as a social phenomenon and the authority of the literary text in its representation of this act.

Whereas the dramatic texts enacted, quite literally, the story of the *burlador,* including the end to be preferred—in other words, the dramatist sat in judgment over Don Juan—novelistic representations of Don Juan have a slightly different function. Even though *La Regenta, Dulce y sabrosa,* and *Don Juan* and *Doña Inés* appear to be open-ended, to suspend moral choices or to defer them to the reader, the narrative of these texts is, finally, unequivocal in terms of the *social* aims of seduction. Don Alvaro or Don Fermín might or might not be reprehensible (and the narrative is slippery on these points); Juan de Todellas is charming, to be sure, but perhaps a bit too sly for his own good; Hermano Juan has left his past behind him and turned to good works. But the objectives of seduction are always the same. As Simone de Beauvoir says, "One is not born, but rather becomes, a woman" (301). That becoming is Don Juan's raison d'être, and literary representations of the *burlador* are complicitous in that seductive lesson.

4

Don Juan and the Economy of Desire: Principals of Exchange, Principles of Exclusion

> *Since Freud did not care for music, and Lacan shared the same attitude, this rather suggests the necessity for the contemporary analyst to be concerned with the two areas that make up the myth of Don Juan— meaning and seduction, "message" and virtuosity.*
> —*Julia Kristeva, "Don Juan, or Loving to Be Able To"*

In the preceding chapters, I discussed the exceptional imaginative force that characterizes the figure of Don Juan as well as the role that seduction plays both in terms of the notion of honor and in that of the psychology of the individual in society. Don Juan's story reappears in the critical exegesis of literary texts in a similar scenario of seduction; he is implicated in a set of rhetorical strategies that exercise—in Shoshana Felman's words, that "dramatize" (*The Literary Speech Act* 28)— the power of language to persuade, to dupe, to promise, in short to offer yet another version of the patriarchal ways of the world, of "truth." Moreover, the literary and social implications of seduction and Don Juan indicate that, as a character, Don Juan offers an opportunity for authorial rivalry—judgment by comparison—and immortality. As a figure embodying specific social values, he serves as a domesticating force, as a principle of order in the social chaos that surrounds him.

If the *explicit* topics of the earlier chapters were distinct one from another, because they dealt with critical approximations as they related to the term myth, with the notions of honor and seduction in dramatic representations of Don Juan, and with the psychological and social implications of novelistic treatments of seduction, the *implicit* topic elucidated was constant. In each case, the discussion treated aspects of similarity and difference. Don Juan reveals himself to be many things at once, a Horatian *res communis* or common ground, a Platonic *daemon* or intermediary, a Freudian Eros, a sacrificial victim, a unifying principle. At the level of the literary text, the play of similarity and difference manifests itself in a number of ways as an "anxiety of influence." This anxiety is operative, to be sure, in many critical approximations as well. Yet, in terms of the critical treatments, there is another factor to be considered, namely, the ways in which the explications become one more version of Don Juan's story: the critical treatments are uncannily like their literary catalysts. Likewise, the meaning of Don Juan's story is equally anxiety-provoking, as the many endings proposed by the many authors demonstrate. Finally, as a social force, Don Juan takes that which is different and makes it the same, makes, for instance, Ana Ozores like the other women in Vetusta, at least inasmuch as she gives in to the temptation of seduction and thereby gives up any idea of being independent and different, something apart from the rest.

It is the play of similarity and difference as related to social principles and principles of exchange—particularly exogamy—that I shall explore here in two distinct lines of inquiry as a conclusion to the other discussions. Exchange and various notions of economy are at once more significant and less apparent than they might seem to be in terms of Don Juan; in fact, Jean-Marie Apostolidès says, "All exchangers are epitomized in Don Juan" (484). For example, in Tirso's *El burlador de Sevilla* [The Trickster of Seville], Don Juan's word functions in an economy of exchange, Tisbea banters and barters with Don Juan, Ana seeks to establish an exchange of her own and thereby to usurp the power of her father and her king to exchange her as best suits their interests, and Aminta tries to get the best deal for herself. Molière's *Dom Juan* closes with Sganarelle's lamentation of the way that his master abrogates their implicit contractual relationship of master and servant, crying, "Oh! My wages! My wages! Thus everyone is satisfied by his death: the Heaven he offended, the laws he violated, the daughters he seduced, the families he dishonored, the parents he insulted, the women he brought to evil, the husbands he drove to desperation. Everybody is happy. Only I am miserable. My wages, my wages, my wages!" (85). Zorrilla's Don Juan bribes servants into aiding and abetting him in his seductions; López de Ayala's Juan de Alvarado exploits the exchange of social courtesies; Clarín's Don Alvaro and Don Fermín are involved in the political and the religious economies of Vetusta; Picón's Juan de Todellas belatedly purchases Cristeta, giving her money at the end of their brief affair; Azorín's Don Juan and Doña Inés use their wealth to ensure a future for the present. In a number of meaningful ways, then, questions of economy and exchange are implicated in the story.

Whereas this study began with a consideration of critical and theoretical studies of Don Juan and continued with an analysis of the literary texts that gave rise to exegesis, in what follows, I first shall bring the discussion full circle by returning to critical and theoretical considerations of the *burlador* or trickster, this time to those that pertain primarily to the social and psychological concerns found in the literary texts. Then I shall initiate a somewhat different line of argument that involves questions of the social implications of seduction. These two distinct lines of inquiry will be brought together in a broadly historical overview of the shifts that occur in the nature and presentation of Don Juan. The purpose of these different topics is to provide a larger cultural context for the literary and critical versions of Don Juan, to show that the multitude of citations included throughout this study do indeed form part of a more general cultural and social scheme of hierarchy and exclusion that is presented and perpetuated by the written word, of which the *burlador* is but one example.

There are, of course, a number of treatments of Don Juan that emphasize the psychological and social aspects of the scenario of seduction in the contexts of literature and the "real world." But the most interesting are those that form part of a larger perspective of society, be it that of Spain or, more generally, that of the West. Thus, I shall briefly consider an anthropological approach to the question of Don Juan as characterized by Timothy Mitchell's Girardian extrapolation of Julio Caro Baroja's studies of Spanish culture; a psychoanalytic approximation as found in the work of Freud, Rank, and Jung; and a medical model and the philosophical dissent as articulated by Gregorio Marañón and José Ortega y Gasset, among others. These diverse, but not entirely divergent, treatments are discussed not only in a general sense but also in terms of the role played by woman, and in terms of how—and why—the treatment of woman as such brings these distinct views together. Moreover, the views of these theorists ought to be considered in conjunction with contemporary feminist views of literature and literary criticism, psychoanalysis, anthropology, political economy, and social theory as they relate to questions of exchange and seduction. By moving the discussion from literary to theoretical texts, and from there to recent issues pertinent to the ongoing polemic over the feminist project of revising history and society, economics and power, I hope to avoid the impasse characteristic of other treatments of Don Juan. In other words, rather than merely retelling the story of the *burlador*, and thereby implicitly recapitulating its meaning, I hope to show another manner of understanding the nature of Don Juan's story so that the meaning is not simply rendered more apparent, but that the dynamics of the figure, including his imaginative power, are recognized, too.

As a discipline, anthropology falls well within the dialectic of similarity and difference at work in Don Juan; the anthropologist attempts to explain what is particular in a given culture or similar to the cultural life of others. Lévi-Strauss, for example, adumbrates the universal structure of myth and demonstrates the ways in which a specific myth will change as it is adapted and modified by different cultural groups, all the while maintaining its structural integrity though changing, or better, sedimenting, its significance. In *Violence and Piety in Spanish Folklore,* Timothy Mitchell explores "the extent to which Spain's cultural history has been marked by the urge to isolate supposed characteristics of the 'race' for purposes of glorification or decontamination, a process that is tantamount to the invention of said traits" (5). He derives the specific model with which he works from Julio Caro Baroja's concept of "sociocentrism" (see Caro Baroja, "El sociocentrismo"), which refers to the power of belief in the superiority of one group over another, an idea that Mitchell develops within the framework of René Girard's ritual violence. The argument, then, deals with Spanish folklore and religion—with the cult of Santiago, Spain's patron saint; with religious festivals; with the peculiar strain of Spanish Catholicism; with bullfights. It emphasizes the role that violence and scapegoating play in the Spanish "will to differentiate" as it relates to piety:

> Piety forged in violence constitutes the ultimate referent of the moral codes that sustain the unity of the group and the honor codes that regulate its dealings with others. The devotion to a patron saint that crystallizes in a moment of crisis soon comes to symbolize the devotees themselves. Cults common to Christendom at large are localized and personalized, idiosyncratic procedures for the eradication of "enemies" grow up alongside, and solemn rituals become expedient vehicles of abreaction. (5)

In these terms, the code of honor is viewed as a means to create and to maintain identity in such a way that all dealings reveal and reinforce a process of differentiation. The rituals by which the notion of honor is kept alive become symbols within the culture itself, but are nonetheless attached to some past moment of "originary" violence from which the possibility of differentiation stems.[1] In their present form, these rituals provide a type of catharsis in that "rituals that employ mock or real violence" provide "a sense of *communitas* for the people involved" (38). In Spain, these rituals are particularly common and tend to focus on rivalry, combat, and scapegoating, precisely the literary and social dynamics discussed in relation to Don Juan.

One of the collective cultural products that Mitchell studies in some detail is Zorrilla's *Don Juan Tenorio,* which he reads as an "anonymous" text, given its origins in popular legend and its extreme popularity. The reading of the drama itself is none too startling since Mitchell believes "that Don Juan cannot be understood apart from a specific historical period and a specific society that (1) upholds a series of strict religious norms, (2) associates female honor with chastity, and (3) identifies male honor with aggressive virility and a pugnacious sort of one-upsmanship that can easily come to jeopardize the first two" (172–73). Moreover, woman is seen merely as the means of salvation, as the forgiving mother, symbolically at least, who intervenes on her son's behalf: "Within the polarizing patriarchal mindset . . . Don Juan's salvation *por vía materna* functions. . . . The end justifies the means—the only justice that matters for saintly mothers, as Unamuno said, is pity and love is their only law" (188–89). Yet the linking of *Don Juan Tenorio* with cultural rituals of violence destined to define and to maintain a specific group profile is significant; in this regard the social function of Don Juan—not only in *Don Juan Tenorio* but also in terms of this discussion in *El burlador de Sevilla* and *El nuevo Don Juan* [The New Don Juan]—acquires further social validity. As a scapegoat, Don Juan unifies society against him, serving as the means of differentiation, which, within the Nietzschean context discussed in conjunction with Azorín's novels, becomes the will to power. This Spanish model of self-definition is, in the end, advanced by Mitchell as not just particular, but, perhaps, universal:

> My study has been animated by the desire to unravel the relationship between collective values and collective violence, between social myth and social history. The suspicion that the *condition humaine* might be the Spanish labyrinth writ large

1. Yet, Mitchell cautions, then asserts, "Not all Spanish folklore is to be traced to some past episode of violence or crisis, nor presumably, will all Spanish folklore be susceptible to violent utilization. But those forms of folklore that relate most intimately to the unity of the group do indeed evince such origins and susceptibilities" (36).

has sustained my attempt to develop a research perspective with potential relevance to large group dynamics as well as to small. . . . In the last analysis, Spain's much touted "difference" may reside in its rigorous replication of humanity's fascination with violence as well as its unceasing efforts to master or deceive it. (198)

Thoroughly Girardian in its faith in the importance of an understanding of ritual violence for all of "humanity," Mitchell's consideration of piety as linked to ritual violence moves the study of Spanish cultural artifacts, specifically Zorrilla's *Don Juan Tenorio,* in the direction of larger social questions as they pertain to the shaping of the individual within society, a topic of equal importance in psychoanalytical discussions of individual psychology.

The nature of the group and of what holds it together—here construed as society and social bonds—as well as its role in the development of the individual is, of course, an issue broached rather late by Freud when compared with other aspects of his theories. Still, Freud's *Group Psychology and the Analysis of the Ego* (1921) offers several points worthy of consideration here, since Freud discussed his ideas relative to group psychology with Otto Rank, who was at the same time working on a study of Don Juan.[2] In a footnote to the postscript of *Group Psychology and the Analysis of the Ego,* Freud says, "What follows at this point was written under the influence of an exchange of ideas with Otto Rank" (*Standard Edition* 18:135 n. 1), and he refers in information added to this note in 1923 to one of the earliest expositions of Rank's thoughts on Don Juan, "Die Don Juan–Gestalt" (1922). Likewise, Rank cites Freud throughout *The Don Juan Legend,* and it is obvious that many of Freud's ideas with respect to the formation of a group, the "primal horde," and the development of the individual, especially as related to artistic creation, serve as the basis for Rank's interpretation of the *burlador.*

Freud's *Group Psychology and the Analysis of the Ego* evolves from an earlier consideration of similar topics, *Totem and Taboo* (1913). In the last essay in the earlier text, Freud deals with the origins of totemism in primitive culture—in an admittedly speculative manner—and concludes that, if "the totem animal is the father, then the two

2. See David G. Winter's prefatory remarks to his translation of *The Don Juan Legend* for a discussion of the various versions of Rank's work on Don Juan and the ensuing modifications (Rank x–xi, 25–34).

principal ordinances of totemism, the two taboo prohibitions which constitute its core—not to kill the totem and not to have sexual relations with a woman of the same totem—coincide in their content with the two crimes of Oedipus, who killed his father and married his mother, as well as with the two primal wishes of children" (*Standard Edition* 13:132). This comparison develops into a kind of fable of the originary violence that is responsible for ongoing societal guilt, indeed, for insights that are extended in *Group Psychology and the Analysis of the Ego*.[3]

What is striking in the later essay is the way in which Freud formulates the power of the group, likening it to Eros:

> love relationships (or, to use a more neutral expression, emotional ties) also constitute the essence of the group mind. . . . Our hypothesis finds support in the first instance from two passing thoughts. First, that a group is clearly held together by a power of some kind: and to what power could this feat be better ascribed than to Eros, which holds together everything in the world? Secondly, that if an individual gives up his distinctiveness in a group and lets its other members influence him by suggestion, it gives one the impression that he does it because he feels the need of being in harmony with them rather than in opposition to them—so that perhaps after all he does it *"ihnen zu Liebe"* [an idiom meaning "for their sake," literally, "for the love of them"]. (*Standard Edition* 18:91–92)

If Don Juan can be seen to function *both* as a modern-day Eros *and* as the means by which society defines itself and its values, then Mitchell is quite right to include Don Juan in his consideration of those ritual elements that play a role in Spanish self-definition. More to the point, Freud's invocation of Eros, especially when tied into the social theories of piety elaborated by Mitchell, parallels the notion that Don Juan not only unifies the community against him, but that the individuals give

3. For further elaboration of Freud's ideas, see Herbert Marcuse 55–126; and Juliet Mitchell 361–416. Tobin Siebers points out, "Freud's 'Just-So Story' is often called his greatest theoretical blunder. When seen in the light of a certain tradition, however, the schema reveals another aspect. Robertson Smith, Durkheim, and Mauss all stress the singularity of sacrifice in culture. Freud's primal horde theory should be interpreted as a restatement and elaboration of these contemporary theories; he only presents in another language such central anthropological notions as the 'totemic feast,' 'effervescence,' and 'participation mystique' " (*The Mirror of Medusa* 165 n. 13).

up their personal ambitions, in essence their individuality, in order to further the aims of society.[4]

Freud also offers a means by which to understand the literary dynamics of Don Juan's story in a social context, a point that figures in the conclusion to Rank's study. Although Rank is ostensibly interested in an explication of *Don Giovanni,* which, like Kierkegaard's "A," he regards as the supreme work to deal with Don Juan, there is the lingering impression that the libretto of the opera serves Rank as the occasion for advancing a psychoanalytic perspective on artistic creation. On the one hand, he discusses Leporello as Don Giovanni's double and "ego-ideal," the Statue as a figure of avenging death and the primal father, and the role of women; on the other, he suggests throughout his study that he will add something to the obvious psychoanalytic correlation between Don Juan and the Oedipus complex, as when he remarks

> that the many women whom he must always replace anew represent to him the *one* irreplaceable mother; and that the rivals and adversaries whom he deceives, defrauds, struggles against, and finally even kills represent the *one* unconquerable mortal enemy, the father. This psychological elemental fact has been discovered through the analysis of individuals; yet when psychoanalysis is applied to an extra-analytic theme it can only serve as the starting point for advancing our understanding, rather than as a result that is known in advance and only had to to be confirmed. (41–42)

By the end of *The Don Juan Legend,* however, it becomes apparent that the textual analysis was, indeed, a prop for a psychoanalytic exploration of the Oedipal aspects of the story, even if the emphasis has shifted from *sexual* possession to mere possession itself: "In summary, we may say that the characteristic Don Juan fantasy of conquering countless women, which has made the hero into a masculine ideal, is ultimately based on the unattainability of the mother and the compensatory sub-

---

4. Freud comments in *Group Psychology,* "Social justice means that we deny ourselves many things so that others may have to do without them as well, or, what is the same thing, may not be able to ask for them. This demand for equality is the root of social conscience and the sense of duty" (*Standard Edition* 18:121). Yet Freud also points out that if, before the institution of society, the "members of the group were subject to ties just as we see them to-day . . . the father of the primal horde was free. His intellectual acts were strong and independent even in isolation, and his will needed no reinforcement from others. . . . He, at the very beginning of mankind, was the 'superman' whom Nietzsche only expected from the future" (*Standard Edition* 18:123).

stitute for her" (95). The move from sexual possession to "the exclusive and complete possession of the mother, as once experienced in the pleasure of the prenatal situation and forever afterward sought as the highest libidinal satisfaction" (95) is a twist that corresponds, of course, to Rank's earlier work in *The Trauma of Birth,* where it is claimed that sexuality is an attempt to work through the trauma associated with birth and that, moreover, society has progressed toward patriarchy and the increasing marginalization of women *because* of the painful memories associated with this trauma. This, then, translates into a social and cultural ambivalence toward the mother, which finds expression in Don Juan's story as the simultaneous desire for and repudiation of women.[5]

Curiously, Rank's psychoanalytic interpretation of Don Juan's story, in drawing on Freud's theories of primitive social violence as found in *Totem and Taboo* and *Group Psychology and the Analysis of the Ego,* actually anticipates Jung's own passing references to Don Juan. Rather than associating Don Juan with the trickster—for example, in "On the Psychology of the Trickster-Figure" (1954)—Jung discusses the *burlador* in terms of the "mother complex." In "Psychological Aspects of the Mother Archetype" (1954), Jung comments that "typical effects [of the mother complex] on the son are homosexuality and Don Juanism, and sometimes also impotence. In homosexuality, the son's entire heterosexuality is tied to the mother in an unconscious form; in Don Juanism, he unconsciously seeks his mother in every woman he meets" (par. 162). Within the broad spectrum of psychoanalysis, therefore, Don Juan is viewed not as a trickster, as a strictly social agent, but as an individual suffering from attenuated development who attempts to bind himself ever more closely to a mother figure.

Nevertheless, there is a specifically social aspect to Don Juan's story

---

5. Winter, Rank's translator to English, advances a similar interpretation of Don Juan—by means of *Don Juan Tenorio*—in *The Power Motive.* Winter says, "To sum up my interpretation of the legend: Don Juan seeks fusion with his mother through seducing a series of women; yet he fears this very fusion, because it is also the source of frustration and thus the threat of his own destruction. He cannot separate these two aspects of 'woman,' because they have been complexly bound together by his mother; and so he is driven to pursue both at once. Symbols of this complex combination of attractive and destructive femininity abound in the play: women themselves, the ocean, the statue, the tomb—all seen as incorporating or 'swallowing up.' Don Juan's behavior—seductions, deprecation, bragging, destruction, prestige, insolence—are thus a drive for power to defend against this incorporation, to control the chaotic and confused sources of pain and pleasure" (173).

according to Rank, one that corresponds to Freud's views of creativity. From the outset, Rank signals his interest in various aspects of Don Juan's story, the individual and the social, the material elaborated in the literary appropriations, and the question of artistic form. Concern for creative processes and "the social function of art" (44) turns up again in the context of Rank's arrogation of Freud's fable of the primal horde, where it is the poet who breaks the emotional impasse associated with the aftermath of the primal crime. In assuming the burden of guilt by converting reality into the stuff of fantasy, the poet thereby becomes the hero of his own story.

Freud suggests that the moment of the first epic poem is a move toward differentiation:

> It was then, perhaps, that some individual, in the exigency of his longing, may have been moved to free himself from the group and take over the father's part. He who did this was the first epic poet; and the advance was achieved in his imagination. This poet disguised the truth with lies in accordance with his longing. He invented the heroic myth. The hero was a man who by himself had slain the father—the father who still appeared in the myth as a totemic monster. Just as the father had been the boy's first ideal, so in the hero who aspires to the father's place the poet now created the first ego ideal. . . . The poet who had taken this step and had in this way set himself free from the group in his imagination, is nevertheless able (as Rank has further observed) to find his way back to it in reality. For he goes and relates to the group his hero's deeds which he has invented. At bottom this hero is no one but himself [the poet]. (*Standard Edition* 18:136)

With respect to Don Juan, Rank asserts apropos of Tirso's *El burlador de Sevilla:*

> the first Don Juan poet (whether or not he might have been a historical personality) has given us the psychological meaning of the vengeance of death, and has embodied this meaning in a dramatic figure that is both eternal, and yet, as we have seen, capable of metamorphosis. Because of a strong personal and social sense of guilt acting from within, he has fantasized, in addition to the traditional punishment, the crime that psychologically corresponds to it [the serial seduction of women]. Indeed, from the primal situation itself, we have even succeeded in

freely deducing the form of Oedipal orientation that characterizes Don Juan exactly. (105–6)

In this regard, the original story of Don Juan and its subsequent retelling embody the "artistic function of poetic art," which, following Aristotle and Freud, corresponds to "catharsis: presenting in the content of
poetry the primitive complexes of mankind, in their actual state of
repression at any particular time" (120).

The anthropological and psychoanalytical models are thus similar in
that they both deal with the *social* importance of Don Juan's story in
terms of differentiation, the one by means of the self-definition of a
group, the other by emphasizing the role that the individual—the poet
and Don Juan—plays in channeling the guilt in the form of art's social
function. Moreover, both relegate woman to a paradoxically secondary
role, immaculately maternal rather than procreatively sexual. If literature serves a broadly social function in these discussions, it is also
important to note that there is a tacit assumption being made with
respect to the topic of Don Juan, be it implicit on the part of the anthro-
pologists and explicit on that of the psychoanalysts. That assumption is
nothing other than the *reality* of Don Juan and the *fact* of his effects
upon society.

The question of Don Juan's historical existence is one that is
broached throughout critical assessments of the figure, and it lies at
the heart of Gregorio Marañón's work on Don Juan.[6] A medical re-
searcher and clinician interested in aspects of human sexuality and
social development, Marañón devoted considerable intellectual energy
to the elaboration and defense of his views of the *burlador*. His first
foray into the field of criticism surrounding Don Juan was with the
1924 essay "Notas para la biología de don Juan" [Notes for the Biology of Don Juan], an essay substantially similar to a lecture given
that same year at the Royal National Academy of Medicine of Madrid
under the title "Psicopatología del donjuanismo" [Psychopathology of
Don Juanism]. He continued to develop and to restate his ideas, principally in the 1928 prologue to Francisco Agustín's *Don Juan en el
teatro, en la novela y en la vida* ("La vejez de don Juan" [Don Juan's
Old Age]), in the 1933 prologue to Manuel Villaverde's *Carmen y don
Juan* ("Más sobre don Juan" [More on Don Juan]), and in the 1939
lecture "Gloria y miseria del conde de Villamediana" [The Glory and

6. Gonzalo R[odríguez] Lafora also speculates as to the "real" Don Juan. He both
disagrees with Marañón and Pérez de Ayala as to the physical type (33–38) and offers his
own clinical record of this "person" (64–71).

Misery of the Count of Villamediana], which was subsequently published in 1940.

In the essay of 1924, Marañón proposes to examine Don Juan from
the optic of biology, because "Don Juan is not, as we all know, an ideal
creature but a being of flesh and blood, with his own particular anat-
omy and physiology; we might add, with his own personal clinical
history" ("Notas," *Obras completas* 4:75). The reason for Marañón's
interest is both clinical and moral. He sees in Don Juan a "myth" of
virility that induces men to act in a manner counterproductive to the
aims of the individual and of society:

> The majority of men, including those men of an extensive biologi-
> cal culture, ignore the fact that they are dealing with a myth [of
> virility] and they submit themselves without reflection to its
> consequences. And they situate the masculine ideal in the vain
> determination of wanting to convert into a perennially burning
> fire that which is merely a spark, as bright as it is brief, that
> shoots out here and there, not always when hoped for and often-
> times when least expected. ("Notas," *Obras completas* 4:77)

By aspiring to incarnate this myth of virility, men fall into the gravest
of errors. The man who does nothing but seduce women is but half a
man ("un varón a medias" ["Notas," *Obras completas* 4:78]) and is
somehow mentally deficient and of fragile moral fiber. He seduces because he is unable to do anything else, and this reveals the problem for
Marañón; "Don Juan is . . . unfit for social struggle" ("Notas," *Obras
completas* 4:80), which means that, as such, he is not masculine and
ought not to be seen as the masculine ideal. The "real" man, according
to Marañón, is someone suspiciously similar to Marañón himself, who,
in a rejoinder to José Ortega y Gasset, says, "My will has always been
feeble and incapable of yielding to almost any temptation" ("Gloria,"
Obras completas 3:545):

> It will surprise many that the man par excellence is not an
> impenitent hunter of women, but an industrious and active
> man, frequently monogamous, oftentimes shy and even a re-
> cluse in a state of voluntary chastity. But this is, in fact, the
> truth, and one must repeat it often and wave it as a banner in
> the battle against Don Juanism. The most virile man is the one
> who works the most, he who best conquers other men, and not
> the Don Juan who tricks poor women who are naturally disposed
> beforehand to allowing themselves to be deceived. ("Notas,"
> *Obras completas* 4:83)

Additionally, Marañón goes into detail with respect to what has been identified as the "effeminacy," if not to say homosexuality, of Don Juan, which is, in fact, his lack of virility. He even attempts to refute the notion that the *burlador* is a model of masculine beauty by turning to an endocrinological explanation that emphasizes just how homely Don Juan ought to be. When carried to their extreme, the characteristics adduced by Marañón "give way to a type of acondroplastic dwarf, who, beneath his grotesque appearance usually conceals an incredible aptitude for love" ("Notas," *Obras completas* 4:89).

There is, however, another equally pressing aspect associated with the problem of Don Juan to which Marañón turns his attention: woman. For Marañón, the truth of Don Juan's story is that it only *seems* as if the *burlador* were pursuing women. It is really the other way around; the women pursue their seducer ("Notas," *Obras completas* 4:80). Indeed, "because woman habitually attracts and courts the man, in the case of the Don Juan, he is the one who sweeps away the woman, who allows himself to be courted by her" ("Notas," *Obras completas* 4:84). Yet it is not a question of *all* women pursuing Don Juan; "women sensitive to Don Juanism will watch him pass by with indifference" ("Notas," *Obras completas* 4:89). Women who duplicate Don Juan in terms of an abnormal sexual desire—because, of course, woman's "sexual appetite" is normally much smaller than that of man—and women who suffer from "troubled minds" or are "hysterics, with muted instincts" ("Notas," *Obras completas* 4:91): these are the two types of women who are attracted to a Don Juan.

Marañón is unequivocal on this point and he goes so far as to reiterate that "no normal woman, in possession of her head and her desires, has ever been seduced by a Don Juan" ("Notas," *Obras completas* 4:92). What underlies Marañón's assessment of Don Juan and his moral concern for the dangers of the myth of a "superman" of virility is a thoroughgoing misogyny that relegates woman to the category of muse, even though it might appear that Marañón holds progressive beliefs with respect to women and their role in society. In "Gloria y miseria del conde de Villamediana," Marañón alludes to the cyclical nature of civilization—and, therefore, of the vicissitudes of Don Juan—in words that echo some of Picón's thoughts on the matter of relations between the sexes:

> I myself realize that Don Juanism, which twenty years ago was a pathetic problem for men and women of that time, has now almost ceased to be troublesome. Don Juan continued to represent man's odd and ostentatious, at times heroic, reaction to the

organization of sexual life. And this organization is today totally different. I said different and not new, because love is always already invented, lived, and spoken from time immemorial. This same present moment has already been lived by men. . . . The present mode of social forms of human love is typical of critical moments in history; and today, without question, is one of these critical moments. It consists of unlimited liberty in terms of carnal love and of an increase in the social influence of women. ("Gloria," *Obras completas* 3:546)

Marañón lets this comment slip by without elaboration. But in "Más sobre don Juan," he clarifies his views regarding the question of woman. Beginning by announcing the imminent death of Don Juan, Marañón discusses his view of progress, which results in a conspiracy against Don Juan because of the "man's instinct" and the "feminine soul." Because women are overcoming their sense of inferiority, with its "pronounced accent of masochism," all of society will progress to the point that Don Juan will no longer serve as a model of virility:

The greatest revolution and the most typical of our time is precisely this one: woman's conquest of the dignity of her sex, a transcendent phenomenon, much more important than the greatest political and economic cataclysms, if somewhat obscured by the foolishness of the majority of women who are feminists. At the hands of authentic women, antifeminists, those for whom the progress of their sex consists of becoming more and more like women, the boastful race of the Tenorio will be extinguished by asphyxiation. And we will have contributed to this those of us who, out of love for woman herself and out of pride for our own virile dignity, might have wanted to drive out of each man the most removed trace of the Don Juan. ("Más," *Obras completas* 1:547–48)

To his credit, Marañón advocates an end to the "masochistic" inferiority historically attributed to women and to all hints of Don Juanism in men. He also sees a future in which there is no Don Juan, when there will be "a simple and clear sexual life, free of myths of this or that meaning" ("Notas," *Obras completas* 4:93). But his comments are situated in the context of a vigorous antifeminism and an endorsement of an essentialist view of woman, in "authentic women, antifeminists." In this sense, the traditional moral values expressed by Marañón in his discussions of Don Juan inscribe social relations between the sexes in terms of *difference,* of masculine instinct and the feminine soul, from which one could extrapolate a series of like oppositions as determined by culture.

If it seems that Marañón's views and prejudices are easily dismissed upon closer scrutiny, such is not the case, at least in the context of early twentieth-century Spain. At first glance, the philosopher José Ortega y Gasset's observations with respect to Don Juan, especially those in which sly references to Marañón are made, seem to differ from those of the medical doctor. In "Vitalidad, alma, espíritu" [Vitality, Soul, Spirit] (1924), Ortega remarks in passing that Don Juan "is neither so simple nor so easy to dismiss as my dear Marañón presumes" (*Obras completas* 2:464) while in "Divagación ante el retrato de la marquesa de Santillana" [Digression While Standing Before the Portrait of the Marquesa de Santillana] (1918) he opines, "Don Juan's vice is not, as a plebeian psychology would suppose, that of brutal sensuality" (*Obras completas* 2:693). Ortega's petulance as regards Marañón's views becomes most forceful in "Para una psicología del hombre interesante: conocimiento del hombre" [Toward a Psychology of the Interesting Man: Knowledge of Man] (1925):

> Everybody thinks that his is the correct or true interpretation of him—of Don Juan, the most recondite, most abstruse, most acute problem of our time. The fact is that, with few exceptions, men can be divided into three classes: those who believe they are Don Juans; those who believe they have been Don Juans; and those that think they could have been, but didn't want to. The latter are the ones who are inclined, with worthy intention, to attack Don Juan and perhaps to decree his demise. (*Obras completas* 4:468–69)

Ortega takes Marañón to task for decreeing the death of Don Juan and, in the process, accuses the doctor of harboring seductive tendencies, to which Marañón replied with his "will . . . always feeble and incapable of yielding to almost any temptation."

It is difficult to give an idea of how sensitive and provocative an issue Don Juan was in the period between the world wars. Marañón's views can be contrasted with those not only of Ortega y Gasset but of Ramiro de Maeztu (who reads Don Juan as a symbol of dynamic—yet frivolous—energy), Hernani Mandolini (who arrives at "conclusions diametrically opposed to those of Marañón—with all of our limitations and with all of the respect that we owe the illustrious physiologist" [326], conclusions that reaffirm Don Juan's masculinity), and Gonzalo

Lafora (who disagrees with Marañón *and* Pérez de Ayala *and* Ortega y Gasset). In truth, the psychological aspects of Don Juan as an individual as well as his effects on society had stimulated comment from the late nineteenth century on, and in strikingly similar terms. In Armand Hayem's *Le Don Juanisme* (1886), a study of the *burlador* as a psychological principle, Don Juan is associated with superior intelligence and ability, and he is, once again, inevitably eternal: "he is eternal and we will find him in the hereafter, if one still finds these men to seduce and women to be seduced" (125). The view of sexual difference as opposition detected at work in Marañón's accounts can be found in Hayem's, in the men that seduce and the women that are seduced, and even in the act of seduction itself: "Seduction, if it is not an art, is nothing but violence" (26). Art or violence, culture or nature, man or woman, all are oppositions involved in descriptions of Don Juan and of society.

These oppositions are to be found in Ortega's discussions, too; his ideas about Don Juan begin—and end—where those of others have. Ortega asserts in the essay "Amor en Stendhal" [Love in Stendhal] (1926) that "Don Juan is not the man who makes love to women, but, rather, the man to whom women make love" (*Obras completas* 5:568). At least initially it seems as if this observation is of but slight importance to an understanding of Ortega's views, but it is a point to which we shall have cause to return. In general, then, Ortega sees in Don Juan a figure allied with spontaneity who stands in opposition to reason and rationalism, in a word, culture, which is represented for Ortega by Socrates. Ortega's explanation in *El tema de nuestro tiempo* [The Topic of our Time] (1923) of this opposition is similar to Nietzsche's paradigm of the tensions between a cult of Dionysus and the vision of Apollo in his *Birth of Tragedy*, in that Ortega posits a moment in history—that he associates with Socrates—at which reason comes to dominate spontaneity. This shift from one mode of being to another results in our culture in a "duality in our existence, because spontaneity cannot be overcome; it can only be arrested as soon as it arises, can be detained and covered over by this second life, a reflexive gesture, which is rationality" (*Obras completas* 3:176).

According to Ortega, humanity finds itself at another important juncture in its history, precisely that point at which it must rediscover and recuperate its spontaneity. Thus, "*the topic of our time* consists of submitting reason to vitality, of situating it within the biological, subordinating it to spontaneity" (*Obras completas* 3:178). In a manner analogous to that of the cyclical view of life espoused by Nietzsche, spontaneity again becomes important to mankind; Don Juan, as the maximum representative of such spontaneity in our culture, regains his importance as a cultural symbol. This leads Ortega to cite Nietzsche in the conclusion of his essay and to propose an ethical twist to the figure of Don Juan:

> The hour has irremissably arrived at which life will submit its demands to culture. "Everything that we today call culture, education, civilization, will have to appear before the infallible judge Dionysus," Nietzsche said prophetically in one of his early works.
>
> Such is the irony of Don Juan, an equivocal figure that our age continues to refine, to polish, to the point of endowing him with a precise meaning. Don Juan turns against morality, because morality had earlier rebelled against life. Only when there exists an ethic that takes account of, as its first principle, vital plenitude, will Don Juan be able to surrender himself. But this implies a new culture: biological culture. *Pure reason will have to yield its empire to vital reason.* (*Obras completas* 3:178)

In this revealing passage, Ortega finds in Don Juan a possible articulation of a new culture: the *burlador* is pure spontaneity and vitality. This view is all but identical to that of Ramiro de Maeztu, for whom Don Juan is raw energy and power devoted to pleasure, to caprice. Yet Maeztu concludes his own discussion of Don Juan with an invocation not of Nietzsche the father, but of God, and with the possibility that there is no higher truth than that of man:

> The conservation of energy is an elemental obligation [*deber elemental*]. It is a higher obligation to employ our energy in fostering knowledge and love among men. But if these obligations have no foundation, if there does not exist a Creditor with the right to oblige us to pay our debts, if there are no debts and happiness is the supreme law, let us waste our energy on caprice, because this is pleasure, and let us proclaim once and for all that Don Juan is right. (*Don Quijote, Don Juan y la Celestina* 106)

On the one hand, both Maeztu and Ortega see in Don Juan a vital force, be it called energy or spontaneity. On the other, and in contrast to Maeztu, Ortega finds a synthesis of reason and spontaneity in a shift from "pure reason" to "vital reason," a shift that will entail if not the death then the renewed subdual of Don Juan.[7]

---

7. It is in the ideas of Ortega, of course, that Carlos Feal finds his greatest inspiration for his utopian version of Don Juan. For Feal, "Don Juan rises once again on his own

The opposition at work in Ortega's account seems to be resolved dialectically, in that spontaneity gives way to reason, which in turn will give way to "vital reason." Yet this dialectical synthesis is not operative in the more practical domain of social life. Ortega succinctly affirms that "Don Juan is the man who, before woman, is nothing but a man—not a father, not a husband, not a brother, not a son" ("Meditación del marco," *Obras completas* 2:308), a view that echoes Tirso's *burlador* who says in the opening scene of *El burlador de Sevilla* that he is "a man with no name" (line 15). Don Juan is, then, man, pure and simple, and, furthermore, the essence of man apart from those social ties that define him in relation to women. Likewise, Ortega elsewhere affirms, "The role of woman, when she isn't anything but woman, is to be the concrete ideal ('enchantment,' 'illusion') of the man. Nothing more. But nothing less. . . . So woman is woman to the extent that she is an enchantment or ideal. A perfect mother is probably an ideal mother, but being a mother is not to be ideal" ("Epílogo," *Obras completas* 3:326). Before woman, Don Juan is man; before man, woman is "the concrete ideal."

As posited by Ortega, the difference between man and woman would not be so remarkable if it were not much more significant and fundamental to his view of things. In passages that are virtually interchangeable with those of Marañón, Ortega carefully circumscribes woman in terms of her function as *merely* a woman. For example, he begins the epilogue to Victoria Ocampo's *De Francesca a Beatrice* with a question, virtually the same question that seems to structure novelistic discourse on women, "But what is woman when she is nothing 'but woman'?" (*Obras completas* 3:323). He answers his question only after considering the nature of "ideals"; immediately after concluding that "woman . . . is to be the concrete ideal. . . . Nothing more. But nothing less," Ortega goes on to express surprise, indeed, horror, at the thought that women would be anything but "ideal" women:

> It is incredible that there might be minds so blind as to admit that woman could influence history as much with the electoral vote and a doctorate as she does with the potent magic of illusion. Because there does not exist in the human condition a biological working so sure and effective as the faculty possessed

---

ruins as a form of utopia. . . . This is the final moment of self-completion, one that points not to the past, but to a beyond, a future time, irremissably future" (5). Yet Feal's utopian future time, *"irremissably* future," is somewhat less optimistic than Ortega's claim that "The hour has irremissably arrived at which life will submit its demands to culture."

by woman to attract man, nature has made of this the most powerful ploy in selection and a sublime force for the modification and perfection of the species. (*Obras completas* 3:327)

If women are responsible for the modification and perfection of all mankind, seemingly an important task within Ortega's framework of social progress, it must be emphasized that theirs is a particularly strange role in the great scheme of things. Political influence and education are not important for women; nor will influence and education allow women to play a significant part in the development of society. As Ortega notes, "Masculine excellence stems, then, from *making and doing* [*en un hacer*]; that of woman in *being and existing* [*en un ser y en un estar*]. In other words, the value of man derives from what he *makes and does* [*por lo que hace*]; woman for what she *is* [*por lo que es*]" (*Obras completas* 3:329). Once again, the essence of woman is to be a woman; in fact, it is her essence ("*ser*") *and* her existence ("*estar*"). But that is also her role in social progress:

> Thus it is explained that the culture and perfecting of the woman have a trajectory different from that of man. While the progress of the male consists principally of making things better each time—in science, art, law, and technical fields—the progress of woman consists of her making herself ever more perfect, of her creating in herself a new type of femininity that is more delicate and demanding. (*Obras completas* 3:330)

Ortega's views on Don Juan differ from those of Marañón, but the underlying assumptions are, if not identical, similar. Marañón speaks of the "foolishness of the majority of women who are feminists" and claims, "At the hands of authentic women, antifeminists, those for whom the progress of their sex consists of becoming more and more like women, the boastful race of the Tenorio will be extinguished by asphyxiation." Ortega also views woman in terms of an ongoing struggle for feminine perfection and implicitly censures those who would support women's suffrage. Under the guise of difference—intellectual difference, competing interpretations—we find the same principle, that of hierarchy and exclusion.

These three different approaches to Don Juan—Mitchell's anthropological discussion of ritual violence; the psychoanalytic interpretations; the medical and philosophical readings—have in common not only the same topic, Don Juan, but also the same dynamics of similarity and difference at the heart of which is a surprisingly consistent misogyny, be it in the form of structural marginalization within the theories relating to Don Juan or in the underlying ideological assumptions with respect to sexual difference and social roles. In this sense, Don Juan's role is doubly related to difference in that he serves as a principle of differentiation at the level of the group (as the means by which society unifies itself) and at the level of patriarchal social structures (as the means by which sexual difference is presented as natural and then absolutely upheld).

To be sure, there is the suggestion in the literary texts themselves—which is echoed in the critical and theoretical treatments—that Don Juan is not necessarily the seducer. As pointed out earlier in terms of Byron's *Don Juan,* the Byronic hero is characterized by his excessive passivity. Similarly, Edmond Rostand suggests that women play along with Don Juan, allow him to seduce them:

DON JUAN.	But I seduced them—
GHOSTS.	After we persuaded you!
	. . . .
DON JUAN.	But I spent my life—
DEVIL.	Believing you were the first To corrupt the hearts that I had already rehearsed!
DON JUAN.	But my seductions—
DEVIL.	"Oh how I seduce," Says the iron to the magnet. It's no use!
ANOTHER GHOST.	You happened to be the only man in sight Who offered his services, either day or night.
ANOTHER GHOST.	Oh, how we used to laugh at you, Don Juan!
	(602–3)

Even more extreme is the notion that women want or *need* a Don Juan, as in Pérez de Ayala's double novel *Tigre Juan* and *El curandero de su honra* [Tiger Juan and The Physician of His Honor], in which Herminia flees from her husband Tigre Juan to the arms of the local— yet effeminate and, in truth, indifferent—Don Juan, Vespasiano, because she needs to see in her husband aspects of the *burlador.* Marital bliss for Herminia ensues when she feels herself abased; after she is reconciled with her husband, he tells a neighbor of how his wife begs for more abuse:

The desperate suffering of those twenty-four hours when I thought I had lost you (it is Herminia who speaks) have left in

me a sad and gloomy void. . . . In that short time, suffering became a necessity for my soul. I rejoiced in my torment; I savored
it as if it were an elixir of happiness, because in suffering for you
I began to be worthy of you. My suffering was my idol. But you
did not let me suffer enough. I hunger to be humiliated by you.
Fall in love, Juan, with another woman, with a trivial and passing love. I will imagine that it is eternal love. I will once again
think that I have lost you. I will suffer for you. What pride!
When you return to me, I will continue to live with the anguish
of losing you, and my happiness will be complete. Humiliate me,
Juan, make me suffer! (*Obras completas* 4:782)

Though humorous and no doubt intended as such, this passage is remarkable in its combination of anterior literary treatments of Don
Juan and in its subtle assertion of the innate—and, for the male ego,
innately salutary effects of—masochism in women. We can detect
Zorrilla's Doña Inés, who will suffer from and then save Don Juan;
López de Ayala's Paulina, for whom redeeming a sinner is the highest
goal of woman; Clarín's Ana Ozores, who imbibes the poisonous filter
associated with Alvaro Mesía and then implores him to swear his eternal love; and Picón's Cristeta, for whom marriage represents the beginning of the end. Yet the manner of presentation is, in fact, identical to
that of the critical and theoretical texts we have discussed: it is, however real in the context of the novel, a masculine fantasy of the desires
of women, a sort of wishful thinking that inscribes sexual difference in
terms of hierarchy, not similarity or equality. Pérez de Ayala's novelistic diptych humorously replicates the assumptions underlying the all
too serious contemporary discussions of Marañón and Ortega y Gasset.

These humorous yet serious assessments and approximations correspond, quite closely in fact, to a four-panel cartoon appearing in the
Madrid Cómico in 1884 (16 March 1884, Figs. 1–4).[8] Cast as a history
of "raptos" or abductions, the cartoon deals with mythology (Fig. 1),
with the fifteenth and nineteenth centuries (Figs. 2 and 3)—in terms
strikingly similar to the abductions and seductions in Zorrilla's *Don
Juan Tenorio* and Picón's *Dulce y sabrosa* [Sweet and Savory]—and
with the as yet to come twentieth century (Fig. 4). Progressing from a
scene in which Paris carries Helen off on foot to a scenario in which an
aging seducer carries his paramour toward a waiting carriage, the
future holds a scenario in which women will abduct men. As the se-

8. I am grateful to Lou Charnon-Deutsch for bringing this cartoon to my attention
and for providing me with the reproductions.

Fig. 1.   Antes de Jesucristo
                           pasa la escena.
                           Así robó . . . ¡tunante!
                           Paris á Elena.

[Even before Jesus Christ this scenario occurred. Thus did Paris—the
rogue!—steal Helen.]

FIG. 2.   Costumbres *puras* del siglo quince.
Trepa el alféizar el trovador,
salta la dama, cógela en brazos
y escapan luego, locos de amor.

[*Pure* (and *chaste*) customs of the fifteenth century: The troubadour scales the wall, the lady leaps, he takes her in his arms, and they escape, mad with love.]

FIG. 3. Siglo presente: Un simón,
una intención del demonio,
y en seguida ¡á la estación!
Los pescan, y . . . ¡matrimonio
per saecula *seculón!*

[The present century: A horse-drawn carriage, a diabolical intention, and off they go to the station. They are caught and it is matrimony *per saecula* unending.]

FIG. 4.   Y como progresamos
                    rápidamente,
                    así serán los raptos
                    del siglo veinte.

[And as we rapidly progress, such will be the abductions of the twentieth
century.]

ducer grows older, women become more assertive; man becomes the passive plaything, once again the child carried by a maternal—yet sexual—figure, the phallic mother representative of men's hopes and fears, paralleling the historical trajectory of Don Juan elucidated in the literary treatments.

In these broadly social interpretations of Don Juan we can see many of the same strategies at work as in the critical versions. As a principle of differentiation and exclusion, Don Juan has a peculiarly dual function that is, in fact, concealed by the illusion of equality in exchange that pervades the many versions of this story. He is, of course, a principle of differentiation at the level of the group, a principle of exclusion and hierarchy within the group itself. Yet there is always the sense that social organization, as both presented and understood in the literary and the critical treatments, is predicated on the basis of egalitarian and free exchange, much as Marx ironically describes his "Eden of the innate rights of man" (*Capital* 1:176). According to Marx, this illusory realm of free exchange is based on

> Freedom, Equality, Property and Bentham. Freedom, because both buyer and seller of a commodity, say of labour-power, are constrained only by their own free will. They contract as free agents, and the agreement they come to, is but the form in which they give legal expression to their common will. Equality, because each enters into relation with the other, as with a simple owner of commodities, and they exchange equivalent for equivalent. Property, because each disposes only of what is his own. And Bentham, because each looks only to himself. The only force that brings each of them together and puts them in relation with each other, is the selfishness, the gain and the private interests of each. Each looks to himself only, and no one troubles himself about the rest, and just because they do so, do they all, in accordance with the pre-established harmony of things, or under the auspices of an all-shrewd providence, work together to their mutual advantage, for the common weal and in the interest of all. (*Capital* 1:176)

This is precisely the type of problem explored by Michel Serres, who suggests Don Juan as an example of capitalism gone awry, in that the *burlador* always seeks the maximum profit for his investment; he buys on credit, offers his word, and attempts to escape making a final payment.[9]

Consider the opening scene of Tirso de Molina's *El burlador de Sevilla* yet again. Earlier, I suggested that this scene presents the two enigmas on which the subsequent dramatic action is based. It also sets forth the basic social principle that Don Juan incarnates:

ISABELA.	Duque Octavio, por aquí podrás salir más seguro.
DON JUAN.	Duquesa, de nuevo os juro de cumplir el dulce sí.
ISABELA.	¿Mis glorias, serán verdades, promesas y ofrecimientos, regalos y cumplimientos, voluntades y amistades?
DON JUAN.	Sí, mi bien.

(lines 1–9)

[ISABELA.	Duke Octavio, you will be able to leave more safely through here.
DON JUAN.	Duchess, I once again swear to you to fulfill my sweet promise.
ISABELA.	All of my dreams will come true? The promises and offers, presents and courtesies, desires and friendships?
DON JUAN.	Yes, my precious.]

The opening scene of the first drama in which a Don Juan appears named begins with an exchange of sexual favors for a promise of marriage. In other words, Don Juan, a principle of differentiation and exclusion, is, moreover, a principal and ambulatory principle of exchange. The illusion is that both the Duquesa Isabela and Don Juan— in anticipation of *all* of the scenarios of seduction in *El burlador de Sevilla*—act as free agents; in Marx's terms, "each enters into relation with the other, as with a simple owner of commodities, and they ex-

9. Stendhal says that "Don Juan disclaims all the obligations which link him to the rest of humanity. In the great market-place of life he is a dishonest merchant who takes all and pays nothing. The idea of equality is as maddening to him as water to a rabid dog; this is why pride of birthright becomes Don Juan's character so well. With the idea of equality of rights vanishes that of justice—or rather, if Don Juan comes of an illustrious stock, such vulgar notions would never have entered his head" (173).

change equivalent for equivalent." Indeed, Marx's view of commodity exchange is strikingly similar to the sacramental rite of marriage, in that the two principals involved are "constrained only by their own free will" and "they contract as free agents, and the agreement they come to, is but the form in which they give legal expression to their common will."[10]

It would seem that this notion of exchange is so obvious as to be superfluous. But the idea of the equality of the individuals involved in exchanges is so prevalent as to merit comment here. In their presentation and critique of neo-classic economic theories, the protagonist of which is "rational economic man," Martin J. Hollis and Edward J. Nell assert that, according to the neo-classicist, "the market place is not a battlefield but an orderly shopping centre where, even if the odd customer is short changed or the odd item shop-lifted, people in the long run get what they pay for and pay for what they get" (216). As Nancy C. M. Hartsock trenchantly explains this position, "Exchange is voluntarily engaged in, and therefore must be mutually profitable and nonexploitative. The argument about the mutual profit of interaction is closely linked to the assumption that all exchanges are voluntary and therefore must be engaged in for gain" (23).

Hartsock demonstrates how this basic idea turns up in social theory as well, as in Peter M. Blau's exchange-oriented discussion of courtship and love. To be sure, Blau admits to a certain selfishness that is characteristic of love when he remarks, "Love appears to make human beings unselfish, since they themselves enjoy giving pleasure to those they love, but this selfless devotion generally rests on an interest in maintaining the other's love" (76). Yet the mere fact that he identifies courtship and love as a "social exchange" and describes the process in terms of an economic marketplace undercuts the sanguine nature of his analysis. For Blau, " 'Social exchange,' as the term is used here, refers to the *voluntary* actions of individuals that are motivated by the returns they are expected to bring and typically do in fact bring from others" (91; my emphasis); such exchanges, which will eventually result in marriage,

10. My use of the term *commodity* differs slightly from that found in traditional Marxist formulations and derives, as do other aspects of my discussion, from Nancy C. M. Hartsock's *Money, Sex, and Power: Toward a Feminist Historical Materialism,* in which Hartsock insightfully demonstrates how exchange theory dominates discussions of social and political theory. Although Hartsock's reading of Marx might be considered somewhat aberrant by orthodox Marxists, her formulations in her critique of capitalist versions of exchange theory are, broadly speaking, consistent with recent tendencies in feminist studies.

are understood as mutually enabling social contracts between individuals acting as equals.[11] Thus, concludes Hartsock:

> As he [Blau] describes it, the courtship market is an orderly and voluntary exchange between participants who face each other on fundamentally equal terms. Each has a fixed good the other wants; and each is both a producer and a consumer of the goods in question. [First,] Blau ignores the assymmetry of the double standard for male and female behavior, and the phallocratic relations of domination this expresses—the fact that *he* could only be the buyer and *she* the seller. Second, Blau's account focuses on a transaction between two individuals, and he presumes that the important terms of their interaction are set by the individuals involved. (49)

In fact, such transactions serve, as we have seen, *not* the interests of both individuals involved, but society itself. In terms of *El burlador de Sevilla* as in other versions of Don Juan's story, the women are always the seller, Don Juan the buyer, who buys on credit and then refuses to honor his obligation.

If Don Juan is a principle of exchange in patriarchal society, then the primary commodity in which he deals is, of course, women, or, perhaps, male desire for women. This assertion follows on Claude Lévi-Strauss's basic observations with respect to kinship and on feminist reinterpretations of this anthropological position. Kinship and the circulation of women bear careful consideration for an understanding of the nature of Don Juan's role in society as well as of the shifts in emphasis in and significance of Don Juan's story. If Don Juan is an economic principle

11. It is surprising the extent to which Blau's presentation gives the lie to a fundamentally patriarchal view of this type of exchange. Even his choice of words gives a peculiar slant to his ideas. Blau comments: "If most girls in a community were to kiss boys on their first dates and grant sexual favors soon afterwards, before the boys have become deeply committed, it would depreciate the price of these rewards in the community, making it difficult for a girl to use the promise of sexual intercourse to elicit a firm commitment from a boy, since sexual gratifications are available at a lesser price. The interest of girls in protecting the value of sexual favors against depreciation gives rise to social pressures among girls not to grant these favors readily" (80–81); "Flirting, moreover, gives rise to expectations that must later be fulfilled to maintain the love relationship. The conduct of the flirtatious girl implies that although she may not yet be ready to let the boy hold her hand, continued association with her would ultimately bring these and much greater rewards. The implicit promises made in the course of flirting put subsequent pressures on lovers to live up to the expectations they have created and begin to provide at least some of the rewards promised" (82).

regulating desire and promoting social order, then he is, in essence, the very principle of society and social organization itself.[12]

Lévi-Strauss's theories of kinship are clearly linked to Marcel Mauss's theory of prestation as found in *The Gift,* the central insight of which is that something given entails an obligation, something to be given in return. Because the acceptance of a gift is a challenge to one's honor, a challenge to repay a debt, Mauss comments, "Food, women, children, possessions, charms, land, labour, services, religious offices, rank—everything is stuff to be given away and repaid. In perpetual interchange of what we may call spiritual matter, comprising men and things, these elements pass and repass between clans and individuals, ranks, sexes and generations" (11–12). Lévi-Strauss modifies Mauss's stance somewhat and claims that women are a special kind of commodity in culture, which can be identified as *patriarchal* culture: a "fundamental difference exists between the women who are exchanged and the goods and services which are also exchanged. Women are biological individuals, that is, natural products naturally procreated by other biological individuals. Goods and services on the other hand are manufactured objects" (*The Savage Mind* 123). Women are not of particular significance because they are "biological individuals . . . naturally procreated by other biological individuals," but, rather, because their primary function is that of procreation itself. Men, by controlling women, can control the functioning and ongoing stability of society. Moreover, the exchange of women is, for Lévi-Strauss, constitutive of the fundamental difference between nature and culture, because it operates in opposition to incest, in concert with the central tenet of civilization, the incest taboo: "The prohibition of incest is less a rule prohibiting marriage with the mother, sister or daughter, than a rule obliging the mother, sister or daughter to be given to others. It is the supreme rule of the gift, and it is clearly this aspect, too often unrecognized, which allows its nature to be understood" (*The Elementary Structures of Kinship* 481).

The importance of the exchange of women has to do with the establishment of kinship ties between clans. Because by giving something— a woman—to another clan, the donor can expect something in return,

12. Hartsock says, "Commodity exchange, because it structures the vision of the ruling class, structures the self-understanding of society as a whole. . . . It should, then, come as no surprise that theories of social life in capitalism frequently take exchange and competition to be fundamental and see the relation of buyer and seller as the prototypic form of social interaction. These are indeed the dominant material relations for at least the capitalist class, and, through their dominance, of society as a whole" (133).

there is in terms of kinship a lasting tie between the two groups that transcends the immediate family and creates an enduring social bond. Juliet Mitchell comments, "it is not the family but the structural relationships *between* families that constitutes the elementary form of human society; that distinguishes human society from primate groups. Furthermore, it is not what is given, but the act of exchange itself that holds any society together" (*Psychoanalysis and Feminism* 374). Hartsock goes somewhat further and suggests that the differences between the commodity exchange of goods and of women lie precisely in the lasting relationships between the participants of exchange:

> Unlike the exchange of commodities, it [the exchange of women] transforms all participants in the transaction. The buyer or seller of a commodity remains buyer or seller after the purchase/sale, but after a woman is exchanged, those who were strangers are now affines, and the woman herself becomes part of another lineage, a married woman, an adult. Every participant occupies a different place afterward. Dualism still reverberates through the transaction, but it is a more complex and contradictory dualism, which transforms not just the social status of the object in question but all other oppositions as well. Yet they remain oppositions within the social synthesis created by the exchange of women. (275)

In one sense, everything is the same, but different. Because there is a dualism inherent in the exchange of women, there is a difference between two groups that is to some extent overcome by the establishment of kinship ties. Yet the primary difference appears to inhere in woman herself, and in all of the other terms of binary opposition with which she can be and is associated.

Lévi-Strauss's exposition of the exchange of women in primitive society has had important implications in feminist theories of social organization. In an extensive comparison of the theories of Freud and Lévi-Strauss, Gayle Rubin has proposed that patriarchal society is dependent upon "the traffic in women," upon man's assertion of control over the social and biological destiny of woman. Rubin claims, in a manner uncannily similar to Aristophanes' myth of the circle- or double-men in the *Symposium*, that "Gender is a socially imposed division of the sexes. It is a product of the social relations of sexuality. Kinship systems rest upon marriage. They therefore transform males and females into 'men' and 'women,' each an incomplete half which can only find wholeness when united with the other" (179). By identifying gender—literally, sexual difference construed as socially absolute and necessary—as the central force behind the exchange of women as a commodity, Rubin articulates the means of understanding kinship in terms of modern, capitalist society. This move is important: Sherry B. Ortner, in her review of Juliet Mitchell's *Psychoanalysis and Feminism,* criticizes Mitchell for a kind of historical blindness in her assumption of Lévi-Strauss's kinship theories. Ortner asserts:

> it has probably become apparent that one would be hard put to apply Lévi-Strauss' alliance theory in any illuminating way to the structure of modern society, since modern society more or less turns Lévi-Strauss on his head. Social alliance as expressed through the medium of marriage is virtually a nil factor in modern social organization (except perhaps among the aristocracy), while the nuclear family, which Lévi-Strauss dismissed as a sort of accidental by-product of the alliance system has, in modern society, tremendous substantiality and significance. (176)

Rubin, however, successfully shows how Lévi-Strauss's model of kinship can be related to Freud's reading of Oedipus:

> The precision of the fit between Freud and Lévi-Strauss is striking. Kinship systems require a division of the sexes. The Oedipal phase divides the sexes. Kinship systems include sets of rules governing sexuality. The Oedipal crisis is the assimilation of these rules and taboos. Compulsory heterosexuality is the product of kinship. The Oedipal phase constitutes heterosexual desire. Kinship rests on a radical difference between the rights of men and women. The Oedipal complex confers male rights upon the boy, and forces the girl to accomodate herself to her lesser rights. (198)

The move from a feudal society based on kinship to a capitalist system in which the basic unit is the nuclear family can still be seen to depend on sexual difference. The one important departure has less to do with alliance than with labor and the sexual division of labor. Rubin notes, "The division of labor by sex can therefore be seen as a 'taboo': a taboo against the sameness of men and women, a taboo which exacerbates the biological differences between the sexes and thereby *creates* gender" (178).[13]

13. Not everybody accepts Lévi-Strauss's theories and their elaboration by Juliet Mitchell and Gayle Rubin without qualification. See, for example, Sherry B. Ortner's review of Mitchell's *Psychoanalysis and Feminism* and, especially, Hartsock, who dis-

Women are important as a caste—for lack of a better term—even in capitalist society because they are a source, in and of themselves, of cheap labor and because they produce future workers, as Marx and Engels as well as contemporary social theorists all realize. Haunani-Kay Trask postulates, "Women are indeed exchanged, but not because of their mysterious signification. They are exchanged because they reproduce the species, because they continue and thereby ensure life. In this view, biology is transformed by concrete relationships (the sexual division of labor) into a daily experience of subordination" (37). Zillah R. Eisenstein thus theorizes, "Within a capitalist patriarchal economy—where profit, which necessitates a system of political order and control, is the basic priority of the ruling class—the sexual division of labor and society serves a specific purpose. It stabilizes the society through the family while it organizes a realm of work, domestic labor, for which there is no pay (housewives), or limited pay (paid houseworkers), or unequal pay (in the paid labor force)" (30). As a result, Eisenstein notes:

> The bourgeoisie as a class profits from the basic arrangement of women's work, while all individual men benefit in terms of labor done for them in the home. For men, regardless of class, benefit (although differentially) from the system of privileges they acquire within patriarchal society. . . . The ruling class desire to preserve the family reflects its commitment to a division of labor that not only secures it the greatest profit but also hierarchically orders the society culturally and politically. (31)

Although we seemingly have moved far from a consideration of Don Juan as a social principle, as a principle of exchange, this excursus was necessary. First, it is important to note the prevalence of the privileging of male perspective in social theory—as in discussions of Don Juan. Not only is there a privileging of perspective, an inevitable hierarchy, there is a concomitant desire to obscure this hierarchy behind the notion of equality, sometimes understood as complementarity. In this sense, it is worthwhile to point out that patriarchy is not merely a fact of life, but an ideology, too, which has meaningful consequences for the ways in which we understand the issues of perspective and representa-

---

cusses Lévi-Strauss, Simone de Beauvoir, and Rubin in a set of appendices to her book (267–301). See also Diana Adlam who concludes her "savage and even pertinent" (96) discussion of treatments of "capitalist patriarchy" by remarking that "[s]ocialist feminism can do without a theory of capitalist patriarchy" (101); and Linda Nicholson.

tion. As Teresa L. Ebert avers in a generally Lacanian discussion of patriarchy and postmodern feminist theory:[14]

> ideology is the dynamic operator that organizes signifying prac-
> tices and attempts to fix and limit the representations, meanings,
> and subjectivities they produce according to the requirements of
> the symbolic order. . . . Ideology is thus misrepresentation, not in
> that it is a false version of some originary "real" or that it stands
> in opposition to the "truth" or an "objective" science outside ideol-
> ogy (as in Althusser's theory), but in that it *represents* itself and
> its signifying practices as "natural," unified—even global—
> totalities free of contradictions. It conceals not only its own incon-
> sistencies but also its own construction through signification.
> (26–27)

Second, the prevalence of this dichotomized understanding of man and woman is central to most, if not all, social theories. Trask believes that this is a given of male theories of social organization, a notion that dominates from antiquity to the present:

> Freud's mythic horde revolves around an archetypal struggle
> with the castrating father later killed by his jealous sons, who
> then possess his property in common, including all women.
> Locke's contractarian brotherhood arises in opposition to the des-
> potism of the natural father and his patriarchal family: "egalitar-
> ian" society is egalitarian because man's properties (his person,
> the fruits of his labor, his women and children) are protected from
> other men. Aristotle's polity is built from the patriarchal house-
> hold: the rule of man over woman, parent over child, master over
> slave. His model of government is familial domination. No matter
> how solidarity between men is established—through Freudian
> guilt, Lockean contract, Aristotelian citizenship—civilization is
> seen to develop from male groupings. Women, the first victims,
> are not members of the patriarchal fraternity; they are its prop-
> erty, the sexual spoils of war. (31)

Once understood as a constant in explanations and theories of society, which are explanations of the way things are, and why, this masculine

14. See also Teresa de Lauretis's discussion of representation and ideology, particularly as they relate to issues of gender, in *Technologies of Gender,* especially the first two
chapters, "The Technology of Gender" (1–30) and "The Violence of Rhetoric: Considerations of Representation and Gender" (31–50).

viewpoint can be linked to seduction, as an attempt to persuade, to coerce, to bribe, to dupe individuals into playing their appropriate roles in society, into fulfilling their social functions as determined by culture. Yet this attempt at persuasion conceals itself in the notions of complementarity (equality as difference) and pluralism (equality in difference) such that persuasion is seductive, and insidiously so.

The seductive nature of persuasion and its corollary, exclusion, figure in Ellen Rooney's recent politicized discussion of contemporary literary theory. Rooney points out that there is an illusion of equality at work in theories of pluralism that eventually tends toward hierarchy and the exclusion of principles that, paradoxically enough, operate on the basis of exclusion. Therefore,

> pluralism is that which goes without saying. By positing a critical community unified by the assumption that every reader is theoretically amenable to persuasion, pluralisms inevitably reinscribe traditional notions of the reader and the author as unified subjects, *transparently equals,* at work in *a homogeneous critical field* [my emphasis]. These assumptions make an irreconcilable divergence of interests *within* the critical community an unthinkable form of discontinuity. Armed with this strategy, pluralism can hope to recuperate any critical account (feminist, minority, marxist) that emphasizes otherness, difference, conflict, or discontinuity: within the problematic of general persuasion, the absent or excluded term is exclusion itself. No discourse that challenges the theoretical possibility of general persuasion, no discourse that takes the process of exclusion to be necessary to the production of meaning or community . . . can function within pluralism. (4–5)

The paradox is obvious. Pluralism, which masquerades in a general sense as a tolerance of difference, excludes that which would oppose it: exclusion. There are, then, limits to the freedom of interpretation suggested by pluralism, a limitation imposed on the number and types of pluralisms, on the possibilities of persuasion. Although Rooney's exposition is linked to the politics of literary interpretation, her insights are valid in larger cultural arenas; indeed, with appropriate changes, the passage cited above can be read as a gloss on Marx's "Eden of the innate rights of Man." Persuasion operative within the politics of literary interpretation can be used as a model for the politics of persuasion as it pertains to the interpretation of a number of cultural models, among them Don Juan, the seducer par excellence.

Not surprisingly, Rooney links her discussion of pluralism with seduction—via Jane Gallop's claim of the synonomy of seduction and the Law[15]—by remarking that "the law masks its own omnipresent seduction," which means that "seductive reasoning is the practice of pluralism: the problematic of general persuasion imposes a regime of general seduction or seductive reasoning which is in a certain sense not veiled" (57). But Rooney could also have commented on Felman's views of seduction, which, in the end, very nearly approximate Ebert's notion of patriarchy as an ideology involved in a process of self-presentation that both conceals and discloses its aims. Seduction thereby becomes the operative rhetorical strategy within patriarchal culture, the means by which patriarchy controls the dissemination of its ideas and represents its hegemony. As inscribed in difference, similarity excludes that by which it would in turn be excluded, all the while insisting on persuasion as a means of concealing the exclusionary aspects of its strategies.

With respect to Don Juan, then, his story must be seen as patriarchy's seductive attempt to represent its own aims. An ongoing elaboration of the ways in which the masculine subsumes the feminine, the vicissitudes of Don Juan mirror those of patriarchy and the historical shifts from feudalism to capitalism and beyond, and of the social shifts from kinship structures to the nuclear family. Just as the world in which seduction occurs changes and is changed, the figure and the nature of seduction are transformed; the social and cultural contexts of seduction are modified as economic and social substructures undergo changes of far-reaching implications.

In this light, Tirso's *El burlador de Sevilla* evidences a somewhat contradictory ideological aesthetic, as Anthony J. Cascardi points out. An example of Golden Age theater, *El burlador de Sevilla* is poised generically at the confrontation between the old and the new, which Cascardi notes has to do with,

15. In the course of *The Daughter's Seduction: Feminism and Psychoanalysis,* Jane Gallop—following Luce Irigaray—establishes an analogy between the relationship of the analyst and analysand, on the one hand, and the father and daughter, on the other. Thus, she discusses how "the law which prohibits sexual intercourse between the analyst and the patient actually makes seduction last forever. The sexually actualized seduction would be complicitous, nuanced, impossible to delineate into active and passive roles, into the anal logic so necessary for a traditional distribution of wealth and power. But the 'lasting seduction' of the law is never consummated and as such maintains the power of the prohibited analyst. The seduction which the daughter desires would give her contact with the father as masculine sexed body. The seduction which the father of psychoanalysis exercises refuses her his body, his penis, and asks her to embrace his law . . ." (75).

on the one hand, a culture in which interpersonal relationships are determined by kinship ties and by bloodlines, in which actions are evaluated according to an archaic heroic ethos, and in which social functions and roles are sedimented into near static hierarchies; on the other hand, a culture in which the categories that determine personal worth are based largely on standards of possessive individualism . . . in which the central cultural myths are those of personal and social progress (the latter to be achieved largely through the technological domination of nature and through the medium of free economic exchange). ("Don Juan and the Discourse of Modernism" 152–53)

The result of this tension between the traditional and the modern is a drama in which there is a simultaneous acceptance and repudiation of the new. Cascardi concludes, "The psychological mobility of Don Juan, which is perceived as a threat to the ethical foundations of society, is overcome once it is discovered that within it lies an extreme concern for honor, the very basis of self-consciousness in a 'traditional' world" (155–56).

El burlador de Sevilla therefore articulates a moment at which traditional notions of value, in relation to individual worth as it translates into honor, are being replaced by what Cascardi refers to as "free circulation" (162). The commodity value attached to women remains constant even as the nature of the *meaning* of that value alters in conjunction with the shift from the kinship structures characteristic of feudalism to the (bourgeois) family associated with capitalism. In other words and as seen in this culture, women are of value as a commodity even as the understanding of their worth and use changes to adapt to a new sense of the economy of exchange; the value of women is paramount even as there occurs a shift in the meaning that is attached to that value and in its expression. Moreover, as Apostolidès demonstrates in terms of Molière's *Dom Juan*, a discussion that could serve as well for *El burlador de Sevilla:*

Although the market structure is in place, the economic vocabulary is not yet well-established. . . . By participating in the elimination of Don Juan, the group of protagonists (and the spectators) tries to reject the new generalized principle of circulation and exchange. Thus, it economizes its collective guilt by finding a scapegoat for the transgressions which have thrown traditional society out of joint. . . . his annihilation will make possible the movement from the Christian feudal world to the market world. (490)

To begin to understand the ways in which the value of woman as a commodity changes within patriarchal society and culture is to begin to understand the vicissitudes of Don Juan. In *El burlador de Sevilla* the commodity value of woman as an object of exchange is similar if not identical to that suggested by Lévi-Strauss in relation to kinship structures. There is a sense that matrimony is productive in that it helps to establish, to monitor, and to maintain social stability. Don Juan, as a principal in the economy of exchange that rules society in the world portrayed in the *comedia,* incarnates the principle by which desire is channeled in a socially "procreative" fashion. Nonetheless, Cascardi quite rightly remarks that "desire never is eliminated; it is only repressed or 'managed' with greater or lesser success, just as the damaged honor of Isabella, Ana, Aminta, and Tisbea may be forgotten but never repaired" ("Don Juan and the Discourse of Modernism" 162). Because desire can never fully be mastered, it remains as problematic as honor, and in direct relationship to it, too: to "manage" desire is to conspire to uphold the honor of the family name, the patronym. Seduction thereby supports the concept of honor as a principally male attribute linked to the comportment of women, first, by acknowledging its importance, and second, by acquiescing to its social priority.

Over the course of the eighteenth and the nineteenth centuries in Spain the historical and social paradigms shift so as to accomodate a somewhat different view of woman and honor, one that allows women the authority of domesticity while carefully circumscribing their lives and activities outside of the home. However, the notions of social and personal honor are still very much in evidence, if slightly transformed, and they find support in the changing views of the individual and of property that accompany the rise of the nuclear family. In essence, what occurs is the extension of aristocratic ideals relative to individual ownership of property and the exchange of women— particularly as these are made manifest in culture—to the domain of the middle class, and from there eventually to the proletariat. As Philippe Ariès has shown, the shift from kinship structures to the nuclear family begins to take place as early as the fourteenth century, with the advent of new concepts of childhood. Yet it remains until the ultimate hegemony of industrial capitalism for these incipient changes in social structure to reveal themselves as the modern bourgeois family and to transform—but not to attenuate—existing cultural norms.[16] Trask notes:

> The bourgeois ideal of the family transformed precapitalist ideals of courtly love and male supremacy into ideals of romantic love and complementarity between the sexes. Marriage became a partnership in love and common destiny. However, this change in ideals, while reflecting a new direction in the ideology of women's oppression, was really an index of middle-class influence. Although the brutality of women's sixteenth-century status was softened by the development of these ideals, the evolution of male supremacy into romantic love brought a different, more insidious because more disguised form of oppression for women. (53)

In a similar vein, Juliet Mitchell observes that "kinship relationships are preserved as important among the aristocracy (a hangover from feudalism) and the cult of the biological family develops within the middle class. The middle class is thus the heir and progenitor of capitalism not only on the economic level but also on the ideological" (*Psychoanalysis and Feminism* 379). Mitchell concludes, "When, within the *majority* of the population, it is no longer necessary for women to be exchange objects, then the small dominant class must insist on their remaining so—hence we have the bourgeois hypocrisies about the value of the family for the working class" (380).

It ought to come as no surprise, then, that, in the context of nineteenth-century Spanish ideology, Zorrilla's Don Juan falls in love with Doña Inés and attempts to submit himself to the paternal authority of Don Gonzalo, to become a good bourgeois gentleman, and that Doña Inés serves as the spiritual salvation of her beloved Don Juan, becomes the reflection of his desire. Given Spain's patriarchal social structure, this is as it should be. Even more appropriately in the context of nineteenth-century Spanish ideology, López de Ayala's Elena exercises her authority within the domestic domain while submitting to her husband's jealous whims ("¡Nada temas de tu Elena!"). She bears his desire as a written mark of possession and strives to uphold his honor by proving Juan de Alvarado to be nothing more than a hapless

---

16. This is but a suggestion of the nature and kind of changes that take place. On this topic see, among others, Ariès, Frederick Engels, Karen Sacks, Juliet Mitchell, Rubin, and Hartsock.

seducer ("Nada esperes de un Don Juan"). Within this general schema, Clarín's *La Regenta* [The Judge's Wife] exemplifies the extent to which a figure related to Don Juan can be associated with significant aspects of social and political power; and in Picón's *Dulce y sabrosa,* the evolution of Don Juan's seductive nature into a type of monogamous romantic love is complete. Now Don Juan can become fully domesticated, as in Azorín's *Don Juan* and *Doña Inés.* In his guise as "everyman," he is relatively harmless, indeed, he contributes to the well-being of society as a whole.

A significant aspect of the nineteenth- and early twentieth-century literary trajectory to be traced in the texts that treat Don Juan is his increasingly bourgeois nature, which Ignacio-Javier López has linked to a process of "degradation." The differences between Tirso's *burlador* and Zorrilla's Don Juan—marked, to be sure—are not so great as those between the hero of *Don Juan Tenorio* and characters of the later nineteenth century. Juan de Alvarado, Alvaro Mesía, and Juan de Todellas share none of the heroic valor and seductive ardor of their literary forebears. With the possible exception of Clarín's Fermín de Pas, novelistic versions of Don Juan appear infinitely more insignificant, more human, more like Azorín's anonymous Don Juan. Eventually some of these representations of the *burlador* move in the direction of parody and satire, all of which indicates a dual aspect to this shift in the presentation of Don Juan.

On the one hand, Don Juan's increasingly bourgeois nature as seen in novelistic representations of this character corresponds to what realist authors in Spain saw as the appropriate subject matter for their observations. Galdós remarks in an early review essay:

> The middle class, the most neglected by our novelists, is the supreme model, the inexhaustible source. The middle class is today the basis of social order; because of its sense of initiative and its intelligence, it is assuming the leadership of society. In its midst is to be found nineteenth-century man, with his virtues and vices, his noble and insatiable ambition, his zeal to reform, his extraordinary energy. . . . The great aspiration of literary art in our time is to give form to all of this. ("Noticias literarias" 323)

Given Galdós's perspective, it is only to be expected that, when novels take as their protagonists the middle class, Don Juan appears as a bourgeois gentleman, or even common, a tendency noted as early as 1863 by one of the anonymous reviewers of López de Ayala's *El nuevo*

Don Juan. In fact, Galdós's remarks on the strange blend of "virtues" and "vices," "noble and insatiable aspirations," could be read as applying not just to the middle class in general but to Don Juan in particular, and to the Don Juans found in *La Regenta* and *Dulce y sabrosa.*

On the other hand, Don Juan's increasingly bourgeois nature as found in novelistic versions is profoundly insidious, a means of extending the notion and the effects of seduction from the nobility to the middle classes. An ideological tool in the creation and consolidation of middle-class social values and cultural authority, the novel continues to disseminate and to uphold patriarchal norms by rewriting Don Juan into the shift from kinship structures to the nuclear family. This transition is significantly marked in the novels studied here by the status of Ana Ozores and Cristeta Moreruela as *orphans,* as young women severed from the ties of affect characteristic of the nuclear family; only later is it possible to present the flirtatious Jeannette of Azorín's *Don Juan,* equally coquettish as a woman *and* as a daughter.

In this regard, it is no coincidence that the advent of the bourgeois Don Juan is accompanied by incipient critical interest in the character. As Don Juan becomes more individualized, more human—indeed, the psychological principle discussed in Armand Hayem's 1886 study—the need to restate and to justify his cultural validity becomes more pressing. In a manner analogous to the explanation of the artistic elaboration of a moment of originary violence as found in Freud and Rank, the ongoing explanations and interpretations of Don Juan reconstitute his social value. Whereas for Freud and Rank the continual retelling of the original story moves the material further from the precise configurations of its principal meaning, with respect to Don Juan, the critical approximations function as the means by which that material remains vivid and socially meaningful. Rank says:

> the *Burlador* presents a complete reworking of the original material in the direction of the most extreme fantasy wish. He is, as it were, the heroic figure, standing at the beginning of the "poetic" accounts of individual psychology. The later poems, in contrast, appear to correspond to the subsequent legendary elaboration in different ways—not only through the breakthrough of the originally repressed elements on the one hand, and in the artistic interpretation of these elements on the other, but more importantly in a progressive *devaluation of the material* that corresponds to *the conquering of the guilt feelings,* the *denial* of which represent the original Don Juan type. (106)

Without subscribing totally to Rank's view of the meaning of Don Juan, it seems safe to suggest that the ongoing literary and critical treatments of the *burlador* posit the type of progression advanced by Rank's psychological interpretation. The ongoing consideration of Don Juan reveals itself as a form of ideological (mis)representation, as the means by which society conceals—even as it explains and vindicates—itself and its mechanisms.

In other words, the critical approximations of Don Juan's story take up where the literary elaborations leave off. They are, quite simply, yet another version of the same story and are written with the same end in view. Although Julia Kristeva would separate "meaning and seduction" in relation to Don Juan, the " 'message' and virtuosity" ("Don Juan, or Loving to Be Able To" 192), they remain linked. The meaning of Don Juan *is* seduction. For men, the message is one of rhetorical virtuosity, of persuasion; for women, Don Juan's story represents indoctrination and belief, or, at the very least, acquiescence, however reluctant. In this way, the progressively insistent emancipation of Don Juan from the domain of the literary indicates not merely his "popularity" or cultural transcendence, but also the force with which he successfully articulates the aims of patriarchy even as the specific desires associated with the *burlador* shift in relation to changes in society as it is constituted in terms of an interplay between and among economics, politics, culture, and individual aspirations. By drawing Don Juan into the larger realm of social theory, critics continue his hegemony even as they decry his pernicious influence and predict his downfall and death.

As a principal in the many forms of exchange at work in patriarchal society, Don Juan becomes the embodiment of a principle of exclusion, precisely the structuring as binary opposition that characterizes both the literary and critical treatments of the *burlador*. For Kierkegaard, such a system of oppositions is necessary, yet essentially without comprehensible meaning, as the indecisive title *Either/Or* suggests and as is confirmed by the fictional editor who admits that "these papers come to no conclusion" (1:14). Thus, with respect to woman, Kierkegaard's "B" asserts:

> I do believe that you have not grasped in all its inwardness the essence of woman, part of which is that she is simultaneously more perfect and more imperfect than the man. If we wish to characterize the most pure and perfect, we say "a woman"; if we wish to characterize the weakest and most fragile, we say "a woman"; if we want to convey a conception of the spirituality

elevated above the sensuous, we say "a woman"; if we want to convey the sensuous, we say "a woman"; if we wish to character-ize innocence in all its uplifting greatness, we say "a woman"; if we wish to characterize the depressing feeling of guilt, we say "a woman." (2:92)

As the locus of contrary meanings, the concept of woman is, as a signi-fier, terrifically overburdened, is differentiated within itself by the very oppositional structure in which it is caught. Yet to think beyond such oppositions is no easy matter, despite contemporary theoretical appeals to a "third woman."

Likewise, it is difficult to think beyond Don Juan, since he is so thoroughly implicated in social and sexual processes of differentia-tion. In this regard, it is once again appropriate to cite from Kierke-gaard's *Either/Or,* this time from the introduction attributed to "Vic-tor Eremita":

I, too, sometimes have felt quite strangely uneasy when I have been occupied with these papers in the stillness of the night. It seemed to me as if the seducer himself paced my floor like a shadow, as if he glanced at the papers, as if he fixed his demonic eyes on me, and said, "Well, well, so you want to publish my papers! You know that is irresponsible of you; you will indeed arouse anxiety in the darling girls. But, of course, in recompense you will make me and my kind innocuous. There you are mis-taken, for I merely change the method, and so my situation is all the more advantageous. What a flock of young girls will run straight into a man's arms when they hear the seductive name. a seducer! . . ." (1:9)

As "Victor Eremita" notes, Don Juan continually changes his method, which accounts for the vicissitudes and historical variations characteris-tic of his story. Yet it is important to note the ways in which the *burlador*'s strategy of seduction transforms itself in the service of patri-archal ideology. Kierkegaard's seducer points out that "girls will run straight into a man's arms when they hear the seductive name"; it would be naive to think that seduction could either lose its force or function in contemporary society.

Is Marañón correct, then, to predict the death of Don Juan? Probably not. If seduction is linked to meaning, the message to rhetorical virtuos-ity, then Don Juan is not dead; he inhabits the domain of language and persuasion. The place to search for him, or his seductive effects, is in those situations in contemporary society in which such virtuosity is both necessary and valued. Whereas in prior historical moments the drama and then the novel served as ideological tools in the dissemination and perpetuation of specific values intrinsic to the continuation of patriarchal society, the trend in the twentieth century to a culture of the masses and thus mass media assumes a shift from the awareness of literary types—*the* Don Juan—to the recognition of cultural absolutes—*a* Don Juan—and from there to the acceptance of a certain psychological type integral to the whole of social reality: the seducer. Finally, seduction itself—as meaning, message, and virtuosity—remains as the contemporary trace of Don Juan's story.

One measure of the nature of the shift from the literary Don Juan to the prevalence of seduction can be found in twentieth-century literary treatments of the *burlador*'s story. Apart from early twentieth-century versions, which do indeed bring the story up to date, contemporary treatments of Don Juan oftentimes either forgo any temporal indication whatsoever or use a historical focus of one sort or another. To give just two examples, Gonzalo Torrente Ballester's *Don Juan* (1963) is cast as an encounter between the narrator and someone who identifies himself as Leporello. Although the novel ostensibly takes place in the present, there is, vis-à-vis the character Leporello, a historical dimension to the text (fictional to be sure, since Leporello later reveals that he and his "master" are simply playing a game). If Torrente Ballester's novel is, in fact, set in the present, it is nevertheless historical in effect; the author himself, in the prologue to the book, claims that Don Juan is a "fictional character, without the least contact with reality" (10). John Berger approaches the issue from a somewhat different perspective in *G* (1972) by situating his novel in the late nineteenth and early twentieth centuries and not the present, and with reason. Geoff Dyer succinctly explains:

> The historical moment of the Don Juan, as conceived by Berger, comes when a society is stagnant, where every channel for change is blocked. Only, as Berger himself has commented, where women are the undisputed property of men—where men act and women appear—is he a subversive force. He cannot flourish where women themselves are struggling for emancipation since his promise is, ultimately, an intense expression of patriarchal power. In other words, he is dependent on the social organization of gender which his mere presence seems to threaten; he depends on women's powerlessness, on their not

recognizing him as a representative of the power he cannot but exploit. (91–92)

In Berger's view, Don Juan both exploits and supports patriarchal social constraints, particularly when they are explicitly linked to gender and power. Because a figure like Don Juan is meaningful only in the context of a "stagnant" society, twentieth-century literary interpretations of the character must look for a means of re-creating such a social impasse.

One means is that of situating the story in an earlier historical moment. Another means of continuing the representation of Don Juan has been in the essay, in critical and theoretical recuperations of the *burlador*. But far more pervasive in our culture is the emphasis on rhetorical effect, on manipulation and persuasion as seen most obviously in advertising and most insidiously in politics, which can be read as a logical extension of the types of concerns present in Don Juan's story. Individuals enter the marketplace most explicitly when they exchange money for a product, and competition for people in this type of exchange is heated. Yet individuals enter into a similar marketplace when they exchange their support, their votes, for someone who offers them a vision that corresponds to their desires for the future: the "campaign promise," which almost by definition fails to materialize. In this regard, Carlos Feal is mistaken in his assumption that Don Juan can lead us to something "beyond" patriarchy and matriarchy that is indeed egalitarian and desired. In one sense, the seductive rhetoric that characterizes Don Juan takes as its object not merely woman, but *every* member of society; in this sense we are "beyond" the mere duality that is matriarchy and patriarchy. But because the dynamics of seduction as social meaning are so much a part of the fabric of social life, the notion of "beyond" Don Juan is illusory. He has, as Kierkegaard's "Victor Eremita" suggests, changed his method, and his situation is all the more advantageous.

This is not to suggest that acquiescence to the seductive charms of the *burlador* is forever inevitable. As I have attempted to demonstrate here, it is possible to read the texts—literary and critical—that form the ongoing history of Don Juan so as to discover the nature of seduction and its complicity in literary and social honor and, from there, in the workings of society. Such a trajectory illustrates the extent to which seduction is implicated in society, in the ways that we construct and deal with the world. An understanding of this literary and critical trajectory reconfigures the discussion and this, in and of itself, initiates a new way of considering Don Juan. Therefore, we cannot be like Nietzsche's Dionysian man in *The Birth of Tragedy,* the expression of which he found in one of Don Juan's comrades in literary renown, Shakespeare's Hamlet:

> both have once looked truly into the essence of things, they have *gained knowledge,* and nausea inhibits action; for their action could not change anything in the eternal nature of things; they feel it to be ridiculous or humiliating that they should be asked to set right a world that is out of joint. Knowledge kills action; action requires the veils of illusion: that is the doctrine of Hamlet, not that cheap wisdom of Jack the Dreamer who reflects too much and, as it were, from an excess of possibilities does not get around to action. Not reflection, no—true knowledge, an insight into the horrible truth outweighs any motive for action, both in Hamlet and in the Dionysian man. (*The Basic Writings of Nietzsche* 60)

Knowledge must lead beyond the "veils of illusion" that Nietzsche associates with action; and this is the "beyond" that knowledge of Don Juan offers: not a specific program, not a utopia, but an understanding of the mechanisms of seduction as they operate in literature in particular and, by extension, in the world in general. In possessing such knowledge, we can both derive pleasure from and reproach Don Juan, learn from his seductive words and learn to recognize what they represent, the honor of tradition.

Conclusion:
... and the Point of Honor

Dear reader, have we not left off believing in positive evil? And therefore
is it not true that the seducer, invaluable to fiction, is dead? The seducer
and the innocent maid are no more. We live in better days.

—*D. H. Lawrence,* Mr Noon

A number of issues pertinent to a discussion of Don Juan have
already been addressed, but the question of honor remains.
Because the *burlador* or trickster is implicated in the ongoing
processes by which patriarchy institutes and reaffirms its social and
cultural hegemony, honor forms part of this continuing discourse and
perpetuation. In fact, honor is a distinctive aspect of Spanish culture
and, with respect to Don Juan, merits recognition in this context. Yet
honor is also a significant part of the Western tradition. It figures in
accounts of ancient culture, particularly with the advent of Platonic
thought; and these various strains of honor are involved in treatments
of Don Juan.

In Hispanic culture, honor—as *honor* and *honra*—is not merely a
linguistic concept but a social notion that reveals itself as *pundonor*
or a "point of honor." According to the 1737 *Diccionario de Autorida-
des, pundonor* is "that state, according to the various opinions of men,
in which lies the honor or worth [*crédito*] of someone," a definition
that is echoed in the *Diccionario de la Real Academia Española*. A
number of the issues discussed with respect to Don Juan are to be found
in these brief definitions, including honor as a state of being, as popular opinion, and as linked, if indirectly, to commerce. As a principle,
honor is an integral part of the social fabric; therefore, it is not particular to Spanish culture—although the Hispanic concern with honor is
often much more apparent than that of other cultural traditions—but
is part and parcel of patriarchy as we know it.

The ongoing significance of honor in Western culture has been broached in a variety of historical periods and in a number of ways. María Rosa Lida de Malkiel discusses the idea of "fame" in literature of the Middle Ages in Spain by prefacing her presentation with a lengthy consideration of classical antecedents. In *Centuries of Childhood: A Social History of Family Life,* Philippe Ariès treats aspects of honor and fame as he studies the changing nature of the family and its relation to the concept of childhood. In a similarly distinct context Albert O. Hirschman touches on the topic of honor in his study of the conditions giving rise to capitalism by beginning with the basic question of how "commercial banking and similar money-making pursuits become honorable at some point in the modern age after having stood condemned or despised as greed, love of lucre, and avarice for centuries past" (9). Most recently, Leo Braudy—in *The Frenzy of Renown: Fame and Its History,* a study of surprising historical sweep—remarks, "In great part, the history of fame is the history of the changing ways by which individuals have sought to bring themselves to the attention of others and, not incidentally, have thereby gained power over them" (3). Although it is difficult to share Braudy's sanguine view of the historical trajectory of "fame" (in particular, his cheer at what he sees as the dissolution of national traditions thanks to the hegemony of mass media [597]), the scope of his project makes one thing clear. Honor, fame, and glory are all concepts that have to do with the ways in which the individual is viewed in social terms in the world, and all have been important throughout history in the West.

Although honor and its corollaries figure prominently in the Western tradition, their cultural significance probably dates from the introduction of Platonic thought and its situation as the cornerstone of Occidental philosophy and culture. Alvin W. Gouldner suggests in *Enter Plato: Classical Greece and the Origins of Social Theory* that a "centrally, culturally approved value of Greek life, embedded in and influencing its system of stratification, is an emphasis on individual fame and honor. The ultimate hope is for a 'fame undying' " (42). Moreover, Gouldner claims that Plato "at last says openly what Greeks had long wanted but feared to acknowledge—that men wish to be immortal. And Plato promises them immortality. He believes that this is one of their most devout hopes. As he states in the *Symposium,* men's creative activities, both biological and intellectual, are born of a desire for immortality" (367). Many of these same observations are developed in M. I. Finley's *The World of Odysseus,* but in a somewhat more conflictual paradigm of the Greek concept of honor as it manifests itself in the shift from *oikos* to *polis.* Finley points out that " 'Warrior' and 'hero' are synonyms, and the main theme of a warrior culture is constructed on two notes—prowess and honour. The one is the hero's essential attribute, the other his essential aim. Every value, every judgement, every action, all skills and talents have the function of either defining honour or realizing it" (113). Finley goes on to remark that it "is the nature of honour that it must be exclusive, or at least hierarchic. When everyone attains equal honour, then there is no honour for anyone. Of necessity, therefore, the world of Odysseus was fiercely competitive, as each hero strove to outdo the others" (118). Or, as Nancy C. M. Hartsock puts it, "Fame, honor, and glory in both situations [in war and in the peacetime rivalries of the *polis*] were to be gained at the price of another losing *his* fame, honor, and glory" (198).[1]

In the *Symposium,* Plato explores a number of means by which man seeks fulfillment, first in the form of the two Eroses and Aphrodites proposed by Pausanias and developed by Eryximachus, then in Aristophanes' circle- and double-men, and finally in Socrates' discussion of procreation. Aristophanes' myth of divided beings is significant in that he suggests that it is the nature of man to search and to strive for completion, for wholeness: "we are all like pieces of the coins that children break in half for keepsakes—making two out of one, like the flatfish—and each of us is forever seeking the half that will tally with himself. . . . And so all this to-do is a relic of that original state of ours, when we were whole, and now, when we are longing for and following after that primeval wholeness, we say we are in love" (191d, 193; Hamilton and Cairns 544–45).

Aristophanes makes it abundantly clear that man is by nature incomplete and destined to remain as such (which sounds suspiciously like Rank's view of Don Juan as a man in constant struggle to regain possession of the mother). Diotima reiterates this point with respect to desire when she claims that Eros is the desire for that which we lack. Yet her ideas do stand in contrast to those of Aristophanes. According to Stanley Rosen in his authoritative discussion of the *Symposium:*

> A fulfillment of Eros would lead, according to both Aristophanes and Diotima, to the disappearance or overcoming of human na-

---

1. Not surprisingly, women in antiquity were generally excluded from these types of concerns. On the role of women in classical Greece and Rome, see Eva Cantarella; S. C. Humphreys 1–21, 33–57; Claude Mossé; Sarah B. Pomeroy, *Goddesses, Whores, Wives, and Slaves* and *Women in Hellenistic Egypt;* Philip E. Slater; and Marilyn B. Arthur's dated but nevertheless interesting review essay. See also Page duBois's noteworthy consideration of ancient representations of women and the importance of Plato in the shaping of Western thought on the "woman question."

> ture. For Aristophanes, however, man would be transformed into
> the circular creatures spawned by the stars, whose physical gro-
> tesqueness is matched by the psychic distortion of hybris. Man-
> kind would be replaced by a race of monsters. To say the least,
> Aristophanes' conception of original nature is ambiguous and is
> not of something simply good or praiseworthy. The implication
> of Diotima's teaching is quite different in this sense. The fulfill-
> ment of Eros in permanent noetic vision would lead to the trans-
> formation of men into gods: not Homeric or personal deities, nor
> even versions of Aristotle's "thought thinking itself," but imper-
> sonal or selfless spectators of "pure beauty itself." (3–4)

Eros becomes the means by which mankind attempts to overcome what
Rosen calls "the merely human" (5). Love represents man's struggle to
become whole, somehow unified, though Rosen hastens to add that this
struggle, however honorable, is doomed to failure: "if Eros is equivalent to, or defines the essence of, psyche, then man can never possess
but must constantly desire. This means that man is radically temporal" (219).

If man is "radically temporal," then a large part of the struggle for
completion has to do with immortality, with becoming like the gods.
This can occur by means of bodily or spiritual procreation, a distinction
that reappears in Western culture as the traditional Christian dichoto-
mies of flesh and spirit, *cupiditas* and *caritas,* and a topic that Socrates,
via Diotima, addresses in some detail. Diotima begins by invoking
immortality by means of eternity, which then leads her to the topic of
procreation; "propagation . . . is the one deathless and eternal element
in our mortality," all of which means that "love is a longing for immortality," because "men's great incentive is the love of glory, and . . . their
one idea is 'To win eternal mention in the deathless roll of fame' "
(206e, 207, 208c; Hamilton and Cairns 559). Although she admits that
bodily procreation is possible (and is, indeed, the principal means by
which the majority of men strive to obtain immortality), Diotima
leaves little doubt that spiritual propagation is to be preferred: "those
whose procreancy is of the spirit rather than of the flesh—and they are
not unknown, Socrates—conceive and bear the things of the spirit. And
what are they? you ask. Wisdom and all her sister virtues; it is the
office of every poet to beget them, and of every artist whom we may call
creative" (209; Hamilton and Cairns 560). Whereas procreation of the
body entails the love of a woman, procreation of the spirit involves the
love of another man, preferably a beautiful man, since a man's "procreant nature is attracted by a comely body rather than an ill-favored

one" (209b; Hamilton and Cairns 651). According to Diotima, the association of two beautiful spirits will bring into being

> the issue of their friendship—and so the bond between them will be more binding, and their communion more complete, than that which comes of bringing children up, because they have created something more beautiful and less mortal than human seed.
>
> And I ask you, who would not prefer such fatherhood to merely human propagation, if he stopped to think of Homer, and Hesiod, and all the greatest of our poets? Who would not envy them their immortal progeny, their claim upon the admiration of posterity? (209c, d; Hamilton and Cairns 561)

The result of procreation of the spirit is wisdom, and "by far the most important kind of wisdom . . . is that which governs the ordering of society, and which goes by the names of justice and moderation" (209, 209b; Hamilton and Cairns 560). Thus, the social aims attached to immortality and honor are clear. Desire is divided into two distinct types, the one pertaining to the physical and relegated to love of women, the other having to do with the spiritual and the social and deriving from the love of men. In this dichotomous understanding of procreation are to be found the types of oppositions informing much of Western thought, particularly as it has to do with the question of woman and with the role of women in society.

John Brenkman has studied in some depth the conceptual oppositions that lie at the heart of Plato's *Symposium*, in particular the relationship between the concepts of male and female, man and woman. Although Brenkman notes that the opposition between male and female is "apparently extrinsic" to this dialogue, by means of a close reading of the *Symposium* he attempts to recover traces of the feminine and to understand their import. He therefore points out that the "feminine has nothing to do with the highest form of sexual desire—the relation between two men—and is excluded from spiritual love altogether, whether in Pausanias' understanding of heavenly love as the offspring of 'a goddess whose attributes have nothing of the female, but are altogether male' or in Socrates' model of spiritual reproduction as the philosopher's education of a beloved youth" (400). But Brenkman does not rest his argument with this observation. Instead, he presses his inquiry further, with interesting results.

In remarking on the narrative structure of the *Symposium*, which effects a separation of various terms in key oppositions, Brenkman focuses on the link between death and reproduction, or death and fatherhood, as it is related to the temporal and the eternal, commenting:

> The form that Socrates' argument takes permits him to recognize that desire is founded on a lack but at the same time to reaffirm the already established opposition between the temporal and the eternal. Love, even the relatively devalued love for a woman, is situated on the path between the temporal and the eternal; since its real aim is immortality, love, through procreancy, puts the human in touch with the divine and the eternal. Socrates can secure this reconciliation with the notion of [desire as a] lack with the metaphysical oppositions underlying the entire dialogue only by producing a kind of narrative, a fictive temporality. Whereas the relation to death and the relation to reproduction are actually enfolded in a single moment, Diotima separates them and distributes them along a narrative line. The recognition of death comes first, and the idea of becoming a father comes afterward as a means of surpassing that recognition. In other words, the relation to reproduction follows upon and triumphs over the relation to death. (425–26)

Ultimately, Brenkman demonstrates the way in which the feminine, in the guise of the mother, is overcome by the masculine, the way in which spiritual procreation is not merely seen as superior to its bodily other, but as subsuming the feminine aspects attached to such physical modes of reproduction:

> Maternity has become absorbed within paternity. . . . There is a kind of Platonic *Aufhebung* at work here. When the philosophical subject enters the realm of spiritual reproduction, taking as his beloved not a woman but a youth to be educated, the maternal is cancelled and transcended by the paternal and yet conserved within it. . . . Even though Socrates defines desire as a lack, as the failure-to-have or the failure-to-be . . . he must present this lack as a lack to be filled and so abolished. In the scheme of Platonic idealism, love is merely the path along which the philosopher presses his way toward the vision of fullness, and the journey itself gets under way with the *Aufhebung* of the maternal. (449–50)

Within the schema of desire and (pro)creation found in Plato's *Symposium,* the articulation and sublimation of the feminine is so complete as to excise what might be viewed as woman's single social and cultural function, however marginal, of reproduction and mothering, which is to say that the notion of honor is brutally masculine. In the dialectical relationship suggested by Brenkman, woman, the feminine, is both canceled out, or discounted, and included by means of transcendence. At one and the same time, there is an element of exclusion, in inclusion, that carries over into the nature of honor as it operates socially and culturally.

The Platonic distinction between procreation of the body and of the spirit, particularly as it relates to honor and Don Juan, implies two kinds of honor, one that pertains to the individual in society, and one that accrues to an artist or author. The dual nature of honor suggests that Don Juan operates as an agent in the perpetuation of patriarchal society and culture (since he imparts wisdom for the good of the state) *and* as a means of obtaining authorial immortality. Authorial appropriation of Don Juan as a character in a literary text and as the object of interpretive inquiry thereby tends toward the perpetuation of patriarchal ideology even as the seduction associated with Don Juan becomes transfigured in the persuasive nature of the new texts.

My point, then, in the various readings of the critical and literary texts treating Don Juan is that seduction serves the aims of patriarchal society, and that it does so quite well by means of the appropriation and elaboration of the *burlador* and his story. If the earliest version of Don Juan, Tirso's *El burlador de Sevilla* [The Trickster of Seville], appears to be inextricably linked to seventeenth-century Spain, it nevertheless structures and stages subsequent representations of the *burlador* even as it restates and refocuses several dominant cultural truths (a word used here advisedly). The imaginative power of Don Juan, beginning with *El burlador de Sevilla*, is such that he is used to embody in a surprisingly consistent manner both the principles of difference and exclusion and the validity of the status quo.

Is it, however, fitting to speak of "truth" in a discussion of Don Juan? Perhaps not. Shoshana Felman concludes *The Literary Speech Act* and her speculation on the promise in Molière's *Dom Juan* (and in Nietzsche, Lacan, and Austin, among others) by questioning the nature of truth and the referentiality of language:

> Thus Austin, like Lacan, like Nietzsche, like others still, instigators of the historical scandal, Don Juans of History, are in reality *bequeathing* us what they do not have: their *word*, their authority, their promise.

> Enjoyers of language, spillers of ink, Sisyphuses of the ban-
> quet stone, theoretical seducers, the Don Juans of History *flirt*
> with shades, *invite* the statue, seek above all to *make* the ban-
> quet stone talk. . . .
>
> Thinkers of desire, of force, of radical negativity, they do not
> *believe* in the promising animal, but, blasé, they continue never-
> theless to desire, to promise, to commit their naïveté.
>
> Modern Don Juans, they know that *truth is only an act*. That is
> why they subvert the truth and do not promise it, but *promise*
> *themselves to it*. Never considering their own answers to be satis-
> fying, they remain the scandalous authors of the infelicity that
> never ceases to make history. (150)

For Felman, truth is the performance itself, Don Juan's promise as it
is made, not as it is kept or broken, which corresponds to José Ortega y
Gasset's vision of man as *homo faber,* as one whose "masculine excellence stems . . . from *making and doing*" and is opposed to woman, for
whom is it a question of "*being* and *existing*" (*Obras completas* 3:329).
What Felman indirectly endorses, of course, is the ongoing process by
which the feminine is subsumed by the masculine lie of truth. But as
Obdulia eloquently asserts in Clarín's *La Regenta* [The Judge's Wife],
almost in spite of herself, "el mundo no debía ser así. Y no es así. Sois
los hombres los que habéis inventado toda esa farsa" ["life shouldn't be
like that. And it isn't like that. All this farce is just an invention of you
men"] (1:331; 179). Felman recognizes the powerful and problematic
status of the promise in Don Juan's story and in theories of meaning,
its seductive nature, and its constitutive role in the fabulation of history. In fact, she goes so far as to comment, "If myth is, in general, an
allegory of history, the Don Juan myth may become, specifically, an
allegory of the way in which history at once *makes* itself and gives
itself to be *misunderstood*" (144). But, in the end, she fails or forgets to
recognize another of the *burlador*'s lessons, namely, that history is not
self-made, that, as Tirso's *comedia* demonstrates, performance is life-
like, not life itself.

It is the distinction between literature and the world of which it is a
part, between language as written and the social forms of communica-
tion that we undertake as we live in this world, that creates the possibility of the truth of Don Juan. Likewise, acknowledgment of the differences between literary representations of the effects of the *burlador*
and the very real power of seduction in our culture opens the way to a
discussion of Don Juan, seduction, and patriarchal society that does not
necessarily replicate this story as it has already been written. A first

step toward understanding the meaning of Don Juan, his truth, is to admit to D. H. Lawrence's ironic stance regarding "positive evil," to admit to the cultural primacy and significance of seduction and to examine the many forms that seduction can and does take. This admission entails a rejection of Kierkegaard's hesitation with respect to publishing the seducer's papers, since to understand the undeniable force of seduction and its place in patriarchal society and literary tradition does not, in and of itself, render Don Juan and his kind innocuous and hence all the more powerful. Rather, we shall be able to lay to rest the issue of the *burlador* through an understanding and revelation of the social, linguistic, and literary mechanisms by which he is allowed to operate. If, as Nietzsche claims in *Ecce Homo,* immortality is the result of dying "several times while still alive" (*Basic Writings of Nietzsche* 759), it is also possible, as I have shown, to speak of Don Juan without resurrecting his seductive ways. In this way, we can name the "hombre sin nombre" and recognize his function, can name Don Juan and recognize the point of honor.

Works Cited

Abrams, Fred. "The Death of Zorrilla's *Don Juan* and the Problem of Catholic Orthodoxy." *Romance Notes* 6 (1964): 42–46.

Adlam, Diana. "The Case Against Capitalist Patriarchy." *m/f* 3 (1979): 83–102.

Agustín, Francisco. *Don Juan en el teatro, en la novela y en la vida.* Biblioteca de Ensayos 9. Madrid: Paez, 1928.

Alarcos Llorach, Emilio. "Notas a *La Regenta.*" *Archivum* 2 (1952): 141–60.

Alberich, José. "La popularidad de *Don Juan Tenorio.*" *La popularidad de Don Juan Tenorio y otros estudios de literatura española moderna.* Clásicos y Ensayos 23. San Antonio de Calonge, Gerona: Aubí, 1982. 13–24.

Alemán, Mateo. *Guzmán de Alfarache.* Ed. Benito Brancaforte. 2 vols. Letras Hispánicas 86 and 87. Madrid: Cátedra, 1979.

Alonso Cortés, Narciso. *Zorrilla. Su vida y sus obras.* 2d ed. Valladolid: Santarén, 1943.

Altieri, Charles. *Act and Quality: A Theory of Literary Meaning and Humanistic Understanding.* Amherst: University of Massachusetts Press, 1981.

Apostolidès, Jean-Marie. "Molière and the Sociology of Exchange." *Critical Inquiry* 14 (1988): 477–92.

Aquinas, Saint Thomas. *Christian Theology.* Trans. Thomas Gilby. Vol. 1 of *Summa Theologiae.*

———. *The Sacraments.* Trans. David Bourke. Vol. 56 of *Summa Theologiae.*

———. *Summa Theologiae.* 60 vols. London: Blackfriars in conjunction with Eyre and Spottiswoode and McGraw-Hill, 1964–75.

Arce, Joaquín. *Tasso y la poesía española: Repercusión literaria y confrontación lingüística.* ensayos/planeta 25. Barcelona: Planeta, 1973.

Arias, Judith H. "Doubles in Hell: *El burlador de Sevilla y convidado de piedra.*" *Hispanic Review* 58 (1990): 361–77.

Ariès, Philippe. *Centuries of Childhood: A Social History of Family Life.* Trans. Robert Baldick. New York: Knopf, 1962.

Aristotle. *Poetics.* Trans. Gerald F. Else. Ann Arbor Paperbacks 166. Ann Arbor: University of Michigan Press, 1970.

Armstrong, Nancy. *Desire and Domestic Fiction: A Political History of the Novel.* New York: Oxford University Press, 1987.

Arthur, Marilyn B. "Review Essay: Classics." *Signs* 2 (1976): 382–403.

Augustine, Saint. *De Sancta Virginitate.* J.-P. Migne, ed., *Patrologiae cursus completus* 40 (1887): cols. 395–428.

———. *In Joannis Evangelium.* J.-P. Migne, ed., *Patrologiae cursus completus* 35 (1845): cols. 1579–1976.

Austin, J. L. *How to Do Things with Words.* Ed. J. O. Urmson and Marina Sbisà. 2d ed. Cambridge: Harvard University Press, 1975.

Azorín [José Martínez Ruiz]. *Obras completas.* Ed. Angel Cruz Rueda. 9 vols. Madrid: Aguilar, 1947–54.

Barnstone, Willis. "Lope de Vega: Frenzy, Outrage, and Saintliness in Don Leonido, a Prototype of the Famous Lover Don Juan Tenorio." *The Poetics of Ecstasy: Varieties of Ekstasis from Sappho to Borges.* New York: Holmes and Meier, 1983. 275–91.

Barry, Edouard, ed. *El burlador de Sevilla y convidado de piedra.* By Tirso de Molina. Collection Mérimée. Paris: Garnier Frères, 1910.

Barthes, Roland. *Mythologies.* Trans. Annette Lavers. New York: Hill and Wang, 1972.

———. *S/Z.* Trans. Richard Miller. New York: Hill and Wang, 1974.

Beauvoir, Simone de. *The Second Sex.* Trans. H. M. Parshley. 1952. New York: Vintage, 1974.

Benhabib, Seyla, and Drucilla Cornell, eds. *Feminism as Critique: On the Politics of Gender.* Feminist Perspectives. Minneapolis: University of Minnesota Press, 1987.

Bennassar, Bartolomé. "Honor and Violence." *The Spanish Character: Attitudes and Mentalities from the Sixteenth to the Nineteenth Century.* Trans. Benjamin Keen. Berkeley and Los Angeles: University of California Press, 1979. 213–36.

Benveniste, Emile. "Analytical Philosophy and Language." *Problems in General Linguistics.* Trans. Mary Elizabeth Meek. Coral Gables: University of Miami Press, 1971. 231–38.

Berg, Elizabeth L. "The Third Woman." *Diacritics* 12.2 (1982): 11–20.

Berger, John. *G.* New York: Viking, 1972.

Berger, P. "La lecture en Valence, 1474 à 1504." *Mélanges de la Casa de Velázquez* 11 (1975): 99–118.

Blau, Peter M. *Exchange and Power in Social Life.* 2d ed. New Brunswick: Transaction Books, 1986.

Bloom, Harold. *The Anxiety of Influence: A Theory of Poetry.* London: Oxford University Press, 1973.

———. Introduction. *Lord Byron's* Don Juan. Modern Critical Interpretations. New York: Chelsea House, 1987. 1–14.

Blue, William R. *Comedia: Art and History.* University of Kansas Humanistic Studies 55. New York: Peter Lang, 1989.

Bobes Naves, María del Carmen. *Teoría general de la novela: Semiología de* La Regenta. Biblioteca Románica Hispánica 341. Madrid: Gredos, 1985.

Bonachera, Trinidad, and María Gracia Piñero. *Hacia don Juan.* Biblioteca de Temas Sevillanos 32. Sevilla: Ayuntamiento de Sevilla, 1985.

Braudy, Leo. *The Frenzy of Renown: Fame and Its History.* New York: Oxford University Press, 1986.

Brenkman, John. "The Other and the One: Psychoanalysis, Reading, *The Symposium.*" *Yale French Studies: Literature and Psychoanalysis. The Question of Reading: Otherwise* 55–56 (1978): 396–456.

Brent, Albert. *Leopoldo Alas and* La Regenta. *A Study in Nineteenth Century Spanish Prose Fiction.* University of Missouri Studies 24.2. Columbia: University of Missouri, 1951.

Brink, C. O. *Horace on Poetry.* Cambridge: Cambridge University Press, 1963.

Brown, G. G. *A Literary History of Spain: The Twentieth Century.* London and New York: Ernest Benn and Barnes and Noble, 1972.

Brown, Norman O. *Life Against Death: The Psychoanalytical Meaning of History.* London: Routledge and Kegan Paul, 1959.

Burkert, Walter. *Structure and History of Greek Mythology and Ritual.* Berkeley and Los Angeles: University of California Press, 1979.

Byron, George Gordon Byron, Baron. *Byron's Letters and Journals.* Ed. Leslie A. Marchand. 12 vols. London: John Murray, 1974–82.

———. *The Complete Poetical Works.* Ed. Jerome J. McGann. 5 vols. Oxford: Clarendon Press, 1980–86.

Cabrera, Vicente. "Doña Ana's Seduction in *El burlador de Sevilla.*" *Bulletin of the Comediantes* 26 (1974): 49–51.

Cantarella, Eva *Pandora's Daughters: The Role and Status of Women in Greek and Roman Antiquity.* Trans. Maureen B. Fant. Baltimore: Johns Hopkins University Press, 1987.

Caro Baroja, Julio. "Honor y vergüenza (Examen histórico de varios conflictos populares)." *Revista de Dialectología y Tradiciones Populares* 20 (1964): 410–60.

———. "El sociocentrismo de los pueblos españoles." *Razas, pueblos y linajes.* Madrid: Revista de Occidente, 1957. 263–92.

Casalduero, Joaquín. *Contribución al estudio del tema de Don Juan en el teatro español.* 1938. Madrid: Porrúa Turanzas, 1975.

———. Introducción. *El burlador de Sevilla y convidado de piedra.* By Tirso de Molina. Letras Hispánicas 58. 3d ed. Madrid: Cátedra, 1978. 11–28.

Cascardi, Anthony J. "Don Juan and the Discourse of Modernism." *Tirso's Don Juan: The Metamorphosis of a Theme.* Ed. Josep M. Solá-Solé and George E. Gingras. Washington, D.C.: Catholic University of America Press, 1988. 151–63.

———. *The Limits of Illusion: A Critical Study of Calderón.* Cambridge Iberian and Latin American Studies. Cambridge: Cambridge University Press, 1984.

Castro, Américo. *De la edad conflictiva.* 2d ed. Madrid: Taurus, 1963.

———, ed. *El burlador de Sevilla y convidado de piedra.* By Tirso de Molina. Clásicos Castellanos 2. 2d ed. Madrid: Espasa-Calpe, 1922.

———, ed. *El burlador de Sevilla y convidado de piedra.* By Tirso de Molina. Clásicos Castellanos 2. 2d ed. Madrid: Espasa-Calpe, 1922.

Cervera y Jiménez-Alfaro, Francisco. "Zorrilla y sus editores. El *Don Juan Tenorio,* caso cumbre de explotación de un drama." *Centenario del estreno de* Don Juan Tenorio *(1844–1944).* Madrid: Instituto Nacional del Libro Español, 1944. 25–70.

Charnon-Deutsch, Lou. *Gender and Representation: Women in Spanish Realist Fiction.* Purdue University Monographs in Romance Languages 32. Amsterdam: John Benjamins, 1990.

Chatman, Seymour. *Story and Discourse: Narrative Structure in Fiction and Film.* Ithaca: Cornell University Press, 1978.

Cinco ensayos sobre Don Juan. Santiago de Chile: Cultura, 1937.

Ciplijauskaité, Biruté. *La mujer insatisfecha: El adulterio en la novela realista.* Barcelona: Edhasa, 1984.

———. *El poeta y la poesía (Del Romanticismo a la poesía social).* Madrid: Insula, 1966.

Clarín [Leopoldo Alas]. "Mis plagios." *Obras selectas.* Ed. Juan Antonio Cabezas. Madrid: Biblioteca Nueva, 1947. 1227–45.

———. "*La mujer. Defendida por la historia, la ciencia y la moral,* por E. Rodríguez Solís." "Libros y libracos." *El Solfeo,* 21 February 1878.

———. *La Regenta.* Ed. Gonzalo Sobejano. 2 vols. Clásicos Castalia 110 and 111. Madrid: Castalia, 1981. Trans. John Rutherford. Middlesex: Penguin, 1984.

———. *Su único hijo.* Ed. Carolyn Richmond. 2d ed. Austral 104. Madrid: Espasa-Calpe, 1989.

———. "El teatro de Zorrilla." *Palique.* Ed. José María Martínez Cachero. Textos Hispánicos Modernos 26. Barcelona: Labor, 1973. 116–23.

Clarín y La Regenta *en su tiempo. Actas del Simposio Internacional.* Oviedo: Universidad de Oviedo, Ayuntamiento de Oviedo, Principado de Asturias, 1987.

Clavería, Carlos. "Sobre el tema del tiempo en « Azorín. » " *Cinco estudios de literatura española moderna.* Tesis y Estudios Salmantinos 11. Salamanca: Colegio Trilingüe de la Univeridad (Consejo Superior de Investigaciones Científicas), 1945. 47–67.

Clémessy, Nelly. "Roman et féminisme au XIXème siècle: Le thème de la mal mariée chez Jacinto Octavio Picón." *Hommage des hispanistes français a Noël Salomon.* Barcelona: Laia, 1979. 185–98.

Collard, Andrée. *Nueva poesía: conceptismo, culteranismo en la crítica española.* La lupa y el escapelo 7. Madrid: Castalia, 1967.

Cornell, Drucilla, and Adam Thurschwell. "Feminism, Negativity, Intersubjectivity." Seyla Benhabib and Drucilla Cornell, eds., *Feminism as Critique* 143–62.

Correa, Gustavo. "El doble aspecto de la honra en el teatro del siglo XVII." *Hispanic Review* 26 (1958): 99–107.

Crescioni Neggers, Gladys. *Don Juan (Hoy)*. Madrid: Turner, 1977.

Cruickshank, D. W. "The First Edition of *El burlador de Sevilla*." *Hispanic Review* 49 (1981): 443–67.

Dante. *Inferno*. Ed. and trans. Charles S. Singleton. 2 vols. Bollingen Series 80. Princeton: Princeton University Press, 1970.

de Armas, Frederick A. "The Guest of Stone and the Cid: Some Parallels." *Romance Notes* 12 (1971): 381–86.

———. *The Invisible Mistress: Aspects of Feminism and Fantasy in the Golden Age*. Charlottesville: Biblioteca Siglo de Oro, 1976.

———. *The Return of Astraea: An Astral-Imperial Myth in Calderón*. Lexington: University Press of Kentucky, 1986.

de Lauretis, Teresa. *Technologies of Gender: Essays on Theory, Film, and Fiction*. Theories of Representation and Difference. Bloomington: Indiana University Press, 1987.

Derrida, Jacques. "Le facteur de la vérité." *The Post Card: From Socrates to Freud and Beyond*. Trans. Alan Bass. Chicago: University of Chicago Press, 1987. 411–96.

———. "Plato's Pharmacy." *Dissemination*. Trans. Barbara Johnson. Chicago: University of Chicago Press, 1981. 61–171.

———. *Spurs: Nietzsche's Styles/Eperons: Les Styles de Nietzsche*. Trans. Barbara Harlow. Chicago: University of Chicago Press, 1979.

Detienne, Marcel. *The Creation of Mythology*. Trans. Margaret Cook. Chicago: University of Chicago Press, 1986.

———. "Rethinking Mythology." *Between Belief and Transgression: Structuralist Essays in Religion, History, and Myth*. Ed. Michel Izard and Pierre Smith. Trans. John Leavitt. Chicago: University of Chicago Press, 1982. 43–52.

Díaz-Plaja, Guillermo. *Nuevo asedio a Don Juan*. Buenos Aires: Sudamericana, 1947.

Douglas, Mary. "The Meaning of Myth: With Special Reference to 'La geste d'Asdiwal.'" *The Structural Study of Myth and Totemism*. Ed. Edmund Leach. London: Tavistock, 1967. 49–69.

duBois, Page. *Sowing the Body: Psychoanalysis and Ancient Representations of Women*. Women in Culture and Society. Chicago: University of Chicago Press, 1988.

Durán, Manuel. "Azorín's 'Broken Record Device' in *Doña Inés*." *Romance Notes* 4 (1963): 112–16.

———, and Roberto González Echevarría. "Luz y oscuridad: La estructura simbólica de *El burlador de Sevilla*." A. David Kossoff and José Amor y Vázquez, eds. *Homenaje* 201–9.

Durand, Frank. "Characterization in *La Regenta*: Point of View and Theme." *Bulletin of Hispanic Studies* 41 (1964): 86–100.

————. "Structural Unity in Leopoldo Alas' *La Regenta*." *Hispanic Review* 31 (1963): 324–35.

Dyer, Geoff. *The Work of John Berger*. London: Pluto, 1986.

Ebert, Teresa L. "The Romance of Patriarchy: Ideology, Subjectivity, and Postmodern Feminist Cultural Theory." *Cultural Critique* 10 (1988): 19–57.

Eisenstein, Zillah R. "Developing a Theory of Capitalist Patriarchy and Socialist Feminism." *Capitalist Patriarchy and the Case for Socialist Feminism*. Ed. Zillah R. Eisenstein. New York: Monthly Review Press, 1979. 5–40.

Else, Gerald F., trans. *Poetics*. By Aristotle. Ann Arbor Paperbacks 166. Ann Arbor: University of Michigan Press, 1970.

Engels, Frederick. *The Origin of the Family, Private Property and the State*. Ed. Eleanor Burke Leacock. New York: International Publishers, 1972.

Enguídanos, Miguel. "Azorín en busca del tiempo divinal." *Papeles de Sans Armadans* 15 (1959): 13–32.

Entrambasaguas, Joaquín de. "Una guerra literaria del Siglo de Oro. Lope de Vega y los preceptos aristotélicos." *Estudios sobre Lope de Vega*. 2d ed. 2 vols. Madrid: Consejo Superior de Investigaciones Científicas, 1967. 1:63–580, 2:7–411.

La Estrella de Sevilla. Ed. R. Foulché-Delbosc. *Bulletin Hispanique* 48 (1920): 497–678.

Farinelli, Arturo. "Cuatro palabras sobre Don Juan y la literatura donjuanesca del porvenir." *Homenaje a Menéndez y Pelayo*. 2 vols. Madrid: Librería General, 1899. 1:205–22.

————. *Don Giovanni*. Milan: Fratelli Bocca, 1946.

————. "Don Giovanni, note critiche." *Giornale storico della letteratura italiana* 27 (1896): 1–77, 254–326.

Feal, Carlos. *En nombre de don Juan (Estructura de un mito literario)*. Purdue University Monographs in Romance Languages 16. Amsterdam: John Benjamins, 1984.

Felman, Shoshana. *Jacques Lacan and the Adventure of Insight: Psychoanalysis in Contemporary Culture*. Cambridge: Harvard University Press, 1987.

————. *The Literary Speech Act: Don Juan with J. L. Austin, or Seduction in Two Languages*. Trans. Catherine Porter. Ithaca: Cornell University Press, 1983.

————. "Turning the Screw of Interpretation." *Yale French Studies: Literature and Psychoanalysis. The Question of Reading: Otherwise* 55–56 (1978): 94–207.

Fernández, Xavier A. "¿Cómo se llamaba el padre de Don Juan?" *Revista de Estudios Hispánicos* 3 (1969): 145–59.

————. "En torno al texto de *El burlador de Sevilla y convidado de piedra*." *Segismundo* 5–7 (1969–70): 1–417.

————. "Estudio preliminar." *El burlador de Sevilla y convidado de piedra*. By Tirso de Molina. Madrid: Alhambra, 1982. 3–65.

————. "Precisiones diferenciales entre *El burlador* y *Tan largo*." *Homenaje a Tirso*. Madrid: Revista *Estudios*, 1981. 39–406.

Fernández de la Reguera, Ricardo. *Don Juan y Casanova*. Santander: Isla de los Ratones, 1969.

Fernández-Turienzo, Francisco. "*El burlador:* mito y realidad." *Romanische Forschungen* 86 (1974): 265–300.

Finley, M. I. *The World of Odysseus*. 2d ed. London: Chatto and Windus, 1977.

Florit Durán, Francisco. *Tirso de Molina ante la comedia nueva: Aproximación a una poética*. Madrid: Revista *Estudios,* 1986.

Foucault, Michel. *The History of Sexuality*. Trans. Robert Hurley. 3 vols. New York: Pantheon, 1978–86.

Freud, Sigmund. *The Standard Edition of the Complete Psychological Works of Sigmund Freud*. Ed. and trans. James Strachey in collaboration with Anna Freud. 24 vols. London: Hogarth, 1966–74.

Froldi, Rinaldo. *Lope de Vega y la formación de la comedia: En torno a la tradición dramática y al primer teatro de Lope*. Salamanca: Anaya, 1968.

Gallop, Jane. *The Daughter's Seduction: Feminism and Psychoanalysis*. Ithaca: Cornell University Press, 1982.

García Castañeda, Salvador. Introducción. *Don Juan Tenorio*. By José Zorrilla. Textos Hispánicos Modernos 33. Barcelona: Labor, 1975. 9–45.

García Gómez, Jorge. "Notas sobre el tiempo y su pasar en novelas varias de Azorín." *Cuadernos hispanoamericanos* 226–27 (1968): 292–338.

Gelabert González, Juan Eloy. "Lectura y escritura en una ciudad provinciana del siglo XVI: Santiago de Compostela." *Bulletin Hispanique* 84 (1982): 264–90.

Gendarme de Bévotte, Georges. *La légende de Don Juan*. 2 vols. Paris: Hachette, 1911.

Gies, David T. "Don Juan contra Don Juan: apoteosis del romanticismo español." *Actas del Séptimo Congreso de la Asociación Internacional de Hispanistas*. 2 vols. Rome: Bulzoni, 1982. 1:545–51.

———. "*Don Juan Tenorio* y la tradición de la comedia de magia." *Hispanic Review* 58 (1990): 1–17.

———. "José Zorrilla and the Betrayal of Spanish Romanticism." *Romanistisches Jahrbuch* 31 (1980): 339–46.

Gilbert, Sandra M., and Susan Gubar. *The Madwoman in the Attic: The Woman Writer and the Nineteenth-Century Literary Imagination*. New Haven: Yale University Press, 1979.

Gillet, Joseph E. "Cueva's *Comedia del Infamador* and the Don Juan Legend." *MLN* 37 (1922): 206–12.

Girard, René. *Deceit, Desire, and the Novel: Self and Other in Literary Structure*. Trans. Yvonne Freccero. Baltimore: Johns Hopkins University Press, 1965.

———. *The Scapegoat*. Trans. Yvonne Freccero. Baltimore: Johns Hopkins University Press, 1986.

———. "*To double business bound*": *Essays on Literature, Mimesis, and Anthropology*. Baltimore: Johns Hopkins University Press, 1978.

———. *Violence and the Sacred*. Trans. Patrick Gregory. Baltimore: Johns Hopkins University Press, 1977.

Glenn, Kathleen M. *Azorín (José Martínez Ruiz)*. TWAS 604. Boston: Twayne, 1981.

Gold, Hazel. " 'Ni soltera, ni viuda, ni casada': Negación y Exclusión en las Novelas Femeninas de Jacinto Octavio Picón." *Ideologies and Literature* n.s. 4.17 (1983): 63–77.

Goldman, Peter B. "Toward a Sociology of the Modern Spanish Novel: The Early Years." *MLN* 89 (1974): 173–90, *MLN* 90 (1975): 183–211.

González-del-Valle, Luis. "Doña Ana's Seduction in *El burlador de Sevilla:* A Reconsideration." *Bulletin of the Comediantes* 30 (1978): 42–45.

González Palencia, Angel. "Quevedo, Tirso y las comedias ante la Junta de Reformación." *Boletín de la Real Academia Española* 25 (1946): 43–84.

Gouldner, Alvin W. *Enter Plato: Classical Greece and the Origins of Social Theory.* New York: Basic Books, 1965.

Gullón, Germán. "Invención y reflexividad discursiva en *La Regenta,* de Leopoldo Alas." *La novela como acto imaginativo: Alarcón, Bécquer, Galdós, "Clarín."* Persiles 147. Madrid: Taurus, 1983. 123–47.

Gullón, Ricardo. "Aspectos de 'Clarín.' " *Archivum* 2 (1952): 161–87.

Hamerton-Kelly, Robert G., ed. *Violent Origins: Walter Burkert, René Girard, and Jonathan Z. Smith on Ritual Killing and Cultural Formation.* Stanford: Stanford University Press, 1987.

Hamilton, Edith, and Huntington Cairns, eds. *The Collected Dialogues of Plato.* By Plato. Bollingen Series 71. 4th printing. New York: Pantheon, 1966.

Hartsock, Nancy C. M. *Money, Sex, and Power: Toward a Feminist Historical Materialism.* New York: Longman, 1983.

Hayem, Armand. *Le Don Juanisme.* Paris: Alphonse Lemerre, 1886.

Hirschman, Albert O. *The Passions and the Interests: Political Arguments for Capitalism before its Triumph.* Princeton: Princeton University Press, 1977.

Hoffmann, E. T. A. "Don Juan." *Fantasiestücke in Callots Manier.* Ed. Hans-Joachim Kruse. Berlin: Aufbau-Verlag, 1982. 81–95.

Hollis, Martin J., and Edward J. Nell. *Rational Economic Man: A Philosophical Critique of Neo-Classical Economics.* London: Cambridge University Press, 1975.

Horace. *Satires, Epistles and Ars Poetica.* Trans. H. Rushton Fairclough. Loeb Classical Library 194. Cambridge and London: Harvard University Press and William Heinemann, 1929.

Humphreys, S. C. *The Family, Women and Death. Comparative Studies.* London: Routledge and Kegan Paul, 1983.

Irigaray, Luce. *Speculum of the Other Woman.* Trans. Gillian C. Gill. Ithaca: Cornell University Press, 1985.

———. *This Sex Which Is Not One.* Trans. Catherine Porter with Carolyn Burke. Ithaca: Cornell University Press, 1985.

Irwin, John T. "Mysteries We Reread, Mysteries of Rereading: Poe, Borges, and the Analytic Detective Story; Also Lacan, Derrida, and Johnson." *MLN* 101 (1986): 1168–1215.

Jackson, Robert M. " 'Cervantismo' in the Creative Process of Clarín's *La Regenta*." *MLN* 84 (1969): 208–27.

James, William. *The Varieties of Religious Experience: A Study in Human Nature*. Cambridge: Harvard University Press, 1985.

Johnson, Barbara. *The Critical Difference: Essays in the Contemporary Rhetoric of Reading*. Baltimore: Johns Hopkins University Press, 1980.

Jones, Ernest. *The Life and Work of Sigmund Freud*. 3 vols. New York: Basic Books, 1953–57.

José Prades, Juana de. "Estudio preliminar." *El arte nuevo de hacer comedias en este tiempo*. By Lope de Vega. Clásicos Hispánicos 11. Madrid: Consejo Superior de Investigaciones Científicas, 1971. 1–274.

Joseph, M. K. *Byron the Poet*. London: Victor Gollancz, 1964.

Juan Manuel, Don. *El Conde Lucanor*. Vol. 2 of *Obras completas*. Ed. José Manuel Blecua. 2 vols. Biblioteca Románica Hispánica 15. Madrid: Gredos, 1983.

Jung, C. G. *The Collected Works of C. G. Jung*. Ed. Sir Herbert Read et al. 19 vols. Bollingen Series 20. Princeton: Princeton University Press, 1953–68.

———. "On the Psychology of the Trickster Figure." *The Archetypes and the Collective Unconscious*. Trans. R. F. C. Hull. 2d ed. Volume 9, part 1 of *The Collected Works*.

———. "On the Relation of Analytical Psychology to Poetry." *The Spirit in Man, Art, and Literature*. Trans. R. F. C. Hull. Vol. 15 of *The Collected Works*.

———. "Psychological Aspects of the Mother Archetype." *The Archetypes and the Collective Unconscious*. Trans. R. F. C. Hull. 2d ed. Volume 9, part 1 of *The Collected Works*.

Kagan, Richard L. *Students and Society in Early Modern Spain*. Baltimore: Johns Hopkins University Press, 1974.

Kaufmann, Walter. "How Nietzsche Revolutionized Ethics." *From Shakespeare to Existentialism: An Original Study*. 1959; Princeton: Princeton University Press, 1980. 207–17.

Kennedy, Ruth Lee. *Studies in Tirso I: The Dramatist and his Competitors, 1620–26*. North Carolina Studies in Romance Languages and Literature 152. Chapel Hill: University of North Carolina Press, 1974.

Kierkegaard, Søren. *Either/Or*. Trans. Howard V. Hong and Edna H. Hong. 2 vols. Princeton: Princeton University Press, 1987.

———. *Fear and Trembling. Repetition*. Trans. Howard V. Hong and Edna H. Hong. Princeton: Princeton University Press, 1983.

Kirk, G. S. *Myth: Its Meaning and Functions in Ancient and Other Cultures*. Berkeley and Los Angeles: University of California Press, 1970.

———. "On Defining Myths." *Exegesis and Argument: Studies in Greek Mythology and Philosophy Presented to Gregory Vlastos*. Ed. E. N. Lee,

A. P. D. Mourelatos, and R. M. Rorty. New York: Humanities Press, 1973. 61–69.

Kirkpatrick, Susan. *Las Románticas: Women Writers and Subjectivity in Spain, 1835–1850.* Berkeley and Los Angeles: University of California Press, 1989.

Kofman, Sarah. *The Enigma of Woman: Woman in Freud's Writings.* Trans. Catherine Porter. Ithaca: Cornell University Press, 1985.

Kossoff, A. David, and José Amor y Vázquez, eds. *Homenaje a William L. Fichter. Estudios sobre el teatro antiguo hispánico y otros ensayos.* Madrid: Castalia, 1971.

Kristeva, Julia. "Don Juan, or Loving to Be Able To." *Tales of Love.* Trans. Leon S. Roudiez. New York: Columbia University Press, 1987. 191–208.

———. "Motherhood According to Giovanni Bellini." *Desire in Language: A Semiotic Approach to Literature and Art.* Ed. Leon S. Roudiez. European Perspectives. New York: Columbia University Press, 1980. 237–70.

Kronik, John W. "El beso del sapo: configuraciones grotescas en *La Regenta.*" *Clarín y* La Regenta *en su tiempo* 517–24.

Labanyi, Jo. "City, Country and Adultery in *La Regenta.*" *Bulletin of Hispanic Studies* 63 (1986): 53–66.

Lacan, Jacques. *Ecrits: A Selection.* Trans. Alan Sheridan. New York: Norton, 1977.

———. *Le Séminaire de Jacques Lacan. Livre XX: Encore (1972–1973).* Le Champ Freudien. Paris: Seuil, 1975.

———. "Seminar on 'The Purloined Letter.'" *Yale French Studies* 48 (1973): 39–72.

Lacoue-Labarthe, Philippe. "Mimesis and Truth." *Diacritics* 8.1 (1978): 10–23.

Lafora, Gonzalo. *See* R[odríguez] Lafora, Gonzalo.

Laín-Entralgo, Pedro. *La generación del noventa y ocho.* 4th ed. Madrid: Espasa-Calpe, 1959.

Larquié, Claude. "L'alphabétisation à Madrid en 1650." *Revue d'Histoire Moderne et Contemporaine* 28 (1981): 132–57.

Larra, Mariano José de. "El *album.*" *Obras de Mariano José de Larra.* Ed. Carlos Seco Serrano. 4 vols. Biblioteca de Autores Españoles 127–30. Madrid: Atlas, 1960. 2:83–86.

Larson, Donald R. *The Honor Plays of Lope de Vega.* Cambridge: Harvard University Press, 1977.

Lawrance, J. N. H. "The Spread of Lay Literacy in Late Medieval Castile." *Bulletin of Hispanic Studies* 62 (1985): 79–94.

Lévi-Strauss, Claude. *The Elementary Structure of Kinship.* Revised Edition. Trans. James Harle Bell and John Richard von Sturmer. Ed. Rodney Needham. Boston: Beacon Press, 1969.

———. *The Raw and the Cooked.* Trans. John and Doreen Weightman. New York: Harper and Row, 1969.

————. *The Savage Mind.* Chicago: University of Chicago Press, 1966.

————. *Structural Anthropology.* Trans. Claire Jacobson, Brooke Grundfest Schoepf, and Monique Layton. 2 vols. New York: Basic Books, 1963.

Levinson, Marjorie. *The Romantic Fragment Poem: A Critique of a Form.* Chapel Hill: University of North Carolina Press, 1986.

Lida, Denah. "El 'catálogo' de *Don Giovanni* y el de *Don Juan Tenorio.*" A. David Kossoff and José Amor y Vázquez, *Homenaje* 553–61.

Lida de Malkiel, María Rosa. *La idea de la Fama en la Edad Media Castellana.* Lengua y Estudios Literarios. Mexico City: Fondo de Cultura Económica, 1952.

————. "Sobre la prioridad de *¿Tan largo me lo fiáis?* Notas al *Isidro* y a *El burlador de Sevilla.*" *Hispanic Review* 30 (1962): 275–95.

Livingstone, Leon. *Tema y forma de las novelas de Azorín.* Biblioteca Románica Hispánica 141. Madrid: Gredos, 1970.

López, Ignacio-Javier. *Caballero de novela: Ensayo sobre el donjuanismo en la novela española moderna, 1880–1930.* Barcelona: Puvill, 1986.

López de Ayala, Adelardo. *Obras completas.* Ed. José María Castro y Calvo. 3 vols. Biblioteca de Autores Españoles 182. Madrid: Atlas, 1965.

López Pinciano, Alonso. *Philosophia antigua poética.* Ed. Alfredo Carballo Picazo. 3 vols. Biblioteca de Antiguos Libros Hispánicos 20. Madrid: Consejo Superior de Investigaciones Científicas, 1953.

Lowrie, Walter. Editor's Introduction. *Repetition: An Essay in Experimental Psychology.* By Søren Kierkegaard. Princeton: Princeton University Press, 1941. ix–xlii.

MacKay, Dorothy Epplen. *The Double Invitation in the Legend of Don Juan.* Stanford: Stanford University Press, 1943.

Maeztu, Ramiro de. "Don Juan o el poder." *Don Quijote, Don Juan y la Celestina: Ensayos de simpatía.* Colección Austral 31. 11th ed. Madrid: Espasa-Calpe, 1972. 71–106.

Maldonado de Guevara, Francisco. "Dolo malo y dolo bueno (El burlador de la noche)." *Revista de Estudios Políticos* 43 (1952): 61–117.

Mandel, Oscar, ed. *The Theatre of Don Juan: A Collection of Plays and Views, 1630–1963.* Lincoln: University of Nebraska Press, 1963.

Mandolini, Hernani. "Psicopatología del Don Juan." *Revista de Criminología, Psiquiatría y Medicina Legal* 13 (1926): 322–30.

Mandrell, James. "Nostalgia and the Popularity of *Don Juan Tenorio:* Reading Zorrilla Through Clarín." *Hispanic Review* 59 (1991): 37–55.

Mansour, George P. "Parallelism in *Don Juan Tenorio.*" *Hispania* 61 (1978): 245–53.

Marañón, Gregorio. *Obras completas.* Ed. Alfredo Juderías. 10 vols. Madrid: Espasa-Calpe, 1966–77.

Maravall, José María. "Azorín. Idea y sentido de la microhistoria." *Cuadernos Hispanoamericanos* 226–27 (1968): 28–77.

Marcuse, Herbert. *Eros and Civilization: A Philosophical Inquiry into Freud.* Boston: Beacon Press, 1966.

Marías, Julián. *"Doña Inés." Insula* 94 (1953): 1, 9.

Martín Gaite, Carmen. *Usos amorosos del dieciocho en España.* 1972; Barcelona: Anagrama, 1987.

Martínez Cachero, José María. " 'Clarín' y 'Azorín' (una amistad y un fervor)." *Archivum* 3 (1953): 159–80.

———. "Cuando José Martínez Ruiz empezaba . . . 'Clarín' le anunció en 1897, como una de las pocas esperanzas de la literatura 'satírica.' " *ABC* 17 April 1954.

———. *Las novelas de Azorín.* Madrid: Insula, 1960.

Marx, Karl. *Capital: A Critique of Political Economy.* Trans. Samuel Moore and Edward Aveling. Ed. Frederick Engels. 3 vols. New York: International Publishers, 1967.

Mauss, Marcel. *The Gift: Forms and Functions of Exchange in Archaic Societies.* Trans. Ian Cunnison. New York: Norton, 1967.

Mazzeo, Guido E. *"Don Juan Tenorio:* Salvation or Damnation?" *Romance Notes* 5 (1964): 151–55.

McGaha, Michael D. "In Defense of *¿Tan largo me lo fiáis . . . ?" Bulletin of the Comediantes* 29 (1977): 75–86.

McGann, Jerome J. *Don Juan in Context.* Chicago: University of Chicago Press, 1976.

McKendrick, Melveena. "Celebration or Subversion?: *Los comendadores de Córdoba* Reconsidered." *Bulletin of Hispanic Studies* 61 (1984): 352–60.

———. *Woman and Society in the Spanish Drama of the Golden Age.* London: Cambridge University Press, 1974.

Meehan, Thomas C. "El desdoblamiento interior en *Doña Inés." Cuadernos hispanoamericanos* 237 (1969): 644–68.

Menéndez Pidal, Ramón. "Sobre los orígenes de *El convidado de piedra." Estudios literarios.* Madrid: Atenea, 1920. 101–36.

Mérimée, Prosper. *Les âmes du purgatoire. Romans et nouvelles.* Ed. Henri Martineau. Bibliothèque de la Pléiade. Paris: Gallimard, 1951. 351–408.

Migne, J.-P., ed. *Patrologiae cursus completus: Series latina.* 221 vols. Paris: 1844–90.

Mitchell, Juliet. *Psychoanalysis and Feminism: Freud, Reich, Laing and Women.* New York: Pantheon, 1974.

———, and Jacqueline Rose, eds. *Feminine Sexuality.* By Jacques Lacan and the *école freudienne.* New York: Norton, 1982.

Mitchell, Timothy. *Violence and Piety in Spanish Folklore.* Philadelphia: University of Pennsylvania Press, 1988.

Moi, Toril. "The Missing Mother: The Oedipal Rivalries of René Girard." *Diacritics* 12.2 (1982): 21–31.

Moir, Duncan. "The Classical Tradition in Spanish Dramatic Theory and Practice in the Seventeenth Century." *Classical Drama and its Influence: Essays Presented to H. D. F. Kitto.* Ed. M. J. Anderson. London: Methuen, 1965. 191–228.

Molho, Maurice. "Oedipe-Burlador ou la théorie du masque." *Sujet et sujet parlant dans le text (textes hispaniques)*. Actes du Colloque du Séminaire d'Etudes Littéraires. Toulouse: University of Toulouse–Le Mirail Press, 1977. 7–23.

———. "Sur le discours ideologique du *Burlador de Sevilla y Convidado de Piedra*." *Actes du Colloque du Séminaire d'Etudes Littéraires*. Toulouse: University of Toulouse–Le Mirail Press, 1978. Not paginated.

———. "Trois mythologiques sur Don Juan." *Les Cahiers de Fontenay* 9–10 (1978): 9–75.

Molière. *Dom Juan ou le Festin de Pierre. Oeuvres complètes*. Ed. Georges Couton. Bibliothèque de la Pléiade. 2 vols. Paris: Gallimard, 1971. 2:31–85.

Mossé, Claude. *La femme dans la Grèce antique*. L'Aventure Humaine. Paris: Albin Michel, 1983.

Muñoz González, Luis. "*Don Juan Tenorio*, la personalización del mito." *Estudios Filológicos* 10 (1974–75): 93–122.

Nalle, Sara T. "Literacy and Culture in Early Modern Castile." *Past & Present* 125 (1989): 65–96.

Newels, Margarete. *Los géneros dramáticos en las poéticas del Siglo de Oro*. Trans. Amadeo Solé-Leris. London: Támesis, 1974.

Nicholson, Linda. "Feminism and Marx: Integrating Kinship with the Economic." Seyla Benhabib and Drucilla Cornell, eds., *Feminism as Critique* 16–30.

Nietzsche, Friedrich. *Basic Writings of Nietzsche*. Trans. Walter Kaufmann. 1966; New York: Modern Library, 1968.

———. *Daybreak: Thoughts on the Prejudices of Morality*. Trans. R. J. Hollingdale. Cambridge: Cambridge University Press, 1982.

———. *Thus Spoke Zarathustra: A Book for All and None*. Trans. Walter Kaufmann. New York: Penguin, 1978.

———. *The Wanderer and his Shadow. Human, All-Too-Human*. Trans. Paul V. Cohn. Vol. 7 of *The Complete Works of Friedrich Nietzsche*. Ed. Oscar Levy. 18 vols. 1909–11; New York: Russell and Russell, 1964.

Norton, Glyn P. "French Renaissance Translators and the Dialectic of Myth and History." *Renaissance and Reformation/Renaissance et Réforme* n.s. 5 (1981): 189–202.

Oriel, Charles. *Writing and Inscription in Golden Age Drama*. Purdue University Monographs on Romance Languages. Amsterdam: John Benjamins, forthcoming.

Ortega y Gasset, José. *Obras completas*. 12 vols. Madrid: Alianza and Revista de Occidente, 1946–83.

Ortner, Sherry B. "Oedipal Father, Mother's Brother, and the Penis: A Review of Juliet Mitchell's *Psychoanalysis and Feminism*." *Feminist Studies* 2 (1975): 167–82.

Pardo Bazán, Emilia. "Juicios cortos. —*Al primer vuelo. —Dulce y sabrosa.* —*El cancionero de la Rosa*." *Nuevo Teatro Crítico* 1.6 (1891): 53–65.

Parker, A[lexander] A. Introduction. *Polyphemus and Galatea.* By Luis de Góngora. Trans. Gilbert F. Cunningham. Austin: University of Texas Press, 1977. 7–106.

———. "The Spanish Drama of the Golden Age: A Method of Analysis and Interpretation." *The Great Playwrights.* Ed. Eric Bentley. 2 vols. New York: Doubleday, 1970. 1:679–707.

Paterson, Alan K. G. "Reversal and Multiple Role-playing in Alarcón's *La verdad sospechosa.*" *Bulletin of Hispanic Studies* 61 (1984): 361–68.

Peña, Aniano. Introducción. *Don Juan Tenorio.* By José Zorrilla. Letras Hispánicas 114. 4th ed. Madrid: Cátedra, 1983. 11–70.

Pérez de Ayala, Ramón. *Obras completas.* Ed. José García Mercadal. 4 vols. Madrid: Aguilar, 1964–69.

Pérez Firmat, Gustavo. *Literature and Liminality: Festive Readings in the Hispanic Tradition.* Durham: Duke University Press, 1986.

Pérez Galdós, Benito. *Doña Perfecta. Obras completas. Novelas.* Ed. Federico Carlos Sainz de Robles. 3 vols. Madrid: Aguilar, 1970–71. 1:415–511.

———. "Noticias literarias. Observaciones sobre la novela contemporánea en España. *Proverbios ejemplares* y *Proverbios cómicos* [por Ventura Ruiz Aguilera]." *Ideología y política en la novela española del siglo XIX.* Ed. Iris Zavala. Salamanca: Anaya, 1971. 317–31.

Pérez López, Manuel María. "Clarín: ¿maestro?" *Azorín y la literatura española.* Acta Salmanticensia 83. Salamanca: University of Salamanca Press, 1974. 198–202.

Pi y Margall, Francisco. "Observaciones sobre el carácter de D. Juan Tenorio." *Comedias de Tirso de Molina y de Guillén de Castro.* Vol. 12 of *Colección de libros españoles raros o curiosos.* 24 vols. Madrid: Fontanet, 1871–96. xi–lxix.

Picatoste, Felipe. *Estudios literarios. Don Juan Tenorio.* Madrid: Gaspar, 1883.

Picón, Jacinto Octavio. *Ayala: estudio biográfico.* Madrid: Impresores y Libreros, n.d.

———. *Dulce y sabrosa.* Ed. Gonzalo Sobejano. Letras Hispánicas 51. Madrid: Cátedra, 1982.

Pieropán, María Doménica. "Una re-visión feminista del eterno retorno en *Doña Inés* de Azorín." *Hispania* 72 (1989): 233–40.

Pitt-Rivers, Julian. "Honour and Social Status." *Honour and Shame: The Values of Mediterranean Society.* Ed. J. G. Peristany. Chicago: University of Chicago Press, 1966. 19–77.

Plato. *The Collected Dialogues of Plato.* Ed. Edith Hamilton and Huntington Cairns. Bollingen Series 71. 4th printing. New York: Pantheon, 1966.

Poggioli, Renato. "Tragedy or Romance? A Reading of the Paolo and Francesca Episode in Dante's *Inferno.*" *PMLA* 72 (1957): 313–58.

Pomeroy, Sarah B. *Goddesses, Whores, Wives, and Slaves: Women in Classical Antiquity.* New York: Schocken, 1975.

———. *Women in Hellenistic Egypt: From Alexander to Cleopatra.* New York: Schocken, 1984.

Radoff, M. L., and W. C. Salley. "Notes on the *Burlador.*" *MLN* 45 (1930): 239–44.

Ramos-Gascón, Antonio. "Relaciones Clarín-Martínez Ruiz, 1897–1900." *Hispanic Review* 42 (1974): 413–26.

Rand, Marguerite C. "Más notas sobre Azorín y el tiempo." *Hispania* 49 (1966): 23–30.

Rank, Otto. *The Don Juan Legend.* Trans. David G. Winter. Princeton: Princeton University Press, 1975.

Reiter, Rayna R., ed. *Toward an Anthropology of Women.* New York: Monthly Review Press, 1975.

Revilla, Manuel de la. "El tipo legendario del Tenorio y sus manifestaciones en las modernas literaturas." *Obras.* Madrid: Ateneo Científico, Literario y Artístico, 1883. 431–56.

Rice, Miriam Wagner. "The Meaning of Metaphor in *La Regenta.*" *Revista de Estudios Hispánicos* 11 (1977): 141–51.

———. "Metaphorical Foreshadowing in *La Regenta.*" *Hispanófila* 71 (1981): 41–52.

Richmond, Carolyn. "En torno al vacío: la mujer, idea hecha carne de ficción en *La Regenta* de Clarín." *Realismo y naturalismo en España en la segunda mitad del siglo XIX.* Ed. Yvan Lissorgues. Colección Autores, Textos y Temas. Literatura 2. Barcelona: Anthropos, 1988. 341–67.

———. "Las ideas de Leopoldo Alas, 'Clarín,' sobre la mujer en sus escritos previos a *La Regenta.*" *Homenaje al profesor Antonio Vilanova.* Ed. Adolfo Sotelo Vázquez and Marta Cristina Carbonell. 2 vols. Barcelona: Universidad de Barcelona, 1989. 2:523–39.

Riley, Edward C. "The Dramatic Theories of Don Jusepe Antonio González de Salas." *Hispanic Review* 19 (1951): 183–203.

Rivers, Elias L. "The Shame of Writing in *La Estrella de Sevilla.*" *Folio* 12 (1980): 105–17.

Rodriguez, Marie-Christine, and Bartolomé Bonnassar. "Signatures et niveau culturel des témoins et accusés dans les procès d'inquisition du ressort du Tribunal de Tolède (1525–1817) et du ressort du Tribunal de Cordoue (1595–1632)." *Cahiers de Monde Hispanique et Luso-brasilien* 31 (1978): 17–46.

R[odríguez] Lafora, Gonzalo. "The Psychology of Don Juan." *Don Juan and Other Psychological Studies.* Trans. Janet H. Perry. London: Thornton Butterworth, 1930. 19–72.

Rodríguez López-Vázquez, Alfredo. Introducción. *El burlador de Sevilla.* By Andrés de Claramonte ("traditionally attributed to Tirso de Molina"). Teatro del Siglo de Oro 12. Kassel: Reichenberger, 1988. 1–61.

Rogers, Daniel. "Fearful Symmetry: The Ending of *El burlador de Sevilla.*" *Bulletin of Hispanic Studies* 41 (1964): 141–59.

———. *Tirso de Molina:* El burlador de Sevilla. Critical Guides to Spanish Texts 19. London: Grant and Cutler, 1977.

Rogers, Edith. "Surrogates, parallels, and paraphrasings in *La Regenta.*" *Revista de Estudios Hispánicos* 18 (1984): 87–101.

Rogers, Paul Patrick. "Dramatic Copyright in Spain before 1850." *Romanic Review* 25 (1934): 35–39.

Romera-Navarro, M. *La preceptiva dramática de Lope de Vega y otros ensayos sobre el fénix*. Madrid: Yunque, 1935.

Romero, Héctor R. "Consideraciones teológicas y románticas sobre la muerte de Don Juan en las obras de Zorrilla." *Hispanófila* 54 (1975): 9–16.

Rooney, Ellen. *Seductive Reasoning: Pluralism as the Problematic of Contemporary Literary Theory*. Ithaca: Cornell University Press, 1989.

Rosen, Stanley. *Plato's* Symposium. 2d ed. New Haven: Yale University Press, 1987.

Rosolato, Guy. *Essais sur le symbolique*. Collection Connaissance de L'Inconscient. Paris: Gallimard, 1969.

Rostand, Edmond. *The Last Night of Don Juan*. Trans. Dolores Bagley. Oscar Mandel, ed., *The Theatre of Don Juan* 569–622.

Rougemont, Denis de. *Love in the Western World*. Trans. Montgomery Belgion. New York: Pantheon, 1956.

Rousset, Jean. *Le mythe de Don Juan*. Paris: Colin, 1978.

Rozas, Juan Manuel. *Significado y doctrina del* Arte nuevo *de Lope de Vega*. Madrid: Sociedad General Española de Librería, 1976.

Ruano de la Haza, José M. "Doña Ana's Seduction in *El burlador de Sevilla*: Further Evidence Against." *Bulletin of the Comediantes* 32 (1980): 131–33.

Rubin, Gayle. "The Traffic in Women: Notes on the 'Political Economy' of Sex." Rayna R. Reiter, *Toward an Anthropology of Women* 157–210.

Ruiz de Alarcón, Juan. *La verdad sosphechosa*. Ed. Alva V. Ebersole. 3d ed. Letras Hispánicas 49. Madrid: Cátedra, 1980.

Ruiz Ramón, Francisco. *Historia del teatro español (Desde sus orígenes hasta 1900)*. Madrid: Alianza, 1967.

Rutherford, John. *Leopoldo Alas:* La Regenta. Critical Guides to Spanish Texts 9. London: Grant and Cutler, 1974.

Ryan, Michael. *Marxism and Deconstruction: A Critical Articulation*. Baltimore: Johns Hopkins University Press, 1982.

Sacks, Karen. "Engels Revisited: Women, the Organization of Production, and Private Property." Rayna R. Reiter, *Toward an Anthropology of Women* 211–34.

Saíd Armesto, Víctor. *La leyenda de Don Juan. Orígenes poéticos de* El burlador de Sevilla y convidado de piedra. Madrid: Sucesores de Hernández, 1908.

Salgot, Antonio de. *Don Juan Tenorio y donjuanismo*. Barcelona: Juventud, 1953.

Salinas, Pedro. "El nacimiento de Don Juan." *Ensayos de literatura hispánica (Del Cantar de Mío Cid a García Lorca)*. Ed. Juan Marichal. 3d ed. Madrid: Aguilar, 1967. 158–67.

Sánchez, Elizabeth. "From World to Word: Realism and Reflexivity in *Don Quijote* and *La Regenta*." *Hispanic Review* 55 (1987): 27–39.

Sánchez, Roberto G. *El teatro en la novela: Galdós y Clarín.* Madrid: Insula, 1974.

Sánchez-Eppler, Benigno. "Stakes: The Sexual Vulnerability of the Reader in *La Regenta.*" *Romanic Review* 78 (1987): 202–17.

Sánchez Escribano, Federico, and Alberto Porqueras Mayo. *Preceptiva dramática española del Renacimiento y el Barroco.* Biblioteca Románica Hispánica. Textos 3. Madrid: Gredos, 1965.

Scanlon, Geraldine M. *La polémica feminista en la España contemporánea (1868–1974).* Madrid: Siglo XXI, 1976.

Schlossman, Beryl. "(Pas) Encore!—Flaubert, Baudelaire, and Don Giovanni." *Romanic Review* 82 (1990): 350–67.

Sebold, Russell P. *Trayectoria del romanticismo español: desde la ilustración hasta Bécquer.* Filología 10. Barcelona: Editorial Crítica, 1983.

Segal, Charles. *Dionysiac Poetics and Euripides' Bacchae.* Princeton: Princeton University Press, 1982.

———. "Greek Tragedy: Writing, Truth, and the Representation of the Self." *Interpreting Greek Tragedy: Myth, Poetry, Text.* Ithaca: Cornell University Press, 1986. 75–109.

Semprún Donahue, Moraima de. "La doble seducción de *La Regenta.*" *Archivum* 23 (1973): 117–33.

Serrano Plaja, Arturo. "Un no de Don Juan y un no a Don Juan. (Notas sobre *El burlador de Sevilla).*" *Segismundo* 9 (1973): 17–32.

Serres, Michel. "The Apparition of Hermes: *Don Juan.*" *Hermes: Literature, Science, Philosophy.* Ed. Josué V. Harari and David F. Bell. Baltimore: Johns Hopkins University Press, 1982. 3–14.

Shell, Marc. *The Economy of Literature.* Baltimore: Johns Hopkins University Press, 1978.

Shepard, Sanford. *El Pinciano y las teorías literarias del Siglo de Oro.* Biblioteca Románica Hispánica. Estudios y Ensayos 58. Madrid: Gredos, 1962.

Sieber, Harry. *Language and Society in* La vida de Lazarillo de Tormes. Baltimore: Johns Hopkins University Press, 1978.

Siebers, Tobin. *The Ethics of Criticism.* Ithaca: Cornell University Press, 1988.

———. *The Mirror of Medusa.* Berkeley and Los Angeles: University of California Press, 1983.

Sieburth, Stephanie. "Interpreting *La Regenta:* Coherence vs. Entropy." *MLN* 102 (1987): 274–91.

———. *Reading* La Regenta: *Duplicitous Discourse and the Entropy of Structure.* Purdue University Monographs in Romance Languages 29. Amsterdam: John Benjamins, 1990.

Slater, Philip E. *The Glory of Hera: Greek Mythology and the Greek Family.* Boston: Beacon Press, 1968.

Sloman, Albert E. "The Two Versions of *El burlador de Sevilla.*" *Bulletin of Hispanic Studies* 42 (1965): 18–33.

Smeed, J. W. *Don Juan: Variations on a Theme*. London: Routledge, 1990.

Smith, Barbara Herrnstein. "Narrative Versions, Narrative Theory." *Critical Inquiry* 7 (1980): 213–36.

Smith, Paul Julian. *Quevedo on Parnassus: Allusive Context and Literary Theory in the Love-Lyric*. MHRA Texts and Dissertations 25. London: Modern Humanities Research Association, 1987.

———. *Writing in the Margin: Spanish Literature of the Golden Age*. Oxford: Clarendon Press, 1988.

Sobejano, Gonzalo. Introducción. *Dulce y sabrosa*. By Jacinto Octavio Picón. Letras Hispánicas 51. Madrid: Cátedra, 1982. 13–58.

———. Introducción biográfica y crítica. *La Regenta*. By Leopoldo Alas (Clarín). 2 vols. Clásicos Castalia 110 and 111. Madrid: Castalia, 1981. 1:7–58.

———. *Nietzsche en España*. Biblioteca Románica Hispánica. Estudios y Ensayos 102. Madrid: Gredos, 1967.

Spires, Robert C. *Transparent Simulacra: Spanish Fiction, 1902–1926*. Columbia: University of Missouri Press, 1988.

Spitzer, Leo. "En lisant le *Burlador de Sevilla*." *Neuphilologische Mitteilungen* 36 (1935): 285.

Steffan, Truman Guy. *The Making of a Masterpiece*. Vol. 1 of *Byron's* Don Juan. 4 vols. 2d ed. Austin: University of Texas Press, 1971.

Stendhal [Marie Henri Beyle]. "Werther and Don Juan." *Love*. Trans. Gilbert and Suzanne Sale. London: Merlin, 1957. 170–77.

Sturm, Harlan, and Sara Sturm. "The Two Sancho's in *La Estrella de Sevilla*." *Romanistisches Jahrbuch* 21 (1970): 285–93.

Sullivan, Henry W. *Tirso de Molina and the Drama of the Counter Reformation*. 2d ed. Amsterdam: Rodopi, 1981.

Tanner, Tony. *Adultery in the Novel: Contract and Transgression*. Baltimore: Johns Hopkins University Press, 1979.

Tatum, James. *Apuleius and the* Golden Ass. Ithaca: Cornell University Press, 1979.

ter Horst, Robert. "The *loa* of Lisbon and the Mythical Substructure of *El burlador de Sevilla*." *Bulletin of Hispanic Studies* 50 (1973): 147–65.

———. "Ritual Time Regained in Zorrilla's *Don Juan Tenorio*." *Romanic Review* 70 (1979): 80–93.

Tirso de Molina. *El burlador de Sevilla y convidado de piedra*. Ed. Joaquín Casalduero. Letras Hispánicas 58. 3d ed. Madrid: Cátedra, 1978.

———. *Los cigarrales de Toledo*. Ed. Víctor Saíd Armesto. Madrid: Biblioteca Renacimiento, 1913.

———. *El vergonzoso en palacio*. Ed. Francisco Ayala. Clásicos Castalia 31. Madrid: Castalia, 1979.

Todorov, Tzetvan. "The discovery of language: *Les Liaisons dangereuses* and *Adolphe*." *Yale French Studies* 45 (1970): 113–26.

Tonelli, Franco. "Molière's *Don Juan* and the Space of the Commedia dell'Arte." *Theatre Journal* 37 (1985): 440–64.

Torrente Ballester, Gonzalo. *Don Juan*. Ancora y Delfín 235. Barcelona: Destino, 1963.

Trask, Haunani-Kay. *Eros and Power: The Promise of Feminist Theory.* Philadelphia: University of Pennsylvania Press, 1986.

Unamuno, Miguel de. *Obras completas.* Ed. Manuel García Blanco. 9 vols. Madrid: Escelicer, 1966–71.

Valbuena Prat, Angel. *Historia del teatro español.* Barcelona: Noguer, 1956.

Valembois V., Víctor. "El mito de Don Juan en el teatro de la posguerra." *Insula* 361 (1976): 10.

Valis, Noël Maureen. *The Decadent Vision in Leopoldo Alas: A Study of* La Regenta *and* Su único hijo. Baton Rouge: Louisiana State University Press, 1981.

———. *The Novels of Jacinto Octavio Picón.* Lewisburg, Pa.: Bucknell University Press and Associated University Press, 1986.

———. "Order and Meaning in Clarín's *La Regenta.*" *NOVEL: A Forum on Fiction* 16 (1983): 246–58.

———. "Sobre la última frase de *La Regenta.*" *Clarín y* La Regenta *en su tiempo* 795–808.

Valverde, José María. *Azorín.* Barcelona: Planeta, 1971.

Vázquez, Luis. "Documentos toledanos y madrileños de Claramonte y reafirmación de Tirso como autor de *El Burlador de Sevilla y Convidado de piedra.*" *Estudios* 42.153 (1986): 53–130.

———. Introducción biográfica y crítica. *El burlador de Sevilla y convidado de piedra. Estudios* 45.164–65 (1989): 5–97.

Vega Carpio, Lope de. *El arte nuevo de hacer comedias en este tiempo.* Ed. Juana de José Prades. Clásicos Hispánicos 11. Madrid: Consejo Superior de Investigaciones Científicas, 1971.

———. *Los comendadores de Córdoba.* In vol. 11 of *Obras de Lope de Vega.* Ed. Marcelino Menéndez y Pelayo. 15 vols. Madrid: Real Academia Española, 1890–1913.

Vidal, José B. "El tiempo a través de los personajes de *Doña Inés.*" *Cuadernos hispanoamericanos* 226–27 (1968): 220–38.

Vilanova, Antonio. "El adulterio de Anita Ozores como problema fisiológico y moral." *Clarín y su obra en el centenario de* La Regenta *(Barcelona, 1884–1885).* Actas del Simposio Internacional celebrado en Barcelona del 20 al 24 de Marzo de 1984. Ed. Antonio Vilanova. Barcelona: University of Barcelona, 1985. 43–82.

Wade, Gerald E. "The Authorship and the Date of Composition of *El burlador de Sevilla.*" *Hispanófila* 32 (1968): 1–22.

———, and Robert J. Mayberry. "*¿Tan largo me lo fiáis . . .?* and *El burlador de Sevilla y convidado de piedra.*" *Bulletin of the Comediantes* 14 (1962): 1–16.

Wardropper, Bruce W. "*El burlador de Sevilla:* A Tragedy of Errors." *Philological Quarterly* 36 (1957): 61–71.

———. "*La fianza satisfecha,* a Crudely Mangled Rehash?" *MLN* 87 (1972): 200–213.

Warren, Robert Penn. "Pure and Impure Poetry." *Selected Essays.* New York: Random House, 1958. 3–31.

Weinstein, Leo. *The Metamorphoses of Don Juan*. Stanford Studies in Language and Literature 18. Stanford: Stanford University Press, 1959.

Whitby, William M., and Robert Roland Anderson. Introduction. *La fianza satisfecha*. Cambridge: Cambridge University Press, 1971. 1–71.

Winter, David G. *The Power Motive*. New York: Free Press, 1973.

Zorrilla, José. "Cuatro palabras sobre mi *Don Juan Tenorio*." *Recuerdos del tiempo viejo. Obras completas*. 2 vols. Valladolid: Santarén, 1943. 2: 1799–1807.

———. *Don Juan Tenorio*. Ed. Aniano Peña. Letras Hispánicas 114. 4th ed. Madrid: Cátedra, 1983. Trans. William I. Oliver. Oscar Mandel, ed., *The Theatre of Don Juan* 469–538.

Index